CATHOLIC
Sexual Ethics

A Summary, Explanation, & Defense
Second Edition

Rev. Ronald Lawler,
O.F.M. Cap.,

Joseph Boyle, Jr.,

& William E. May

D1293707

Our Sunday Visitor Publishing Division
Our Sunday Visitor, Inc.
Huntington, Indiana 46750

Nihil Obstat:

Rev. Isidore Dixon
Censor Deputatus

Imprimatur:

Most Reverend William E. Lori, S.T.D.
Vicar General for the Archbishop of Washington
June 17, 1998

The *Nihil Obstat* and *Imprimatur* are official declarations that a book or pamphlet is free of doctrinal or moral error. No implication is contained therein that those who have granted the *Nihil Obstat* or *Imprimatur* agree with the contents, opinions, or statements expressed.

Our Sunday Visitor Publishing Division
Our Sunday Visitor, Inc.
200 Noll Plaza
Huntington, IN 46750

International Standard Book Number: 0-87973-952-5
Library of Congress Catalog Card Number: 84-62225

Cover design by Peggy Gerardot
Updated by Tyler Ottinger

PRINTED IN THE UNITED STATES OF AMERICA
952

ACKNOWLEDGMENTS

The authors and publisher are grateful to the following for the use of their materials appearing in this work:

The Division of Christian Education of the National Council of the Churches of Christ for Scripture quotations taken from the *Revised Standard Version, Catholic Edition,* © 1965 and 1966 by the Division of Christian Education of the National Council of the Churches of Christ, except for those appearing in quoted sources such as *Vatican II: The Conciliar and Post Conciliar Documents* and in paraphrased material. All rights reserved.

The Costello Publishing Company, Inc., for quotations taken from *Vatican II: The Conciliar and Post Conciliar Documents* and *Vatican Council II: More Post Conciliar Documents*, Austin Flannery, O.P., General Editor. Reprinted with permission of Costello Publishing Co., Inc., © 1975 by Costello Publishing Company, Inc., and Reverend Austin Flannery, O.P. All rights reserved.

A special debt of gratitude is owed those publishers, authors, etc., for the use of excerpts taken from the works cited in the chapter notes of this book, among them:

Sheed and Ward, *Marriage: Human Reality and Saving Mystery*, by Edward Schillebeeckx, © 1965 by Sheed and Ward, Inc., reprinted with permission of Andrews McMeel & Parker, all rights reserved; Harvard University Press, *Contraception: A History of Its Treatment by Catholic Theologians and Canonists*, by John T. Noonan, Jr., © 1965; McGrath Publishing, *Official Catholic Teachings: Love and Sexuality*, by various popes and their encyclicals, ed. Odile M. Liebard, © 1978; U.S. Catholic Conference, *Declaration on Certain Questions Concerning Sexual Ethics*, by the Sacred Congregation for the Doctrine of the Faith, © 1976; Franciscan Herald Press, *The Way of the Lord Jesus: Christian Moral Principles*, vol. 1, by Germain Grisez, © 1983; Daughters of St. Paul, *Original Unity of Man and Woman: Catechesis on the Book of Genesis*, by Pope Paul II, © 1981; Paulist Press, *Sexual Morality: A Catholic Perspective*, by Philip S. Keane, S.S., © 1977; Farrar, Straus, and Giroux, *Love and Responsibility*, by Karol Wojtyla (Pope John Paul II), tr. H.T. Willetts, © 1981; Raymond Collins, "The Bible and Sexuality I" and "The Bible and Sexuality II," in *Biblical Theology Bulletin*, vols. 7 and 8, © 1977 and 1978.

CONTENTS

Chapter Eight

Chapter Nine

FOREWORD
TO THE SECOND EDITION

It is with joy and gratitude that I commend this new edition of *Catholic Sexual Ethics*. No area is in greater need of clear and eloquent teaching than that of sexual ethics. Faced with the ideologies that are the usual fare in the media and popular entertainment, so many need a clear explanation of the Church's teaching on human sexuality, a teaching that affirms and gives life, a voice which recognizes the dignity of the human person.

The Church has received from the Apostles the solemn command of Christ to announce the saving truth (*Catechism of the Catholic Church*, 2032; *Lumen Gentium*, 17). The Church's teachings on the precious gift of sexuality are indeed *saving*. They are life and mercy for a people led astray! But these teachings need to be proclaimed, taught, and convincingly explained.

This is precisely the service rendered by William May, Joseph Boyle, and Father Ronald Lawler. Integrating the *Catechism of the Catholic Church* and also the Holy Father's teaching since the first edition, the 1998 edition of *Catholic Sexual Ethics* is an important guide for any who are responsible to hand on the Catholic teaching on human sexuality. These three scholars and teacher offer a clear, systematic, and readable summary of the Church's teachings that are drawn from the revelation of Scripture, Tradition, and from the most recent teachings of the Magisterium. *Catholic Sexual Ethics* will be a valuable resource for lay people, for university students, catechists, teachers, parents, priests, religious, and many others.

The work of these authors is a wonderful contribution to the Church's mission of teaching the saving truth. I thank them for this gift, and I ask God to bless all that seek to understand and communicate the Good News of the Church's teaching on human sexuality.

☩James Cardinal Hickey
Archbishop of Washington
May 15, 1998

FOREWORD
TO THE FIRST EDITION

Pope John Paul II has frequently urged scholars to show ever more clearly the origins of Catholic sexual morality. Setting an incomparable example, the Holy Father repeatedly offers to the modern world the vision of the beauty, the realism, and the bracing strength of the Gospel's teaching about human love.

The fact is that Catholic teaching in this area is not clearly understood by many. Hence the need to show in profound ways how securely Catholic moral teaching about human sexuality is rooted in the Gospel, how supportive it is of persons and of personal values, and how much this teaching supports the ethical ideals most needed in contemporary society.

For this reason I am very pleased to welcome this book, and to urge those who are concerned with teaching the Catholic vision of human sexuality to study it carefully.

Catholic Sexual Ethics shows clearly that Catholic teaching on love and sexuality is full of joy and hope. It remembers the liberating power of self-possession made possible by the grace of our Lord, Jesus Christ. It is Christ himself who gives joy and strength in living the life for which we were created in him.

Catholic moral teaching reminds us of where authentic sexual liberation is to be found. Freedom is not found in surrendering to inner and outer pressures. It is found by those who achieve self-possession in Christ, and the power to live as the heart longs to, in ways always faithful to lasting love, to life, to every human good.

✠William Cardinal Baum
Prefect, Sacred Congregation
for Catholic Education, 1985

INTRODUCTION
TO THE SECOND EDITION

This second edition of *Catholic Sexual Ethics* is intended primarily to bring the text, published originally in 1985, up to date. It does so, first of all, by integrating into the text and notes the relevant teaching of the magisterium found in documents promulgated after 1985. Here we should note that the "updated" text of the first edition, published in 1996, featured a new chapter (Chapter 9), offering a summary of six magisterial documents of relevance to sexual ethics published between 1985 and 1995. This chapter, revised to the extent necessary to take into account the fact that the teaching of these documents has now been incorporated into the previous chapters, has been retained for the revised edition, and it now includes a summary of another relevant magisterial document — the Pontifical Council for the Family's *The Truth and Meaning of Human Sexuality: Guidelines for Education Within the Family,* published after the "updated" version of the text had been prepared.

The revision also brings the text up to date by taking into account some of the more significant scholarly literature on issues of sexual ethics and incorporating references to this literature throughout the work. The revised text also integrates our own efforts to develop and strengthen some of the evidence and arguments presented in the first edition.

A major feature of the revised text is the reordering of the first three chapters. Chapter 1 is now given over to a presentation of the Church's teaching on sex; Chapter 2, to the biblical teaching on sex; and Chapter 3, to the understanding of sex in the Catholic theological tradition. In the first edition the present Chapter 1 was Chapter 3, the present Chapter 2 was Chapter 1, and the present Chapter 3 was Chapter 2. We are now convinced that the order followed in the revised edition is the right order, since the Church's teaching on sex gives us an authoritative interpretation of Scripture and of the Catholic tradition. The chapters on the Church's teaching and on the biblical understanding of sex have been extensively rewritten. All the other chapters have been substantively revised in light of recent magisterial teaching, particularly that found in the new *Catechism of the Catholic Church* and in the major writings of Pope John Paul II such as *Veritatis Splendor,* more recent scholarly studies, and our own efforts to strengthen and develop the matter included in the first edition. Of the co-authors, May was primarily

11

responsible for preparing the revised edition; Lawler and Boyle, however, gave him inestimable advice and help on many specific matters. In revising the chapter on the biblical teaching on sex, May was helped greatly by advice given to him by Reverend Francis Martin, professor of Scripture at the John Paul II Institute for Studies on Marriage and Family in Washington, D.C.

This "Introduction to the Second Edition" is followed by the original "Introduction." This has, however, been revised slightly to take into account, first of all, the ordering of chapters in this edition and the inclusion of the new chapter on recent magisterial documents of relevance to the subject. We have also decided to shorten the original introduction by cutting material no longer judged necessary. We believe that the "responsible-relational" view of human sexuality described in the original "Introduction" is still the dominant understanding of human sexuality in our culture. Moreover, now, at the beginning of the new millennium, the idea that sex, gender, sexual morality, and the family itself are all sheerly the result of the social construction of morality and that the sexual "nature" of men and women is, as it were, the raw material for such social construction in becoming more and more dominant among the elite of our society,* and is likely to exert more and more influence in the future on public debates over sex and sexual morality. The challenges raised by the "responsible-relational" view of human sexuality and the "social construction/deconstruction" view of sex, gender, morality, and the family make it all the more imperative to know, appreciate, and defend the Church's teaching on human sexuality, love, marriage, and the meaning of man and woman. We hope that the revised text of *Catholic Sexual Ethics* will help implement this need.

---

*On this see *Sex, Preference and Family: Essays on Law and Nature*, ed. David M. Estlund and Martha C. Nussbaum, New York: Oxford University Press, 1997. (The titles of some essays are revealing: e.g., "Sexual Orientation and Gender, Dichotomizing Differences?"; "The Social Construction and Reconstruction of Care"; "Sexuality and Liberty: Making Room for Nature and Tradition?"; "Beyond Lesbian and Gay: Families We Choose"). See also, Carol Levine, "AIDS and Changing Concepts of the Family," *Milbank Quarterly*, 68, Supplement 1 (1990), 30-46.

INTRODUCTION
TO THE FIRST EDITION

The purpose of this book is to present the teachings of the Catholic Church on questions of sexual morality.

A presentation of Catholic teaching on sexual morality is needed today because many Catholics and non-Catholics alike do not have a clear overall view of this teaching. Even those who know the Church's position on the various controverted issues in sexual ethics do not understand the roots of this teaching and its real human value. Many see it as a set of rules or taboos created by human authorities, or as vestiges of a culture which no longer serves any human needs.

The true character of the Church's teaching on sexual ethics can be understood only if its genuinely personalistic emphasis is grasped. With remarkable uniformity and insistence the Church, over many centuries, has taught that sex is fundamentally a good and wonderful gift of God, and that intelligently ordered sexual activity can be a humanly perfecting and even sanctifying thing. The condemnation of certain kinds of acts, choices, and attitudes bearing on the sexual domain is the result of this conviction about the basic goodness and importance of sexuality, for those things condemned by the Church are the sexual acts and attitudes which harm the human goods at stake in sexual activity. They are treated as gravely wrong because these goods are so central to the person's self-integrity, to the most intimate and fundamental relationships between persons, and to the person's relationship to God.

The Christian view of sexuality stands in stark contrast to many views that have become widely accepted in our culture. Perry London, for example, summarized the change in attitude toward various sexual activities which has occurred over the past few decades. He reported that there have been revolutionary changes in attitude and practice concerning things that have until recently been considered immoral. He concluded that sexual legitimacy is no longer confined to marriage, and that sexual prohibitions might well follow in the way of the now abandoned prohibitions concerning various kinds of food: "If sexual norms were to follow a similar course, then common attitudes and behavior connected with it, like those predominant today with food, might become matters of preference, of health and manners, not of religion and morals."[1] Thus, he says: "It is unclear whether sex will long remain a topic for ethical concerns of any kind in our society."[2]

London, however, is not willing to endorse this trend without some kind of qualification. He believes that there might still be a need to regulate the sex appetite. He argues: "The most important characteristics of sex may finally be that it is so deeply intertwined with affection and that it is still the chief human instrument for making progeny, and these may suggest some limits on its exercise, though they do not reveal the contents of those limits."[3]

From the perspective of Catholic sexual ethics, London's observations are instructive. Intelligent reflection, even from an entirely secular perspective, must acknowledge that sexual activity cannot be treated as a trivial matter, and that the current permissiveness in sexual matters does trivialize sex. Sex is simply too important a part of life to be left as a matter of taste or mere preference.

There are many views about how sexuality is to be regulated so as to avoid its trivialization. Some might wish to see a revival of Victorian prudery or a puritanical denial of the real goodness of human sexuality. Such views, however, involve a denial of what most people correctly see as important human values. A more dominant view nowadays is that sexuality is governed by moral norms, and that these are requirements of its interpersonal character. On this view, the relational character of sexual activity is its most important feature,[4] and thus provides a moral criterion for evaluating sexual behavior. This criterion is the quality of the relationships established and expressed in the sexual activity. By this standard, degrading and exploitative sexual relationships are excluded. Some would add the further condition that the relationship be responsible — that it show care and concern for one's sexual partner, and that it be contraceptive unless a child is expressly desired.[5]

This view of sexual morality might be called the "responsible-relational" view. Besides upholding the conviction that moral norms do bear on sexual activity, this view has the merit of focusing on an undeniably important part of sexual morality, for human beings do establish the most intimate of their interpersonal relationships sexually. However, all human relationships should be responsible and nonexploitative, so this view provides no specific guidance on sexual matters as such. It fails to highlight the special moral responsibilities that flow from concern for the human goods toward which sexuality itself is ordered. It pays insufficient attention to the connection between sexual activity, marital love, and children. It is not surprising therefore that this view tends to approve, in many kinds of circum-

14

stances, premarital sex, masturbation, homosexual activity, and so on, and simply has nothing to say about questions of purity of thought. Its view of personal relations is not broad or deep enough to allow a realistic account of what is specifically at stake in sexual activity.

It is surprising therefore to note how much of the responsible-relational view some Catholic writers have accepted. Most of these writers have stated their views in a careful and circumscribed way. But they have denied some teachings very insistently affirmed by the Church, and have proposed a view of sexuality more in keeping with the responsible-relational view. Catholic writers, of course, are concerned to preserve the special place of marriage in the sexual domain. But even here some are willing to allow — at least as a possibility — the legitimacy of sexual activity outside marriage.[6] These writers also allow the permissibility of contraception,[7] and some would count homosexual behavior in some circumstances as morally acceptable or even praiseworthy.[8]

For many Catholics nowadays, the clear light of the Church's teaching is not brought to bear on the problems of sexual life. The only moral tempering of the sexual exploitation and hedonism of our culture is provided by the responsible-relational view, which can do little to articulate the real grandeur of sexuality or to protect it from the current onslaught. When Catholic moral teachers cannot show clearly what is distinctive about the Christian understanding of sexuality, Catholics are likely to be confused and misled.

It is essential therefore that the Church's teaching on sexual morality be presented in a way that reveals its truth and attractiveness. This book is part of the effort to do this — to fulfill the mandate of Pope John Paul II to reveal "the biblical foundations, the ethical grounds, and the personalistic" appropriateness of the good news about human sexuality which God has commanded the Church to proclaim.[9] Thus, this book will contain an extended exposition of the Church's teaching on sexual morality as well as a theological development of the arguments which support the Church's teaching. This theological argumentation will seek to relate the Church's teaching on sexual morality to the most fundamental concerns of Christian life, and to make clear within the perspective of Catholic faith why the Church's teaching on these matters is important and true.

To achieve these theological and pastoral aims, the book is divided into nine chapters and a conclusion. The first three chapters present a general account of the development of the Church's understanding of human sexuality. The first sets forth the authoritative teaching of the Church on sex; the second, the biblical understanding of sex; and the third, the development of

15

the Catholic theological tradition on sex. The fourth and fifth chapters deal with general issues of moral theology which lie behind many of the specific issues in sexual morality. The fourth is a brief account of the foundations of moral theology; it provides a critique of the method of moral reasoning used by those Catholic writers who do not accept the received teaching on sexual morality. The fifth is a presentation of the Church's teaching on conscience; it focuses on the relationship between Church teaching and the conscience of the Catholic. The sixth chapter is an account of Christian marriage from a moral theological perspective. The next two chapters consider in some detail the specific requirements of chastity; Chapter 7 considers the requirements of chaste love within marriage; Chapter 8 considers the requirements of chastity for the unmarried. Chapter 9 offers an overview of seven major magisterial documents of relevance to understanding human sexuality promulgated between 1985 and 1995. Following the nine chapters the Pastoral Conclusion considers how the Christian message about sexuality is to be presented; it emphasizes both the seriousness of living chastely and the real possibility of living chastely given our union with the risen Lord. His own example of dealing with fallen humankind is proposed as the model for pastoral problems in this area where so much weakness abounds.

This work was begun in 1978 at the urging of Ronald Lawler, O.F.M. Cap. Many unavoidable delays prevented its publication until 1985. It should be noted that these delays were largely beneficial. Perhaps the greatest of these benefits was the appearance of the great body of teaching on the issues at hand by the present pope, John Paul II. His statements and analyses have enriched every aspect of our work enormously. Most importantly, his *Familiaris Consortio* has made clear beyond any doubt that the received teachings of the Church — what the authors of this work have set out to explain and defend in this book — are indeed the authentic teachings of Christ's Church. Dissent on sexual matters is rejected — firmly and clearly — by the Church in this apostolic exhortation. This statement has exceptional authority, for in it John Paul II — as the authentic pastor of the whole Church and as the leader of the college of bishops — hands on received Catholic teaching. The collegiality of *Familiaris Consortio* is very real, since it is the pope's summary and response to the proposals made by the 1980 Synod of Bishops on the problems of the family.

Originally, the group of people involved in preparing this work was quite large. In addition to the authors, the following persons contributed material which has been used in some way in the development of the final product: Mark Dosh; John Harvey, O.S.F.S.; Frederick Jelly, O.P.; Mary

16

Joyce; John Kippley; James Mohler, S.J.; Henry Sattler, C.Ss.R.; and William B. Smith. The authors thank these friends and colleagues for their irreplaceable help. The authors also thank Germain Grisez, whose insight on the issues addressed and whose work on fundamental moral theology and specific issues in sexual ethics has influenced this book greatly. In addition, the authors thank Barbara Boyle, who typed and retyped several versions of a number of the chapters, and Joseph Koterski, who entered a number of chapters into a word processor. The authors owe a great debt to the University of St. Thomas in Houston, Texas, and to the Basilian Fathers there, for providing word-processing equipment, hospitality, facilities for the authors' common work, and encouragement.

Finally, a word about the collaboration which led to this book is in order. Boyle and May drafted most of the chapters as they now appear. Drafts of early chapters often made use of materials provided by the collaborators listed above. Revisions were made on the basis of editorial work done by all three authors but primarily by Lawler. The final text therefore is the joint work of all three authors. All have read and agreed to the text as it appears, to the extent that it is very difficult to say who authored any individual sentence or came up with any specific argument or point. The authors hope that this work will prove invaluable to married and single people, to pastors and marriage counselors, and especially to those individuals who are seeking guidance concerning the Church's stand on sexual ethics.

Chapter One
The Church's Teaching on Sex

I. Moral Theology and the Magisterium

This book intends to present the moral teaching of the Christ and his Church concerning sexual ethics. Catholic moral theology is rooted in faith in Jesus Christ. The Gospels portray Christ telling his followers to teach all the nations "to observe all that I have commanded you; and lo, I am with you always, to the close of the age" (Mt 28:20).

Catholic faith is before all else faith in Christ, who remains with us through his Church, which is the sacrament of his own presence. Much of what we believe can also be shown to be true by good reasoning. Not all persons, however, are capable of freely assimilating such proofs, while the gift of faith in Christ is far more accessible and is more decisive than any philosophical argument.[1]

Christ is the one Teacher upon whose word all faith depends (Mt 7:29, 11:27). In a special way he himself teaches his faithful today through the teaching office (magisterium) he has willed to be in the Church until the end of time. He has given it authority to speak in his name. The mission of the magisterium is to guard and hand on, with divine authority, the truth and salvation brought to us by the Lord. The Second Vatican Council declared that the "task of giving an authentic interpretation to the Word of God . . . has been entrusted to the living teaching office of the Church alone" (*Dei Verbum*, no. 10). This teaching office, first given to St. Peter and the other apostles, is now, by the will of Christ, entrusted to the pope and the bishops who teach in communion with him.

The Church presents and always has presented many moral teachings with entire assurance, expecting her sons and daughters to believe and live by this teaching. She does not expect this because popes and bishops are so humanly wise, but because through them Christ himself guards the faith and its saving truths — truths necessary if we are to live worthily as children of God.

According to Catholic faith, the magisterium invested in the college of bishops under the headship of the pope *always* teaches with the authority of

Christ — a more-than-human authority. At times this teaching office proposes matters, whether of faith or morals, infallibly, i.e., with divine assurance that what is proposed is absolutely true and is to be held definitively. Teachings proposed in this way are to be given the assent of faith (cf. *Lumen Gentium*, no. 25). At other times, it teaches matters of faith or morals *authoritatively and as true*, but not as divinely guaranteed to be true. Although teachings proposed in this way do not require the assent of faith, they are to be received with a "religious assent of will and mind," and all the faithful, including pope, bishops, ordinary lay people, and theologians, are to accept these teachings as true and to shape their lives and actions in conformity with them[2] [this matter will be taken up in more detail in chapter 5].

The Church teaches infallibly in matters of faith and morals through the solemn definitions of councils and *ex cathedra* pronouncements of supreme pontiffs. But she also teaches infallibly through her ordinary teaching by the bishops of the Church in union with the pope, when they agree in teaching that something of faith or morals is to be held definitively.[3]

The Church's magisterium is capable of teaching infallibly and authoritatively precisely because it is the instrument by which the Spirit of Christ preserves the Church in his saving truth, and prevents the Church from wandering from this truth. The apostolic preaching, through which the saving truth given by our Lord was communicated to the apostolic Church, was, as Vatican Council II affirmed,

> To be preserved in a continuous line of succession until the end of time. Hence, the apostles, in handing on what they themselves had received, warn the faithful to maintain the traditions which they had learned either by word of mouth or by letter (cf. 2 Thes 2:15); and they warn the faithful to fight hard for the faith that had been handed over to them once and for all (cf. Jude 3). What was handed on by the apostles comprises everything that serves to make the People of God live their lives in holiness and increase their faith. In this way, the Church, in her doctrine, life, and worship, perpetuates and transmits to every generation all that she herself is, all that she believes (*Dei Verbum*, no. 8).

The Spirit's work within the Church is not, of course, limited to his guidance of the pope and bishops. The Spirit also guides and instructs the many people within the Church who seek to penetrate God's revelation more deeply and to live worthily as God's children. Theologians, philosophers, mystics, and ordinary good people are helped by the Spirit in their attempts to understand, live, and explain the faith. But they can hold and proclaim the faith securely and shape their lives in accord with its truths only when they take care to teach and live in conformity with the guidance of the teaching office of the Church, for that office alone has been charged with the supervision of public teaching in the Church, and it alone has the God-given authority to make secure, final judgment in matters of faith and morals. Christ has confided to the magisterium the task "to preserve God's people from deviations and defections and to guarantee them the objective possibility of professing the true faith without error" (*Catechism of the Catholic Church*, no. 890). It is for this reason that the Second Vatican Council declares that "in forming their consciences the faithful must pay careful attention to the sacred and certain teaching of the Church. For the Catholic Church is by the will of Christ the teacher of truth. It is her duty to proclaim and teach with authority the truth which is Christ and, at the same time, to declare and confirm by her authority the principles of the moral order which spring from human nature itself" (*Dignitatis Humanae*, no. 14).

Theologians have an indispensable role to play within the Church, for they can help all the faithful — including pope and bishops — come to a deeper and richer understanding of the faith and of the requirements of the Christian way of life. But they are *not* charged with the direct pastoral responsibility for the care of souls, for this has been entrusted to the magisterium. Theologians are not vested with the authority of Christ. The matter can perhaps be put this way: do not *believe* theologians; rather, consider the evidence and arguments that they offer to support their positions, and be grateful to them when well-founded positions they take help deepen one's faith; but do not listen to them if they take positions contrary to those proposed by Christ's shepherds. As St. Thomas Aquinas, surely a model for theologians and for the faithful, put the matter, "we must abide by the pope's judgment rather than by the opinion of any theologian, however well versed he may be in divine Scriptures."[4]

It is therefore critically important for us to summarize what the teaching office of the Church has taught and does teach about marriage and sexual morality. It is necessary to consider the Church's teaching on sexual morality within the context provided by her teaching on marriage. This is so because the Church clearly recognizes that it is only within marriage that human persons and the precious goods which human sexuality is to serve can be adequately respected and realized. This will be done in considerable detail in Chapters 6, 7, and 8 where we will develop a theological account of the Catholic view of marriage and the concrete requirements of chastity. In this chapter we will summarize what the Church teaches about the goodness and holiness of marriage, what the Church teaches about sexual activity within marriage, and what it teaches about the immorality of sexual activity that is not authentically marital. This will be done so as to highlight some of the essential points of Catholic sexual teaching, and to make clear the seriousness, constancy, and nonarbitrariness of this teaching.

II. The Goodness and Holiness of Marriage[5]

The Church has always taught that the union of man and woman in marriage is a good and holy thing. It is good because, as Scripture makes clear, God himself instituted marriage and gave it its defining characteristics. It is holy because the Lord Jesus made marriage a sacrament of his spousal union with his bride, the Church, and a source of grace.

The Church clearly affirmed the goodness of marriage in the face of the attacks on marriage by the various forms of Gnosticism which appeared through the centuries. As early as 340, a council of bishops meeting in Gangra (in Asia Minor, in what is now modern-day Turkey) stated: "If anyone disparages marriage, shuns a faithful and God-fearing wife who sleeps with her husband, and speaks as though she cannot enter the kingdom of God, let him be anathema."[6] Similarly, the Second and Fourth Councils of the Lateran in 1139 and 1215 defended the goodness of the marital union against the challenge of the medieval neo-Gnostics.[7] In 1208 Pope Innocent III insisted that Catholics "believe that the husband with his wife can be saved."[8] And these declarations from the local council of Gangra, the Second and Fourth Councils of the Lateran, and Pope Innocent III are simply illustrative of the universal teaching of the Church; other magisterial documents on marriage prior to the great Council of Trent contain the same praise for marriage as a good and holy reality.[9]

Although from her very beginning the Church has lived in virtue of the power of the seven sacraments instituted by Christ, time was needed for developing clearly, in the light of faith, what precisely a sacrament itself is, and which gifts of Christ are sacraments in that sense. Concretely, thanks to the witness of the Fathers, it is clear that marriage was always regarded as a source of the graces needed by spouses in order to live a holy life and that it is a symbol of the union between Christ and the Church. Nonetheless, the detailed development of the Church's teaching on the sacramentality of marriage took place over many centuries.[10] Long before the sacramentality of marriage was solemnly defined, marriage was recognized in the Church as a true sacrament. In 1439 the Council of Florence explicitly affirmed that marriage was not only humanly good but also one of the seven sacraments instituted by Christ. This council also affirmed as Catholic teaching that "three blessings are assigned to matrimony. The first is the procreation and education of children for the worship of God. The second is the fidelity that each of the spouses must observe towards the other. The third is the indissolubility of matrimony, indissoluble because it signifies the indivisible union of Christ and the Church."[11]

The Council of Trent in the sixteenth century was not faced with a challenge to the inherent goodness of marriage but rather with the denial of its sacramental character and indissolubility. In a solemn dogmatic proclamation, this Council reaffirmed the divine institution of marriage and its later elevation by Christ to the dignity of a sacrament. The decree *De doctrina sacramenti matrimonii* began by calling to mind the divine institution of marriage, at the very beginnings of the human race, established as a unique and indissoluble bond between one man and one woman: "The first parent of the human race, under the inspiration of the Divine Spirit, proclaimed the perpetual and indissoluble bond of matrimony when he said, 'This now is bone of my bones, and flesh of my flesh. . . . Wherefore a man shall leave father and mother and cleave to his wife: and they shall be two in one flesh' (Gen 2:23; see Eph 5:31)."

Moreover, in order to give spouses the help necessary, given man's fall from grace, to make marriage a road to holiness Christ made of it a sacrament, which produces grace: "Christ himself, who instituted the holy sacraments and brought them to perfection, merited for us by his passion the grace that brings natural love to perfection and strengthens the indissoluble unity, and sanctifies the spouses. The Apostle Paul intimates this when he says: 'Husbands, love your wives, just as Christ also loved the Church, and delivered himself up for her' (Eph 5:25); and he immediately adds: 'This is a great mystery — I mean in reference to Christ and to the Church' (Eph 5:32)."[12]

In the centuries since Trent there have been many challenges to the Catholic teaching on marriage. None of these is an explicit denial that marriage is a good institution, but many of these challenges involve the belief that marriage is a purely human institution which can be changed by human decision so that it need not be regarded as permanent but can be considered as allowing for divorce and remarriage, or that it can be understood as a relationship between persons with no necessary order to the begetting and educating of children. Within the past decade some have even claimed that there can be marriage between persons of the same sex.

In response to these and other challenges, popes in recent centuries have reaffirmed the divine origin of marriage and the sacramental character of Christian marriage. They have done this to emphasize that the human meaning and the supernatural significance of marriage are threatened by the various proposals to change the character of marriage or to alter sexual morality. Thus, for example, Pope Leo XIII in 1880 affirmed very clearly that marriage was instituted by God, that it is indissoluble, and that as one of the seven sacraments it provides special graces to spouses.[13]

In 1930, fifty years later, Pope Pius XI issued his comprehensive encyclical on Christian Marriage, *Casti Connubii*. He solemnly reaffirmed Catholic doctrine that God is the author of marriage, that Jesus raised Christian marriage to the dignity of a sacrament, that it is indissoluble and blessed with the goods of children, fidelity between the spouses, and indissolubility. Noting the errors and vices opposed to marriage and marital love, he repudiated as intrinsically immoral abortion, contraception, adultery, and divorce. He emphasized that the beauty and dignity of marriage can be secured only by adhering to the divine plan for marriage and doing so by having recourse to prayer and to the sacraments, by docility to magisterial teaching, and by preparing adequately for marriage.

A major element in *Casti Connubii* was Pius's teaching on the beauty of conjugal love, the "soil" which enables conjugal fidelity to flourish. This love, which is presented as the vital principle of marriage, is meant to inform the whole of married life and reaches its perfection in conjugal charity, which leads the spouses to imitate the holiness of Christ himself.[14]

Although he wrote no encyclicals on marriage, Pope Pius XII took up issues concerning marriage in many of his addresses, in particular his "Addresses to Newlyweds" and to various organizations of Christian families. He reaffirmed Catholic teaching on marriage as a divine institution and sacrament of the new law, considering in particular issues of conjugal sexual morality (see the following section).[15]

The Second Vatican Council, in response to the developing modern attitude that marriage is whatever society or individuals may choose to make it, attractively reaffirmed and developed Catholic teaching on marriage. First, it presented Christian marriage as a specific vocation to holiness, affirming that Christian "spouses are fortified and, as it were, consecrated for the duties and dignity of their state by a special sacrament; fulfilling their conjugal and family role by virtue of this sacrament, spouses are penetrated with the spirit of Christ and their whole life is suffused by faith, hope, and charity; thus they increasingly further *their own perfection and their mutual sanctification*, and together they render glory to God" (*Gaudium et Spes*, no. 48).

Second, it developed significantly the understanding of the role of conjugal love in the structure of marriage, clearly showing that this love is the animating principle of marriage. It is manifested at the very beginning of marriage in the act of marital consent, through which a man and woman give themselves unreservedly, completely, and irrevocably to one another as husband and wife. It is present in principle throughout the whole of married life, a love always possible for spouses to give and one that they are obliged to deepen and foster in their daily life.

Third, Vatican Council II insisted that there can be no true contradiction or conflict between the requirements of authentic marital love and the great good of having and raising children. It insisted that by its own inner dynamism conjugal love is ordered to the procreation and education of children, a gift crowning and perfecting the love of the spouses.

In continuity with the Catholic tradition the Second Vatican Council reaffirmed the truth that God is the author of marriage, that he has endowed it with "various benefits and ends in view" (*Gaudium et Spes*, no. 48) — namely, the procreation and education of children, spousal fidelity, and indissoluble unity.[16] While insisting that marriage comes to be only when a man and a woman freely consent *to be* husband and wife by giving themselves irrevocably to one another, the Council emphasized that the *nature* of marriage is not subject to human choices but has been definitively determined by God.[17] Consequently, the "sacred bond" of marriage, which comes into being when the man and the woman freely give themselves to one another through an "irrevocable" act of the will, perdures and is not "dependent on human will" (*Gaudium et Spes*, no. 48).

Pope Paul VI succinctly summarized the key elements of the Second Vatican Council's teaching on marriage in his 1968 encyclical *Humanae Vitae*. In his Encyclical, Paul VI stressed the competence of the magisterium to interpret authoritatively the divine law, both natural and evangelical, and reaffirmed strongly Catholic teaching on contraception.[18]

Pope John Paul II, even prior to becoming Supreme Pontiff, had devoted himself extensively to the study of human sexuality, sexual morality, marriage, and the family.[19] Immediately upon becoming pope and in order to prepare for the Synod of Bishops in 1980 devoted to the theme "The Role of the Christian Family in the World Today," he began a series of papal Wednesday audiences given over to reflections on the "theology of the body," reflections concerned with human sexuality, the male-female relationship, marriage, and family.[20] Throughout his pontificate he has given hundreds of addresses on marriage and the family and sexual morality.[21] The most important and authoritative document on marriage and the family promulgated by John Paul II, however, is undoubtedly his 1981 apostolic exhortation *Familiaris Consortio*, "The Role of the Christian Family in the World

Today." This document, which John Paul II himself described as a "*summa*" of the teaching of the Church on the life, the tasks, the responsibilities, and the mission of marriage and of the family in the world today,"[22] is divided into four parts.[23] Parts Two and Three are doctrinal in character and beautifully summarize and develop Catholic teaching on marriage and family, particularly as deepened by the teaching of the Second Vatican Council. Pope John Paul II affirms the goodness of marriage as a human reality created by God and takes special pains to explain its holiness. He emphasizes that, by reason of their baptism, "man and woman are definitively placed within the new and eternal covenant, in the spousal covenant of Christ with the Church" (*Familiaris Consortio*, no. 13). Because of this "indestructible insertion" into the new covenant, married love is elevated and enriched by Christ's redeeming power. As a result, the Christian family is a "domestic Church" and, as John Paul II develops extensively in Part Three of *Familiaris Consortio*, is called to play an indispensable role in the redemptive mission of the Church.

In his 1994 *Letter to Families* John Paul II recapitulates many of the themes set forth in *Familiaris Consortio*, emphasizing that the family rooted in marriage has as its task the building up of the "civilization of love," a theme to which he returns in his 1995 encyclical *Evangelium Vitae*, where he stresses that the conjugal love of spouses enables the family to be the "sanctuary of life."[24]

Catholic magisterial teaching on marriage is, finally, concisely set forth in the 1994 *Catechism of the Catholic Church*. It begins its consideration of marriage by summarizing Catholic teaching on the meaning of marriage in God's wise and loving plan for human existence, considering marriage first in the order of creation as a gift from God, then marriage under the regime of sin and under the Mosaic law, and finally, it takes up marriage "in the Lord," that is, marriage as restored to its original dignity and, in addition, raised to the level of a sacrament of grace, insisting that "it is by following Christ, renouncing themselves, and taking up their crosses that spouses will be able to 'receive' the original meaning of marriage and live it with the help of Christ" (no. 1615). It considers the "goods" of marriage — the procreation and education of children, fidelity between the spouses, and indissolubility — as required by the nature of conjugal love, a love that leads to the sanctification of the spouses and, through them, of the world in which they live (cf. nos. 1643-1658).

To conclude this section, we think it most important to emphasize that in the Church's teaching the goodness and holiness of marriage are essentially connected with the great goods intrinsic to marriage: the procreation and education of children and faithful conjugal love. It is precisely in order to protect and promote these great human goods that God created marriage and that Jesus elevated marriage to the dignity of a sacrament, a fitting sign of his life-giving, love-giving union with his Church. Thus, it is not surprising that, when affirming the goodness and holiness of marriage, the Church has regularly emphasized the essential ordering of marriage to the procreation and education of children, and to the fostering and deepening of the love between spouses.[25]

The genuine goodness and holiness of marriage is therefore a constant theme of Church teaching, whether in response to Gnostic claims that marriage is evil or in response to modern claims that its meaning is to be determined by human decision. The character of this God-given goodness is especially important today, because those who wish to change the Church's teaching on sexual morality fail to recognize that this morality is necessary to preserve great and indispensable human goods.

III. Sexual Activity Within the Covenant of Marriage

The Church clearly teaches that marital intercourse is good and holy when the choice to engage in this act is properly marital. As Vatican II has stated: "Married love is uniquely expressed and perfected by the exercise of the acts proper to marriage. Hence the acts in marriage by which the intimate and chaste union of the spouses takes place are noble and honorable; the truly human performance of these acts fosters the self-giving they signify and enriches the spouses in joy and gratitude" (*Gaudium et Spes*, no. 49).

This teaching of the Second Vatican Council, as we shall show in the chapters to follow, is by no means new. It is rooted in the biblical understanding of the bodily, personal union between husband and wife (cf., for instance the Song of Songs), and was clearly recognized by the great theologians of the Middle Ages. It gradually received greater attention in magisterial teaching over the last few centuries. Clearer teaching on this matter was occasioned by the development of modern secular humanism with its often distorted views about the goodness of sexual pleasure and other forms of human fulfillment. Especially in this century the popes have sought to clarify the authentic goods of human sexuality fostered and protected by the covenant of marriage in the face of the hedonistic and subjectivist values of secular humanism. The secular humanist view of values has enough of the truth in it to make it appear initially plausible, and it has become dominant in much of modern western society; but its shortcomings make it a real threat to the genuine humanism, rooted in a profound respect for the inviolable dignity of human persons, which the Church proclaims.

To stress the authentic goodness of marital love, Pope Pius XI taught that the decision of the spouses to engage in the marital act can be virtuous, even when they know that procreation is impossible. He recognized that "the cultivation of mutual love" is a worthy purpose in such circumstances.[26] Pius XII taught that spouses may rightly and gratefully seek the pleasure which accompanies their marital intercourse. He carefully distinguished his position from the condemned view that marital intercourse may be properly sought *solely* for the sake of pleasure.[27] He clearly taught, however, that the Creator in His goodness and wisdom has willed to make use of the work of the man and the woman to preserve and propagate the human race, by joining them in wedlock. The same Creator has arranged that the husband and wife find pleasure and happiness of mind and body in carrying out that noble mission. Consequently, the husband and wife do no wrong in seeking out and enjoying this pleasure. They are accepting what the Creator intended for them.[28]

Pius went on to articulate the Church's basic standard for evaluating these pleasures, which is, in fact, the Church's basic standard for evaluating sexual activity: "This, therefore, is the rule to be followed: the use of the natural, generative instinct and function is lawful in the married state only, and in the service of the purposes for which marriage exists. It follows from this that only in the married state and in the observation of these laws are the desires and enjoyment of that pleasure and satisfaction allowed."[29] The purposes to which he refers are, of course, the goods pursued in the marital act — the good of offspring and the good of faithful marital love.

The moral norm stated by Pius XII has been reaffirmed by the Second Vatican Council and subsequent popes. Vatican II emphasized that decisions about sexual activity within marriage should be guided by objective criteria. These criteria should be "drawn from the nature of the human person and human action," and should "respect the total meaning of mutual self-giving and human procreation in the context of true love" (*Gaudium et Spes*, no. 51). The Council Fathers continued by stressing that spouses would be able to honor these criteria and respect these goods only by seriously practicing the virtue of marital chastity.

Paul VI makes a similar point in *Humanae Vitae*. He teaches that any marital act which separates the procreative from the unitive significance of marriage and the marital act is wrong. This separation is wrong because one cannot properly respect and foster these goods if one deliberately separates them, when one intentionally repudiates either one. Thus Paul VI rejected contraceptive acts because by freely choosing to contracept one intentionally repudiates the procreative meaning of the marital act, severing it from its unitive meaning, and by so doing harms both of them. He also rejected sexual acts imposed on one's spouse without regard for his or her condition or legitimate desires, since such sexual acts fail to respect the good of marital union.[30] The teaching of *Humanae Vitae* has been vigorously reaffirmed by John Paul II, most notably in *Familiaris Consortio*.[31]

John Paul II has provided a succinct, clear, and powerful summary of the Church's teaching on this matter in the following passage:

> Sexuality, by means of which man and woman give themselves to one another through the acts which are proper and exclusive to spouses, is by no means something purely biological, but concerns the innermost being of the human person as such. It is realized in a truly human way only if it is an integral part of the love by which a man and a woman commit themselves totally to one another until death. The total physical self-giving would be a lie if it were not the sign and fruit of a total personal self-giving, in which the whole person, including the temporal dimension, is present; if the person were to withhold something or reserve the possibility of deciding otherwise in the future, by this very fact he or she would not be giving totally (*Familiaris Consortio*, no. 11).

The *Catechism of the Catholic Church* clearly reaffirms this teaching of Pope John Paul II.[32]

To conclude this section it is worth noting an observation of Pius XII which forms an important part of the evaluation of modern attitudes toward sexuality on the part of recent popes. Pius disputed the popular view that "happiness in married life is in direct proportion to the mutual enjoyment of marital relations." He recognizes, as we have seen, that sexual pleasure adds to the joy of marriage; but he also teaches that it is not basic. Marriage has far greater goods to rejoice in. "Happiness in marital life," he wrote, "is in direct ratio to the respect husband and wife have for each other, even in the intimate act of marriage."[33] They respect each other by treating each other as irreplaceable persons, committed to a common life in which each fosters the uniquely exclusive conjugal love for each other and the great goods of marriage.

IV. The Immorality of Sexual Activity Outside the Covenant of Marriage

In proclaiming the norms of sexual behavior rooted in God's law and in respect for the inviolable dignity of human persons and the goods of human sexuality, the magisterium has always taught, as the previous section has indicated, that it is seriously wrong to choose to engage in any sexual activity that is not authentically marital. From the first days of the Church, pastoral leaders taught, as Scripture had, that those who engage in fornication, gross indecency, and sexual irresponsibility ". . . shall not inherit the kingdom of God" (Gal 5:19-21). Moreover, the magisterium has always proposed its teaching on these matters as being the teaching of God himself, as revealed in Scripture. This is clearly shown by both the *Roman Catechism*, promulgated after the Council of Trent in the sixteenth century and in use until the present century, and by the *Catechism of the Catholic Church*, written in response to Vatican Council II and promulgated by John Paul II, who describes it as "a sure norm for teaching the faith."[34] The *Roman Catechism*, in condemning adultery, fornication, prostitution, and homosexual acts, listed them as violations of the sixth commandment — that is, as acts prohibited by Scripture.[35] The *Catechism of the Catholic Church* begins its treatment of the sixth commandment and its requirements by citing Exodus 20:14 and Deuteronomy 5:18, where we read, "You shall not commit adultery," and Matthew 5:27-28, where Jesus says "You have heard that it was said, 'You shall not commit adultery.' But I say to you that every one who looks at a woman lustfully has already committed adultery with her in his heart." It goes on to condemn as absolutely immoral and opposed to the virtue of chastity and the dignity of marriage the sins of masturbation, fornication, pornography, prostitution, rape, homosexual acts, adultery, divorce, and polygamy, incest, and "free unions" (see the *Catechism of the Catholic Church*, nos. 2351-2359, 2380-2391, 2396, 2400). From earliest times the magisterium has regarded masturbation and contraception among the grossly indecent and sexually irresponsible acts which exclude their perpetrators from God's kingdom.[36]

The reasons for these teachings are spelled out in later chapters. But it is clear that the Church presents this teaching as based not only on the most serious of reasons but also on the basis of her faith in God's revelation. She has received a teaching from God which she must proclaim both to be true to her mission and to protect the dignity of human persons and human sexuality. This teaching expresses a loving concern to preserve the real meaning and goodness of marital love and to foster human dignity in intimate personal relations. Pope John Paul II has articulated these considerations as follows:

> The only "place" in which this self-giving [of man to woman] in its whole truth is made possible is marriage, the covenant of conjugal love freely and consciously chosen, whereby man and woman accept the intimate community of life and love willed by God Himself, which only in this light manifests its true meaning. The institution of marriage is not an undue . . . imposition of a form. Rather, it is an interior requirement of the covenant of conjugal love which is publicly affirmed as unique and exclusive, in order to live in complete fidelity to the plan of God, the Creator. A person's freedom, far from being restricted by this fidelity, is secured against every form of subjectivism or relativism and is made a sharer in creative Wisdom (*Familiaris Consortio*, no. 11).

The kind of reasoning exhibited here will be developed further and applied to particular sexual activities in the final chapters of this work. The point here is simply that the Church's teaching on sexual matters is always presented both as the revealed will of God, and also as eminently reasonable. The Catholic vision of sexuality teaches a way of living sexually which is liberating and genuinely good for human beings. Those who reflect carefully in the light of faith can see and experience this for themselves.

Chapter Two
The Biblical Teaching on Sex

In its *Dogmatic Constitution on Divine Revelation* Vatican Council II declared: "All the preaching of the Church, as indeed as indeed the entire Christian religion, should be nourished and ruled by sacred Scripture" (*Dei Verbum*, no. 21).

The study of the biblical teaching on human sexuality is then appropriate and necessary, for Scripture is the primary fount of the Church's teaching. This chapter will offer a review of this teaching, based on the work of excellent contemporary exegetes and biblical theologians, and of other persons qualified to expound on the biblical teaching on human sexuality, marriage, and the morality of freely chosen sexual acts.

I. The Old Testament

The Old Testament is not, nor was it intended to be, a textbook either on morality in general or on sexual morality in particular. But it is the record, written under divine inspiration, of God's revelation to his chosen people, preparing them and the whole of humanity for his definitive revelation in and through the life, death, and resurrection of his only-begotten Son made man, Jesus Christ. As such, it articulates fundamental truths about God himself and the created universe, and in particular, about human life and destiny, and the special relationship of friendship that he wills to exist between himself and human beings and between men and women. It reveals to us too the source of what Pope John Paul II terms "a fundamental disquietude in all human existence,"[1] namely, the disobedience of our first parents and its devastating effects on human persons and human sexuality, and it likewise points ahead to the One who will be our Redeemer. It is not surprising, therefore, that the Old Testament contains fundamental truths about human sexuality and its place in human life and the divine economy. These truths, as we shall see, have lasting significance and are relevant today.

The Context of Old Testament Teaching on Sex

The proper perspective for understanding the Old Testament's teaching on sexual matters is provided by the fundamental concerns of this first stage of divine revelation. These concerns cluster around the Hebrew awareness of the reality of God, his holiness, and his covenant with the people Israel and, through them, with all humankind. The God of Israel, utterly unlike the "no gods" of their pagan neighbors, is a holy God. He is good, and he cares about the moral quality of our actions. Israel's conviction about the holiness and moral character of the one true God is reflected in the life of the people. The Old Testament itself explicitly claims that in sexual matters its ways are in sharp contrast to the practices of the surrounding peoples (cf. Lev 18:3, 24-30; cf. also Gen 34:7; Jgs 19:30; 2 Sam 13:12).[2] Indeed, as John L. McKenzie has observed, "the *morality of sex* is far more rigorous in Israel than among its neighbors. It is not merely fanciful to see in this a reflection of the character of Yahweh himself in contrast to the gods and goddesses of the fertility cults. Sexual license profanes the holiness of a God who is above all sexual processes."[3]

The Hebrews saw sexuality primarily in moral terms, and they understood morality in the light of their faith in God and in the light of what was taught them in God's name. Morality thus understood was primarily a way of response to the love of the all-holy God as revealed to them in the various covenants God offered them. All of human life, including sexual life, was seen as a worshiping service of God. This was so because God, who gave to human persons the gift of life and of sexuality, wanted his people to be holy, as he is holy.

In this summary of Old Testament teaching on sex, attention will center first on the first two chapters of Genesis, the "beginning," to which Jesus himself referred in his response to the question about divorce posed to him by the Pharisees (cf. Mk 10:2-12; Mt 19:3-12). For these chapters describe God's original design for human existence, human sexuality, and human marriage. The third chapter of Genesis is also central inasmuch as it treats of the disobedience of our first parents, and the terrible effects of their sin on human existence, human sexuality, and the relationship between men and women. Following the analysis of these Genesis texts, other teachings of the Old Testament on sex will be summarized.

Genesis 1-2: Human Sexuality and Marriage

The first two chapters of Genesis, the "creation accounts," are central for understanding the teaching of the Old Testament on marriage and human sexuality. These chapters, which contain the stories of what Pope John Paul II has called the "beatifying beginning of human existence,"[4] have been shaped into a harmonious whole, although they include two distinct accounts — the Priestly narrative of Genesis 1:2-2:4a, and the Yahwist narrative of Genesis 2:4b-24. Though these two accounts differ in many ways, they share certain central common themes. Thus, for instance, each was written in a deliberate effort to counter the stories of human origins current among Israel's pagan neighbors, in particular, the myth of Baal and its accompanying fertility cult. That account of human origins and of human life and sexuality was utterly incompatible with faith in the God of Abraham, Isaac, and Jacob because it divinized human sexuality and portrayed the gods as sexual beings, capable, like men, of the unrestrained passion of lust.[5] Other features common to the two accounts will be noted below. But first we will summarize and comment on the key teachings of each account.

Genesis 1

The narrative of Genesis 1, attributed to the Priestly tradition (chronologically later than the Yahwist tradition that is the source of Genesis 2), expresses many great truths about human persons, human sexuality, and marriage.[6] First, it unequivocally affirms the fundamental equality of man and woman as persons made in the image and likeness of God, and uses the Hebrew word `adam (man) as a generic term, not a proper name, to refer to both the man and the woman: "So God created man [`adam] in his own image, in the image of God he created him; male and female he created them" (Gen 1:27). Each is a different but complementary epiphany or revelation of God himself, whose full image is found in their communion.[7]

Another great truth expressed by Genesis 1 is that human sexual activity is not something divine. It is not something that God engages in, nor is it a means of currying favor from the gods, as it was understood to be in the fertility cults. Sexuality, rather, is a great and good gift of God to human persons, male and female. Through their sexuality men and women image him in the world.[8] Moreover, through their responsible exercise of their sexual powers in the pursuit of the great goods toward which sexuality is ordered, they honor God.

A third great truth of this account is that God is the author of marriage. Genesis 1 speaks not only of God's creation of man, male and female, but also of his creation of marriage. Indeed, it was in the first Adam, the first human beings, male and female, "that God himself constituted the essential structure of marriage between man and woman — the structure that we should expect to encounter in every marriage."[9]

34

A fourth great truth of this account of human origins is that human fertility is a blessing, not a curse: "And God blessed them, and God said to them, 'Be fruitful and multiply, and fill the earth and subdue it' " (Gen 1:28). The marital union is one upon which the blessing of fertility can descend. Children are a gift from God, the fruit of his blessing.[10]

Genesis 2

The narrative in Genesis 2, stemming from the earlier Yahwist tradition, is more poetic in character. It too contains many truths about human existence, human sexuality, and marriage.[11] Unlike the text in Genesis 1, which speaks of the simultaneous creation of male and female and which uses the term `adam (man) to designate both, this passage speaks first of the creation of man as male and uses the word `adam to identify this male. This being is alone in the universe, utterly different from and superior to the other animals. None of these is his equal; he exercises authority over them all. This authority is symbolized by his being given the power to name all the animals (cf. Gen 2:19-20).[12] To give the first man a "helper fit for him," that is, a being equal in dignity to him, the Lord God then makes the "woman," fashioned from the man's own ribs.

A first magnificent truth that Genesis 2 articulates is the complementary character of man and woman, who are made for each other and meant to live in an intimate communion of persons. The very first words of the man (`adam) in this text ("this at last is bone of my bones . . .") are a short poem expressing, in wondrous delight, a vision of the relation meant to exist between man and woman.[13] The helper, the woman, is a person equal to the man ( `adam), but she is not his clone. She is woman (*ishshah*) because she is taken from man (*ish*), but differs from him. Communion is between two likes who are yet unlike. In naming her, moreover, the man (`adam) himself assumes a new name (*ish*). Sharing bone and flesh forms a totally human basis for an interpersonal and covenantal relationship made possible by God's action.[14] The woman is given to the man by God. Without her the man, in his solitude, is in a situation that is "not good." She is taken from him and given to him so that, together, they may be what they cannot be alone. There is a complementarity between them that permits them to form a true communion of persons when they become "one flesh," cleaving to each other as husband and wife.

"Cleaving" (Gen 2:24) implies a devotion and an unshakable faith between humans: it connotes a permanent attraction that transcends genital union, to which, nevertheless, it gives meaning. There can be no mistaking the author's intention. He concludes his narrative by interpreting the divinely ordered sexual differentiation and the sexual drive within the perspective of a permanent social union between man and woman.[15]

Genesis 2 also suggests the great truth that marriage comes into being when a man and a woman "give" themselves to one another by a free act of irrevocable personal consent. Pope John Paul II says of this text:

> The very formulation of Genesis 2:24 indicates not only that human beings, created as man and woman, were created for unity, but also that precisely *this unity, through which they become "one flesh," has right from the beginning a character of union derived from a choice.* We read, in fact, that "a man leaves his father and his mother and cleaves to his wife." If the man belongs "by nature" to his father and mother by virtue of procreation, he, on the other hand, "cleaves" by choice to his wife (and she to her husband).[16]

A third great truth about man and woman as created by God and prior to their disobedience is expressed in the remark that ". . . and the man and his wife were both naked, and were not ashamed" (Gen 2:25).[17] By stating that the man and the woman were naked and felt no shame, the author refers to a mode of existence for the man and his wife beyond our experience. He indicates that they have a distinctive form of integrity, which permitted a spontaneous and unveiled communication between them. This truth, central to the teaching of Genesis 2, is what John Paul II seeks to communicate by speaking of the "nuptial meaning" of the body.[18] Since the naked bodies of both the man and the woman, the husband and the wife, perfectly manifest their dignity as persons and, because of their complementarity, the "gift" that each is for the other, they feel no shame.[19]

Another truth that Genesis 2, like Genesis 1, makes clear is that God is the author of marriage. Genesis 2, as Johannes Bauer emphasizes, proclaims "monogamy as ordained and willed by God."[20] Genesis 2 does not explicitly talk about the procreative nature of the marital union, but it nonetheless presupposes it. Genesis 2 forms a literary unit with Genesis 3 and 4, and Genesis 4:1 affirms that "Now Adam knew Eve his wife, and she conceived and bore Cain, saying, 'I have gotten a man with the help of the LORD.' " This shows that "the establishment of the first family was the solution to the man's need for social life and for a race to fulfill his commission. . . . In creating woman and coupling her with the man, God created one flesh that could be the source of the family."[21]

36

Genesis 3

The third chapter of Genesis, also from the Yahwist tradition, tells of the primordial sin by the first man and woman. As a result of their sin — their rebellion against God — the man and the woman find themselves alienated from God, from each other, and even from their own sexuality. They now experience shame over their nakedness, for after their sin ". . . the eyes of both were opened, and they knew that they were naked" (Gen 3:7). Concupiscence had entered the human heart. As a result, one can truly say: "Man, alas, is not such a perfect being that the sight of the body of another person, especially a person of the other sex, can arouse in him merely a disinterested liking which develops into an innocent affection. In practice, it also arouses concupiscence, or a wish to enjoy concentrated on sexual values with no regard for the value of the person."[22]

The "nuptial meaning" of the bodies of men and women has, as it were, been veiled; concupiscence makes itself felt.[23] The man begins to lord it over his wife, whose social and cultural oppression begins. The treatment of women as inferior to men within Israelite society is the consequence of sin.[24] In his original creation, God intended that man and woman should live harmoniously, in peace and unity. The evil which disrupted their daily lives, even in their most intimate aspects, was the result of human sin.[25]

Key Old Testament Teachings on Sex

First of all, throughout the Old Testament marriage is presented as something holy and good; and sexual union within marriage is portrayed as good when it is mindful of God and his covenant. All this is brought out nicely in the prayer Tobias offers before consummating his union with Sarah:

"Thou [God of our fathers] madest Adam and gavest him Eve his wife as a helper and support. From them the race of mankind has sprung. Thou didst say 'It is not good that the man should be alone; let us make a helper for him like himself.' And now, O Lord, I am not taking this sister of mine because of lust, but with sincerity. Grant that I may find mercy and may grow old together with her" (Tob 8:6-9).

In addition, the prophets, beginning with Hosea and continuing through Isaiah, Jeremiah, and Ezekiel, saw in human marriage a fitting symbol of the covenant between God and his people. In using this image, the prophets were more interested in articulating the truth about God's love, forgiveness, and mercy than they were in spelling out the nature of a loving marriage. Nonetheless, as Schillebeeckx has pointed out, the use of this image by the prophets involves a "reciprocal illumination" of the human meaning of

37

marriage. Their use of this image speaks to us not only of the utterly faithful love of God for his people but also the normative reality of marriage — the divinely intended, faithful, and exclusive union of husband and wife.[26]

It is true that the understanding of marriage among the Hebrews was imperfect. The husband was permitted to divorce his wife, but she was not permitted to divorce him; women were regarded as inferior to men; and there was a double standard for adultery. A married man committed adultery only if he had sexual relations with the wife of another man or with a maiden betrothed to another, but he was not judged guilty of adultery if he had sexual relations with an unbetrothed maiden, a harlot, or slave girl (cf. Deut 22:28-29). But any sexual relations on the part of a married woman or betrothed virgin with any man other than her husband was considered adultery.

These inequalities were rooted in socioeconomic factors within Hebrew society and reflect its patriarchal ethos.[27] While it is true that husbands who had intercourse with prostitutes, unbetrothed maidens, or slave girls were not considered to have committed adultery, their infidelity is severely criticized by the prophets (Mal 2:14-15) and in the Wisdom literature (e.g., Prov 5:15-20).[28] There is abundant evidence in the Old Testament that the very nature and purposes of human sexuality require husbands and wives to be faithful to one another.[29] The story of Joseph and Potipar's wife (Gen 39), the episode of Abimelech and Sarah (Gen 20), and in particular the teaching set forth in the Wisdom literature give the reasons why adultery is incompatible with married life. Thus it is clear, for instance, from a reading of Proverbs 1-9 that "sexual fidelity is . . . a symbol of one's attachment to Lady Wisdom," and the upright Israelite man was urged to be attached to Lady Wisdom.[30]

Moreover, the insistence by the prophets (above all, Hosea, Isaiah, Jeremiah, Ezekiel) that the marriage of man and woman is a sign of God's utterly faithful love for his people led to the idea that fidelity was central to a covenanted marriage. This fidelity was so highly valued that restrictions were developed so that a wife could not be too easily abandoned by her spouse. "Marriage," above all, "was to be experienced from the standpoint of an unconditional faith and confidence in Yahweh, since this was the very core of the covenant of grace and it was in this way that man was to express his response to Yahweh's love."[31]

Although fornication is not explicitly condemned in the Old Testament, the rich meaning of sexual union was appreciated ever more deeply by the prophets and the authors of the Wisdom literature. The latter repeatedly counsels husbands and wives to be faithful to one another and speaks glowingly of the happiness of a marriage marked by lifelong fidelity. The advice given young men, especially in the Wisdom literature, strongly supports a negative evaluation of fornication or premarital sexual activity.[32]

The Old Testament vehemently condemns bestiality and homosexuality as reprehensible and abominable. Since human sexuality is ordered to the personal relationship of marriage and the good of children, sexual commerce with a beast is utterly repugnant. To engage in bestiality is to be guilty of a most grievous crime (Ex 22:19; Lev 18:23, 20:15-16; Deut 27:21).

Contemporary biblical scholars differ as to why homosexuality was so strongly condemned in the Old Testament (cf. Lev 18:22, 20:13), and offer different interpretations of the story of Sodom and Gomorrah in Genesis 19. But it is clear that the Old Testament unequivocally condemns homosexual acts as an abomination, a form of idolatry, and a base attempt to gain sexual power. Moreover, the motive for the moral condemnation seems to be the nature of homosexual acts themselves.[33] There is no explicit distinction made between homosexual orientation and homosexual acts in the Old Testament; judgment was made about the acts.

The older Catholic tradition (Fathers, scholastics, manualists) frequently appealed to the Onan story (Gen 38:8-10) to show that the Old Testament condemned masturbation and contraception. A number of contemporary exegetes[34] suggest that Onan was punished not because of any sexual sin but because he violated the Levirate law, according to which he was obliged to help his widowed sister-in-law Tamar have a child in order to continue his brother's line. This interpretation, although popular today, is sharply challenged by other scholars. Closely analyzing the language used to describe Onan's offense, they point out that God punished him both because of *what* Onan chose to do — to waste his seed on the ground was a perverse sexual act — and because he did this for a base purpose or *end*, namely, to deprive his dead brother of progeny.[35]

II. The New Testament

The principal message of the New Testament is that the long-awaited good news, heralded by the prophets, is now with us. God himself, through the person of his only-begotten Son made man, Jesus Christ, is establishing his reign of justice, peace, and love, bringing his people and all humankind redemption and salvation. Indeed, God, in and through Jesus, in a most wonderful and unexpected way, is making possible a new kind of intimate friendship and life with himself. God has saved us, through the life, death, and resurrection of Jesus. In and through union with Jesus we are freed from the slavery of sin, and from the "hardness of heart" (cf. Mt 19:8; Mk

39

10:5) that had prevented post-Adamic man from honoring God's will regarding marriage. In and through union with Jesus we can overcome concupiscence and recover the "nuptial meaning" of the body and live lives worthy of the holiness to which we are called.[36]

Here we will show how this new way of understanding the meaning of human existence impacted the New Testament's teaching on sex by considering (1) New Testament teaching on virginity, (2) Jesus' teaching on marriage and sexual morality, and (3) the teaching of St. Paul on marriage and sexual morality.

New Testament Teaching on Virginity

The new way of understanding human existence central to the Gospel — the "good news" of our redemption in and through Christ — is clearly manifested in the new evaluation of virginity and celibacy. The Jews of the first century — with the exception of the ascetic Essenes — believed that a life of celibacy was abnormal, perhaps even sinful. According to the rabbinical schools of the time "no man may abstain from keeping the Law, 'Be fruitful and multiply,' unless he already has children; according to the school of Shammai, two sons; according to the school of Hillel, a son and a daughter."[37] Yet Jesus was himself a virgin and highly commended virginity or celibacy for the Gospel's sake to his disciples. In like manner St. Paul encourages those Christians of Corinth who were able to embrace the life of virginity for the sake of the kingdom, arguing that virginity, like marriage, is a great gift from God.

Today, some claim that the prominence given to the virginal state by Paul and other New Testament writers is simply a contingent, culturally-conditioned aspect of the apostolic age. It was favored simply because the early Christians thought that Jesus' second coming was imminent — hence, why marry at all?[38] But this opinion is not supported by a careful study of the New Testament's teaching on virginity for the sake of the kingdom. The whole point of the New Testament teaching is that we must put first the requirements of God's kingdom — his reign of justice and love — and everything must be seen in this light. Jesus makes this clear in his teaching on the indissolubility of marriage (see below) and his absolute prohibition of divorce. How difficult his teaching must have appeared to husbands and wives abandoned by their spouses, but surely among the "eunuchs for the sake of the kingdom" were husbands and wives so abandoned. Yet, because of the requirements of the kingdom of God — of the requirements of his love — such persons had to remain celibate.[39]

Schillebeeckx notes the richness of New Testament teaching on virginity. Although Paul's views on the subject were set in the context of his expectation that Jesus would soon return in glory, his overriding concern was to impress upon his converts the radical transformation of human life effected by Jesus' saving deed and our new life in the Risen Lord. Thus, as Schillebeeckx accurately observes, Paul wanted to encourage Christians to be self-sacrificing enough to embark on the charism of total continence. . . . It is inconceivable that some " 'new existential experience,' the discovery of new aspects of marriage which escaped those who experienced it at an earlier period, should make the New Testament vision of Christian celibacy appear relative or incomplete in any respect. . . . Christianity will never be able to close its ears to the authentic biblical call to total abstinence as a possibility that forms an intrinsic and essential part of Christianity itself."[40]

This shows us that the basic perspective from which the New Testament approaches all questions of human existence, including those concerned with human sexuality, is that provided by our new life in Christ. With Christ we have "died" to sin and are risen to a new kind of life. This new and richer life is possible only because of his redemptive death and resurrection and our union with him through baptism. We are indeed "new creatures" for we have been regenerated through the waters of baptism. We are now, in, with, and through Christ, members of the divine family, led by his Spirit, able to call his Father "our Father," called to be holy even as the heavenly Father is holy.

New Testament Teaching on Marriage and Sexual Morality

The New Testament takes for granted Old Testament teaching on the goodness of sexuality and the beauty of faithful marriage. But the New Testament is concerned above all with showing how marriage, sexuality, and indeed everything human, have been inwardly transformed and deepened by the new life brought to us by Jesus.

Jesus' Teaching on Marriage and Sexual Morality

Jesus' teaching on these matters needs to be put into the context of his teaching on the moral life in general. This is provided by his Sermon on the Mount (Mt 5:1-7:28) and in particular his teaching on the Beatitudes.[41]

This is the framework within which Jesus set forth his teaching — brief but very significant — on marriage and sexual morality. In his teaching on divorce (Mt 19:3-12; Mk 10:2-12; Lk 16:18) [42] Jesus first reaffirms the goodness of sexuality and marriage as taught by Genesis. By including in their versions of our Lord's teaching explicit references to both Genesis 1:27 (Mt 19:4; Mk 10:6) and Genesis 2:24 (Mt 19:5; Mk 10:7), the evangelists indicate that for Jesus the sexual differentiation of man into male and female is part of God's plan of creation and that marriage is the only proper "place" for genital union to take place.[43]

Several features of Jesus' teaching here are particularly striking. First of all, he unequivocally condemns both divorce and remarriage. He insists that "remarriage" after divorce is not a marriage at all but adultery. As Schillecbeeckx has rightly emphasized: "Christ not only expressly condemned divorce (showing, in other words, that the indissolubility of marriage is a *moral* obligation); he also said that any divorce that might possibly take place had no effect whatsoever on the bond of marriage itself (pointing out, in other words, that the indissolubility of marriage is an *objective* bond)."[44] Second, he clarified and developed the Old Testament teaching on the fundamental equality of woman. He stated that the one who divorced his wife and married another committed adultery against his wife. This is particularly clear in Mark's account: "Whoever divorces his wife and marries another, commits adultery against her" (Mk 10:11). Thus, any double standard of the sort tolerated in the Old Testament was firmly excluded: adultery was a very serious evil, and since remarriage after divorce was adultery, it was obviously a serious violation of God's wise and loving plan for human existence.[45]

Matthew's account of Jesus' teaching contains an *apparent* exception when it says, "whoever divorces his wife (lewd conduct is a separate case)" (Mt 19:9). The Greek word translated here by "lewd" is *porneia* (cf. Mt 5:32). Traditionally, in the Fathers, Scholastics, and post-Tridentine manuals, it was understood that unchaste conduct could permit separation from bed and board, but not dissolution of the union with freedom to marry again. But modern scholarship has shown that in this text the Greek term *porneia* specifically refers to an *unlawful or invalid* marriage. As one scholar, Johannes Bauer, says: "*porneia* means an unlawful marriage, in particular marriage between blood relations, as was practiced among the gentiles and regarded among them as lawful. Such marriage relationships, which could sometimes be found among applicants for baptism, had to be dissolved, and this could give the impression of a divorce such as had been forbidden by Jesus. The Matthean redaction is an attempt to meet this problem as it arose in gentile Christian circles."[46]

Thus this text cannot be interpreted as an "exception clause" to the teaching of Jesus on the indissolubility of marriage.

Jesus and Woman's Equality With Man. Jesus' gracious dealings with women further illustrate his concern for their human and personal dignity and their fundamental equality with men. For example, his treatment of the Samaritan woman at the well reveals an open friendliness not expected in first-century Palestine (Jn 4:27). And his response to the woman taken in adultery, although it makes clear his firm teaching that adultery is seriously wrong, shows his kindness and mercy in a context in which righteous indignation was a more common reaction.

Jesus' Emphasis on Interior Attitudes and Dispositions. The focus on internal dispositions and the emphasis that morality comes from the "heart," from the inner core of a person, is absolutely central to Jesus' teaching on sexual morality. It is reflected in the catalog of vices Jesus presents (Mt 15:19; Mk 7:21-22). These vices proceed from the human heart and profoundly defile the human person in a way that eating "unclean food" could not. In the list provided by Mark there are several sexual sins, among them adultery (*moicheia*), fornication (*porneia*), and sensuality (*aselgeia*). The list found in Matthew includes adultery (*moicheia*) and fornication (*porneia*). New Testament scholars recognize that it is difficult to determine precisely the nature of the different kinds of sexual offenses designated by some of these terms, in particular by *porneia* ("fornication") and by *aselgeia* ("sensuality"). Nonetheless, it is clear that the authors of these Gospels present Jesus as teaching that adultery (*moicheia*, whose meaning is not disputed) is not the only act of a sexual nature that must be considered sinful and utterly opposed to God's wise and loving plan for human existence. There are many others. Moreover, although *porneia* was frequently used in the New Testament to speak of prostitution or incest, this term was definitely used in the New Testament to include acts properly designated by the English term *fornication*, which is today sometimes referred to as "premarital" sex. Such sexual behavior was certainly condemned by the New Testament.[47]

St. Paul on Marriage and Sexual Activity

The writings attributed to St. Paul provide another most important source of New Testament teaching on marriage and human sexuality. In his First Letter to the Corinthians, Paul, who is keenly aware of the effect of concupiscence on human persons and on our need for redemption, nonetheless reaffirms the basic goodness of human sexuality and the goodness and holiness of marriage. In 1 Corinthians 7 he clearly affirms that marriage is the way willed by God for men and women to exercise their sexuality. It is the only legitimate means of satisfying the call inscribed in nature and of mastering the disorder of the passions (cf. 1 Cor 7:2).

43

Moreover, in 1 Corinthians 7 Paul clearly recognizes that Christ's coming has inwardly affected the whole reality of marriage, so that it is now incorporated into God's economy of grace. This is reflected in the following passage: "If any brother has a wife who is an unbeliever but is willing to live with him, he must not divorce her. And if any woman has a husband who is an unbeliever but is willing to live with her, she must not divorce him. The unbelieving husband is consecrated [literally "made holy"] by his believing wife; the unbelieving wife is consecrated by her believing husband. If it were otherwise, your children should be unclean; but as it is, they are holy" (1 Cor 7:12-14).[48]

Paul says that if the unbelieving spouse wishes to separate, then the believing spouse can let him or her depart, but, speaking to those who have married "in the Lord," he writes: "To those now married . . . I give this command (though it is not mine; it is the Lord's): a wife must not separate from her husband. If she does separate, she must either remain unmarried or become reconciled to him again. Similarly, a husband must not divorce his wife" (1 Cor 7:10-11).[49] Commenting on this important passage, Pierre Benoit has justly said: "We understand by this the prohibition of divorce such as we find it in the Gospels on the lips of Jesus . . . [who], returning to the will of the Creator . . . declared that in the Kingdom of God he was inaugurating divorce was not allowed. It is this command of the Lord that Paul solemnly repeats with his apostolic authority. He knows that human weakness can involve serious difficulties between married persons. He admits, therefore, not without hesitation, the possibility of a separation, but without remarrying."[50]

The Letter to the Ephesians[51] (5:22-32) immeasurably deepens the prophetic presentation of marriage as a reality symbolizing the covenantal relationship between God and his chosen people. It teaches that the marriages of those who marry "in the Lord" are meant to symbolize and make present the life-giving, love-giving, grace-giving union of Christ and his bride the Church. It is thus a text that figures largely in the development of Catholic teaching on the sacramentality of marriage.[52]

Other key texts of St. Paul dealing with human sexuality are 1 Corinthians 6:15-20 [53] and 1 Thessalonians 4:3-6.[54] A key term in both of these passages is the Greek word *porneia*, which, as we have seen, can signify a wide range of immoral sexual acts or "lewd conduct," including incest and prostitution (which seems to be its central meaning in 1 Cor 6). But there can be no doubt, as important biblical scholars (e.g., Silverio Zedda and others) have demonstrated[55] that this term is used by St. Paul to exclude all non-marital genital intercourse.

44

St. Paul and the Fundamental Reason Why Christians Must Avoid Sexual Sins. Moreover, and this is supremely important, the fundamental reason leading Paul to the judgment that all non-marital genital intercourse is gravely immoral and unbecoming a Christian is that it is utterly irreconcilable with *the* most fundamental moral norm of the Christian life, namely, our call *to be what we are!, i.e., children of God himself, called to live worthily as those who have been "purchased at a price," recreated in the image of Christ.* As new beings in Christ, we must let Christ be formed in us and live in us, and we cannot do this if we freely choose to perform immoral sexual acts.[56]

Homosexuality. Paul's brief discussion of homosexuality in Romans 1 is also noteworthy. He does not argue that homosexuality is wrong. He sees that as evident. He treats homosexual practices as being both sinful in themselves and part of the punishment for disbelief. Homosexuality is therefore presented as an evil, a distortion of human life which follows from sin (Rom 1:26-27).

Summary

The New Testament teaches that chastity is required of every Christian, male or female, married or unmarried. Because sexuality is a good gift from God, God shows us in the fullness of his revelation in Jesus that its proper use is to be highly prized and its abuse severely condemned. The Letter to the Hebrews sums it up well: marriage is to be held in honor by all; the marriage bed is to be kept undefiled; God will judge adulterers and fornicators (Heb 13:4).

Chapter Three
Sex in the Catholic Tradition

Catholics are the heirs of a long theological tradition. Over the centuries there has been careful reflection on human sexuality and sexual morality in the light of the Scriptures. From apostolic times to the present, Catholic scholars, saints, and pastoral leaders have sought to understand, in the light of God's revealing word, the meaning of human sexuality and the norms of sexual morality. During this long history, errors have unquestionably been made. It is, however, important to note the *kind* of errors made by the tradition, and the kind not made. Thus, for instance, some of the Fathers of the Church mistakenly believed, for a variety of reasons, that sexuality would never have been used in a state of innocence. But errors of this kind did not mislead the Christian people in their efforts to lead chaste lives. None of the Fathers, none of the Scholastics, indeed no theologian in the Catholic tradition up to the very recent past, ever claimed that the Church is in error in saying that fornication or adultery or masturbation is always gravely wrong. While it is not surprising to discover some rather strange opinions by theologians over such a long period of time and in the development of a complex history, what is truly remarkable and striking is the profound unity one discovers: the same basic Catholic teaching on sex everywhere. This history is also a story of the development in doctrine toward a clearer understanding of the nature of sexuality as revealed by God and uncovered by human reflection. The growth in the Church's understanding of human sexuality has not been haphazard but systematic, for it has been directed by an awareness of fundamental truths about human nature and destiny which are grounded in Scripture, proclaimed by the teaching authority of the Church, and gradually refined by the developing theological tradition.

This tradition teaches now, and has always taught, that the union of man and woman in marriage is good, indeed holy. It teaches now, and has always taught, that the virtue of chastity is necessary for all persons, male and female, married and unmarried, so that they might fully have freedom of self-possession and not be controlled by unworthy sexual desire. It teaches now, and has always taught, that some specific sorts of sexual activity —

fornication, adultery, contraception, and sodomy, for instance — are simply incompatible with the way of life appropriate for a person who has become one body with Christ through baptism, and whose body is a living tabernacle of God.

It is, of course, impossible in a brief section of a book such as this to provide a detailed history of the developing Catholic theological tradition on sex. A satisfactory history on this subject has never, in fact, been written.[1] Still, it is possible to note the major claims about human sexuality and sexual morality that have been central to this developing tradition, and to specify some of the principal developments that have taken place.

I. Early Christian and Patristic Thought

To understand the sexual attitudes expressed by the earliest Christian writers one must first of all be aware of the context in which they wrote. They lived in an age of great sexual licentiousness — an age whose similarities to our own are unmistakable. The early Christian writers were keenly aware that the teachings of the New Testament on marriage, virginity, and chastity were radically opposed to the sexual outlook and practice of the pagan world. Thus, their thought must be understood in the context of their interaction with a society in which prostitution was widespread; divorce, contraception, abortion, and infanticide were common; and chastity for males was considered out of the question.[2]

In addition to the debauchery and disregard for human life prevalent in the Greco-Roman world of the time, the early Christians likewise faced a religious challenge in the various Gnostic movements of the day. Gnosticism at times posed as a variant of the Gospel, but it was a mystery religion more influenced by contemporary philosophical ideas than by the Gospel. It claimed a "saving" knowledge quite opposed to the Christian message. The Gnostics were metaphysical dualists, and therefore held that matter itself was evil. Consequently, they held that the human body and sexuality were evil. They despised marriage and, in particular, the procreation of new life through marital union. Although they advocated sexual abstinence for the "elite," they did so not because they thought that such abstinence might be required by God's will or by a proper regard for the goods of human nature but because they regarded sexual union as defiling. Since total abstinence was difficult for most people, however, some Gnostics conveniently taught that the non-elite could freely engage in all kinds of sexual activities for the sake of the exquisite experience of pleasure that they might bring, as long as they took care to ensure that no new life was generated.[3]

47

Facing these two evils, the early Christian writers drew on the teaching of the Gospels and Paul to instruct the faithful and to articulate Christian attitudes toward sex. While extolling a virginity that would be chosen for the sake of God's kingdom, they taught that marriage itself was something good because it had been divinely instituted and had been blessed by Jesus' presence at the wedding feast of Cana (Jn 2). Irenaeus, for example, writing in the second century, repudiated the views of the Gnostics, saying: "Saturninus and Marcion, who are called 'the Continent,' preach abstinence from marriage, frustrating the age-old creation of God and implicitly finding fault with Him who made human beings male and female so that they could reproduce themselves. They introduced abstinence from what they describe as 'animal-like,' ungrateful as they are to Him who made everything, God."[4] In similar fashion St. Clement of Alexandria wrote: "if marriage . . . is a sin, I do not see how a person can say he knows God when he says that the law of God is a sin. But if 'the law is holy,' then marriage is holy."[5]

In their desire both to encourage the faithful to live chastely and to repudiate Gnostic dualism, the early Christians stressed the procreative purpose of marriage and of human sexuality. Thus, Justin the Martyr, another second-century apologist, declared that "we Christians either marry with but one thought, to beget children, or, if we refuse to marry, we are completely continent."[6] Similarly, Athenagoras of Athens[7] and Clement of Alexandria wrote that marriage is for the sake of children. Clement, writing from a center of Gnosticism and a city notorious for its sexual licentiousness, appealed to the teaching of the Stoic philosophers in stressing the procreative purpose of marriage. Yet it needs to be said that Clement and other Christians who appealed to Stoic thought were not themselves Stoics. They were Christians, and they had already adopted the view that marriage and sex are meant for procreation from their reading of the Scriptures.[8] Clement, who with other Fathers praised virginity as a preferable state of life for Christians, also noted that married persons have more trials. But these trials could themselves serve growth in virtue.[9]

The great value of virginity and the procreative purposefulness of sex and marriage were also emphasized by the Fathers of the fourth and fifth centuries. Athanasius is typical of them in his encouragement of the young to choose a life of virginity for the sake of the Gospel. All of these writers — including Jerome and Augustine in the West, and John Chrysostom and Gregory Nazianzus in the East — see Christ as the founder of Christian virginity. They teach that the life of the virgin is to be preferred to marriage insofar as those who choose the virginal state rightly have fixed their concern on eternal realities and are already living in the anticipated end time.[10]

While they praised highly a life of virginity, these Fathers nonetheless recognized that marriage too is good, and that proper sexual relations within marriage can be morally good. Like earlier writers, they commonly found marital relations good precisely because they can lead to the procreation of children. In their reading of Genesis they saw the good of procreating children as *the* purpose of marriage. As several of them noted, it was, after all, in view of generating human life that God had given Eve — a woman — to Adam as his helpmate instead of another male.[11]

There was nonetheless in these Fathers an anxiety about sex. This anxiety was caused not only by the sexual depravity they witnessed in the lives of the pagans but also by their understanding of Scripture, in particular the story of the fall of our first parents. In the third chapter of Genesis, Adam and Eve are described as being ashamed of their nakedness after eating the forbidden fruit. The Fathers saw in this a sign that sexual appetite in particular had been wounded by sin.[12]

Some of the Fathers were so suspicious of the sexual appetite that they believed it became operative only after the fall. These Fathers — among them Gregory of Nyssa, John Chrysostom, Theodoret, and John Damascene[13] — believed that God had originally intended to generate life in some nonsexual way. Foreseeing, however, that Adam and Eve would fall, he had providentially endowed them with sexual powers that would be used after the fall. This view, to be sure, was not commonly held, and was vigorously repudiated by many. Still, its presence in some of the Fathers is sufficient to show us the caution with which some of them regarded sexual activity. This caution was not based on the conviction that sexual activity was evil in itself but on the conviction that it had been profoundly wounded by mankind's fall.

These Fathers saw sexuality as lying at the root of the conflict so eloquently spoken of by Paul when he described his inability to do the good he willed, and when he distinguished between the law of his mind and the law of his members. The Fathers blamed the loss of rational control over sexual activity on the impairment brought about by original sin. In sexual matters desires frequently seemed to overpower reason. Thus, even within marriage there is need to make sure that reason dominates, lest man be led to sin by unruly desires. Clement of Alexandria wrote: "The man who has taken a wife in order to have children should also practice continence, not even seeking pleasure from his own wife, whom he ought to love, but with honorable and moderate desire, having but one intention, children."[14] The Fathers were thus led to stress the procreative end, or purpose, of marriage, for this wonderful purpose provides married couples with a reasonable ground for the choice to have sexual relations. With this purpose in mind they can moderate their desires and bring them under reason's rule.

Still, there was in Scripture, particularly in the teaching of Paul on marriage in 1 Corinthians, another purpose of marriage. Paul suggested that marriage could allay the concupiscence experienced by humankind as a result of Adam's sin. Among the Fathers, Lactantius in the West and John Chrysostom in the East explicitly affirm that marital relations for the purpose of avoiding concupiscence are licit.[15] These authors do not expressly affirm that marital relations may be chosen as a way of fostering or expressing love between the spouses, but they do say that marital relations may rightfully be chosen in order to alleviate sexual desire and to avoid fornication. In addition, Chrysostom wrote beautifully about Christian marriage as an image of Christ's bridal union with the Church.[16]

What all this shows is that it was difficult for these Fathers to articulate a balanced sexual morality within the context provided by the twin evils of sexual licentiousness and Gnostic hatred of matter and marriage. The whole aim of the Fathers was to instruct the faithful in the Gospel of salvation. They saw, and rightly so, that sexual immorality, to which humankind is easily inclined, is a form of idolatry, for it is, as Paul had taught, a desecration of a human person who has become, through baptism, one body with Christ and a living temple of the Holy Spirit. Likewise, the Fathers believed that sex in itself, as created by God, is good, as is marriage.

From the Scriptures they had likewise learned that through Adam's sin all men had been harmed, for now the power of sin enslaved all mankind, disrupting the interior harmony of the human person and rendering humans incapable of ordering their desires — in particular, their sexual desires — as they must be if evil is to be avoided. Thus, in their efforts to combat, on the one hand, sexual immorality, and, on the other, Gnostic contempt for marriage and the generation of human life, they quite naturally found it necessary to stress one important truth about sexuality and marriage, namely that these good gifts of God are intended for the generation of new human life.[17]

St. Augustine

The thought of St. Augustine is especially important for several reasons. First of all, Augustine wrote more extensively about sexual and marital issues than did other Fathers.[18] Second, his influence, particularly on later theologians in the Western Church, has been and continues to be profound. It is fashionable today to portray Augustine as something of a pessimistic villain in the history of Christian theological reflection on sex, with some even accusing him of a latent Manicheism — that is, of an essentially Gnostic viewpoint which regarded sex as evil.[19] But these charges are unfair. There were, as shall be noted, limitations in Augustine's thought. But they are far from gross errors, and they should not cause us to forget the important contributions he has made to our understanding of human sexuality and of marriage.

In his early writings as a Catholic Augustine was inclined to accept the view of some Greek Fathers that marriage and the sexual generation of human life would not have existed in Paradise (the Garden of Eden).[20] But the mature Augustine rejected this opinion, saying: "I do not see what could prevent there having been honorable marriage and an immaculate marriage bed in Paradise. . . . God could have arranged that, without any restless burning of sexual desire, . . . children would be born."[21] Obviously Augustine did not believe sex and sexual desire as such to be evil, though some claim that he did.[22] Following the Letter to the Hebrews, Augustine believes that marriage is to be held in honor, but he also shares this epistle's concern that the marriage bed "be undefiled" (Heb 13:4). He believes that this defilement occurs when desire is disordered, when it is a "restless burning."

Augustine held that concupiscence is the source of this restless burning. Concupiscence, which exists in us as a result of Adam's transgression, is not the same as original sin.[23] Rather, concupiscence is *caused* by original sin and *inclines* us to sin. Original sin itself, from which concupiscence arises, is clearly distinct from concupiscence because baptism completely removes original sin, whereas its effect and punishment, concupiscence, remains.[24] Augustine clarifies the relationship between concupiscence and actual sins of human beings in his commentary on a passage from the Letter of James in which we are told that "everyone is tempted by being drawn away and enticed by his own concupiscence. Once concupiscence has conceived, it gives birth to sin" (Jas 1:14-15). "These words," Augustine wrote, "distinguish the thing brought forth from the one giving birth. But concupiscence gives not birth unless it conceives; it does not conceive unless it entices, that is, unless it obtains willing consent to commit evil."[25] Thus, concupiscence may be called sin "by a certain figure of speech" (that is, by metonymy), since it comes from sin and leads to sin.[26] But since sin as such exists only in the will, it is not sin in the strict sense.[27]

According to Augustine, concupiscence distorts all our natural desires. These desires are good in themselves; but, as a result of original sin, they are now prone to seek their own proper objectives in a disordered way. Thus, for Augustine, concupiscence is a privation whereby our natural appetites or desires are bereft of their proper subordination to the rule of reason, and, thus deprived, tend to lead human beings away from God to the pursuit of worldly things in a sinful way.[28]

Augustine taught that, in virtue of our freedom and the grace of God poured forth in our hearts through Christ,[29] we are capable of resisting the enticements of concupiscent desire and of choosing and doing the good. We choose what is good when we "use" created goods, including our natural desires, for the purposes for which they have been created. Such "use" is not to be understood in any narrow utilitarian sense but simply in the sense that things to be used must be treated in a way that recognizes their true worth. The goods of this world are to be used and not "enjoyed" as if they were the final objects of human desire, for these are created and limited goods in which our hearts are not to take final rest. These created goods are ordered among themselves and are ordered ultimately to the Uncreated Good, God. He alone is our end — the one in whom our hearts will find rest. He alone is the Being that is to be "enjoyed" in the true sense of that word.[30]

Augustine explains how the goods of human sexuality are to be properly used in his discussion of marriage, for it is within marriage that these goods can be realized fully and rationally. Marriage, for Augustine, is a very good thing, and the goods of marriage provide the standard for proper sexual activity. His classification of the goods of marriage as the good of offspring, the good of fidelity, and the good of indissoluble unity became a classic source for the Christian discussion of marriage and chastity.[31]

Before taking up Augustine's teaching on the goods of marriage, however, it is most important to emphasize that he clearly distinguished *pleasure*, including *sexual pleasure*, from the evil of sinful concupiscence. He insisted that sexual pleasure, sought temperately and rationally, is not and cannot be termed concupiscence.[32] And he contrasts the lawful pleasure of the conjugal embrace with the unlawful pleasure of fornication.[33] In short, Augustine is not, as some people like to portray him, a pessimist who condemned all sexual pleasure as evil.[34]

For Augustine, offspring is the first and most obvious good of marriage. "What food is to the health of man, intercourse is to the health of the race."[35] This good does not consist merely in the physical generation of life. "Marriage was instituted so that the chastity of women would make children known to their fathers and fathers known to their children. True, it was possible for men to be born of promiscuous and random intercourse with any women at all, but there could not have been a bond of kinship between fathers and children."[36] The good of offspring, for Augustine, means the giving of life to persons who are called to a life of surpassing joy and friendship with God. Augustine says: "By offspring is meant not merely their begetting, but the receiving of them lovingly, the nourishing of them humanely, and the educating of them religiously."[37]

The great good of marital fidelity required, for Augustine, not only fidelity in sexual intercourse for the sake of procreating children but also mutual service in sustaining each other's weakness so that each may avoid illicit intercourse.[38] It is in conjunction with these two goods of marriage that Augustine discusses the morality of sexual union within marriage. Since procreation is "the primary, natural, and legitimate purpose of marriage,"[39] it is evident that conjugal union chosen to serve this good is completely without any fault. It is, indeed, a "chaste activity."[40]

The good of fidelity requires that spouses be faithful to each other, avoiding fornication and adultery. Augustine, like Lactantius and Chrysostom, is mindful of Paul's teaching in 1 Corinthians that people are to marry if they cannot exercise self-control, for "it is better to marry than to burn [with concupiscent desire]" (1 Cor 7:9), and that married couples are "not to deprive each other, except perhaps by consent, for a time that [they] may give themselves to prayer and return together again lest Satan tempt them because they lack self-control. But this I say by way of concession, not commandment" (1 Cor 7:5-6). But whereas Lactantius, Chrysostom, and Damascene — in speaking of the rightfulness of marital union "to avoid fornication" — imply that marital union for this purpose is unqualifiedly good, Augustine teaches that a spouse who requests marital relations precisely in order to avoid fornication is guilty of a venial sin. By "venial sin" Augustine means the sort of sin to which all of us are daily susceptible and of which we cannot claim to be free without lying (cf. 1 Jn 1:8); it is the sort of sin that is forgiven when we recite the Lord's prayer.[41] "In marriage, intercourse for the purpose of procreation has no fault attached to it; but intercourse for the purpose of satisfying concupiscence, provided it is with a spouse, is but venial fault because of fidelity; adultery or fornication, however, is a mortal sin."[42]

Many find this teaching of Augustine distasteful and demeaning to marriage. Yet Augustine's teaching perhaps shows a deeper appreciation of the human reality of marriage than does that of Lactantius, Chrysostom, and Damascene, for in holding that there is some minor fault when spousal relations are sought for the precise purpose of allaying desires and avoiding fornication, Augustine suggests that a basic good of marriage is itself not directly being sought but only indirectly fostered by avoidance of an activity that is seriously disordered. What is being sought in this type of

53

intercourse is precisely the allaying of a desire and the avoiding of an evil to which the desire may lead. It is hardly an act which precisely expresses conjugal fidelity or, in modern terms, conjugal love. Augustine did clearly teach that the spouse who serves the good of conjugal fidelity by consenting to marital relations to meet the need of the spouse seeking relations for this purpose is choosing something perfectly good, for this spouse is choosing to serve the good of marital fidelity. Marital intercourse in the service of a real good is itself good.

Where Augustine can be faulted is in his failure to consider that spouses can choose to have marital relations for the precise purpose of expressing their fidelity, their love. With his predecessors, he sees as the possible purposes of marital union (1) the generation of children and (2) the serving of the good of fidelity when one spouse blamelessly agrees to marital union when the other spouse seeks it, with venial fault, expressly as a way of avoiding illicit intercourse. He does not explicitly entertain the possibility that both spouses might choose marital relations precisely as a way of showing their fidelity, their love.

Nevertheless, there is some evidence that if Augustine had considered this possibility, he would have approved it. For instance, in one place he wrote: "Surely we must see that God gives us some goods which are to be sought for their own sakes, such as wisdom, health, friendship; others which are necessary for something else, such as learning, food, drink, sleep, marriage, sexual intercourse. Certain of these are necessary for the sake of wisdom, such as learning; *others for the sake of friendship, such as marriage or intercourse*"[43] (emphasis added). Obviously, there is here the suggestion, one that will be made explicit in the development of the Catholic theological tradition, that spouses can rightly choose marital union as a way of showing their friendship. This would involve no unworthy motive and no sin. Unfortunately, however, Augustine himself did not proceed in this way. Rather, he conceived marriage not as something good in itself, like wisdom and friendship, but only as something instrumentally good, specifically as a means toward friendship. Moreover, the friendship he had in mind was the friendship that could exist between fathers and their sons, not the friendship between husband and wife.[44]

The third good of marriage discussed by Augustine is the bond of indissoluble unity between husband and wife. Although he did not use his term for this bond — the Latin word *sacramentum* — in precisely the same sense in which the Church now uses the word "sacrament," Augustine nonetheless attributed to marriage two characteristics which make it a true sacrament. First, he taught that Jesus Christ himself instituted this symbolic representation of his union with the Church,[45] and second, he taught that grace is given to the spouses in virtue of this institution.[46]

In his own understanding of the good of *sacramentum* in marriage Augustine first stressed that it was a holy bond. He based the permanence of marriage on the moral obligation of married persons to honor this sacramental bond, but this holy bond is itself rooted in the sacramental sign which reveals the meaning of marriage. Marriage is a human reality pointing toward the mystery of God's love for man, a love made real by Christ's indissoluble union with his bride, the Church.[47] Marriage symbolizes and draws strength from that union.

Augustine taught that every marriage has a natural bond requiring that it not be dissolved, but the marriage of Christians has more than this natural bond. Its indissolubility is also rooted in something even more profound; for Christians, marriage is a reality profoundly touched by the love between Christ and his Church. Christian marriage must be as indissoluble as this love.[48]

Augustine held that any act of adultery or faithlessness violated the good of fidelity, but such an act could not rupture the indissoluble unity between the spouses. The good of fidelity requires the spouses to be faithful to each other and to abstain from any form of sexual immorality; the good of the *sacramentum* excludes that adultery which would be involved in an invalid marriage after separation.[49]

Augustine's analysis of the goods of marriage has provided the Church with a powerful analytical device for understanding both the human significance and the salvific importance of marriage and human sexuality. Later theologians and the magisterium even till the present time make use of a framework whose full implications Augustine did not grasp.[50] Augustine's study of sexual morality therefore, even though it has limitations, is an important step in the development of the Church's understanding of sexual morality.

II. The Teaching of the Medieval Theologians

Between the death of Augustine in 430 and the flowering of scholarship in the universities of the twelfth and thirteenth centuries, Western Europe experienced great social upheaval and disarray as a result of the fall of the Roman Empire and the migrations of the Germanic, Frankish, and Celtic peoples. During these centuries dedicated communities of monks both preserved the cultural heritage of the past and worked to evangelize the pagan peoples and to instruct the Catholic faithful in the Christian way of life.

These monks, as the penitential books they wrote show, regarded marriage as good and holy. They informed the people of the immorality of nonmarital sex, and instructed couples about the immorality of contraceptive, anal, and oral intercourse, and the wickedness of abortion.[51] Some of their views were too rigoristic — for instance, their prohibition of marital intercourse during certain seasons of the year, on holy days, and prior to receiving communion.[52] However, these positions were only peripheral to their central teaching, and can perhaps be understood as a function of the difficult times in which they lived. The core of their teaching on sexual matters was not something specific to their cultural situation but rather a set of admonitions and prohibitions which were already present in patristic and scriptural times. Thus, for example, the condemnation of sexual activity outside of marriage is not unique to the monks and their penitentials but was already the common teaching of the Church and was proposed as such by the monks. The teaching of the Fathers of the Church on sexual matters as well as their understanding of the relevant biblical texts had already become normative for Christian life.

The great contribution of the medieval Church to the developing understanding of human sexuality came during the period of the High Middle Ages when theological activity reached a high point of creative achievement, especially in the works of Doctors of the Church like St. Thomas Aquinas and St. Bonaventure in the thirteenth century. Although their cultural situation was very different from that of the Fathers of the Church almost a millennium before, some of the challenges they faced were quite similar to those the Fathers had to deal with. A new form of Gnosticism developed during the High Middle Ages, particularly in the south of France. Albigensianism, Catharism, and Bogomilism constituted a movement which, like the older forms of Gnosticism, held marriage in contempt. This contempt had the standard Gnostic rationale: matter was taken to be evil, and marriage was bad because it was the basis for the generation of new life.

The great medieval theologians also faced a challenge not unlike that presented to the Fathers in the form of pagan sexual licentiousness. The ideal of "pure" or "romantic" love proposed by some of the troubadours was, in effect, an endorsement of romantic sexual activity separated from marriage and procreation, for these troubadours not only emphasized something very good — the love between man and woman — they also glorified sexual pleasure within the context of romance. Far more important, they showed no appreciation for the good of procreation. In this last respect they were influenced by the Gnosticism of the age.[53] This movement had considerable appeal, especially to the wealthier classes, and had the effect of creating within medieval culture a kind of neopaganism.

56

These two challenges — of Gnosticism and neopagan licentiousness — form the background for the thought of the medieval theologians on sexual morality. Their creative responses to these challenges led them to develop a body of work that deepened the Church's understanding of human sexuality in a real way, for their response to the anti-humanism of the Cathars and Albigenses required an affirmation of the Church's concern for human values, and their response to the hedonism of the heterodox troubadours required a careful sifting of opinions about what really is good for human beings.

Furthermore, this work of clarification took place within the context of an unprecedented effort to systematize the teaching of the Church and to present it as a coherent whole. Thus, in the great theologians of the Middle Ages, there is not only a creative response to serious challenges to Christian life and teaching but also an attempt to see this response within an overall account of Christian doctrine. This effort was carried out within the context of acceptance of the Church's received teachings on moral matters, and of heavy reliance on the Fathers of the Church, and especially on St. Augustine. Augustine's teaching on sexual morality was particularly influential, and his discussion of the goods of marriage was the framework for thinking about marriage. It is not surprising therefore that the medieval theologians unanimously affirmed the goodness of marriage and the excellence of properly ordered sexual activity, and that they unanimously condemned those acts which attacked the great goods of marriage. They counted all such disordered acts as "unnatural."

The Evil of Acts Which Attack the Goods of Marriage

Three principal lines of argument were developed by medieval theologians to show the moral evil of nonmarital and "unnatural" sexual activity. The first was an argument from the authority of the Scriptures and the Fathers. This was advanced, for instance, by the twelfth-century theologian and bishop Peter Lombard, whose *Sentences* were used as a textbook for teaching theology from 1157 until 1550, and were commented on by all the great theologians of the thirteenth century. In discussing the sixth commandment, Lombard observed, citing Augustine, that this commandment required one not to have sexual union except within the marital covenant.[54] He also held that any sexual activity fully contrary to the purpose of marriage and of the sexual differentiation of the species into male and female was a gravely sinful violation of this commandment.[55]

A second line of argument, developed at length by the medieval theologians in their discussion of the natural law written in the hearts of mankind and discernible by right reason, was that the prohibited forms of sexual activity violated not only the law divinely revealed by God but also the natural moral law written in our hearts.[56] Bestiality, sodomy, contraceptive intercourse, and other forms of "unnatural sex" were judged to be wrongful in a special way insofar as they violated the order God had called into being by making humankind a species sexually differentiated into male and female and therefore capable of giving life to new human beings through acts of sexual intercourse.[57] These sins were judged to be unnatural in a stronger sense than other sins, including other sexual sins. All evil actions were held to be unnatural insofar as they are contrary to the order of right reason, that is, to the demands of rationally ordered activity which properly respects the goods of human nature. But unlike other sins, these particular sexual sins were held to be unnatural in a further sense, since they violated the most basic, God-given purpose of human sexuality. For this reason, they were held to be more seriously wrong than acts of sexual intercourse outside of marriage. These latter sins too were judged to be gravely sinful because such acts as adultery and fornication contradicted both God's divine law and the requirements of right reason. But sins of sodomy and the like were judged to be more gravely sinful because their peculiar unnaturalness violated divine and natural law in a radical way.

The teaching of medieval theologians that such sexual sins as masturbation, sodomy, and contraception are more perverse, as sexual sins, than fornication or adultery or even rape (the former were said to be *contra naturam* whereas the latter were said to be *praeter naturam*), angers many people today. But this teaching must be understood properly. The medieval theologians are claiming that certain kinds of sexual sins more seriously offend the virtue of chastity than do others. They are not saying that these sins are for this reason less grave as sins than adultery or rape, for instance. After all, adultery and rape are very serious violations of the virtue of justice as well as being violations of the virtue of chastity. Thus, as a sin, rape is far more serious than masturbation or homosexual sodomy because it not only offends chastity but also gravely violates justice.

Thomas Aquinas, in arguing that nonmarital sexual union is contrary to the demands of the natural law insofar as it acts against the good of offspring, provides an argument characteristic of this second line of reasoning: "The end [or purpose] of the exercise of the genital organs is the generation and education of children; therefore, every exercise of these powers which is not properly ordered (*proportionatus*) to the generation of children and the education to which they have a right is of itself disordered."[58] Thus, sexual intercourse outside of marriage is excluded, for it is only in marriage that human life can properly be given, nurtured, and educated in the love and worship of God.

The medieval theologians also taught that nonmarital sexual behavior violated the fidelity spouses owe to each other. Bonaventure presents this teaching in a passage which reveals the growing appreciation by the medieval theologians of the love that is meant to exist between husband and wife: "In matrimony there is indeed a singular kind of love (*amor singularis*) which is not possible to be shared with others; naturally, therefore, a husband is jealous of his wife with respect to this, that she love no one else and that she love him in this act, and similarly the wife is naturally jealous of her husband in this respect."[59]

A third line of argument used by some of the medieval theologians to show that every kind of sexual union outside marriage and every kind of "unnatural" sexual act is morally wicked was based on the nature of concupiscent desire. This argument, which they believed to be rooted in biblical and patristic teaching, focused on the inclination to evil that exists in human beings as a result of original sin. According to this view — one expressed by many authors, including Lombard, Aquinas, Bonaventure, Albert the Great, and the authors of the *Summa of Brother Alexander*[60] — all our desires, good in themselves, have been corrupted by original sin. But sexual desires, they held, have been corrupted and indeed infected by original sin in a special way. Of itself the disorderliness of human sexual desire is not a moral evil, for moral evil can arise only when free personal consent is given to evil. But it is an evil we experience as a penalty. This restless itching for sexual gratification in a disorderly way exists in us as a result of original sin.[61] As a result of this we are tempted to do evil deeds in order to satisfy disorderly desires.

But according to the argument advanced, particularly by writers like Peter Lombard and Bonaventure,[62] God has in his goodness given us a remedy to help us avoid the evil to which we are prone as a result of this restless itching. That remedy is marriage. Before the fall, it had been instituted — as Lombard says — to be an office of nature, something good. Indeed now, as Paul and the Fathers had taught, it exists as a holy sign or sacrament pointing to the mystery of Christ's love for his Church. But in our present state, as Paul taught in 1 Corinthians 7, marriage also serves as a remedy for allaying the burning desires of concupiscence.[63] The great goods of marriage noted by Augustine, and, in particular, the good of offspring, serve to rectify sexual desires.[64] These goods cannot be properly and adequately realized outside of marriage, for children can be conceived but not properly cherished outside of marriage, and a kind of fidelity is possible but not

59

the reality of a firm and unshakable union in a single life. Consequently, this argument continued, any choice to exercise one's sexual powers outside of marriage is morally wrong. Such acts may satisfy strong and natural desires; but they are not the remedy which God has provided.[65]

These three lines of argument advanced by the medieval theologians to explain the Church's received teaching on sexual morality were not meant to provide a rationalistic proof of the immorality of nonmarital and unnatural sexual activity. They do not seek to replace faith by philosophical argumentation. Rather, these arguments were proposed as a way of understanding, from within the faith, the sexual teaching based on Scripture and handed down through the Church. If these arguments are taken on their own terms they are very weighty, even if some of their details must be revised or even rejected. The power of these arguments within the perspective of Catholic faith becomes even clearer when their connection with the Church's affirmation of the goodness of marriage is spelled out.

The Goodness of Marriage

As the inheritors of Christian tradition, the medieval theologians unequivocally affirm the goodness of marriage. Like the Fathers they regard this matter as settled in Scripture. God himself instituted marriage by creating humankind as he did; and Christ blessed it at the marriage feast of Cana. This theme is sounded throughout the period. It was clearly articulated by Peter Lombard. When discussing the question of the goodness of marriage, he is content to refer simply to the patristic teaching, ably summed up by Hugh of St. Victor, the first medieval theologian to set forth in detail a theology of marriage.[66] Hugh had written: "That marriage is a good thing is proved not only from the fact that the Lord is said to have instituted it in creating our first parents but also because Christ himself took part in the marriage feast at Cana, commending the nuptials with a miracle by changing water into wine. . . . Therefore it is quite evident that marriage is a good thing."[67]

Thus far the medieval theologians reaffirm and make their own the patristic teaching on the goodness of marriage. Where they go beyond the Fathers is in developing a deeper appreciation for all the goods of marriage and conjugal intercourse.

The Goods of Marriage and the Meaning of the Marital Act

Augustine's teaching on the threefold good of marriage — progeny, fidelity, and indissoluble unity — was, as noted already, fully accepted by the medieval theologians. They regarded the indissoluble unity to be the good that marriage is, the good that man and woman bring into being when they freely choose to be husband and wife.[68] The medieval theologians saw the bond of unity not only as a moral obligation but also as having ontological significance. This bond is not only a sign of the indissoluble unity between Christ and his Church but also a reality within marriage. The marriage really participates in this mystery of divine love. It becomes a union so profound that only death can dissolve it. Moreover, it is accompanied by graces intended to assist spouses in living their marriages faithfully and generously.[69] It is for this reason, the medieval theologians taught, that marriage between Christians is a true sacrament of the Church. Ecumenical councils of the Church also affirmed this teaching.[70]

The other two goods of marriage — fidelity and progeny — were held to be the goods that marriage *intends*, that is, they are goods which the spouses promise to give and honor in their shared lives as they make the free consent that constitutes them as husband and wife and brings into being their indissoluble unity.[71] Adultery and contraceptive intercourse violate the goods of fidelity and progeny by undermining and wounding them. Such deeds violate the good of the indissoluble bond of marriage as well, but since this bond is the very reality of marriage itself, it cannot be broken by them. Marriage itself cannot be dissolved by these or any other sins.[72]

The medieval theologians, with Augustine and the other Fathers, held that marital intercourse for the sake of having children — that is, with the intention of begetting progeny — is completely justifiable. Indeed, they commonly taught the conjugal act ordered to this good was an act of the virtue of religion, insofar as its end was the generation of life that was to be brought up in the love and worship of God.[73]

Likewise, the medieval theologians followed Augustine in teaching that it was a venial sin for a spouse to seek sexual union merely as a way to avoid fornication, while the spouse who consented to marital union for this purpose was free of all sin.[74]

But the medieval theologians developed Augustine's teaching in this matter by focusing on an idea only implicit in his writings — namely, that the spouses could rightly choose to unite in marital coition in order to foster and express the good of fidelity. To choose marital union for this purpose, writers like Thomas Aquinas and Bonaventure maintained, is a truly virtuous act, an act of the virtue of justice.[75] In fact, Aquinas argued that a husband ought to anticipate his wife's desires in this matter and offer to give himself to her in sexual union in order to cherish this good.[76]

There is even, on Aquinas's account, a suggestion that the sexual expression of the good of fidelity by husband and wife participates in the sacramental character of the marriage. Thus, St. Thomas writes: "A human act is good in two ways. In one way, by moral goodness, which the act has from the goods which make it a right act. In the case of the marital act, fidelity and progeny do this. . . . In another way, by sacramental goodness: this factor causes an act to be not simply good but also holy. And the marital act has this goodness from the indissolubility of the union, for in this regard it is a sign of the union of Christ and the Church."[77] It is not surprising therefore that Aquinas regarded sexual intercourse for the sake of fidelity to be a meritorious act.[78]

A procreative intent is not, then, necessary for marital acts to be virtuous, holy, and meritorious. To choose conjugal intercourse for the sake of the good of fidelity is to choose to do something exceedingly good. Of course, Aquinas and other writers who justified marital union as an expression of the good of fidelity regarded it as wicked to act *contrary* to the good of offspring — that is, to act contraceptively. But in the medieval theologians there is clear and explicit recognition of the "non-procreative" purposes of marital sexual union.

It is true that Aquinas, Bonaventure, and other medieval theologians who justified marital union as a way of fostering the good of fidelity taught that the act in question was an act of the virtue of justice, of the justice that husband and wife owe each other. They did not, ordinarily, speak of it as an act of conjugal love, but their thought was clearly open to fuller development in this direction. This is strongly suggested by Bonaventure when he speaks of the "singular love that is meant to exist between husband and wife, a love expressed in that act," namely, in the marital act. In this passage love is explicitly related to marital union. St. Thomas Aquinas speaks in a similar way about the special character of the friendship between spouses. He affirms this to be the highest friendship, and clearly supposes that marital intercourse is integral to it; his concern is to affirm that sexual intercourse is not the whole of marital friendship.[79]

A similar emphasis can be found in the teaching of the *Summa Fratris Alexandri*. This work is specially significant because it is not the work of an individual author (Alexander of Hales, to whom it was attributed) but is rather the compilation of many theologians representing "the spirit of the Franciscan thirteenth-century school of theology at the University of Paris."[80] The authors of this work consider an objection to the appropriateness of the human race's derivation from the first pair of humans by way of sexual intercourse. The objection is that this mode of derivation only serves to increase the intensity of carnal love, which is an "impediment" to spiritual love. To answer this objection the authors of the *Summa Fratris Alexandri* distinguish three types of love: carnal love, natural love, and spiritual love. They maintain that "natural love," which is carnal love purged of all lust, is no obstacle to spiritual love; on the contrary, "spiritual love should come to be through natural love, and natural love is meant in turn to be perfected by the spiritual love toward which it disposes."[81] The authors of this work go on to speak of the loving embrace of husband and wife — obviously a reference to sexual union between spouses — as symbolizing the union of the soul with God "both as to the intensity of that union and its fruitfulness."[82]

It is clear therefore that the medieval theologians enhanced the Church's understanding of the values involved in marriage by their development of the teaching that fidelity was one of the goods of marriage, and by their explicit recognition of the value of marital friendship and its relationship to sexual intercourse.

These developments quite naturally led to a more positive evaluation of the status of sexual pleasure than Christian tradition had accepted, but the medieval theologians did not, for the most part, articulate these implications. Thomas Aquinas, however, did make several points that are important in the development of a more balanced view of the moral status of sexual pleasure. Like the other medieval theologians, Aquinas affirmed the common teaching of the Church that sexual intercourse solely for the sake of pleasure was sinful. He maintained that it would be mortally sinful if one's sexual interest in one's wife would be so exclusively aimed at finding pleasure that he viewed her really as only a sex object or object of lust, not as a wife, as one with whom he was lovingly committed to honoring the great goods of marriage. But he rejected as absurd the more rigorous position that it is better to repudiate or merely tolerate the pleasure of marital intercourse.[83] His view on this matter follows from his realistic and warmly human evaluation of pleasure and its role in human life. With Aristotle, he held that pleasure is a natural accompaniment and perfection of a human action. As such the moral character depends on the moral status of the action it accompanies. Thus, the pleasure of a morally good act is itself morally good and worthy of pursuit as part of a good activity. The pursuit of pleasure becomes morally suspect only if it inclines one to act in ways that are somehow unreasonable or disordered. Aquinas's analysis of pleasure provides the ground for a more realistic appreciation of sexual pleasure.[84]

III. Post-Medieval Catholic Thought

In this section our purpose is by no means to attempt even a brief history of the development of Catholic theological thought on sexual morality from the Middle Ages to the present. Rather, we hope only to indicate the continuity of the Catholic theological tradition, and to note briefly some of the principal developments that have taken place since the end of the age of high Scholasticism.

The continuity of the Catholic theological tradition from the death of St. Thomas Aquinas in 1274 until the 1960s is remarkable. For nearly eight hundred years Catholic tradition has affirmed unanimously and with one voice that marriage is good; that genital sexual activity outside marriage, whether through adultery, fornication, masturbation, homosexual activity, or bestiality, is gravely sinful; and that within marriage some sexual acts — notably contraception and acts leading to orgasm apart from sexual intercourse — are seriously wrong. Germain Grisez and John Ford, S.J., surveyed forty-two manuals on moral theology in common use during the nineteenth and twentieth centuries for their teaching on contraceptive intercourse. All the authors studied unanimously held that such behavior was gravely sinful.[85] Nor is it surprising that these authors taught as they did, for in branding contraceptive intercourse as seriously wrong they were simply reaffirming the centuries-old teaching of the Church, a teaching which the Fathers, the Scholastics, and their modern successors found rooted in the Scriptures as understood by the Church.[86]

The same authors examined by Ford and Grisez likewise unanimously teach that all forms of nonmarital sexual activity (fornication, adultery, rape, sodomy, masturbation, etc.) are serious moral evils, contrary both to the natural moral law and to the law divinely revealed by God. Again, there is nothing surprising in this teaching.

In the 1960s some Catholic theologians began to question the received teaching on contraception; and in 1966 several prominent moral theologians — in preparing a report for the Papal Commission for the Study of Problems of Population, Family, and Birthrate — urged that contraceptive intercourse could be morally justifiable for married couples.[87] In advocating this view, these authors rejected the claim that the principles upon which they justified contraception for married couples could be used to justify anal or oral intercourse for married couples.[88] These theologians held, in accord with the theological tradition, that nonmarital modes of sexual activity were immoral. Likewise, they agreed that sexual activity between spouses must be directed toward sexual intercourse — that seeking orgasm outside of natural intercourse was seriously wrong even for married couples. They thought that allowing contraception for married couples under narrowly described circumstances would not compromise the rationale for these proscriptions.

Recent history shows that they were mistaken, for subsequent Catholic theologians — among them Michael Valente[89] and the authors of *Human Sexuality: New Directions in American Catholic Thought*[90] — were willing to draw the conclusion that the principles justifying contraceptive intercourse for married couples likewise can be used to justify nonmarital sexual activity and deviant sexual activity within marriage. As Charles E. Curran has noted: "History has clearly shown that those who were afraid that a change in the teaching on contraception would lead to other changes [in the teaching on sexual morality] were quite accurate."[91] Curran seems to have recognized that a radical change in principle was needed to justify contraception, and that such a change is bound to have wide effects.

It is not our purpose here to enter into the current dispute concerning the morality of contraception and other types of sexual activity. Subsequent chapters of this volume will be concerned with these issues. What is relevant here is that those contemporary theologians who justify contraception, and with it various kinds of sexual activity condemned by the received teaching of the Church, themselves recognize that their teaching markedly contrasts with the theological tradition as expressed in the writings of theologians prior to the 1960s. No theologian, from the time of the apostolic writers until the 1960s, even suggested that sexual activities of the kinds justified by these writers could be morally legitimate.

This aberrant development is not, however, the only development in the Church's sexual teaching in recent centuries and decades, for there has been a genuine development in the Church's understanding of the purpose of human sexuality *within* marriage on the part of post-medieval theologians. There has been, throughout the modern period, a deepening appreciation of the significance of marital intercourse as an expression of love. This growing appreciation of marital love in no way contradicts the theological tradition but authentically develops themes which were suggested by the medieval theologians and present in Christian consciousness from the start.

As noted above, the medieval theologians clearly recognized that procreative intent was not necessary for marital intercourse to be morally good, and even meritorious and holy.[92] The medieval teaching that marital intercourse undertaken in order to express the good of marital fidelity developed through the modern period into the explicit recognition that marital intercourse can be rightly chosen as a way to foster and nourish spousal love.

Even before the medieval period came to an end, Nicolas Oresme, a theologian who became bishop of Lisieux, wrote warmly about the love between husband and wife, a love that is displayed in their marital act. The teaching of Oresme, who wrote about the middle of the fourteenth century, has been summarized as follows:

The union between man and woman in marriage is fully natural. It is meant to spring from love and to be grounded upon love — a love that is productive of an intensity of joy and pleasure, that makes equals of man and woman and makes each to be supreme in the other's affections. The marriage act is good if decently and lovingly engaged in. It has purposes beyond generation. . . . Sin may enter into the union, but if the union is of reason and is basically good, there is no need to worry about it. It is only when love becomes 'bestial' — when one is intent only upon his isolated pleasure — that there is cause for concern.[93]

Oresme's conception of the value of sexual intercourse between spouses as expressive of their mutual love is foreshadowed by the work of St. Thomas Aquinas, St. Bonaventure, and other medieval writers. It was to be developed and more fully articulated only in the nineteenth and twentieth centuries in the works of thinkers like Jean Gury and Dietrich von Hildebrand.[94]

Another element in the development of Catholic theologians' appreciation of marital intercourse has been the explicit recognition that spouses may legitimately seek pleasure in the marital act. Here too there is a development anticipated by medieval authors. We have already noted that the principles of Thomas Aquinas are open to this recognition, and his great commentator, Thomas Cardinal Cajetan (1469-1534), explicitly recognized that spouses may legitimately seek pleasure in conjugal union. Like Aquinas, he taught that spouses were obliged to seek conjugal union as spouses, that is, as acting for one or the other of the goods of marriage, and that pleasure is the natural perfection of the act, as beauty is the bloom of youth. But he added that spouses ought to give God thanks for the pleasure that marital union brings, thus suggesting that sexual pleasure was a legitimate object of marital activity.[95] He taught, however, that an explicit or actual intent to foster one or the other of the goods of marriage, such as the aim of nourishing faithful love, also had to be present for the act to be morally good.

Subsequent theologians like Thomas Sanchez (1550-1610) and Alphonsus Liguori (1696-1787) taught that this last condition was too stringent. They held that it was sufficient for the proper respect for these goods, and thus for the moral goodness of marital intercourse, that spouses seek marital union *as spouses*.[96] Their teaching became the common heritage of nineteenth- and twentieth-century theologians. In other words, spouses need not *explicitly* intend their marital act to further either the good of procreation or of marital fidelity. A habitual intent to respect these goods — to seek marital union as spouses — was sufficient, although of course, it would be seriously wrong for them to repudiate either the good of *proles* or the good of *fides*.

In short, there has been development since the time of the Middle Ages in the Church's understanding of human sexuality and the role, within marriage, of conjugal intercourse. As one would expect in the legitimate development of God's revelation, this development has many antecedents in the earlier tradition. The medieval notion that spouses could rightly choose marital union as a way of expressing their marital fidelity was a development of ideas found in St. Augustine. The more modern teachings that marital union is a way of expressing the singular love between the spouses and that it is by no means wicked for spouses to take delight in their conjugal union but that it is rather quite proper for them to seek this pleasure *as spouses* are foreshadowed by and rooted in the teaching of the great Scholastics. Another sign of the real continuity and legitimacy of the post-medieval theological developments in sexual morality is the unwillingness of modern theologians to question or compromise the received teaching that it is seriously wrong to seek sexual union within or outside of marriage in ways that deliberately fail to honor any of the goods of marriage.

In sum, even the briefest of surveys of the theological tradition's developing teaching on sexual morality shows beyond all doubt that there is real continuity and development in the Church's understanding of human sexuality. This development has taken place within a framework of moral norms which are not questioned or rejected but better understood as the moral thinking of the Church unfolds in response to new situations. This framework is never presented as a mere imposition of divine or human authority but as an inherent requirement of authentic human life. One of the most important aspects of the development of doctrine on sexual matters has been the ever-clearer articulation of the connection between the specific requirements of Christian sexual morality and the basic moral principles of Christian living. Today it has become clearer than ever before that Christian sexual morality is no more and no less than the implication of the logic of love — what love of God and of neighbor requires in this area of human life.

Chapter Four
Patterns of Thinking in Moral Theology

Christian life is not primarily the following of a moral code. It is, most fundamentally, living as adopted sons and daughters of God. This new life is made possible by the redemptive activity of Jesus. It essentially involves participating in God's own life, in living freely in ways that God's grace makes possible. This grace is God's altogether free gift.[1]

Christian Life and Morality

Still, it is clear that Christian life involves a morality. Specific ways of living are appropriate for those who live the life of charity, and some ways of living, some choices and actions, are simply incompatible with this life. This is revealed in the covenants which God made with the people of Israel and their ancestors. All the covenants required that God's people keep his commandments. Jesus reaffirms and develops this Old Testament emphasis. He tells us that we must keep his commandments if we are to be saved (Mt 19:17-19).[2] The moral implications of Jesus' message are so central to it that they appear prominently in the original proclamation of the Gospel; they appear in the heavily moral emphasis of the early Pauline epistles, as they do in all later Catholic teaching.

Jesus did not show his concern with morality only by his teaching. He came to redeem sinners, and their salvation required much more than articulating moral truth. He died and rose for them, to give them power to live a new life. Those who would respond to Jesus' invitation to new life were required to have a change of heart, a conversion. The free cooperation of those who would follow Jesus must include repentance for their sins (Acts 2:38), and a resolve to live unselfish and upright lives, doing all that love requires (1 Jn 3). Thus, the life of the Christian involves a moral component. The Christian, like Christ himself, must obey the commands of the Father and so live in a way befitting one who has become a new kind of creature.

Christian faith offers important helps toward living as authentic love requires. First, it helps believers to know what God's will is. Then it gives power to live in the good ways in which God wishes us freely to walk.

The Church has always taught the moral vision of Christianity with confidence, for the Church is convinced that authentic Catholic morality is true and good, that this morality serves love, reveres the person, intelligently resolves difficult problems, and faithfully responds to Gospel requirements. In this chapter we cannot provide an exhaustive study of the principles underlying this moral vision.[3] But it is possible — and sufficient for our purposes — to consider the most basic principles of Christian morality in order to reveal their basic soundness and relevance. These principles provide a rationale for understanding the received teaching of the Church on sexual morality. Moreover, they make it plain that the current challenge to this teaching both by various groups outside the Church and by some Catholics is neither rationally defensive nor compatible with basic truths of revelation.

This chapter contains four major sections. The first is a discussion of the most basic principles of Christian morality. The second is an account of the human values or goods, recognized by human intelligence and celebrated in Scripture, which are the grounds for moral norms. The third considers how moral norms are based upon the goods discussed in the second section. Since there is considerable debate among Catholic theologians about how moral norms are justified and applied, this section will constitute the bulk of the chapter. In it we will present a critical discussion of the moral theory most often used to justify dissent from the Church's teaching on sexual matters, the theory called proportionalism. The fourth section is a discussion of the importance of human actions and choices in the economy of salvation.

I. The Basic Principles of Catholic Moral Reasoning

To understand Christian morality one must reflect on the importance of free choice and the reality of divine and human love. A correct understanding of these two principles is especially important in a treatment of sexual morality, for mistaken ideas about love and freedom are often at the root of people's distorted views about human sexuality.

Freedom. The word "freedom" has several related senses.[4] Two of these are especially important for the Christian, namely the liberty of the children of God and free choice. The "liberty of the children of God" speaks of God's merciful gifts of grace which enable the Christian to escape from the dominance of sinful desire and selfishness. Free choice is a gift flowing from man's very nature. It is presupposed by the Judeo-Christian notion of moral responsibility. It would be useless to study sexual ethics if human beings were so dominated by irrational forces that they could not come to know and to choose intelligent and good ways to direct their sexual lives, or if God did not provide the power for people to live in these excellent ways. Both kinds of freedom are therefore important. We will focus on free choice in its relation to moral principles.

A person makes a free choice when he or she selects one from a set of practical options. A choice is free when the person's own choosing determines which of the available options the person will select. In other words, all the factors determining the outcome of the choice, other than the person's own choosing, are not sufficient to determine which selection is made. A free choice is made when a person could choose this or that, and the person himself determines which alternative he will perform.[5]

Free Choice in Scripture and Tradition

The reality of free choice is explicitly affirmed in Scripture: "It was he who created man in the beginning, and he left him in the power of his own inclination. If you will, you can keep the commandments, and to act faithfully is a matter of your own choice. He has placed before you fire and water: stretch out your hand for whichever you wish. Before a man are life and death, and whichever he chooses will be given to him" (Sir 15:14-17). This biblical teaching has also been explicitly affirmed by the authentic teaching of the Church.[6] Furthermore, free choice is implicit in a number of biblical themes: sin and punishment, conversion and repentance — all presuppose free choice. As St. Thomas Aquinas noted: "Counsels, exhortations, precepts, prohibitions, rewards, and punishments would be in vain" if mankind lacked free choice.[7]

In his encyclical *Veritatis Splendor*, Pope John Paul II emphasized the truth that human acts have moral significance because at their heart is a free, self-determining choice. They "do not produce a change merely in the state of affairs outside of man, but *to the extent that they are deliberate choices,* they give moral definition to the person who performs them, determining his *profound spiritual traits.*"[8] Indeed, it is in and through free choices that one shapes one's own life.[9]

We rightly prize freedom. God wishes us to live in freedom, for it is above all by virtue of free actions that we please God and shape good lives in time and for eternity. Freedom is not opposed to that law which directs one to what is really good and fulfilling, that empowers us, gives us freedom to do what is best for us.[10] Freedom does not mean the power or right to "make good" what is not good. God is the author of the moral law; but it is not an arbitrary law, alien to our hopes. God enables us to see the goodness of it, both naturally (in the gift of awareness of the natural law) and through the gifts of divine revelation.

Grace. The biblical affirmation of free choice is not opposed to the equally strong biblical emphasis on the importance of God's grace and the inability of fallen human beings consistently to do good without God's help. Human free choice can be exercised for good or for evil, but in the present condition of mankind it cannot be consistently used for good without the help of God's grace. However, the effect of God's grace on human lives does not override or cancel human freedom. God works through human freedom as he does through all the capacities of human nature.

Limitations on Free Choice. Similarly, the affirmation of free choice in revelation does not involve the denial that many factors affect human behavior and inhibit the exercise of free choice. The work of social scientists in recent decades confirms the common-sense judgment that pressures of various kinds often limit human freedom. The Christian tradition recognizes that not all human behavior is free. Sexual conduct is especially affected by passions and pressures, and often one does not know what measure of freedom was involved in a given act.

Nevertheless, the view that all or most human behavior is determined by factors other than choice has no basis in experience and is irreconcilable with the revealed truth that people are in fact responsible for their acts and the basic direction of their lives. Even in this world of many pressures, God made human beings capable of free choice.

The Law of Love. The moral teachings of Christianity express the requirements of love. Both the Old and the New Testaments insist that love is the foundation of all morality. Jesus declared unequivocally that every other commandment flows from the two greatest commands: that we should love God above all things and our neighbor as ourselves (Mt 22:34-40).

The love commandments play a central part in God's providential plan for mankind, for they direct human beings to a sharing of life and good things with God and with other human beings that is closely related to God's loving purpose in creating mankind. He who is Love itself — sharing divine goodness within the perfect community of the Trinity — wishes to share this love with us creatures by making us his children. This love between God and creatures cannot be realized unless human beings live in such a way as to be open to this wonderful fellowship.

The basic norms of Christian morality are therefore in no way arbitrary. They do not restrict our freedom but are addressed to it.[11] They are proposed to us by a loving God to assist us to live as intelligent love would choose to live.

To make clear the connection between specific moral norms and the love commandments — thus revealing the necessity and nonarbitrariness

71

of these specific requirements — we shall reflect on the human goods, the basic perfections of human nature which God desires us to promote and respect.

II. The Human Good

God loves us and wishes us to flourish in all that is really good. He wishes our lives and actions to be good, for authentic love always wishes the beloved to flourish in what truly enriches and fulfills the beloved. This perfection cannot be merely something that happens to intelligent creatures — but rather is something persons must freely and intelligently achieve by their own actions. Hence, God's love for us must include the demand that we show an intelligent concern for what is truly good for us.

Today there is much pessimism about the fundamental roots of a good life. Skepticism and relativism lead many to hold that nothing is really good, or knowable as really good. Christian faith, however, confidently teaches human beings what is really good. It also teaches that we can know the nature of goodness, even without the help of revelation, and that people can know the real goods that are so precious that they make all moral striving worthwhile.

The Nature of Goodness. Difficult moral questions, like those in sexual ethics, cannot be resolved without an understanding of the most basic ideas, such as "good" and "bad," and without a grasp of the richness of the human values that underlie all our striving. Reflection upon why we call some things, actions, or experiences good and others bad makes clear that the meaning and application of the terms "good" and "bad" are not arbitrary. "Good" does not refer simply to whatever a person prefers or recommends or likes. Most people have asked, or at least can understand, the question, "I like it, but is it good?" This question supposes that the goodness of something is not simply constituted by one's liking it.

Thus, common sense, reflection, and experience support what Christian faith affirms on this matter: there are reasons rooted in reality for calling some things "good" and others "bad." God, the Creator of all, has willed that human beings should be able to participate in his creative activity by their free actions. This is possible only because he has created an intelligible order in which some realities can be recognized as truly valuable and worthwhile. Life, truth, beauty, friendship, peace, and so on are good; what undermines, harms, and attacks them is bad.

The Objectivity of Goodness. Human creativity operates within this divinely established set of values. It cannot create the very goodness of these values. But human beings can grasp the real goodness of these values, and by choosing rightly can create worthy human lives in which the goodness God made accessible can flourish. Thus, human beings can choose to do certain things and to live in a certain way; by their choices they make themselves the kinds of persons they become, but they cannot by their willing it make any kind of action whatsoever to be good.[12] Whatever they choose must have at least some appearance of good; but a good human action, one that tends to make the one who does it a good person, requires, as we shall see, much more.

What Makes Human Life Good? A good human life therefore is one in which a person is fully perfected in all the dimensions of his or her personality. It is a rich life of human flourishing. Whatever contributes to that flourishing is to that extent good.[13] Being a good person is an essential part of this full human perfection, for one is a good person in virtue of making morally good choices, and this is the part of human flourishing that is most properly human, most properly a form of self-perfection. Moral norms are the standards for choosing well. They are the guidelines for that part of human flourishing that is within our own power to realize. This is why being moral is the same in the end as being good. Being moral is not, in the last analysis, a matter of rules and regulations but of the demands of our own self-perfection, a perfection that God desires because it is good for us.

The Nature of Evil. This general account of the meaning of goodness throws light on the problem of evil. Christian faith believes that all things are made by an infinitely good God who is free and loves our freedom. There are evil deeds, persons, and things, but evil does not have the substantial reality of goodness. Evil in any reality is not a positive and substantial factor in it. The evil in any reality is the lack of proper perfection in it, an absence of the good that should be present. There is evil in the world because things can fail to have the fullness of reality they were meant by their Creator to possess. The worst and most bitter of evils — the evil of deliberate, malicious actions — flows not from God's creative will but from the refusal of the creature to let his or her free acts have the fullness of being that God commands and makes possible but does not force upon the person. It would be a serious mistake to imagine that any sexual sin is evil because sex itself, or pleasure, or passion, is inherently evil or suspect. The things God made are very good. This understanding of the relationship of good and evil is important for Christian ethics generally and for sexual ethics in particular. Any form of Gnosticism which denies the fundamental goodness of physical reality or of human bodily life must be rejected as inconsistent with the basic truth that all of God's creation is very good.

The Goods of Human Nature. The human good is that which perfects and completes human nature. Human persons are dynamic, reaching their fulfillment by actively participating in real goods like truth and friendship. This section is concerned with developing an account of those objective values that make up this human good. These values — basic goods of human nature — are revealed by reflection on the basic motives of human action. Some of them are noted in *Gaudium et Spes*, no. 39:

> When we have spread on earth the fruits of our nature and our enterprise — human dignity, brotherly communion, and freedom — according to the command of the Lord and in his Spirit, we will find them once again, cleansed this time from the stain of sin, illuminated and transfigured, when Christ presents to his Father an eternal and universal kingdom "of truth and life, a kingdom of holiness and grace, a kingdom of justice, love and peace." Here on earth the kingdom is mysteriously present; when the Lord comes, it will enter into its perfection.[14]

This powerful manifesto of Christian humanism lists as intrinsic components of the Lord's kingdom a number of basic human concerns which are not unique to Christians. All persons and cultures pursue goods like these. Truth, life, justice, love, and holiness are not valued by Christians only but by all men and women. These values are not always properly realized and respected in the individual and social activities of humankind, but they do comprise a good deal of the basic motivation for human action and enterprise. These values motivate us at this basic level precisely because they are the basic components of human perfection. By doing things which realize these values we are perfected and completed as human beings.

The Goods of Human Communities. Perhaps the most obvious of these basic goods are those realized in the relations between persons and within communities. Such things as love and friendship, justice and peace, are among the most basic concerns of all persons. They are also among the most highly regarded human realities in Scripture.[15] These values are characteristics of persons and communities based on the relationships the persons establish among themselves and with those outside the community and with God himself. It is clear that these goods are realized primarily in the commitments of persons to relate decently to one another and to have good and friendly relationships. It is also clear that these goods can be, and often are, sought not as a means to any further goal but as part of what makes life rich and meaningful. Even those who treat others unjustly by

74

manipulating or oppressing them desire some genuine friends and some real human mutuality. The deep human significance of the charge that one does not really care for another but is merely using the other, shows that people understand that a true human relationship is meant to be a basic, noninstrumental value within human life, precious in itself and not a mere means of pursuing other goals. Clearly, the interpersonal goods perfect a dimension of human nature, for we are by nature social beings; a satisfactory human life without friends and decent relationships is simply unthinkable.[16]

Other Basic Goods. Goods perfect other aspects of human nature. Since human beings are complex creatures made up of intellects and wills, minds and bodies, emotions and convictions, it is part of human perfection to harmonize and integrate these elements. This good has a number of aspects, so it is called variously self-integration, authenticity, integrity, practical reasonableness, or, simply, peace.[17] It is the good realized in the cardinal virtues of prudence, temperance, and courage.[18] Consequently, this good is very important for sexual morality, since this good is almost always affected when decisions about sex are made.

Knowing the truth is also a basic human good. Human persons pursue truth not only for pragmatic reasons but also for its own sake, simply because it is good to know; and it is good because the capacity to know is a basic aspect of human nature. Scripture and Church teaching clearly endorse the goodness of knowledge.[19]

Finally, human life itself is a basic good of human nature. Without life the human person does not exist. This does not mean, however, that life has value only as a means or as the context for the realization of other goods. Life is good in itself. To be alive is good, and to flourish in biological life by being healthy and by passing life on to new generations is a perfection of this basic good. The goodness of human life is explicitly and implicitly affirmed in Scripture and in the lives of faithful believers down through the centuries.[20]

This listing of basic human goods is not meant to be exhaustive.[21] It is, however, sufficient for present purposes because it reveals the goods that are most often at stake in sexual activity. Moreover, this discussion makes clear that the human good is not a specific finite goal or achievement but something that is realized in different ways in the actions of individuals and communities. No individual or group can realize all the human goods. That is why choices are necessary. Still, it is possible to make our choices in a way that shows proper regard for all that is humanly good. Moral norms show the way to this proper regard.

The Goodness of Pleasure. Our discussion of the human goods up to

75

this point is obviously incomplete, for we have not yet considered pleasure. Common experience indicates the basic goodness of pleasure. All human beings desire pleasure in one form or another. Thus, unless human desire is utterly perverse, pleasure must be good. It is unthinkable that God, who created mankind out of love, should have created us with utterly perverse desires.

But common experience also reveals another, darker side of pleasure. For the lure of fleeting, empty, and even destructive satisfactions is an undeniable part of the human condition. Many spouses have deeply hurt those they love, and wounded their own lives, by servile pursuit of adulterous pleasure. The desire for pleasure can lead us away from things we know to be good — even from good things to which we would like to remain deeply committed. Pleasure, in short, can enslave us.

Thus, pleasure has a complex character: it is a good thing but one which — more than other good things — can lead us astray. Consequently, any account of pleasure which implies that it is essentially a bad thing, or that it is always entirely good, must be rejected as oversimplified.

Hedonism. The tendency in our culture is toward an uncritical overestimation of the goodness of pleasure. This cultural tendency has found a number of theoretical formulations. Perhaps the most important of these is the familiar philosophical doctrine of hedonism. For the hedonist, the point of all human effort and action is pleasure of some sort. Thus, pleasure is not simply the highest good; it is the only thing that is desirable for its own sake. Nothing is counted as good except to the extent that it causes pleasure.

This doctrine correctly emphasizes the goodness of pleasure; but, like all extreme views, it vastly oversimplifies the human experience of this complex phenomenon. As careful students of human motivation from the time of Plato and Aristotle have noted, the goodness of the desirable things in life cannot be explained simply in terms of their capacity to cause pleasure. Some good things are not pleasurable, at least not in most circumstances; and they are good and desirable even when they do not give pleasure, even when they are quite unpleasant. It is good to struggle to protect one's friend, even when the pain and tension of the effort are so great that one cannot enjoy the nobility or praiseworthiness of one's fidelity.

Moreover, other things than pleasure are truly good. Pleasure simply is not the ultimate point of all human action, the basis for all motivation.[22] It is good to pursue and honor truth and justice, even when one's efforts have no pleasurable resonance. Ideally the pursuit and realization of these and other human goods will be pleasant, but they are not recognized as good only to the extent that they lead to pleasure. Trials, hardship, and pain must be endured by one who truly cherishes the goods of human persons. The fidelity of Job and the obedience of Jesus unto death show how good persons pursue what is really good without expecting to taste pleasure in their efforts.

Examples like these show that the direction of Christian thought about pleasure is profoundly anti-hedonist. But being opposed to hedonism is not being opposed to pleasure, for hedonism says that only pleasure is ultimately good, and this is a false theory. It does not follow that pleasure is not fundamentally a good thing.[23] Thus, the Christian evaluation of pleasure is not a rejection of its goodness but a critical, realistic understanding of its complex reality and motivational complexity.

Evaluating Pleasure. According to this understanding, the good actions and efforts in human life can be and ideally are pleasurable. But they are not good because they give pleasure. Such activities tend to give pleasure because they perfect some dimension of the human person. So, pleasure is a good thing, but it is not the very meaning of goodness nor is it an independent principle of goodness.

This does not mean that actions are always pleasurable in proportion to their goodness, for the amount of pleasure any activity causes depends on many variable conditions.[24] People must work even when they are tired and distracted. Even when the work is noble, they may find no pleasure in it. People must struggle against divided selves — trying to do good when emotion, laziness, or passion is pulling in another direction. So, good activities which under ideal conditions would be pleasant are in fact often not so.

Conversely, activities that are intensely pleasurable can often be destructive and immoral. The adulterer may take great pleasure in acts he knows are destroying his life. Evil but pleasurable acts do have something good about them. They do fulfill some human potentiality but not in an ordered and integrated way. To the extent that such actions are good, they can be pleasant; but to the extent that they block or destroy the full goodness of persons, the associated pleasures will fail to be deeply and enduringly satisfying.

This evaluation of pleasure is based on an understanding of pleasure as a kind of accompaniment to a good activity which completes and crowns the activity. Pleasure therefore is closely related to what is good, but it is not the primary component in the goodness of humanly good activities. The presence of pleasure indicates something good in the activity, though not necessarily total goodness. Its absence does not indicate a lack of real goodness. In determining the goodness of an action, therefore, the emphasis must be on the character of the action itself and not on the quality of the accompanying experiences of pleasure and pain.[25] This is the case in the sexual domain as elsewhere. A morally good sexual act is in no way suspect because of its great pleasure. This pleasure is an appropriate concomitant of the act's overall goodness. Similarly, the pleasure of an immoral sexual act is not itself bad. What is bad is the act itself, and the willingness to yield to disordered desire for gratification in acts that by striking against the authentic goods of human persons are unreasonable.

III. From Human Goods to Moral Norms

The good person acts out of love, pursuing what is really good out of love of God, of neighbor, and a right love of self. Since it is possible to pursue good things in evil ways, the task of moral thinking is to discover how to love good things rightly, and to pursue them properly.

The Second Vatican Council urged moral theologians to show more clearly how Christian morality is based upon the Scriptures, and how moral theology throws light on the vocation of Christians and the obligation to bring forth fruit in charity for the life of the world (*Optatam Totius*, no. 16). Thus, the Council Fathers called for a renewal in moral theology which would make clearer its connection with the fundamental realities of Christian life. This call for renewal presupposed recognition that there were deficiencies in the ways many theologians of recent centuries explained the moral teachings proclaimed by the Church. In the decades and centuries prior to the Vatican Council, the moral teachings of the Church, especially her insistence on moral absolutes, were sometimes presented as legalistic restraints on living which impose merely extrinsic limitations on persons, telling them only the minimum necessary for escaping grave sin.[26]

As the Fathers of Vatican II suggest, the shortcomings of moral theology in the years prior to the Council are not problems in Catholic moral teaching itself but in its presentation and theological explanation. The basic way of overcoming these difficulties is a thoroughgoing recognition that moral norms are, as the Gospel insists, requirements of intelligent love of what is really good. Once this point is accepted, the objection that traditional moral teaching is some form of authoritarian imposition loses its force. At best, such an objection can be addressed to certain theological formulations — not to the substance of Catholic moral teaching.

Making Good Moral Choices. The problem facing us in this section concerns the standards and procedures for arriving at the judgment that a certain choice — a certain proposed human act — is morally good or bad. We have already seen that the love commandments require a concern and

78

respect for human goods, but we have yet to see how that concern is translated into specific practical norms and procedures of moral thinking.

Since Pope John Paul II explicitly addressed this problem in his encyclical *Veritatis Splendor*, we will begin by noting briefly pertinent teaching of that encyclical.

The Teaching of Pope John Paul II

Early in his encyclical John Paul II emphasizes that the commandments of the so-called "second tablet" of the Decalogue, those concerned with our neighbor, are rooted in the more basic commandment to love our neighbor, and he explicitly relates love of neighbor to unyielding respect for basic human goods. "The different commandments of the Decalogue," he writes, "are really only so many reflections of the one commandment about the good of the person, at the level of the many different goods which characterize his identity as a spiritual and bodily being in relationship with God, with his neighbor, and with the material world. . . . The commandments . . . are meant to safeguard *the good* of the person, the image of God, by protecting his *goods*."[27]

Later on he says that reason attests that certain kinds of human acts, specified by the object freely chosen,[28] "are by their nature 'incapable of being ordered' to God." Why? Because "they radically contradict the good of the person made in his image. These are the acts which, in the Church's moral tradition, have been termed 'intrinsically evil' (*intrinsece malum*); they are such *always and per se*, in other words, on account of their very object, and apart from the ulterior intentions of the one acting and the circumstances."[29]

Corresponding to these intrinsically evil acts are absolute moral norms, i.e., specific moral norms that admit of no exceptions, e.g., the norms prohibiting adultery, the intentional killing of innocent human persons, etc.[30] In fact, John Paul II says that the "central theme" of his encyclical is the reaffirmation of the universality and immutability of absolute norms proscribing intrinsically evil acts.[31]

Consequently, in this encyclical John Paul rejects the thesis, sustained by those defending consequentialist and proportionalist moral theories, "which holds that it is impossible to qualify as morally evil according to its species — its 'object' — the deliberate choice of certain kinds of behavior or specific acts, apart from a consideration of the intention for which the choice is made or the totality of the foreseeable consequences of that act for all persons concerned."[32]

Proportionalism

In *Veritatis Splendor,* John Paul II repudiated two kinds of moral theories denying the reality of moral absolutes and intrinsically evil acts in the sense in which these terms are understood by the magisterium of the Church, identifying these theories as "consequentialism" and "proportionalism."[33] Our attention will focus on proportionalism because this is an accurate term for describing the position of Catholic theologians holding the views regarding moral absolutes and intrinsically evil acts rejected by Pope John Paul II. Early in the development of their position, it is true, some of these theologians described their theory as consequentialistic.[34] However, when the charge of "consequentialism" was leveled against them, many immediately countered by asserting that, unlike secular consequentialists, for instance, utilitarians, they did not claim that consequences are the *only* criterion for determine whether an act is morally good or not. One must, they insisted, take into account not only the consequences of the act but its nature as well. All this must be taken into account in judging the morality of an act.[35] In subsequently developing their position, these theologians made it more can more clear that proportionalism is a more accurate description of their theory.

Their theory is called proportionalism because of its emphasis on the proportion of good and evil in actions. According to proportionalism, an act which would otherwise be immoral can be justified morally if the overall good or evil involved in doing the action compares favorably with the overall good or evil which the available alternatives would bring about. Thus, its basic principle can be called the principle of the greater good, or more commonly, the principle of the lesser evil.

Proportionalism, then, is a method of moral thinking according to which a person ought to choose that alternative course of action which promises the greater proportion of good over evil.[36] In other words, proportionalists believe that intelligent concern for the human goods requires an assessment of all the good and evil involved in alternative possibilities for action. The purpose of this assessment is to determine, prior to choice, which of the alternatives promises the greater good or the lesser evil. This determination tells us which of the alternatives we morally ought to choose.

The proportionalist method is considered applicable to any moral problem, but the Catholic theologians who make use of it tend to limit its application in various ways. This method is, however, used in an unrestricted form by many secular moralists. These thinkers are usually called "consequentialists," and they tend to treat the principle of the lesser evil as the single basic moral principle. The most widely known form of consequentialism is utilitarianism. In its classical versions this secular form of ethics held that there is really only one good that human action pursues, pleasure; and it taught that men ought always pursue that which leads to "the greatest happiness of the greatest number."

Catholic proportionalists are far from being pure utilitarians. The whole context of their thinking is Christian, not secular. Generally they acknowledge the objective goodness and distinctive reality of each of the kinds of basic goods that we have noted above. Thus, they reject the oversimplified identification of the human good with pleasurable experience.[37] They also rightly reject any suggestion that individual rights can be subordinated to the interests of society. Most importantly, proportionalists acknowledge that there are some moral absolutes — for example, that one should never seek to lead another into sin. Thus, they admit significant limitations on the applicability of the proportionality principle.[38]

But proportionalists distinctively hold that the most common moral absolutes traditionally taught by the Catholic Church — and, even now, insistently taught by the magisterium — are not valid. Ordinarily these moralists hold, against the received teaching of the Church, that not every act of contraception is immoral, that not every act of homosexuality or fornication is objectively wrong, that not every intentional taking of innocent human life is absolutely prohibited.

Proportionalists typically hold that no kinds of acts, when defined in purely descriptive language, that is, language that includes no morally evaluative terms, are *always* wrong, or *intrinsically evil in a strong sense*. If one were to mean by murder an unjust slaying of an innocent person, then they would agree that every murder is indeed wrong, for the characterization of the killing as unjust is sufficient to settle its immorality. But the direct slaying of an innocent person is not held to be absolutely and in every possible circumstance wrong. Such an act does not include evaluative terms in its description, and it is conceivable that in some extreme circumstances such an act would be determined to be the lesser evil. In those circumstances killing would be a morally good act.

Proportionalists recognize, of course, that there are some alternatives for action that, although not excluded because they are by definition morally bad, are likely to cause greater harm in almost all circumstances. To use one of their examples, it would be wrong to force a retarded child to have sexual relations. Such a norm is a "practical absolute" which is "virtually exceptionless." But, as these phrases suggest, the norm here is not absolute in principle. This, or any other act characterized in purely descriptive terms, might under some circumstances we cannot now think of be thought to be the lesser evil, and thus the correct thing to do.[39]

81

The proportionalist supposes that there is a radical difference between actions characterized evaluatively and actions characterized only in descriptive terms. This difference depends upon one of the most fundamental distinctions in the proportionalist approach — that is, the difference between moral evil and premoral, physical, or ontic evil. Moral evils are essentially morally bad choices and acts. By definition such acts may not morally be done. Thus, proportionalists would not allow the use of their method to justify an action already determined to be morally evil. One important implication is that we should never act deliberately to cause another to commit sin.

Premoral evil refers to the deprivation of some good that is due a person or a thing; premoral evils are really bad, but they are not as such immoral. Sickness and death are premoral evils. They are obviously bad, but not as such immoral. The question is whether choices deliberately to cause premoral evils are morally bad choices. The proportionalist answer is that a choice of what is premorally evil can be morally justified if there is a proportionate reason — if choosing or intending that evil is the way to realize the lesser evil in the situation.

As a leading proportionalist has put it: "Where a higher good is at stake and the only *means* to protect it is to choose a non-moral evil, then the will remains properly disposed to the values constitutive of the human good. . . . This is to say that the intentionality is good even when the person, reluctantly and regretfully to be sure, intends the non-moral evil if a truly proportionate reason for such a choice is present."[40]

Thus, we have in the basic logic of the proportionalist method a ground for rejecting much of the Church's received teaching on sexual matters, for much of this teaching is about acts that can appear to affect only premoral goods, and it is possible to think of many situations in which the lesser evil will seem to require that one deliberately harm or fail to respect these goods.[41]

Recent popes, synods, and episcopal conferences have very frequently reaffirmed the validity and importance of moral absolutes in the Church's traditional sense.[42] And, as we have already seen, Pope John Paul II vigorously reaffirmed this teaching in *Veritatis Splendor*.[43] The *Catechism of the Catholic Church* likewise insists that there are intrinsically evil acts prohibited by absolute moral norms.[44] Thus, it has become characteristic of proportionalists to hold that one need not assent to these teachings of the magisterium on specific moral matters. They hold this, even though the Church has taught these things with such force and in such insistent ways that many theologians believe they have been taught infallibly by the ordinary magisterium.[45] Proportionalists argue that these teachings are proposed

82

only by a fallible magisterium, and that it is licit to dissent from the most insistent teaching of the ordinary teaching authority of the Church, if one has sufficient reasons.

Arguments for Proportionalism. Of the many arguments adduced in favor of proportionalism, two seem especially important.

The first is a philosophical argument that the fundamental principle of proportionalism is *evidently true.* Proportionalists argue that if one were not required to choose the greater good, or the lesser evil, the alternative would be that one would be obliged to choose the lesser good or greater evil. This alternative is patently absurd.[46] The self-evidence of the proportionalist principle is said to be confirmed by the fact that it is the natural, obvious way to determine the right course of action, as the actual moral thinking of good people reveals. The good person will certainly concede that he ought not do what leads to a greater balance of evil over good; that is to say, he instinctively judges as a proportionalist. The reason for this conviction is that morally serious persons care about what is really good, and this concern, if it is to be thoroughly reasonable, must justify the principle of the lesser evil.

The second major argument for proportionalism is that just as serious individuals make use of the proportionalist principle in their moral thinking so also does the Church. Thus, the adoption of proportionalism by Catholic thinkers, they claim, is a modest and legitimate development of moral themes already used by the Church, even if only implicitly. This argument is often supported by examples of the role of proportionality in the just-war theory and as one of the conditions of the principle of double effect.[47]

This development of moral teaching is especially appropriate today, so the argument goes, for a variety of reasons. As noted already, Vatican Council II called for a renewal in moral theology. In particular, the Council seems to have called for a more humanistic and less legalistic approach to morality. Proportionalism seems to many to be the proper response to this need in the life of the Church. It seems to be the worst sort of rule worship, the most uncaring legalism, for a person to refuse to do an act necessary for avoiding great harms simply because it is prohibited by a moral absolute taught by the Church. Pastoral reasons are also cited in support of the legitimacy of this development. People today will not and cannot accept the moral absolutes that so burden people in the new circumstances of a greatly changed world.

Difficulties in Proportionalist Arguments. The claim that the proportionalist principle of the lesser evil is self-evidently true cannot be sustained. This principle supposes that it is possible to determine which

83

alternative has the better or the less bad effects overall. To make this determination it must be possible to "commensurate" in an unambiguous way
goods and evils at stake in human actions. It must be possible, in other
words, to rank, measure, or compare the goods and evils at stake. One must
be able to tell how much harm to one good is offset by the realization of
some other good. Unless one can do this, the proportionalist method simply cannot work as a rational procedure of moral decision-making. This
commensurating of goods cannot be rationally carried out. As Pope John
Paul II says, "everyone recognizes the difficulty, or rather the impossibility, of evaluating all the good and evil consequences and effects — defined
as pre-moral — of one's own acts: an exhaustive rational calculation is not
possible. How then can one go about establishing proportions which depend on a measuring, the criteria of which remains obscure?"[48]

Thinkers within the broad tradition of consequentialism have tried for
centuries to show how human goods are commensurable but have never
provided an account which is both analytically satisfactory and consonant
with the common experiences of deliberation and choice. On the contrary,
common experience shows that the goods at stake when a person must
make a choice — the very situation in which moral guidance is needed —
are not commensurable. It is because the goods between which we must
choose are incommensurable that we must in the end settle what we shall
do by choosing. Powerful philosophical and theological arguments have
been developed which show that the common experience of the incom-
mensurability of goods must of necessity reflect the reality of human motivation and choice.[49]

Moreover, there are other problems with this method, problems about
how to determine the consequences, how many consequences to consider,
and so on, which have led many non-Catholic moralists to abandon
consequentialism altogether.[50] It is somewhat ironic that Catholic thinkers
have adopted a method of moral thinking that has been for over a century
the centerpiece of secular humanist thinking at the very time when many
secular moralists were despairing of its ability to withstand the objections
raised against it.[51]

Those who deny the self-evidence of the basic proportionalist principle are in no way proposing that we are ever expected to choose the greater
rather than the lesser evil. The claim is that proportionalists have selected
an incoherent way to distinguish the greater and the lesser evil. Thus, what
a proportionalist might claim to be the lesser evil really is not shown by
proportionalist procedures to be the lesser evil.

An example can clarify this. If a woman is considering having a direct abortion, she would, if following the proportionalist approach, list the central good and bad effects of deciding to have the abortion and of deciding to forgo it. Among the bad effects is that she would be choosing to kill directly and deliberately her own unborn child. Among expected good effects might be that she preserves her own mental and physical health, or that she saves the peace, unity, or financial integrity of her family. But how could she objectively add and subtract among goods and evils so diverse? Is the acknowledged evil of having the abortion such that it can be outweighed by the goods one anticipates by having it? How could she determine this? Her feelings might lean one way rather than the other, but the need is for a norm that will give rational, objective guidance in such situations.

A leading proportionalist tries to deal with this difficulty as follows: "In fear and trembling we commensurate"; "we *adopt* a hierarchy."[52] This approach seems to concede that there is no rational way to determine the lesser evil. It proposes that one adopt, that one choose for oneself, a hierarchy of goods, as a way of rating the worth of the various goods. One cannot do it objectively; but one *decides* how one will weigh alternatives; then one chooses in the light of the subjective evaluation that one has given. What this means is that one does not discover what is morally good; one decides what one shall call good by an arbitrary assessment.

One can indeed arbitrarily select ways of assigning values to the various incommensurable goods: of holding, for example, that the direct slaying of one's unborn child is an evil, nonetheless is less an evil than the sum of the evils which would follow if one did not have the abortion. However, this is evidently not a serious moral argument; it is a patent act of rationalization. One does not learn or discover that one's moral evaluation is the right one; rather one arbitrarily decides to adopt a standard of evaluation that will make one's preference turn out to be the right course.

This objection to proportionalism does not imply that the phrase "lesser evil" has no use in the moral thinking of decent people, for it surely does play such a role. But "lesser evil" does not have only the one meaning given to it by proportionalists. Some people, for example, think that the morally right course of action is always good, even when it has very sad and tragic consequences. Such persons might express this conviction by saying that the right course of action is the lesser evil, while never for a moment supposing that doing what violated a moral absolute could be the greater good or the lesser evil.[53] What the preceding argument precludes is only the specific use of the notion of lesser evil within the proportionalist method. It is by no means clear that morally decent people make use of this conception of lesser evil in their moral decision-making.

The second argument for proportionalism is also unsatisfactory. Proportionalism is a far more radical position than its defenders acknowledge it to be. It encourages rejections of moral norms that seem to be infallibly taught in the Church, and of positions that certainly cannot be legitimately rejected by Catholics, even if they are not infallibly proposed. Thus, proportionalism cannot be a legitimate development of Catholic moral teaching. The basic problem is that proportionalism leads to the denial that many of the moral absolutes taught by the Church are in fact true moral absolutes. Its history suggests that this is essential to its whole program, for it developed within the Church during the early 1960s as a rationale for justifying some use of contraceptives. This denial of moral absolutes taught insistently by the Church involves a denial of a basic moral principle — namely, that one must not do evil that good might come of it. This principle, as enunciated by St. Paul (Rom 3:8) and taught by the Church over the centuries, excludes the possibility of overturning moral absolutes by appeal to consequences, and this is exactly what proportionalism enjoins us to do.

Thus, it is implausible to maintain that a principle so opposed to what is fundamental in Church teaching can really be a development of that teaching. The precedents cited in favor of this claim are unimpressive. The fact that Christian tradition made use of some considerations about proportionality in some sense does not provide evidence for the claim that Christian tradition implicitly used or endorsed proportionalism, for it is not clear that proportionality was understood as a weighing of values, and even more importantly, such considerations were never used to overturn moral absolutes but only to settle issues in which it was clear that no moral absolute was at stake.[54]

Proportionalism therefore is not authentic development of received Catholic morality but a radical rejection of its central positions. Its claims to be the reasonable way to avoid legalism and to deal with pastoral problems are therefore suspect. Unless one supposes that any approach to morality that holds for moral absolutes must be legalistic, then it is by no means clear that proportionalism is the only way to avoid it. Caring deeply for persons and their goods does not mean attempting impossible ways of calculating and weighing the consequences of acts.[55] Utter fidelity to persons and their goods seems to imply an absolute refusal to do kinds of acts that will harm them by attacking directly basic goods in them. And this refusal implies a rejection of the basic principle of proportionalism. Similarly, pastoral love for the faithful is not shown by encouraging them to reject authentic (and perhaps infallible) Church teaching, and to live in

86

ways that the Fathers and saints have always said would separate one from the love of Christ. Even today it is an "eminent form of charity" to present Catholic teaching fully and persuasively, and to give every assistance to live in accord with its excellent norms.

A final difficulty with proportionalism should also be noted. It is the development of a criticism of consequentialism highlighted by secular moralists — namely, that consequentialist forms of thinking tend to be demoralizing in a number of ways.[56] Pastoral experience confirms the reality of this criticism. When the faithful are told that acts like those of adultery or fornication are not absolutely and always wrong but could be upright acts when proportionate reasons are really present, the faithful are deprived of bracing supports ordinarily necessary to strengthen them in the emotional and intellectual turmoil they experience at the time of temptation. If people are convinced that their own selves, their own moral identities, depend upon unswerving fidelity to moral principles, they have a defense lacking to those who are convinced that there is some way to rationally justify taking a course of action toward which they are inclined, although they know them to be unworthy.

The experience of our time shows how much human rights are threatened when small exceptions to necessary defenses of rights are allowed. For instance, few people wished the massive abortions now overwhelming the world. At first it was urged that some abortions be permitted "for very good reasons." But if abortions are permissible when the calculation of goods and harms permits it (a calculation that cannot be objectively valid; a calculation that will be mightily affected by hopes and fears), then the nonobjective nature of the calculation called for almost certainly leads to the terrible consequences brought about by abortion. Clearly, as John Paul II rightly insists,[57] there can be no inalienable rights when there are no exceptionless duties.

Proportionalism therefore is inadequate as an approach to moral thinking for Catholics. Instead of providing guidance for the care and love of persons and their goods, proportionalism demands that human beings achieve a kind of knowledge only God could have, and undertake a responsibility for the consequences of actions that only God's providence can have. Instead of fidelity to the limited but real commitments we all have and to the moral absolutes which mark the boundaries for proper human participation in God's providence, proportionalism tells us to look further — to consider all the effects, to put on a scale things that reflect in irreducible ways God's infinite goodness. This may seem noble to some, but it overreaches, taking as our own what we must trust to God's loving concern.

Our moral thinking must not suppose that we can extricate ourselves from the tragedies and evils of human life; only God's healing re-creation can do that. But we can be faithful, can have hearts and wills completely faithful to the goodness which God so loves and, in the end, will restore. Proportionalism, sadly, corrupts that fidelity.

The Morality of Principles

We give the name "Morality of Principles" to the broad approach within Catholic moral theology which, on the one hand, seeks to meet the challenge of Vatican II for renewal in moral theology and, on the other hand, seeks to maintain continuity with the received teaching of the Church on moral matters and with the best of the moral thinking in the theological tradition.

This approach might also be called the "natural law" approach, and this is the way John Paul II and the *Catechism of the Catholic Church* identify it.[58] We identify it as "the morality of principles" to distinguish our approach, which is definitely based on St. Thomas's teaching on natural law,[59] from other theories of moral law also bearing the name of "natural law" approaches, for instance, the kind of natural-law theory rooted in the thought of Francis Suarez.

The primary way in which the morality of principles maintains continuity with the tradition of Catholic moral teaching is by insisting on the truth and centrality of moral absolutes. This approach holds that the specific moral norms taught by Christian tradition as valid in every instance do indeed have such universal applicability. Such norms as "never directly kill the innocent" and "never commit adultery" are held to be true, always binding, and nontrivial. There can never be any objectively good reasons for violating specific principles such as these. This, of course, is not taken to imply that no moral norms have exceptions. Most norms do have exceptions. "Keep your promises" and "obey all just civil laws" are true general norms, but there are certainly circumstances in which the good person recognizes that they do not apply.

The renewal of moral theology called for by Vatican II does not lead to an abandonment of the norms always taught in the Church but rather to a fuller understanding of why these norms are essential to the fabric of authentic Christian living. To reject moral absolutes and the rich tradition of moral thinking developed for applying and refining them would not be to renew Catholic morality but to discard it.

The renewal of moral theology is therefore understood within the morality of principles as an effort of deeper understanding and fuller appreciation of the significance of moral life within the economy of salvation. It is an effort to see how moral activity relates to the saving work of Christ, to the eternal destiny of Christians, and to the true humanism which faith has always held and Vatican II explicitly proclaimed. Thus understood, renewal in moral theology looks deeper into the sources of faith and into Catholic tradition to overcome a presentation of morality either as merely legalistic rules and regulations imposed by God or the Church, or as a set of directives which rationalistic arguments might establish.

The morality of principles therefore does not defend Christian moral teaching, including the teaching on moral absolutes, in a legalistic way. One must not avoid blasphemy or homosexual acts regardless of the consequences of one's faithfulness to the rule simply because one superstitiously venerates rules. Nor is the universality of the rule grounded merely in some command of God, who perhaps inexplicably demands faithfulness, even when more harm than good would appear to follow from faithfulness to the precept in a given situation.

Faith confirms that there are moral absolutes but also insists that moral absolutes are the requirements of love. The moral absolutes taught by the Church are not iron rules or nonrational demands. They are intelligent directives, guiding us to live in accord with the requirements of love for neighbor and reverence for what is really good. Hence, proponents of the morality of principles point out that it is always wrong to do such deeds as faith has proscribed absolutely because acts such as these are incompatible with the good of persons whom God calls us to love and absolutely respect. To do such acts is always to act in ways contrary to the full perfection of human persons and communities, and so it is to act in ways unworthy of persons created in God's image and called to act as he does — never willing evil, never harming love, and always respecting the dignity of persons. Human goods are not ideals that dwell apart; they are the fulfillment of human persons, and flourish only in persons. Hence, to act so as deliberately to harm a basic human good is to act against the fulfillment of a human person. And that is incompatible with loving the person.

The preceding argument in defense of moral absolutes is characteristic of the approach taken by those who hold for the morality of principles. But since this is a broad approach and not a single theory, not all who take this approach would develop the argument in exactly this way. Some would emphasize the dignity of persons, and how this dignity cannot be respected unless certain absolute rights and obligations are honored. Others would perhaps focus more on the precious human relationships and meanings that will be distorted unless these absolutes are accepted. But all versions of the

89

morality of principles hold that moral absolutes protect what is most precious, lasting, and valuable in human life. In this sense they are all profoundly humanistic; all are variations on the theme that genuine love requires a care and respect for persons which absolutely excludes certain kinds of actions, namely those that harm persons by attacking the goods prefective of them, manipulate them, or disregard their true dignity.

The contrast between proportionalism and the morality of principles is perhaps sharpest at this point, for while both are concerned for human persons and their goods, this concern is understood very differently by each. Unlike proportionalism, the morality of principles does not suppose that the demands of love can be captured by a single simple moral principle, like the principle of the lesser evil. More important, the morality of principles does not require the mistaken assumption that the goods of human persons can be calculated and measured on a single scale. The tradition's concern with a hierarchy of values was never construed as a scale on which one could calculate the lesser evil as a ground for moral judgment.

The recognition that human goods are not calculable in the way proportionalism supposes does not mean that there can be no rational way to honor and respect them. Quite the contrary. We do not truly honor the precious goods of human persons when we are willing to harm them because doing so would, as we think, bring about the lesser evil. The morality of principles is serious about not harming human goods, and demands that in our acts we respect and honor each of them. Of course, we cannot in a given act immediately promote and pursue all that is humanly good; but we can always do acts in such a way that all the goods of human nature are respected and honored. Our fidelity to the whole good of human persons is often revealed not so much by the goods we seek but how we respect the goods that are not our immediate concern. The basic principle of the morality of principles, expressed in religious terms by the love commandment, can be formulated therefore as a principle of respect for the entire human good. We must always act in such a way as to be open to integral human fulfillment.[60]

Concern for the goods of persons is not therefore realized by trying, as it were, to create a world in which the maximum possible amount of good is realized but in making ourselves persons who humbly cherish and respect all that is good. This is not an attitude of contempt for the harms and tragedies which befall human beings, nor is it an attitude of self-righteousness that cares only for moral rectitude and not at all for human problems. It is, rather, realism about the multifarious character of the human good and our limited ability to make the world good. It is humility which recognizes that the solution to the problem of evil is not human action but God's healing re-creation. It is confidence that God will restore all that is really good and that we shall be part of the re-creation if only we cooperate by maintaining the steadfast loyalty revealed by Jesus and his saints, even in the face of failure and tragedy.

The morality of principles therefore is a form of humanism; but it is one in which the true good of man is seen in its full and proper perspective — the perspective of the kingdom of God made possible by Jesus' human acts and God's loving response to them. Thus, it is an approach to moral thinking which is fully open to the larger and deeper meaning of human existence made possible by the revelation of Jesus. In this respect, it compares favorably with the rather narrow, secular, and this-worldly emphasis of proportionalism.

Moral absolutes are only one ingredient in a morality of principles; but they have always had a distinctive place in Catholic moral thought. Even the most corrupt societies have known that adultery is generally harmful, and that divorce is destructive of the basic human community. But Christian thought has been distinctive in teaching that one should not commit adultery, slay the innocent, or seek divorce and remarry even for the most splendid reasons, even to avoid the most bitter consequences. Christian faith has seen that there are in fact evil kinds of deeds, deeds that always involve assaults upon the love of persons. Such deeds must never be done; there can be no "proportionate reason" for doing them. We must not do evil that good may come of it. We must not do even a small evil because a great good seems destined to come of it, or because a great harm can be avoided by doing it. (St. Thomas More was right in judging that he should not affirm by oath false statements already so affirmed by virtually all the religious leaders of England, even though it seemed that little harm and slight additional scandal would come of it, and even though his own life, his family's hopes, and the possibility of influencing the king for the better might be salvaged by doing the evil.) John Paul II has made explicit the connection between moral absolutes and martyrdom.[61] He also repeats the teaching of twentieth century popes that moral absolutes are necessary for a decent society in which basic human rights are recognized, cherished, and protected.[62]

The morality of principles respects the rich complexity of serious moral thinking. It realizes that a good moral act involves more than doing a good kind of deed, or avoiding a perverse kind. It involves more than having good intentions in what we do, and more than seeking to avoid harmful consequences. St. Thomas Aquinas articulated what might be called a "principle of completeness" for evaluating human actions which required that good actions (like good persons and good realities of every kind) must be complete in their goodness.[63] According to this principle, clearly affirmed by The *Catechism of the Catholic Church* and by John Paul II,[64] every aspect of the act must be morally good: a single moral flaw, whether in the kind of action one does, or in the intentions with which it is done, or in the consequences of other circumstances with which it is done, is sufficient to render the act morally bad.

This principle does not prohibit actions because they have a tragic or unfortunate aspect to them; that would make most actions in this fallen world impossible. The integrity required is the integrity of a wholly upright will, of one who is unwilling to do whatever is contrary to a complete and intelligent respect for what is really good. Acts and other realities are morally bad to the extent that they lack any essential trait needed for their integrity and fulfillment. Thus, for example, if an act promises so much harm, and to do little good, in its outcomes, one who respects the Golden Rule will not do the act even if it be of a good kind and done with a good intention. One cannot merge these factors together and judge that one may do a bad kind of act, or approve an act done for a perverse intention, if one perceives that the act, considered in all its features, will have a greater balance of good consequences or aspects over bad ones. *Each* of the moral determinants must be good, or the act will not be a good one; it will not otherwise be faithful enough to what love requires.

IV. Good Deeds and Good Consequences

Christian faith has always been more concerned that the faithful do excellent actions and so live morally excellent lives than that they produce many good effects in the world, or have wonderful things occur in their lives. Our lives are constituted far more by what we do than by what happens to us.

Many people in today's world find this aspect of Christian faith to be very puzzling. Modern secular humanists and, in particular, secular consequentialists reject it altogether, for consequentialists believe that it is not actions but the overall effects of actions that are morally most important. Christian ethics, of course, does not deny that we have some responsibility for the predictable effects of our actions but maintains that our actions themselves are the center of moral life.

The *Centrality of the Chosen Action*. Classical Catholic thought stresses the centrality of action because our free actions are the existential center of our lives. In our freely chosen acts we not only affect the world and other persons but also shape our own personalities and character. By choosing to do certain actions we determine ourselves to be one kind of person rather than another; we make ourselves to be friends of God by responding to his grace and freely loving all that is good, or we choose actions incompatible with love of God and fellowman.[65]

Of course, we do not choose only actions in the narrow sense. We also make large-scale choices that tend to establish the broader outlines of our lives: our vocations, our professional identities, and our basic relationships with other persons. And the measure of the responsibility we have for the wide range of consequences of our actions varies with the ways we relate ourselves to those consequences.

Intended Actions and Unintended Side Effects. What we deliberately choose to do and the ends we deliberately make our own have an especially great importance. Clearly we do not, in every free choice and action, deliberately choose all that flows from such choices and acts: all the side effects, all the other things left undone, and so on. What is foreseen to come about as a result of our choices — but is not itself chosen — is voluntary in a way; but it is not itself freely chosen. It is accepted or permitted but not positively willed. The voluntary acceptance of side effects is not self-determining in the way free choices of the objects and ends of our acts are.[66]

This difference is the basis for the crucial distinction in Catholic morality between what is directly willed or intended and what is indirectly willed or outside the person's intention. To deny the moral significance of this distinction, as proportionalists often do, is to deny something fundamental to Catholic morality.[67] For if one rejects this distinction, and holds that there is no moral difference between directly willing or doing evil and indirectly causing it, one would have to concede that it is permissible at times to do evil, and that there really are no moral absolutes. For it is scarcely deniable that even good people do, and cannot escape doing, acts from which bad effects flow. A parent who saves his or her child from the violent assault of an attacker may be able to do this only by a protective act that causes great harm or death to the assailant, however unintended that harm may be. But if every act that causes harm is morally indistinguishable from an act in which the harm is directly done or intended by the agent, then the absolute moral prohibition of directly doing evil would be meaningless.

To deny the moral significance of the distinction between directly doing and indirectly causing (or permitting) evil is unreasonable. Anyone can see how different is the personal attitude toward evil in two cases: one in which the agent chooses only good, and allows evil to happen as the unintended effect of his or her actions when there are weighty reasons for doing so; and the very different case in which one fixes the heart upon doing or achieving the evil as a means toward some end. Even God, in creating this good world, which is filled with adventures of freedom and responsibility, permitted the free evil deeds of his creatures (which he in no way directly willed to bring about). If there is no difference between permitting evil and setting one's heart on it, God must set his heart on evil. But such a conclusion is not only absurd, it is blasphemous. It is possible for persons to set their hearts only on good. Permitting evil is not choosing it. Choosing evil can never be justified; permitting evil, while obviously not always justified, can sometimes be justified.

Thus, it is not necessarily a violation of the Thomistic principle of completeness to accept bad consequences of actions. One should, of course, avoid acts having very harmful consequences, if one can morally do so. But if the alternative to accepting bad consequences is to choose to do an immoral act, one must endure the bad consequences, for to choose to do evil is to set one's heart against what is good, and to determine oneself as a person who rejects what the love of God and neighbor requires.

The End Does Not Justify the Means. Catholic teaching has always held that it is a terrible flaw in an action — and a horrible tragedy for the one who does it — to do evil directly for any reason. Even if the most precious and necessary goods could not be achieved except by doing a deed that directly does even a small evil, the good man should not do that deed. He must care to make the world good; but the most important good he is to do, the most pressing service he has, in making the world good, is to make his own heart good, by doing only good actions. If he cannot achieve goods he loves by good actions, he has no morally good way to achieve them. Yet he can rightly hope in God, if, living rightly, he does what good he can do well, and trusts God to realize the goods that he himself cannot achieve in acting well.[68]

Good Actions, Good Character, and Fundamental Option. Some protest against the traditional emphasis on freely chosen actions. They argue that actions alone are not the center of moral life. Character, or the basic and enduring moral orientation of the person, has a more profound significance. This has led some moral theologians to locate the basic self-determination of persons not in free choices but in a fundamental or transcendental freedom which cannot be found in any discrete choice but rather in the fundamental orientation of a person's entire life. This fundamental option, and not our free choices, is said to be what determines our basic response to God, our very moral identities, and thus our eternal destiny.[69]

This theory is correct in emphasizing that our lives can and should be organized by a fundamental commitment which shapes and orders all our life in response to God's call. But, as Pope John Paul II has taught, fundamental option theory is mistaken, however, in holding that this basic commitment does not flow from the free, deliberate choices of our ordinary moral life but is rather the fruit of an allegedly profound, somewhat mysterious act at a deeper and ineffable level of freedom.[70]

Choices are spiritual realities and not physical events like the performances that carry them out. As Pope John Paul II has made clear, our free actions have not only a transitive aspect in which an event in the world is caused but also a nontransitive aspect which remains in the human self and determines the kind of person the agent is.[71]

Free choices therefore have enduring effects and in this enduring aspect are the basis for the virtues which form the fabric of a good life. The virtuous person is fundamentally one who has made the right free choices, and has made them in such a way that his or her entire personality, desires, reactions, and beliefs are integrated around these good choices.[72] So Christian morality is not too "act-oriented" but recognizes the importance of a life of integrated and stable commitment to the Lord's work.

Still, the Church also emphasizes that the discrete choices of a person's life are the root of personal self-determination and responsibility. Human action is trivialized if we fancy that a single choice moved by grace cannot be important enough to merit salvation or tragic enough to lose it.[73] Thus, a single free choice can change the fundamental orientation of a person's life, as the Good Thief changed his fundamental option on Good Friday.

The freedom of our choices is that whereby we determine ourselves; it is the locus of the "soul making" which is the center of the moral life. It is the part of our natures which perhaps most fully images the supremely free Creator of all; it is the part of us which allows us to be friends of God, not because we were in any way constrained or forced to be such but because we ourselves choose to be his friends. This freedom, however, has its burdens that make us want to hide from its full reality. We must, as the Church has always taught, use that freedom well; we must make hard choices but only good ones — choices to do actions that intelligently show that we love and cherish all that is good.

Chapter Five
Conscience: Its Meaning, Formation, and Relationship to Church Authority

"But every person must follow his own conscience!" Christian faith holds that this statement expresses an important truth about morality.

This statement, unfortunately, is often misunderstood. Many take it to imply that personal conscience is the only thing a responsible person must be concerned with; in other words, that one need not be concerned with the objective principles of morality discussed in the previous chapter.

This implication is entirely unwarranted. The good person will care very much that his or her conscience guides him or her correctly to what is really good to the extent that he or she can discover it. For the upright person is concerned with doing authentically good actions, not only actions that now seem right or appear good. Such a person is concerned with knowing and doing what is truly good.

In this chapter we shall first note certain important distinctions in the uses of the word "conscience." Then we shall consider the duty to follow one's conscience. Finally, we shall treat of the principles for forming a Christian conscience, and of the relationship between the personal conscience of a Catholic and the authoritative teaching of the Church.[1]

I. Different Meanings of the Term "Conscience"

The word "conscience" has a number of distinct but related meanings. In this section we will first consider conscience in the psychological sense — the conscience described by psychologists as related to parental norms, guilt feelings, and other nonrational factors. Second, we will analyze conscience as the moral evaluation of a particular action. Third, we will consider conscience, as a personal grasp of correct moral principles and ways of thinking morally. Finally, we will consider a current account of the relation between moral principles and specific moral judgments — the theory of transcendental conscience.

Psychological Conscience. "Psychological conscience" is essentially related to feelings of moral approval or disapproval. Virtually everyone experiences at times — at least with respect to some important actions — either the security of some inner approval of one's decision, or the anxiety of a condemnation within the depths of one's own being. For example, a woman who had been trained from childhood to be submissive might feel that she is being immoral if she does not do just what her husband desires. This emotional self-condemnation might persist even if upon critical reflection she judges it right to behave as she does.

Guilt feelings stirred up by the inner mechanisms of psychological conscience have a great impact on one's life, and they have been widely discussed by psychiatrists. Freud's notion of the superego is one explanation of psychological conscience.[2] Conscience in this sense involves the internalization of parental and social norms and even of traditional taboos. Thus, conscience in this sense is the result of a process of psychological conditioning. The spontaneous reactions, impulses, and feelings associated with psychological conscience may, of course, be more or less healthy and realistic; they may at times be pathological.

Because conscience in this sense is shaped largely by nonrational factors, and is frequently found to condemn what is not wrong or to approve what is wrong, it cannot of itself provide decisive moral guidance. There can be no obligation to obey conscience in this sense. But psychological conscience is one of the factors that a mature and conscientious person will evaluate in the light of moral principles. A person's critical moral judgment must determine the validity of the impulses of psychological conscience.

Particular Moral Conscience. Sometimes "conscience" refers to one's considered judgment about the morality of a particular act. This judgment is the result of the attempt to know what is truly right, and it is this judgment that Catholic moral tradition most often calls "conscience." Conscience in this sense does not refer to feelings of approval or disapproval but to reflective moral judgment. Since the judgment of conscience is the result of the thoughtful evaluation a person makes about the moral goodness or badness of a particular action, it can be called "particular moral conscience." The judgment involved can be about an act one is considering doing (technically called *antecedent conscience*) or about an act that one has already done (*consequent conscience*).[3] In each case one is attempting to speak the moral truth about some action of one's own: "Is this particular act really a morally good act or is it an evil act?" The person responds to such questions in judgments of conscience like these: "I should not do this, because it would be wrong" or "What I did was good." It is in this sense — in the sense of a judgment about the rightness or wrongness of particular acts that St. Thomas Aquinas and much of Catholic tradition after him use the term "conscience."[4] Conscience in this sense can be defined as one's best judgment as to what in the circumstances is the morally right thing to do. Thus the *Catechism of the Catholic Church* says: "Conscience is a judgment of reason whereby the human person recognizes the moral quality of a concrete act that he is going to perform, is in the process of performing, or has already completed."[5] Similarly, Pope John Paul II writes: "The judgment of conscience is a *practical judgment*, a judgment which makes known what man must do or not do, or which assesses an act already performed by him. It is a judgment which applies to a concrete situation the conviction that one must love and do good and avoid evil."[6]

It is important to note that since the judgment of conscience is an act of the intellect, it cannot merely be a feeling or a personal decision to act or live in a certain way. This is not to say that the affective or existential dimension is unimportant in the moral life or that the feelings of an upright and integrated person are irrelevant in making judgments of conscience.[7] The point is simply that living morally requires the conviction that given acts either are or are not truly in accord with correct moral standards. Concern for the truth is essential. Intelligent judgments, not feelings or choices, should direct the lives of mature persons.

It is precisely because the judgment of conscience is one's best judgment about what one should do that a person is morally obliged to act in accord with his or her conscience.[8] We shall consider this matter more fully in our discussion of the duty to follow conscience.

General Moral Conscience. A person's awareness of the basic principles for making moral judgments is also often called "conscience." In this sense, conscience is one's personal awareness of the most basic moral truths.[9] It is in this sense of the term that one's conscience can be said to be an awareness of the law of God written in the human heart (Rom 2:14-16), and it is in this sense too that conscience refers to our awareness of ourselves as moral beings, summoned to seek the truth about our lives and to live them in accord with this knowledge. This dynamic thrust of our personality is called "transcendental conscience" and will be discussed below. Vatican II refers to conscience in this general sense when it affirms that conscience is that through which man "sees and recognizes the demands of the divine law" (*Dignitatis Humanae*, no. 3).[10]

Conscience in this sense grasps the norms that will guide one in evaluating particular actions. Thus, it is by this general conscience that a person knows that one should do good and avoid evil; that one should aim at harming no one; that one should love God and neighbor; and that one must never do deeds that are of their nature base, that always attack basic goods in

98

ourselves or other persons.[11] Conscience likewise knows that the Ten Commandments follow from these basic principles and must be understood in the bracing way that faith has understood them.[12] The mature and responsible person grasps also, in intelligent conscientious reflection, more detailed moral precepts that can be seen to be true from a right understanding of basic moral principles and of the Ten Commandments. Thus, typical adult Catholics grasp personally not only the broad truth that killing innocent people is wrong but also the more specific truths that abortion and suicide are always wrong.

In a famous paragraph of the *Pastoral Constitution on the Church in the Modern World*, the Fathers of Vatican II stated the importance of conscience in the sense we are now discussing. They also make reference to the particular judgment of conscience and show its connection with our awareness of the moral law and of ourselves as moral subjects impelled to seek the truth. The Council Fathers say:

> Deep within his conscience man discovers a law which he has not laid upon himself but which he must obey. Its voice [that is, the voice of this law],[13] ever calling him to love and to do what is good and to avoid evil, tells him inwardly at the right moment: do this, shun that. For man has in his heart a law inscribed by God. His dignity lies in observing this law, and by it he will be judged. His conscience is man's most secret core, and his sanctuary. There he is alone with God whose voice echoes in his depths. By conscience, in a wonderful way, that law is made known which is fulfilled in the love of God and of one's neighbor. . . . Hence, the more a correct conscience prevails, the more do persons and groups turn aside from blind choice and try to be guided by the objective standards of moral conduct. Yet it often happens that conscience goes astray through ignorance which it is unable to avoid, without thereby losing its dignity. This cannot be said of the man who takes little trouble to find out what is true and good, or when conscience is by degrees almost blinded through the habit of committing sin.[14]

This statement by the Council sums up many of the points we have been considering. First, conscience involves an awareness of something objective and truly good — a law which man does not give himself but discovers. Second, moral conscience, in the sense of man's best judgment about what he is to do, must be obeyed — even when it is mistaken. Man will be judged according to the law which conscience knows, and the very dignity of man consists in submitting to this law, that is, in doing what he perceives to be good. Third, the invincible ignorance which causes the conscience of an upright person to err is firmly distinguished from the ignorance of one who does not sufficiently care about finding the truth concerning what is right, and from the blindness of one whose conscience is dulled by habitual sin.

Conscience, understood in this sense, presents us with an objective standard of morality. We have a duty to obey this standard precisely because we perceive in the light of faith and of natural intelligence that it is directing us toward what is authentically good. It is, of course, possible for us to be ignorant of at least some part of this standard, or to make use of it in inadequate ways. But we cannot escape responsibility for these shortcomings if we are not serious about discovering what is truly right. "Certainly," as John Paul II says, "in order to have a 'good conscience' (1 Tim 1:5), man must seek the truth and must make judgments in accordance with the same truth."[15]

Transcendental Conscience. The morally mature person recognizes that feelings and social conventions do not determine what is morally right and morally wrong. We know that our own moral feelings can be misguided and that societies can be more or less corrupt, and at times incline us to approve what no truly good person should approve. The morally serious person is convinced that questions of right and wrong cannot be settled arbitrarily but need to be determined in accordance with the truth. Precisely because of this realization that moral conscience in its authentic sense is concerned with moral truth, some contemporary theologians have developed an account of moral awareness which they call "transcendental conscience." One of the leading proponents of this theological view, Walter E. Conn, has suggested that conscience can best be considered as "the dynamic thrust toward self-transcendence at the core of a person's very subjectivity, revealing itself . . . as a demand for responsible decision in accord with reasonable judgment."[16] Summarizing the work of developmental psychologists such as Erik Erikson, Jean Piaget, and Lawrence Kohlberg, and relying heavily on the philosophical and theological studies of Bernard Lonergan, Conn properly rejects any normative significance to conscience understood in a merely psychological sense. In his opinion, the term "conscience" refers basically to the *whole person* as a moral self, as a being inwardly impelled to act responsibly in accordance with the truth.

Conn and theologians like him are surely correct in emphasizing that conscience, in its moral sense, is intimately linked to our quest for truth. Human persons are unique in that they are question-asking beings, anxious to discover the truth not only about the physical world in which they live but even more the truth about what they are to do if they are to become fully the beings they are meant to be. In her teaching, the Church clearly recognizes this unique characteristic of human existence. More significantly, she explicitly uses the term "conscience" in speaking of the human person's inner drive to discover the truth about human action and being. In a remarkable passage in Vatican Council II's *Declaration on Religious Liberty*, the Council Fathers first note that "the highest norm of human life is the divine law itself — eternal, objective, and universal, by which God orders, directs, and governs the whole world and the ways of the human community." Then they continue by saying:

> God has enabled man to participate in this law of his so that, under the gentle disposition of divine providence, man may be able to arrive at a deeper and deeper knowledge of unchangeable truth. . . . It is through his conscience that man sees and recognizes the demands of the divine law (*Dignitatis Humanae*, no. 3).[17]

Thus, there are grounds for saying that conscience refers to the inner dynamism of the human person impelling the individual to discover the truth about what is to be done and what he or she is to be. Conscience is therefore "a special and very fundamental mode of self-awareness — the awareness of 'how it is with oneself.' "[18] But conscience does more than reveal the gap between what we are and what we ought to become. It is also a summons to realize our full humanity.[19]

The vision supporting this understanding of conscience seems to be behind Pope Pius XII's metaphorical description of conscience as the "inner core and sanctuary of a man, where he is alone with God,"[20] a description which both the Second Vatican Council and Pope John Paul II have made their own.[21]

The theory of transcendental conscience focuses on several essential aspects of general moral conscience. Despite this, however, the theory of transcendental conscience, as proposed by Conn and others, does not adequately explain the whole of moral awareness. The fundamental weakness in Conn's position is this: it misrepresents the relation between the particular judgment of conscience and the knowledge of basic moral principles. An uncritical acceptance of certain popular philosophical assumptions leads

101

the proponents of this theory to suppose that the natural awareness of morality does not contain any principles having definite implications. Conn argues that the judgment of conscience, while it is not arbitrary, cannot be derived in an objective way from the general principles of conscience.[22] Instead, he argues that authentic moral living "is determined neither by absolute principles nor by arbitrary creativity relative to each situation: authentic living, rather, is defined by a normative structure of consciousness which demands that a person respond to the values in each situation with creativity that is at once sensitive, critical, responsible, and loving."[23]

No one, of course, would advocate responding to moral situations in ways that are insensitive, uncritical, irresponsible, or unloving. But the question concerns the *criteria*, or *norms*, whereby one can know whether one's response is critical, responsible, sensitive, and loving. And Conn's position seems to make conscience itself the norm. It makes conscience altogether autonomous and beyond criticism, because in rejecting the proper role of principles it makes conscience an almost mystical and unanalyzable component of the person. However, one may acknowledge the dynamic thrust of basic moral awareness and yet hold that the basic structures of moral consciousness grasp principles of the sort the Church has held all along to be the basis of moral judgment. Unless there are such principles, it is hard to see how the "dynamic thrust toward self-transcendence" could be determined to be a movement toward authentic self-transcendence, for without critical principles it could become a dynamism toward self-destruction or self-deception.

Moreover, if there is no definite connection between the basic demands of being fully human and particular actions, it is hard to see how one of the basic facts of moral experience can be explained, for the phenomenon of moral evil is essentially one in which one is aware that one is choosing contrary to the concrete implications of the moral law. If the moral law has no definite implications, and all we have to guide our choices is the dynamic thrust of consciousness, it is difficult to grasp any intelligent patterns whatsoever in the workings of conscience.[24]

II. The Duty to Follow One's Conscience

As we have already seen, a person has the moral duty to act in accordance with his or her own judgment of conscience. "The judgment of conscience," Pope John Paul II writes, "has an imperative character: man must act in accordance with it."[25] Surely a good person must do what he or she decisively judges he or she truly should do. Nonetheless, since the obligation to follow one's conscience is so frequently misunderstood, it will be of value to extend our discussion of this important topic.

Even if one thinks that one would suffer great losses, or fail to gain important goods if one should follow the demands of conscience, one's duty is to act as one has conscientiously judged one must act. Even if the most august authorities, political or religious, should command one to act in a way that conscience — understood as one's firm and honest moral judgment — forbids, then such authorities should not be obeyed. This evident truth, one clearly affirmed by Catholic theological tradition and by the teaching authority of the Church,[26] must however be clearly distinguished from the question whether one who is *inclined* to make a particular moral judgment of conscience ought not be prepared to change it if any authoritative teaching of Christ or his Church begins to make one aware that one's own former opinion was incorrect.

It is important to recognize that the duty to follow one's conscience is intelligible only when conscience is understood in the sense of a *judgment of conscience* — the best judgment one can make about the truly good thing to do in the circumstances. Merely psychological conscience can generate no such duty.

It is, moreover, important to recognize that a person's judgment of conscience can be more or less mistaken. Any judgment is the result of a person's attempt to discover the truth. Such attempts can fail, especially when one attempts to discover the truth about complex matters. Of course, this is not to say that our attempts to discover the truth about particular moral matters always fail; we are often justifiably certain that we have succeeded.[27]

Our judgments of conscience are not therefore *infallible*.[28] One might perhaps be inclined to think of one's judgment of conscience as infallible if one thought of conscience as a kind of "moral sense" which grasps or intuits the moral qualities of acts, except that this intuitionistic view of conscience is not defensible. It is inconsistent with the common experience of the complexity of the process leading to the judgment of conscience, and with the awareness each of us has of noting and correcting mistakes in the formation of his or her conscience. Clearly, it conflicts with the approach to moral thinking taken by the greatest Catholic teachers and endorsed by the magisterium.[29] Moreover, the moral qualities of acts are not like the observable features of physical things and events: the rightness or wrongness of a particular act is not an observable feature of the act in the way that the size of this page is an observable feature of this page, and cannot be as simply observed as such features can be.

103

Thus, one's judgment of conscience can be mistaken. However, this does not change the fact that a person is obliged to follow his or her final judgment of conscience, for in such a case one honestly believes that a certain course of action is morally required, and to refuse to act in accord with one's judgment in such a case would be to refuse to act in the way one personally believes to be morally required.[30] The morally upright person will, of course, earnestly seek to see to it that his or her judgments of conscience are true. Such a person will seek to ground his or her judgments of conscience upon a solid basis of moral principles understood in the light of faith. Thus, "it is always from truth that the dignity of conscience derives. In the case of the correct conscience, it is a question of the *objective truth* received by man; in the case of the erroneous conscience, it is a question of what man, mistakenly, *subjectively* considers to be true."[31] Moreover, such a person will, when unable to reach secure answers personally, seek counsel from those he knows to be trustworthy and wise guides to good moral life.

If a person does not make efforts of this kind, he or she bears the responsibility for his or her mistaken judgments of conscience. The mistake in such a person's judgment is attributable to his or her own neglect. At times this mistake may be attributable to previous bad choices that an individual has made. Such sinful choices, as Vatican Council II reminds us in the passage cited previously, can frequently "blind" conscience, and the blindness in question is voluntary, at least in its cause. Thus, a seriously convinced — even "sincere" — racist is not innocent if his racist sentiments and judgments are the result either of his own negligence in seeking the truth about this matter, or of his deliberate choices not to discover this truth.[32]

Thus, the duty to follow one's conscience means that we have an obligation to act in accordance with our own best judgment of what is right in the circumstances. This obligation also requires that in arriving at this judgment, we have struggled to discover the truth, that we have sought to inform our conscience. As the American bishops put the matter in their pastoral letter on the moral life:

> We must have a rightly informed conscience and follow it. But our judgments are human and can be mistaken; we may be blinded by the power of sin in our lives or misled by the strength of our desires. "Beloved, do not trust every spirit, but put the spirits to a test to see if they belong to God" [1 John 4.1]. Clearly, then, we must do everything in our power to see to it that our judgments of conscience are informed and in accord with the moral order of which God

104

is creator. Common sense requires that conscientious people be open and humble, ready to learn from the experience and insight of others, willing to acknowledge prejudices and even change their judgments in light of better instruction.[33]

Thus, we shall now turn to consider the question of informing a Catholic conscience.

III. The Formation of a Catholic Conscience

As noted earlier, the goal of the judgment of conscience is to arrive at a knowledge of what truly is to be done in the concrete. An essential basis for this judgment is each person's awareness of the general principles of the moral law, already discussed above (under the heading of "General Moral Conscience," page 98). These general principles, however, need to be specified and applied to the concrete circumstances of a person's life. While some applications are relatively easy, others are very complex. If one realizes that every intentional killing of an innocent person is wrong, and if a given act is readily seen to be an instance of intentionally killing an innocent person, then it is clear that this act is wrong. But there are cases in which it is very difficult to tell whether the killing is intentional or the person innocent in the relevant sense. Moreover, many moral norms are nonabsolute. For example, there are times when the rule that just civil laws are to be obeyed does not apply. Thus, guidance for the concrete choices which make up a person's life does not follow simply from general moral principles.[34]

Forming one's conscience therefore involves two types of activity. First, one must grasp the implications of the basic principles of morality; second, sensitive to all the significant features of one's situation, one must learn how to apply these norms so as to form reasonable judgments of conscience.

Every person must use thoughtful intelligence in making such judgments. The Catholic, knowing that one of the central purposes of revelation is to assist him or her in seeing how to live wisely, will accept what Christ teaches through his Church. As the Fathers of Vatican II state: "However, in forming their consciences the faithful must pay careful attention to the sacred and certain teaching of the Church. For the Catholic Church is by the will of Christ the teacher of truth. It is her duty to proclaim and teach with authority the truth which is Christ and, at the same time, to declare and confirm by her authority the principles of the moral order which spring from human nature itself."[35]

Thus, God's revelation in Scripture and Christian tradition as explained and articulated in the teaching of the Church, together with the expression of this teaching in the example of the saints, and the struggles of our ancestors in faith, as well as the Catholic's natural insight into morality — all these together provide the Catholic with reliable guides to form his or her conscience.

Moreover, in making use of these various elements by which God reveals his plan, the Catholic will treat them as forming an integral whole. Such a person will read Scripture as a Catholic and will understand the demands of his or her natural insight into moral issues in light of the whole of revelation and the Church's actual living of the faith.

These sources are not regarded by the Catholic as extrinsic sources of information or as external constraints upon his or her conscience. The revelation of Jesus is accepted by an intelligent and mature believer as the fundamental framework in which he or she organizes his or her life and understands his or her existence. "The authority of the Church," as John Paul II says:

> When she pronounces on moral questions, in no way undermines the freedom of conscience of Christians. This is so not only because freedom of conscience is never freedom "from" the truth but always and only freedom "in" the truth, but also because the magisterium does not bring to the Christian conscience truths which are extraneous to it; rather, it brings to light the truths which it ought already to possess, developing them from the starting point of the primordial act of faith. The Church puts herself always and only at the *service of conscience*, helping it to avoid being tossed to and fro by every wind of doctrine proposed by human deceit (cf. Eph 4:14) and helping it not to swerve from the truth about the good of man, but rather, especially in more difficult questions, to attain the truth with certainly and to abide in it.[36]

The moral law is not an alien law. For each person, it expresses the demands of his or her own humanity. The divine law is not an extrinsic and foreign ordinance.[37] Rather it presents the moral requirements of the Gospel to which the believer is freely and gladly committed. In other words, the divine law presents requirements that lie at the heart of a believer's inner life.

Cardinal Newman, in his famous *Letter to the Duke of Norfolk*, points out how precious is the service of the Church in clarifying for us the bracing law of God:

> The sense of right and wrong, which is the first element in religion, is so delicate, so fitful, so easily puzzled, obscured, perverted, so subtle in its argumentative methods, so impressible by education, so biased by pride and passion, so unsteady in its course, that, in the struggle for existence amid the various exercises and triumphs of the human intellect, this sense is at once the highest of all teachers, yet the least luminous; *and the Church, the Pope, the hierarchy are, in the divine purpose, the supply of an urgent demand*[38] (emphasis added).

Thus, the appropriation of these sources by Catholics seeking to form their consciences is a development of their initial Catholic commitment. If one is to be a Catholic, one cannot form one's conscience in any other way. The bishops of Ireland observed: "It is impossible to separate allegiance to Christ from obedience to the teaching Church. One cannot be his disciple while disregarding those to whom he has given a share in proclaiming and teaching his Gospel."[39]

IV. The Relationship Between Catholic Conscience and Catholic Teaching

The well-formed Catholic conscience, as we have just seen, draws light from the Scriptures and Christian tradition as these are understood and proclaimed by the magisterium and witnessed by the lives of good Christian people. It is thus unlikely that faithful Catholics will discover any serious conflict between the teaching of the Church and their particular judgments of conscience or their general approach toward making such judgments. And surely, as the *Catechism of the Catholic Church* reminds us, "personal conscience and reason should not be set in opposition to the moral law or the Magisterium of the Church."[40]

Furthermore, if a Catholic finds a measure of conflict between some of his or her convictions and the teaching of the Church, this conflict will be *within* that person's conscience, and not a conflict between the person's conscience and an alien authority. This is true because the teachings of the Church — as far as the believing Catholic is concerned — are teachings of a faith he or she has freely accepted and made his or her own. They enter into the formation of the believing Catholic's conscience.

But if this is so, how can we explain why many Catholics today — according to various surveys — have accepted moral views, particularly regarding matters of sexual morality, that contradict Church teaching? Several factors are relevant. The Church's teaching on contraception, for example, has not been effectively presented by many priests and theologians in recent years. Moved by the pressures of the world, it is easy for people to cease believing what is not earnestly preached. Moreover, while many Catholics realize that the Church *officially prohibits* contraception and other disordered sexual activities, still those same Catholics may not perceive that the Church firmly *teaches* in the name of Christ that such conduct is immoral. Some, indeed, may have been induced to think that "official" proscriptions of the magisterium are not Church teachings in the strict sense. They are said to lag behind the "real" mind of the Church, which is allegedly found in the experience of select members of the faithful, especially that of those Catholics who have rejected insistent teachings of the magisterium.[41]

Before examining these confusing situations, it is important to note the essential freedom and autonomy of the mature Catholic. He or she draws light from faith, but this does not mean blind acceptance of the judgments of Church leaders. There are many pronouncements by pastors, theologians, and even by bishops, that are merely private opinions which a conscientious Catholic might, after sufficient reflection, appropriately set aside.

Moreover, the precepts of the moral law taught by faith are always in some measure general precepts which can be applied in the concrete circumstances of life only through the conscientious deliberation of the individual person. Often this deliberation will have a creative element which cannot be anticipated in general precepts. While this personal deliberation is sometimes simple, the necessary reflection is at times much more difficult. For example, most people have a number of positive duties — to work at one's profession, to say one's prayers, to teach one's children, and so on. In many instances one must judge which duty one is to act on now, if many real duties seem to require attention at the same time. The individual himself or herself must make the judgment in such cases.[42]

In cases such as these the individual's judgment of conscience cannot be deduced from the general norms taught by the Church. One must learn prudence to guide one's life; no simple rules given by authority can substitute for this practical thinking. But there is no genuine *conflict* here between such a person's conscience and the teaching of the Church.

Conflict between personal conscience and Church teaching arises only

108

when a person judges in a way he or she knows to be contrary to the firm teaching of the Church. When conflict arises, the person faces a difficult choice: either follow the Church's teaching, which, when it has been personally appropriated, becomes a living factor within that person's conscience, or reject that teaching — that part of one's own conscience — in favor of the personal judgment that opposes it. In the next section we will consider how it is reasonable for a Catholic to resolve such conflicts.

V. May Personal Judgment Be Preferred to the Teaching of the Church?

There has been much talk in recent years of the problem of conflicts between personal conscience and the teaching of the Church. Great care must be taken to state this problem precisely. For one who has Catholic faith, who has acquired a happy, personal certainty that the Lord teaches and guides us in the teaching of the Church, the insistent message of Catholic faith is not something alien to conscience. Thus, one does not first form one's conscientious judgment, and then compare that with the teaching of the Church, and finally make another judgment about what to do. Church teaching is there from the beginning in the formation of conscience.

The difficulty arises concretely in something like the following scenario: A couple is faced with a decision about family planning and considers contraception as a possibility. The spouses become aware that the Church teaches that contraception is always gravely wrong, but they also become aware that many people do not believe this — including Catholics. They know that some people argue against the Church's teaching, and make the case that the use of contraception can be responsible, liberating, and even enriching. The question really facing such a couple is a decision about how the two of them should form their consciences. Should they form their conscience in accord with insistent Church teaching? Or should they shape it in the light of opinions they might favor, or might find persuasive, even though they contradict the teaching of the Church? The question therefore is not simply whether one may follow conscience when it contradicts Catholic teaching — it is the more fundamental question of how one is to form one's conscience. Should conscience be shaped by Church teaching, or by opinions contrary to this teaching?

Before 1960 there was unanimity among Catholic theologians and pastors on this point. It was common teaching that one who has the gift of faith must form his or her conscience in the light of faith's teachings. Since such faith is known by the believer to be true and to guide us toward what is really good, it would be unreasonable, foolish, and wrong for one to live in ways contrary to the teachings of the Church. It would be contrary to one's deepest interests to do so. Vatican II, expressing the received teaching of the Church on this matter, tells us:

> Bishops who teach in communion with the Roman Pontiff are to be revered by all as witnesses of divine and Catholic truth; the faithful, for their part, are obliged to submit to their bishops' decision, made in the name of Christ, in matters of faith and morals, and to adhere to it with a ready and respectful allegiance of mind. This loyal submission of the will and intellect must be given, in a special way, to the authentic teaching authority of the Roman Pontiff, even when he does not speak *ex cathedra* in such wise, indeed, that his supreme teaching authority be acknowledged with respect, and sincere assent be given to decisions made by him, conformably with his manifest mind and intention (*Lumen Gentium*, no. 25).

Moreover, the Council made it clear by the way it taught that the moral teaching of the Church includes not only very general principles but also specific moral norms. For example, its own teachings on sinful forms of family planning, and on crimes against human life such as abortion, euthanasia, and genocide are stated in specific and categorical terms which are unmistakably intended to guide consciences and are proposed in the name of Christ.[43]

There can be times, of course, when the Catholic is strongly inclined to form his or her conscience in accord with principles which would be much more convenient than the teachings of the Church, or which would accord with philosophies in some way alien to Catholic belief. When tempted to consider whether it might be permissible to commit adultery in some circumstances, one might very much want to use the principle that adultery can be justified when there are good enough reasons, and might be inclined to think that in the situation those reasons were present. The question, however, is not whether such situations arise but whether it can ever be justified to adopt principles of the kind mentioned. The American bishops, following Vatican II, answer this question negatively, and provide the basic reason which faith always has held:

> The Holy Father and the bishops in communion with him have been anointed by the Holy Spirit to be the official and authentic teachers of Christian life. For Jesus "estab-

lished His holy Church by sending forth the apostles as He Himself had been sent by the Father" (cf. Jn 20:21). He willed that their successors, namely the bishops, should be shepherds in His Church "even to the consummation of the world" [*Lumen Gentium*, no. 18]. It is their office and duty to express the teaching of Christ on moral questions and matters of belief. This special teaching office within the Catholic Church is a gift of the Lord Jesus for the benefit of all His followers in their efforts to know what He teaches, value as He values, and live as free, responsible, loving, and holy persons. As Christ says, "He who hears you, hears Me" [Lk 10:16]. The authoritative moral teachings of the Church enlighten personal conscience and are to be regarded as certain and binding norms of morality.[44]

Moreover, the *Catechism of the Catholic Church* insists that "the law of God entrusted to the Church is taught to the faithful as the way of life and truth. The faithful therefore have the *right* to be instructed in the saving divine precepts that purify judgement and, with grace, heal wounded human reason. They have the *duty* of observing the constitutions and decrees conveyed by the legitimate authority of the Church."[45]

In the face of this clear teaching of the Church, a number of contemporary theologians have argued that in the formation of conscience it is permissible to follow personal opinions that contradict the teaching of the Church. Most of these have been developed by theologians who reject the firm teaching of the Church on various questions in sexual ethics.

In support of their position, these revisionist thinkers advance the following arguments. (1) The Church has in fact never infallibly proposed any specific moral norm. (2) It is, in fact, beyond the competency of the Church to teach infallibly on specific moral issues. (3) The authoritative but noninfallible teachings of the Church may be mistaken, and so Catholics have the right to reject them when they are conscientiously convinced that the teachings are wrong.

Infallible Teaching and Specific Moral Norms

Those who encourage dissent from the Church's insistent moral teaching ordinarily suppose that they are urging changes in the noninfallible teaching of the Church. In arguing that some acts of contraception or adultery are permissible, they recognize that the Church has taught acts of those kinds to be seriously wrong, but they take it for granted that this teaching is not infallible. Frequently, they point out that it has not been the practice of the Church to make solemn definitions about specific moral points, and it is true that the great body of Catholic moral teaching has not been solemnly defined.[46]

However, as Vatican II has pointed out, there is a form of infallible teaching distinct from proclaiming solemn definitions. The bishops of the Church teach infallibly when they teach authoritatively in matters of faith and morals; "they are in agreement that a particular teaching is to be held definitively and absolutely," even though they are "dispersed throughout the world but preserving . . . amongst themselves and with Peter's successor the bond of communion" (*Lumen Gentium*, no. 25). Indeed, appealing to this precise text of *Lumen Gentium*, Pope John Paul II has made it lucidly clear in his encyclical *Evangelium Vitae* that the Church's teaching on the absolute inviolability of innocent human life from direct, intentional attack, and the intrinsically grave evil of all intentional killing of innocent human beings, as in abortion and euthanasia, has been infallibly proposed by the ordinary and universal magisterium.[47]

Clearly, it is one of the chief duties of the Church to teach the faithful "how they are to live and please God" (1 Thes 4:1). The Church's teaching on basic issues in sexual ethics in her ordinary magisterium has been most firm over the centuries. The Church has regularly insisted that her teaching about divorce, contraception, fornication, and the like is not a mere teaching of men but a teaching of the Lord himself.[48] With virtual unanimity the teachers of the Church have held and handed on the received teachings on sexual morality, and have presented them as unconditional requirements of salvation. When the Church teaches with such firmness and unanimity in the name of the Lord, it seems inescapable that she is exercising the infallibility of the ordinary magisterium as delineated by Vatican II.

For this reason, highly respected theologians have argued at length that the Church's ordinary magisterium concerning contraception meets these conditions for infallible teaching spelled out by Vatican II.[49] Hence, as we shall see more fully in Chapter 7, the Church's teaching on the immorality of contraception is in all likelihood infallible. And the arguments used by these theologians would seem to apply to other teachings of the Church on sexual matters, for the bishops of the Church have taught with equal firmness, with the same kind of unanimity over centuries, and as teachers who hand on what Christ requires for salvation, when they have taught on topics like adultery, masturbation, and so on.

A few theologians respond that the Church is simply not competent to teach infallibly about the morality of specific kinds of action. They would admit that the Church could infallibly teach general principles of morality, such as that people must love one another, or that the faithful must put fidelity to the Gospel before worldly success. But they insist that the Church cannot infallibly teach such specific norms as adultery is always wrong or one must never directly kill the innocent.[50]

Aside from the fact that this position is clearly incompatible with the teaching of Pope John Paul II in *Evangelium Vitae*,[51] the arguments for this position are surprisingly weak. They rely too much on the supposed authority of a relatively small group of dissenting scholars, and on assumptions about moral teaching that presuppose proportionalism. The main argument is that it is impossible for a universally stated Church teaching to take into account all the details needed for a judgment that adultery or contraception is always wrong. If proportionalism were a correct way of understanding moral thinking, then it would be impossible for the Church to absolutely exclude certain kinds of acts as immoral. If a particular act of adultery could be upright when the good effects of doing it in its concrete circumstances outweighed the bad consequences, then the Church would have to look into all the details of every conceivable act of adultery before she could reasonably teach that every act of adultery is seriously wrong. But the Church does not suppose that the mistaken theory of proportionalism is correct, and then proceed to teach only those things which proportionalism can justify. She teaches instead, and has always taught, that there are moral absolutes. Some acts, just by being the human acts they are, are disordered; they cannot be acts of intelligent and faithful love.[52]

Serious reflection on the history of the Church's moral teaching shows that her most firm and insistent moral teachings have been concerned with the specific moral issues about which the dissenting theologians think decisive teaching is impossible. If anything is characteristic of the whole tradition of Catholic moral teaching, it is the constant and insistent proclamation that certain kinds of acts — adultery, contraception, abortion, direct killing of the innocent, and so on — are always seriously wrong. Her teaching on the broad moral principles which justify specific norms has often been less insistent and precise. Scholars have been allowed great discretion in explaining how specific norms follow from the basic principles of love, and why they are always binding. But these variations in theological reasoning have always been carried out within the conviction of the Church that the moral absolutes proclaimed are always true.

If there are more general principles that have been insistently taught by the Church, none has been more firmly taught than this: that one must never do evil that good might come of it (cf. Rom 3:8). This principle is appealed to again and again as part of the defense of moral absolutes. It is the reason why moral absolutes may not be set aside when the consequences of following them are very difficult to accept. In other words, it is the basis for rejecting the proportionalism which denies the competency of the Church to teach infallibly on specific moral questions.

Another reason given to support the claim that the Church cannot teach infallibly on specific moral questions is that such teachings cannot have the clear connection with divine revelation that is required for infallible teaching.[53] But there are two major flaws in this claim. First, this claim supposes that no specific choice can be essential for salvation. However, the Church, reading Scripture in the light of Christian tradition and with the aid of the Holy Spirit, judges that specific choices are essential to Christian life. In particular, the Church holds that some specific choices fail to show the love the Gospel requires in such a way that they exclude from membership in the community of divine love those who make the choices and refuse to repent. Even if there is no independent argument to show how and why such choices must separate one from the love of God, it cannot be denied that the Church has held that they do.

The second flaw in this position is suggested by the first, for the position supposes that unless one can demonstrate how and why a given teaching is related to divine revelation, one is not justified in thinking that it is. The fact that the Church presents it as such is not taken as decisive evidence that a teaching is essentially related to revelation; independent theological explanation of the connection is necessary. This assumption is rationalistic in a way that is contrary to the actual practice of the Church. When there is some dispute about whether something is of revelation — for example, whether Jesus is consubstantial with the Father — the Church does not seek to settle the question by consulting scholarly opinion. In fact, in such disputes there is often a lack of scholarly consensus, and even a body of scholarly opinion favoring the view that the teaching in question is not essentially related to revelation. To settle such questions the Church must rely on the exercise of the teaching office of the pope and bishops. Their determination settles whether or not a point of Christian teaching is essentially connected with revelation. The task of the theologians is to articulate this connection, to help us understand it, and not to determine whether or not it exists.[54]

In short, it would not be responsible to assume that the Church's most firm teaching about specific moral matters is not infallibly proposed by the Church's ordinary magisterium. As the *Catechism of the Catholic Church* says: "The authority of the Magisterium extends also to the specific precepts of the *natural law*, because their observance, demanded by the Creator, is necessary for salvation. In recalling the prescriptions of the natural law, the Magisterium of the Church exercises an essential part of its prophetic office of proclaiming to men what they truly are and reminding them of what they should be before God."[55]

Dissent From Authoritative Teaching

The focus of theological dissent in the last thirty years has been on the authoritative moral teaching of the Church. In spite of the fact that in recent years competent theologians have made a powerful case that the teachings rejected are for the most part infallibly proposed, most dissenters have not even considered the possibility that what they reject might be infallible. This possibility completely changes the contour of the debate about the status of the Church's received teachings on sexual matters. Clearly, it deserves continuing, careful study. Another question, however, must also be considered, namely whether the dissenters are correct in thinking that dissent from authoritative but noninfallible teaching is justified.

Until the disputes of the last thirty years, all theologians acknowledged that the authoritative judgments of the Holy See in moral matters were practically decisive. Even when its teachings were not infallibly proposed, they were taken to be binding on the consciences of the faithful, who were required to give them internal religious assent. Not surprisingly, such teachings were not lightly made. They were understood as the teachings of Christ, proclaimed by his vicar, the pope, for the sake of guarding the whole Church from serious moral harm.

But in recent decades some theologians have formulated arguments to justify both doctrinal dissent from authoritative teaching and practical dissent which allows formation of conscience in ways contrary to this teaching. We will consider briefly three of the central arguments for the position that such rejection of authoritative Church teaching is justifiable.

The first argument asserts boldly: "It is the common teaching of the Church that Catholics may dissent from authoritative, noninfallible teachings of the magisterium when sufficient reasons for doing so exist."[56] However, this assertion finds no justification within Church teaching or widely accepted theological opinion other than the recent opinions of those very theologians who wish to justify their own dissent from received teaching. Appeal is often made to the teaching of the "approved authors," and, in particular, of the approved authors who wrote on the binding force of authentic teaching in the years prior to Vatican II. During the Council a discussion of the binding character of noninfallibly proposed teachings took

115

place. It was part of the discussion leading to the articulation of *Lumen Gentium*, no. 25. Conciliar officials referred to the teachings of the approved authors as normative in this matter. But when we examine the writings of these approved authors,[57] we find that they do not speak of a *right to dissent*, or of a right to guide consciences in ways opposed to authentic teaching. To be sure, they do argue that one might justifiably *withhold assent* provisionally from noninfallibly proposed teaching under certain stringently defined conditions. But withholding a positive act of assent provisionally, while continuing to study the matter with a willingness to accept magisterial teachings on the issues in question, is very different from dissenting actively from these teachings.[58]

Here it is worth noting the teaching found in the 1990 *Instruction on the Ecclesial Vocation of the Theologian* issued by the Congregation for the Doctrine of the Faith. This document clearly distinguishes between *questions* that theologians (and others) may raise about such Church teaching and *dissent* from such teaching. It judges that questioning can be compatible with the "religious submission of will and intellect" which Vatican II requires, but it firmly and unconditionally repudiates dissent from such teaching as incompatible with "religious submission" and irreconcilable with the vocation of the theologian.[59]

The second argument given to justify dissent from authoritative but noninfallible Church teaching was that the "atmosphere," or "spirit," of Vatican II made such great changes in the Church that dissent could now be justified. This claim, however, has proved impossible to sustain in the face of what Vatican II actually says — namely that the faithful are to assent "with a ready and respectful allegiance of the mind" to the authoritative teaching of the Church even when it is not proposed infallibly.[60] Admitting that the explicit teaching of the conciliar documents — in particular, of *Lumen Gentium*, no. 25 — forbids dissent, some argue that this conciliar teaching represented "a very dated and very discussable notion of the Church's teaching office."[61] That is, matters have changed since Vatican II spoke. But since the Council, the magisterium has continued to teach that one may not dissent from authentic teaching. Thus, the teaching of the Church on this question remains what was proclaimed at the Council, what has always been held within the Church: the faithful are expected to give internal assent to authoritatively proclaimed teachings in faith and morals.[62]

A third line of reasoning to justify dissent from noninfallible but authoritative Church teaching is that good sense and integrity permit such dissent. This line of reasoning seems to underlie much of the theological dissent of recent years, although explicit arguments for it are not well de-

116

veloped. Noninfallible teachings, it is argued, are fallible — that is, they can be mistaken. Hence, it would be foolish and wrong to demand conformity to them from intelligent people who are reasonably convinced by arguments for contrary positions.

This familiar argument is remarkably weak if evaluated in the light of faith. In matters which touch salvation it is essential that the faithful be able to walk in secure ways. Faith knows that there is no more secure way of discovering how we are to live and to please God than by attending to what the Church has constantly taught. This is not to say that there are not reasons that many find plausible for accepting opinions contrary to constant and insistent Church teaching. Those who defend the permissibility of some acts of fornication or some homosexual acts can give reasons for these positions that many people find persuasive. But it would surely be an exaggeration to pretend that such arguments give to anyone a real certainty that the enduring teachings of the Church, which also have strong rational defenses, are mistaken.

The conviction that the Church's teachings on moral matters are mistaken is not based on irrefutable rational arguments. This conviction has a number of sources. It can be based on the appeal of persuasive but far from infallible forms of secular thinking, on cultural and social pressures, and on an uncertain hope that life might be happier if Church teaching were set aside. None of these or similar sources provide a reliable basis for rejecting Church teaching. Thus, the requirement that one follow the Church's teaching does not involve a demand that a person violate what his or her own intelligence has discovered. The grounds for rejecting Church teaching are far more fallible than the reasons a believer has for accepting this teaching.

Even if the teaching of the Church on a given point is not infallibly proposed, it is presented in a way that makes it a far more reliable guide than any other a Catholic might have. Moral debates, in areas in which persons have an emotional stake, are notoriously difficult. Where faith does not give guidance, we see astonishing and virtually irreconcilable differences on even the most basic moral issues. Those who believe that Christ the Lord remains always with his Church, teaching and guiding through those he authorizes to speak in his name, have far better reasons for accepting the teaching of the Church than they could ever have for accepting the novel and dubious arguments whose persuasive power is largely based on the insecure prejudices of a secular culture.

We pointed out earlier that a person has an obligation to follow his or her conscience, even though a person's conscience is not infallible. The reason is that a rightly formed conscience provides the best, though still imperfect, guide for action that a person can have. The role of the authoritative but noninfallible teachings of the Church in the formation of conscience is analogous. This teaching is not infallible, but it is the best guidance a person could have. To set it aside in favor of more pleasing but less sure guides is irresponsible; it is a failure to form one's conscience in the way most likely to lead to judgments that are true.

Many fail to formulate the issue this way because they suppose the Church's teaching on moral issues is not a matter of Christ's truth but rather of policies, decisions, or rules laid down by ecclesiastical leaders. This misunderstanding of the Church's teaching is a form of legalism. The Church's moral teaching is not simply a set of rules adopted by men. It is teaching based on prayerful and thoughtful reflection of the whole Church on the moral guidance found in divine revelation. It is proclaimed by those who have a duty to hand on and guard what God entrusted to the Church for the salvation of mankind; and it is teaching guided and protected by the Spirit Jesus promised to his Church. Thus, even when the teaching in question is not infallibly proposed, it should be thought of in terms of truth — not simply in terms of decisions which are more or less sensible. In these terms, the authoritative teaching of the Church makes a powerful, rational claim on the loyalty of believers, for this teaching is most likely to be true.

Other Arguments to Justify Rejecting Authentic Church Teaching

The two general positions just considered — the claim that Church teaching on specific moral questions is never infallible, and that dissent from noninfallible teaching is legitimate — are the basic reasons given for preferring personal judgment to Church teaching. There are, however, other arguments for this conclusion which are often used in conjunction with the two central arguments. We will consider four such arguments briefly.

The first of these is based on the claim that the Church's traditional teaching on questions on sexual ethics is "physicalist" or "biologistic." The objection is that the natural-law theory on which traditional teaching is based left "moral man at the mercy of his biology. He had no choice but to conform to the rhythms of his physical nature and to accept its determinations obediently."[63] That is, the arguments for many of the Church's moral teachings proceed according to the following faulty pattern: since nature tends to act in this way, men have a duty to act in this way (that is, according to the way nature acts). While it can be admitted that some of the theo-

118

logical arguments used in the past to show that certain types of actions were immoral were poor,[64] this does not of itself show that the *conclusions* to which those arguments led were false, for a Catholic is to give assent to Church teachings, not because of the philosophical-theological arguments scholars in any age use to support this teaching but because this teaching is proposed by those who have been divinely appointed as the authentic interpreters of the "Word of God, whether in its written form or in the form of Tradition" (*Dei Verbum*, no. 10).

Moreover, it is by no means the case that all who have developed arguments for the Church's received teaching have employed some form of objectionable physicalism. The writings on sexual morality by Pope John Paul II, which are used throughout this book, are clearly not physicalistic; they articulate a form of Christian personalism. In fact, in his encyclical *Veritatis Splendor* Pope John Paul II directly confronted the claim that the Church's moral teaching, particularly on questions of human life and sexual ethics, is physicalistic. He compared the claim to "certain ancient errors [Gnosticism, Manicheanism] always . . . opposed by the Church," and judged it incompatible with the Church's teaching on the unity of the human person and on the respect due to such basic human goods as bodily life and integrity.[65] The arguments of St. Thomas Aquinas, often strangely taken as the paradigm of physicalism by opponents of traditional teaching, do not follow the flawed logic of physicalism, for the main concern in these arguments is not the physical structure of acts as such but their finality, and the way they relate to the human goods at stake. For example, disordered sexual behavior is called unnatural because one engaging in such acts is unreasonably choosing in a way that harms or ignores the human good of procreation.

The second of the arguments for rejecting Church teaching in the formation of conscience is that the dignity of conscience requires it.[66] Of course, one morally ought to do what one finally judges to be right. It is also true that governments and other institutions having coercive power should not use this power to force people to act in ways opposed to their conscience. It is this obligation to respect individual conscience — especially in religious matters — which the *Declaration on Religious Liberty* of Vatican Council II articulates so forcefully.

Neither of these truths is, however, relevant to the justification of a Catholic's preferring his or her personal judgment to the teaching of the Church, for the liberty of conscience to which the Council document refers is not a liberty of the individual Catholic to set aside the teaching of the Church. As we have seen, the relationship of the teaching of the Church to the individual conscience is in no way analogous to that of the power of public authority and the individual conscience. The teaching of the Church is not a power alien to the conscience of the Catholic; it enters essentially into the formation of a Catholic's conscience. Moreover, there is no question here of coercion; the question is about the legitimacy of the procedure of one who is a Catholic and who nevertheless sets aside the teaching of the Church.

The "dignity" to which the Fathers of Vatican II refer is the dignity of a person who obeys in a Catholic way the law revealed by conscience.[67] One who accepts a moral teaching opposed to the teaching of the Church is not clearly behaving in a Catholic way, unless, of course, one is truly in invincible ignorance. For a Catholic, a primary source in seeking the truth in moral matters *is* the teaching of the Church.

The third line of argumentation for preferring personal judgment is that the "sense" of the faithful, or their practical experience, provides a better source for knowing what faith requires of them in their moral lives than does the "official" teaching of the "hierarchical" magisterium.[68] It is true that the *sensus fidelium* — the lived, experienced consent of the faithful to the truths of Catholic faith — is one source of our knowledge of the faith and its requirements. But the notion of "consent or sense of the faithful" needs careful analysis. It does not mean that any opinion of any believer is to be taken as normative, for members of the Church can be tempted to forsake the teachings of the Church and to conform to the pressures of the world around them, sometimes with excellent intentions. Nor does "*sensus fidelium*" refer to the opinions of some believers when they disagree with others, and especially when they disagree with the multitude of believers who still hold fast to what has been held by the overwhelming number of the faithful to be God's word down through the centuries.[69] To say that the sense of the faithful meant either of these things would be to replace doctrinal faith with some sort of relativism. It would pretend that what the Church over many centuries has taught to be the enduring word of God is in our age unacceptable. The sense of the faithful must reflect what the believers have in common; it is a sense true to the faith that has been authentically proclaimed in the Church. It is not to be confused with transient convictions rooted in philosophies and visions of life received from sources alien to the Church.

The final argument to support preference for personal judgment to Church teachings is based on an appeal to the "magisterium of theologians." This argument rightly supposes that theologians have a kind of teaching office within the Church based on their scholarly competence. But the argument wrongly proceeds to give the theologians an authority similar in practice to that of the magisterium of pope and bishops. Thus, some insist

120

that the hierarchy must not teach in a binding way if the consensus of theologians is not in agreement with them. Lacking such agreement, the pronouncements of the magisterium are not binding.[70]

Some have suggested that when the hierarchy and the theologians disagree, the faithful may follow a new version of probabilism — that is, when some scholars reject authentic teaching, one may live by their opinions. However, classical probabilism taught that scholarly opinion lost its authority if it was opposed to the teaching of the Holy See.[71]

This argument supposes that the theological community is in overwhelming agreement in rejecting received teachings of the Church on sexual matters. But this supposition is false. There is nothing like a true consensus of theologians favoring theological dissent. Increasingly, theologians have come to recognize that their mission is to serve the magisterium of the Church, and that this mission cannot be carried out unless they responsibly accept the authentic teaching of the Church.[72]

Theologians do have a special office within the Church, and it is not improper to call this office a *magisterium*.[73] However, positions which contradict the received teachings of the Church simply cannot have normative status within the Church, for while there is an authentic mission for theologians within the Church, and while they can indeed teach us in significant ways, their role within the Church is clearly subordinate to that of those who are divinely appointed teachers of the faith, namely the pope and the bishops in communion with him. The life of faith is not primarily guarded by scholars. It is a gift of God, proclaimed first of all by the authentic witnesses who are successors to his apostles. One of the greatest theologians of all time expressed this point precisely. Addressing the issue of conflict between theological opinions and the teachings of those divinely appointed to express the mind of Christ within the Church, St. Thomas Aquinas unambiguously declared: "We must abide rather by the pope's judgment than by the opinion of any of the theologians, however well versed he may be in divine Scriptures."[74] He speaks here the judgment of the great family of Catholic theologians.

Thus, the effort to justify a Catholic's putting aside the firm teaching of the Church in favor of his or her own judgment does not succeed. The final moral evaluation of an action by a Catholic must be the judgment of his or her Catholic conscience. There is no way to maintain the authenticity of this conscience without holding faithfully to the insistent moral teaching of the Church. In the light of what faith teaches, the mature Catholic freely and intelligently guides his or her conscience toward what is really good — what following Christ requires.

121

Chapter Six
Chastity, Christian Marriage, and Virginity

The first three chapters of this book summarized the teaching of the Church, of Scripture, and of the Catholic moral tradition on marriage and questions of sexual morality. The fourth and fifth chapters considered the general moral issues which must be faced by those trying to reach responsible and true judgments about how they should act, not simply in the sexual area but in all the areas of human existence. These teachings of God and his Church, as well as these general moral considerations about moral reasoning and decision making, must be brought to a focus to make it clear how they provide the needed guidance for making correct decisions about sexual matters. This application of Catholic teaching to particular questions of sexual ethics will be carried out in some detail in Chapters 7 and 8 of this work.

Before developing this detailed application to specific moral questions, however, it is necessary to consider the virtue of chastity and its relationship to the basic vocations of Christian life. This consideration is necessary because chastity is the virtue by which a person integrates his or her sexuality into his or her own Christian life. All Christians, of course, have the common vocation to holiness, to be saints (*Lumen Gentium,* nos. 39-42). But each individual Christian has his or her own unique personal vocation, his or her own indispensable part to play in carrying on the redemptive work of Christ.[1] One's personal vocation is one's particular way of responding to God's call and of following Christ; it should be the organizing factor in the life of each Christian. One of the dimensions of our lives which must be integrated with our personal vocation is our sexuality, for sexuality is a powerful force within us. It can be used intelligently in the service of Christian love; but it can also be used for self-gratification, and then it becomes a source of personal disintegration, which compromises the organization of life in response to vocation. The virtue of chastity is therefore necessary for mature Christian living.

Of course, the chastity of a consecrated religious or of a single person in the world is very different from that of a married person. But they are not totally different realities: both require that sexual desire be permeated by love and guarded by self-possession; both involve the appreciation of sexuality as a gift to be used intelligently in the service of what is really good.

This chapter therefore will consider the virtue of chastity in general and its realization in the two most fundamental vocations of Christian life: marriage and virginity, whether voluntarily chosen for the sake of the kingdom or freely accepted as God's way of calling one to fulfill one's vocation. Thus, this chapter will provide the immediate framework for the discussion of the specific questions of sexual morality which will complete this work.

I. Chastity and Our Sexual Life

It is a commonplace saying that human persons are sexual beings. Human beings are members of a species that is sexual: every human being is either a male or a female. This biological fact about human nature is not, however, simply of biological significance — for sexuality, as Pope John Paul II has noted, is "by no means something purely biological, but concerns the innermost being of the human person as such."[2] In other words, being male or female is not simply an accidental or unimportant aspect of a human person, nor is it something whose significance is simply cultural. The sexuality of men and women affects them not only in obvious physical ways but also psychically, intellectually, and spiritually. Sexual differences make possible the complementarity and special friendship between men and women — relationships that in a host of ways are connected to the economy of salvation: man and woman he made them; in his image he made them.

Human persons are not spirits who happen to have bodies attached. Each one is a living flesh of a kind that is inherently sexual. This is not to deny that the human person has an immortal soul, a spiritual dimension which other animals lack. It is to say, rather, that this soul is a part or dimension of the entire human person — a part that is essentially related to the bodily reality of which it is a principle. The soul of a man is his soul and thus inherently male; the soul of a woman is her soul and thus inherently female. Thus, human sexuality is a modality affecting our entire being as persons.

Sexuality is, in fact, "a fundamental component of personality, one of its modes of being, of manifestation, of communicating with others, of feeling, of expressing and of living human love."[3] This capacity for love as self-giving, rooted in the being of man and woman as sexual persons, is incarnated, as it were, in their bodies. As John Paul II has said, "The human body, with its sex, and its masculinity and femininity, seen in the very mys-

123

tery of creation . . . includes right 'from the beginning' the 'nuptial' attribute, that is the *capacity of expressing love: that love precisely in which the man-person [and, vice versa, the woman-person] becomes a gift* and — by means of this gift — fulfills the very meaning of his being and existence"[4] (emphasis added). The sexuality of man and woman is, thus, complementary in character.[5]

Human sexuality is not, of course, simply a fact about human nature that must be observed objectively, from the outside, as it were. It is experienced — long before it is analyzed or understood — as a dynamic tendency or urge within us. We experience it as an impulse orienting us toward love and affection with other persons, particularly to persons of the other sex. We experience it too as a dynamic tendency having existential significance, inasmuch as it is bound up with the being or existence of the entire human species, with the generation of new human persons.[6] Obviously, sexuality as experienced in this way has a specifically genital component which is distinct from, although by no means separated from, our generic sexuality.

Because we are sexual, genital beings, it is natural that we respond to the sexual values incarnate in other persons, particularly in those of the opposite sex. It is natural too that there should arise within us sexual desires, accompanied at times by intense feelings of affection. These natural desires are in themselves good, for they are a part of our human nature created by God, and, when properly integrated into the personal vocation to which God calls every person, they play an irreducible role in the self-perfection which is each person's contribution to the kingdom of Christ.

These desires, however, also present a challenge because they elicit powerful emotions which sometimes resist rational control, particularly because of concupiscence. Our sexual desires, indeed, our sensuality or natural tendency to respond to the sexual values of the body, in particular, the body of a person of the opposite sex, are natural to us as bodily, sexual beings. But as a result of original sin concupiscence has entered the human heart. Because of concupiscence human beings, male and female, are inclined to "hanker after" these sexual values, divorcing them from the person and viewing them as objects of potential enjoyment.[7] In other words, our sensuality and sexual desires, under the influence of sinful concupiscence, can lead us to treat persons as objects of sexual gratification and not as irreplaceable and nonsubstitutable persons with whom we must join in a community that respects the dignity of all.

There is likewise the danger that sentimentality and superficial feelings of affection may blind us to reality and cause us to lose sight of the

124

authentic goods at stake in sexual activity. We may, because of sentimental affection, be prompted to say "I love you," when in reality what we love is the feeling of warmth and affection that we experience in a particular person's presence.[8] There is also the danger that we will become possessed by our sexual desires and inclined to act in accord with them and not in accord with the objective demands of intelligent love. Possession by such desires is incompatible with the self-possession of the mature and integrated person, and makes impossible the use of sexuality as part of a free and intelligent gift of self. What is compelled by passion cannot be a free gift.

Sexual desire and emotional affectivity are part of the raw stuff out of which authentic human love can be shaped, but this material needs to be shaped intelligently if it is to become integrally and fully a component of love.

To achieve this goal the virtue of chastity is necessary. Put briefly but neatly, chastity is a virtue that "frees love from selfishness and aggression."[9] It can be more fully described as a virtue concerned with the intelligent and loving integration of our sexual desires and affections into our being as persons, enabling us to come into possession of ourselves as sexual beings so that we can love well — and so that we can touch others and allow ourselves to be touched in ways that respect fully the goods of human existence, and the irreplaceable persons in whom these goods are meant to flourish. A brief explanation of this description will now be given.

Chastity is a virtue. A virtue is a stable character trait or disposition. Virtues therefore are not actions or feelings, for these are passing and often momentary. Virtues last, and like other traits that are not naturally given, they must be acquired over a period of time and are not readily lost. Virtues are those character traits which enable a person to do well what is morally good. Virtues enable a person to know what is right and to do it without excessive struggle. Thus, virtues are the extension of a person's morally good choices throughout his or her entire personality; they integrate a good person's entire self around what is best and most central in his or her personality.[10]

Our powers of intellect and will must be developed; they must put on muscle if they are to properly guide our lives. The virtues are the developed orientations of the self which enable these powers to do their proper jobs. But virtues are not only traits of the mind and will, they also develop and perfect the other aspects of our personalities so that they are able to respond readily and joyfully to the directions of our intelligence and will.[11]

The mark of a virtuous person is not simply that he or she does the right things. To be virtuous a person must do the just or courageous or temperate thing in the way a just or courageous or temperate person would do it — that is, with the promptitude and joy that mark such a person's good actions.[12] Thus, a virtuous person does not act from fear and out of a merely automatic routine but freely and autonomously.[13] Likewise, the virtuous person does not act from external constraint, or out of a conditioned response, but because the virtuous person wants to do the right thing and delights in doing it well.[14]

This can be illustrated if we consider two employers and the justice each exhibits in dealing with employees. One pays his employees a just wage and provides decent working conditions. So this employer does the just thing. But he does so reluctantly, with no real willingness, perhaps because laws require him to provide decent working conditions, or because economic forces constrain him to pay a just wage. This employer lacks the virtue of justice. The other employer does the same things, but he does so because he wants to; he does so willingly, freely, and with enthusiasm. This employer does the just thing justly, that is, virtuously. For him, justice is not an extrinsic constraint but an orientation of his own personality.

The virtue of chastity is an aspect of the cardinal virtue of temperance, which has as its subject matter the pleasures of eating, drinking, and sex. Chastity is the form of temperance concerned with the pleasures of sex. These pleasures are essentially related to touch — in particular, touches involving the exercise of one's genital sexuality — and secondarily all the pleasures which prepare them by stimulating the desire for them.[15]

These pleasures and the desire for them are, as we have already seen, natural. The clamor to satisfy these desires is often vehement. The point of the virtue of chastity is not to flee from these pleasures or to suppress the desire for them. Thus, those who despise chastity as being a renunciation or denial of sexuality are mistaken. Chastity does not deny the goodness of these pleasures or suppress desire for them because chastity, like all virtue, is reasonable. To be reasonable is to care for the goods of human nature, and sexuality is meant to promote and respect these goods. The reasonable person therefore sees in the desires and feelings of our sentient nature something good that can serve the entire good of the human person if intelligently integrated into a life of commitment to what is really good.[16]

Chastity therefore does not seek to suppress or deny sexuality but rather enables a person to put a loving and intelligent order into his passional life, to take possession of his desires so that the whole self can be integrated and at peace. Thus, in a certain way, the emotions and desires themselves participate actively in the moderation coming from intelligence. This moderation becomes, as it were, a kind of connatural eagerness on their part. Our will and intellect do not dictate from without to restless passion. But our emotions and desires spontaneously, as it were, order themselves to the authentic goods of human persons which the person grasps through intelligence and loves through his will. Thus, it is a mockery of chastity to regard it as a life of constant warfare between unruly passion and imperious reason. Chastity, once achieved, is a basis for inner peace and personal integration.[17]

As Karol Wojtyla says, far from being something negative, chastity is above all positive and affirming. Its essence "consists in quickness to affirm the value of the person in every situation, and in raising to the personal level all reactions to the value of 'the body and sex' . . . [it] is above all positive and creative 'from within,' not negative and destructive."[18]

A virtuous spouse therefore will "feel" differently about the marital act with his or her own spouse and about genital sex with another. He or she will recognize — not only intellectually but with his or her whole being as an emotional, affective, passionate person — that the choice to engage in the marital act is one that is good and that the pleasure and joy associated with it are good and noble too. And he or she will recognize — not only intellectually but with his or her whole being — that whatever delight there might be in genital sex with another person is specious, that it does not crown an act that is beautiful and ennobling but rather one that fails to respect the goods perfective of human persons. And virtuous single persons "feel" differently about having sex outside of marriage. They know that this is unworthy of the dignity of human persons not only with their minds but also with their hearts.

Of course, no one achieves the fullness of chastity swiftly without some struggle and effort. For many people, the effort to be chaste is a long struggle with recalcitrant emotion. For these people, there is not the peace and joy of mature chastity. Even here, however, the effort is not without real rewards, for there is an anticipation of the joy of chaste living, a recognition of the goodness of self-possession, and a nobility in seeking goods one cannot fully experience. Moreover, even here the struggle is not an attempt to overcome or suppress emotion but an effort to integrate one's personality in a way that is really rewarding. Thus, even the efforts of the imperfectly chaste are not to be seen as battles in an endless struggle but as the efforts to begin a life of inner tranquillity and self-possession.

The virtue of chastity is one that all human beings need if they are to open themselves to integral human fulfillment and to the precious goods that perfect human existence and human persons. And chastity in no way

127

deadens or repudiates sexuality. Rather, chastity by freeing love from the ultilitarian attitude,[19] enlivens it so that, being "vitally integrated into the person," it "makes the subject capable, on the plane of his passional life, of the self-determination and self-control which characterizes a mind."[20]

Moreover, as the *Catechism of the Catholic Church* reminds us, the virtue of chastity "blossoms in *friendship* . . . notably in friendship with one's neighbor."[21] Because this is so, "chastity . . . also involves a *cultural effort* . . . [and] presupposes respect for the rights of the person."[22]

Jesus, the complete human, provides a striking model of chastity. He is a sexual being, a virile yet affectionate male. His life was full of close and affectionate friendships with men and women alike. Yet Jesus was a celibate, a virgin because of the demands of his personal vocation as redeemer of the world. His example teaches us that the chaste person is the one who has his or her priorities right, who intelligently loves the goods of human nature and integrates his or her affective life into the vocation by which each one of us is called by God to pursue these goods.

In subsequent chapters the requirements of chastity both for married persons and for unmarried persons will be set forth in some detail. Here, the general outline of chaste Christian life will be sketched out by considering how the basic vocations of Christian life promote and protect the goods of human sexuality.

II. Christian Marriage: A Vocation of Chastity

The Christian vocation of marriage provides an important frame of reference for the understanding and development of the virtue of chastity. This vocation is the context within which God calls most men and women to holiness; and even those who are not called to this vocation know from the lives of married friends and relatives that this is a special locus for God's work in saving mankind. Moreover, marriage is the context in which the use of genital sexuality has its proper role in God's plan. So, it is within marriage that the goods to which human sexuality is ordered are properly realized. Since these goods are the basis for chastity, an understanding of marriage is indispensable for understanding chastity.

The Nature of Marriage. To understand chastity within marriage, it is necessary to understand the nature of marriage itself, for the nature of marriage is designed by God to enable people to integrate their sexuality into the service of self-giving and new life. Thus, marriage enables what could degenerate into a selfish and enslaving force to become instead a full and integral part of a life in which the greatest goods of human persons are served, and the love which is God himself is revealed.

128

Marriage is one of the most profound and important aspects of human social existence. Its depths of human meaning and supernatural significance are suggested by the attention it receives in Scripture, by the great theologians, and in the teaching of the Church. The discussions in the first three chapters of this book only begin to explore what faith teaches about this wonderful and mysterious reality. Here, it is possible only to summarize those aspects of Christian reflection on marriage which are necessary for understanding its special role as a vocation of chastity.

All human societies have some institutionalized framework for the begetting and raising of children. Perhaps "marriage" could be used as the name for any of these social arrangements. But the biblical and Christian understanding of marriage does not accept any such arrangements as marriage, for not just any arrangement for having and raising children is conducive to their genuine well-being, or for a promotion of the kind of relationship between men and women that will foster real love and respect between them. The God who reveals himself as our Father, whose love for us is like that of our mother but never failing, will not tolerate just any arrangement for begetting and raising children. So marriage is an institution, but unlike most institutions it does not depend simply on human convention or decision. God himself is the author of marriage. As Pope Pius XI said, reflecting the entire tradition going back to Genesis:

> Let it be repeated as an immutable and inviolable fundamental doctrine that matrimony was not instituted or restored by man but by God: not by man were the laws made to strengthen and confirm and elevate it but by God, the Author of nature and by Christ our Lord by whom nature was redeemed, and hence these laws cannot be subject to any human decrees or to any contrary pact even to the spouses themselves. This is the doctrine of Holy Scripture; this is the constant teaching of the Universal Church; this is the solemn definition of the sacred Council of Trent, which declares and establishes from the words of Holy Writ itself that God is the Author of the perpetual stability of the marriage bond, its unity and stability.[23]

But what is the God-given character of marriage? It is the union of one man and one woman, who mutually give themselves to each other so that they may share an intimate partnership of the whole of their lives until death. Their marital union, which is brought into being by their personal

act of irrevocable consent, is, of its own inner dynamism and nature, ordered to the procreation and education of children and to the fostering of a
special and exclusive kind of love — marital or spousal or conjugal love.
As spouses, moreover, husband and wife form the single subject of a shared
sexual life, and their marital union is fittingly expressed in and by an act
proper and specific to them, the marital act. In this act they become "one
flesh," and come to "know" one another in a unique and unforgettable way.
Through it, spouses symbolize and support all the activities in which they
share intimately their lives with each other and communicate the gift of life
to new human persons.[24]

This divine plan for marriage was obscured and damaged by the sin
described in Genesis 3, with the result that divorce and polygamy disfig-
ured the human reality that God had in mind in bringing marriage into
being (cf. *Gaudium et Spes*, no. 47); but this divine plan has been restored
in an incomparably marvelous way by our Lord and Savior, Jesus Christ.

Although God is the author of marriage and gives to this human reality
its defining characteristics and intrinsic conditions of existence, its
coming-into-being in a particular instance depends on the free, personal
choice of the man and woman who give themselves to each other in marriage. Nothing can take the place of their act of mutual consent. It is this act
that brings their marriage into being and makes them husband and wife. In
and through this self-determining act they give to themselves a new identity: the man becomes the woman's husband, and she becomes his wife,
and together they become spouses.[25] Prior to this act of irrevocable free
consent in which they forswear all others to bestow themselves upon each
other, the man and the woman live their own independent lives; in and
through it they unite their lives, forming a community of sharing that is so
intimate and all-encompassing that they can be said to have one common
life and to be one flesh.

The paramount significance of this act of marital consent is eloquently
expressed in the Yahwist account of the creation of marriage in Genesis 2.
There we read that the man, Adam, on seeing the person equal to himself,
whom the Lord had fashioned for him, cried out: "Here at last is bone of my
bone and flesh of my flesh. . . . For this reason a man shall leave father and
mother and cleave to his wife, and the two shall become one flesh" (Gen
2:23-24).[26] In his perceptive analysis of this passage from Genesis, Pope John
Paul II noted: "The very formation of Genesis 2:24 indicates not only that
human beings, created as man and woman, were created for unity, but also
that precisely this unity, through which they become 'one flesh' has right
from the beginning a character of union derived from choice. We read, in

130

fact, 'a man leaves his father and mother and cleaves to his wife.' If the man belongs 'by nature' to his father and mother by virtue of procreation, he, on the other hand, 'cleaves' by choice to his wife (and she to her husband)."[27]

Since marriage is brought into being through an act whereby the spouses give and receive the "word" or person of the other,[28] it is unconditioned, irrevocable, and dependent for continuation in its being only on the continuation in being of the spouses themselves. Thus, both by reason of its God-given nature and the intention of the spouses, marriage is a relationship which lasts until death.

Moreover, in consenting to be spouses, a man and a woman consent to marriage and to all that it entails. Since marriage is an institution for the procreation and education of children, marital consent involves a commitment to this worthy enterprise. Similarly, they commit themselves to fostering the special love of those who would share a common life and hand on that life to their children. Thus, spouses consent to the special expression of marital love — the self-giving of marital intercourse.[29] All of these commitments are expressed in the consent whereby spouses take each other for richer or for poorer, in sickness and in health, unto death.

This brief account of the nature of marriage reveals the essential goods to which human sexuality is ordered; these are the three goods of marriage articulated by St. Augustine — (1) the bond of unity between the spouses, (2) children, and (3) marital fidelity. The requirements of faithful service to these goods provide much of the concrete fabric of chastity, but even the most general characteristics of Christian marriage just considered indicate some basic aspects of this virtue. First, they show that sexuality is not created for the sake of the satisfaction of individuals on terms they can themselves arbitrarily set. Rather, it serves great human goods which they can personally appreciate, goods they must share in to fulfill their own lives. Sexuality is for the sake of human relationships — precious relationships whose excellence must enlighten and guide our sexual desires, and which have an objective, God-given character.

Second, the essential role of mutual consent in the actualization of a marriage shows that these relationships are fundamentally a matter of the commitment of the whole person. The implication is that desire, affection, and emotion must serve commitment, and are enriched and made more satisfying by doing so. The reality of marriage is in the selves constituted by the mutual commitment to be spouses. The feelings of the spouses should be integrated into this commitment. They are not themselves constitutive of the fundamental reality of the relationship.

Chastity and the Goods of Marriage

As already noted, even the briefest account of the nature of marriage makes clear that marriage is meaningful because it is the context in which very important human relationships can be realized and basic human goods fostered and protected. It is in service to these goods — the goods of marriage first articulated by Augustine[30] — that the fabric of chastity takes shape. A brief review of these goods and their implications for chastity will provide some understanding of that shape.

The good of the sacrament — that is, the indissoluble unity of husband and wife — is the good which constitutes the reality of marriage itself, the bond of union between the spouses. Without this union there is no marriage, no marital giving and receiving, and, so the tradition regards it as the most essential of the goods of marriage.[31] The centrality of this good is closely tied to its sacramental character.

The feature of this good that is morally most important is the indissolubility of the marriage bond. Indissolubility imposes a moral obligation on spouses not to attempt another marriage as long as their partner is alive. This obligation holds even if it is necessary to separate, even if one is deserted[32] — for marriage, as we saw above, is a total joining of two lives into one; the marital commitment is necessarily for life.

In fact, the indissolubility of marriage not only imposes an obligation not to attempt remarriage, but it also makes remarriage in the case of sacramental marriages literally impossible, for the bond of marriage is a reality, not a matter of human convention, and when that bond is created in the life of two Christians, it simply cannot be broken. This bond is intended by God to symbolize the love of Christ for his Church, and as a sacrament of the new covenant it partakes of that divine and human love. And that love cannot be broken by any power in the universe.[33] Thus, as Vatican II teaches, marriage comes to be through the choice of the spouses; but once it has come to be, it does not depend on any choice whatsoever.[34] A spouse can no more become an ex-spouse than a father can become an ex-father, or a mother an ex-mother. They may cease to love each other as spouses should, but they are spouses until death.

In virtue of its being a sacrament of the new covenant, marriage is a special source of grace. A sacrament is a sign which represents a supernatural reality and in some way participates in the reality it signifies. Thus, a sacrament is a means for receiving the grace it signifies.[35] Marriage therefore is a means for the sanctification of the spouses.[36]

The marriage of those who give and receive each other "in the Lord"[37] has present within it not only the power of the spouses themselves but also

132

the power of Christ's love. By virtue of this love their marriage not only can respect the precious goods it is bound to honor, it can also be the bearer of a greater and more healing kind of love. Thus, the marriage of Christians both signifies the love of Christ for his Church and participates in this love. It draws from this love so that it is capable of revealing it in the lives of the spouses.[38]

Christian marriage is capable of being a sacrament in this sense because the partners are already incorporated in Christ in virtue of their baptism. As Pope John Paul II said: "Indeed by means of baptism, man and woman are definitively placed within the new and eternal covenant, in the spousal covenant of Christ with the Church. *And it is because of this indestructible insertion* that the intimate community of conjugal life and love, founded by the Creator, is elevated . . . and enriched by his redeeming power"[39] (emphasis added).

The act of marrying of baptized persons therefore is an act of the Church and a sacrament of the new covenant to which Christ himself is party. As such, marriage enables the love of the spouses to be caught up "into divine love and is directed and enriched by the redemptive power of Christ and the salvific action of the Church, with the result that the spouses are effectively led to God."[40]

Non-Christian marriages are not sacramental in this full sense; but they are not totally separated from its saving reality, for whenever people seek earnestly the human goods of marriage, there is an openness to supernatural blessings not explicitly recognized. Thus, we can say that even the marriages of non-Christians are touched by grace, for the goods sought in such marriages "come from God the creator and are integrated in an inchoative way into the spousal love of Christ for His Church."[41]

The implications for chastity of the indissoluble bond of marriage and its supernatural significance as a sacrament of the new covenant are easy to grasp, for this bond points to the fact that our sexuality is meant to serve a lasting and unbreakable relationship with another person — a relationship that is meant to join the spouses in a common life together. It cannot do this if sexual feelings are not penetrated and guided by intelligent love. Thus, the principle for the use of sexuality is not the exigence of sexual desire or of romantic affection but the demands of lasting commitment. The sacramental character of this bond makes clear that the self-transcendence of marriage is not simply a self-transcendence of each of the spouses for the sake of the common life of their marriage but a contribution to the saving work of Jesus. Thus, their union should be a vocation in which they seek to contribute to the work of Jesus. In particular, their vocation is to signify the great saving union between Christ and the Church. So, chastity is shown to have a vocational, ecclesial dimension.

The procreative good — the good of children — also perfects marriage and generates requirements of chastity but in a way very different from the bond of marriage itself, for the procreative good is one of the goods which fulfills the life of married couples, and toward which marriage is ordered. This good — fulfillment and orientation — is present even when couples are not actually blessed with children. The orientation toward procreation and education of children is implicit in the very fertility of sexuality and in the institutional significance of marriage.[42] Thus, spouses undertake a mission to serve life when they join together in marriage. This service is the natural effect and embodiment of their common life, so perfectly expressed in marital intercourse. Thus, children are "the supreme gift of marriage, and greatly contribute to the good of the parents themselves."[43] Of course, the inherent human significance of procreation is transformed in sacramental marriages, for children are not simply the next generation of the human species, they also are images of God, persons for whom Christ died and rose so that they might become citizens of his kingdom and children of God.[44]

The implications of this good for chastity are perhaps not as easy to see as those of the indissoluble bond of marriage; but they are far-reaching, for the procreative good introduces a new, social dimension to chastity. This good requires a dimension of responsibility for the use of sexuality which goes beyond what is required by the bond of unity alone, for procreation entails responsibility for very dependent persons who made no choice to be a member of a given family. Moreover, this good requires that human sexual activity remain open to new life, and that it be used in such a way as to preserve the delicate balance of community between parents and children.

The third good of marriage is the fidelity of the spouses. This good includes not only the literal fidelity — abstention from adultery — required by the nature of the marital bond and by the procreative good, but it also includes the development of the special love and friendship of the spouses. So, this good is required for the realization of the other goods of marriage but is not simply instrumental to their realization, for the love of spouses is good in itself, a wonderful form of human communion.[45]

Vatican II described marital love as eminently human, inwardly capable of being merged with the divine love of Christ, and utterly distinct from mere erotic attraction. The Council Fathers added that marital love is

134

properly expressed in the chaste union of marital intercourse, that it is faithful and exclusive, and ready for self-sacrifice.[46] In short, this is a love in which all the goods of marriage are realized and celebrated.

The special implications for chastity of the good of fidelity and, in particular, of the love between spouses center on the need for sexuality to serve the needs of others. Genuine love must be ready for self-sacrifice, the antithesis of the self-gratification of sexual indulgence.

The distinctive expression of marital love is the act of marital intercourse. But it would be a mistake to think that marital intercourse is the only expression of marital love. Mutual help, support, and cooperation are also very important. Thus, chastity requires that we order and integrate all of our desires, affections, and aspirations so as to serve the love between spouses that is the foundation of family life. It follows from this, as from the good of procreation, that chastity cannot be limited to the sexual dimension in the narrow sense. All of our familial existence — our entire relationship with our children and our spouses — pertains to chastity. Marital chastity therefore affects in some way the entire existence of husbands and wives, for every part of the life of spouses must be integrated around these basic commitments of married life.

Conjugal intercourse is the act proper and exclusive to spouses. It is an act that singularly expresses conjugal love. It is the act in and through which the spouses *chastely* and intimately, as the Fathers of Vatican II remind us, become one.[47] As marital, this act is open to the goods or blessings of marriage, namely, faithful conjugal love and the procreation and education of children. Indeed, as St. Thomas teaches, the marital act, when chastely and honorably engaged in, participates in the good of the sacrament and can thus be called a "holy" act.[48]

As a marital act, it is a shared act of the spouses. Thus, it is the action which actualizes their common life — realizes their bond of unity. It is the act whereby they literally become one flesh, and come to know each other in the special way of spouses.[49] Since conjugal intercourse is the common act of persons irrevocably committed to each other, it fosters the love and fidelity of marriage, and signifies in a concrete way the union of Christ and his Church.[50]

Marital intercourse also realizes the goods of fidelity and of children. It can do this only insofar as it is truly conjugal, for only thus will it involve the self-giving needed for the responsibilities of parenthood and the common life of spouses.

This self-giving has several aspects that are essential for chastity. First, there must be an openness to children in sexual activity. Without this openness, the lovemaking of the spouses cannot be the full sharing of a common life, for it rejects the embodiment and responsibility of that life. This aspect of marital chastity will be considered more fully in Chapter 7. Second, self-giving must fully respect the person of the other. It must systematically avoid treating the other as an object for one's sexual gratification. Third, self-giving requires that the spouses have possession of their sexual desires so that they can freely offer themselves in marital intercourse. If their lovemaking is simply a response to sexual desire, if, in other words, it is activity to which they are driven rather than one chosen freely as an act of love, it cannot have the essential features of a gift. Something that must be done to satisfy exigent desire cannot be a gift, for a gift must be freely given and therefore must be within one's power to withhold. Thus, periodic voluntary abstinence from marital intercourse can also be an essential part of the self-giving of marital love. This is especially so when the full realization of the goods of marriage requires that the couple forgo intercourse.[51]

These aspects of the self-giving that should characterize marital intercourse are, of course, normative features which are not always realized. In fact, they are difficult to realize in the lives of many couples; but they are the goal toward which all couples must strive if their sexual relationships are not to degenerate into mere pleasure-seeking or to the pretense of genuine love.

III. Marriage, the Christian Family, and Chastity

The family rooted in the marriage of Christian spouses is, as Vatican II reminds us, is "a church in miniature" (*Ecclesia Domestica*).[52] Thus the Christian family, as Pope John Paul II insists, "is called upon to take part actively and responsibly in the mission of the Church in a way that is original and specific, by placing itself, in what it is and what it does as an 'intimate community of life and love,' at the service of the Church and society."[53]

The Christian family provides the home where new human life can take root and develop as it ought to develop. It is, indeed, the "sanctuary of life," whose role in building a culture of life and a civilization of love is, John Paul II says, "decisive and irreplaceable."[54]

Husbands and wives are the primary educators of their own children.[55] As such, they have the obligation, as Vatican II emphasizes, "to give suitable and timely instruction to young people, above all in the heart of their own families, about the dignity of married love, its role and its exercise, so that, having learned the value of chastity, they will be able at suitable age to engage in honorable courtship and enter upon a marriage of their own."[56]

136

Parents must keep in mind that God never obliges them to the impossible. Thus, they can confidently rely on Him for help in carrying out their educational responsibilities toward their children. They can, with God's help, succeed in giving their children, especially through their own example and chaste love of each other, an understanding of "sex that is truly and fully personal," leading them to recognize that "sexuality is an enrichment of the whole person — body, emotions, and soul — and it manifests its inmost meaning in leading the person to the gift of self in love."[57]

IV. Chastity and the Life of Consecrated Virginity

Marriage is an especially important vocation of Christian life for putting the demands of chastity into perspective. Of course, it is not the only vocation of Christian life, nor is it the only one that helps put chastity into proper perspective. The life of consecrated virginity in which a person completely forgoes marital and familial life for the sake of witness to the kingdom is also important for understanding Christian chastity. It may seem that the life of consecrated virginity presupposes values quite opposite to those of marriage. In particular, it may seem that this life rejects the values of sexuality for the sake of higher values. These appearances are misleading, for the two vocations are in fact complementary. Pope John Paul II has explained part of this relationship as follows:

> Virginity or celibacy for the sake of the Kingdom of God not only does not contradict the dignity of marriage but also presupposes it and confirms it. Marriage and virginity or celibacy are two ways of expressing and living the one mystery of the covenant of God with his people. When marriage is not esteemed, neither can consecrated virginity or celibacy exist; when human sexuality is not regarded as a great value given by the Creator, the renunciation of it for the sake of the Kingdom of Heaven loses its meaning.[58]

Because marriage is so good, its renunciation can reveal how truly wonderful is the life of the kingdom to which the virginal life testifies in a special way; but the relationship works the other way as well. The life of consecrated virginity throws light on the character of Christian marriage, for the life of virginity is a response to the unconditioned demands of Christ's kingdom. This makes clear that marriage as a human reality is subordinate to the demands of Christ's kingdom; the basis for judging marriage, as for

137

judging everything else in this world, is this kingdom.[59] Only as a vocation contributing to his kingdom does marriage have an absolute claim on his followers. The desires for gratification and earthly happiness must give way in the face of these demands, and nowhere are these more clearly manifested than in the response to the call to renounce all for the kingdom, for only in Christ's kingdom can each of us and all of us together realize full human perfection, and full sharing of goods with other human beings and God himself in loving communion.

Thus, the full meaning of Christian marriage requires an appreciation of the life of consecrated virginity. As Edward Schillebeeckx has said: "It is no longer possible within the Christian order of salvation, to define marriage perfectly without at the same time calling upon total abstinence for the sake of the kingdom of God as a correlative possibility. . . . Christianity will never be able to close its ears to the authentic biblical call to total abstinence as a possibility which forms an intrinsic and essential part of Christianity itself."[60]

Those who answer the call to the life of consecrated virginity in no way repudiate the goods of married life. Such goods are perfectly realized in the kingdom of Christ to which their lives attest. Moreover, such persons stand as a constant reminder that we can come into full possession of our sexuality without engaging in genital activity, and that we can reasonably engage in sexual activity only within a vocation in which the precious goods of human sexuality are fostered and respected.

V. The Single Life and Chastity

Some men and women, as we saw in the previous section, have the vocation to the consecrated life of virginity. There are, however, many men and women who sincerely desire to marry but unfortunately are never able to do so, and there are others, as the *Catechism of the Catholic Church* reminds us, who "forgo marriage in order to care for their parents or brothers or sisters, to give themselves more completely to a profession, or to serve other honorable ends. They can contribute greatly to the good of the human family."[61]

All these people are, like every human person, called to be chaste. While some of them are involuntarily celibate and have not freely chosen to be celibate either in order to enter the religious life or to serve "other honorable ends," they must all respect and honor the great goods of human sexuality and of human persons in their lives. In a sense, celibacy has chosen them.[62]

Indeed, in contemporary society, such single men and women have an

138

especially important and indispensable role to play in the development of a civilization of love. They are called to show others that chastity is indeed a liberating virtue, one that enables a person to "maintain the integrity of the powers of life and love placed in him."[63] They are called to show the world that happiness in human life is not contingent upon the number of sexual experiences one has but rather on the respect one has for the goods of human existence and of human sexuality.

To sum up this chapter: chastity is an essential virtue of Christian life. It is the virtue by which our sexual dimension is integrated into our lives as followers of Christ. Through this virtue, we are able to reasonably order and direct our sexual desires and emotions so that they serve and do not hinder the vocation to which God calls each of us. Thus, chastity is not a matter of suppressing sexuality but of ordering and integrating so that it can be part of a life of Christian service. In marriage, the marital act, which is exclusive and proper to spouses, is a chaste act, one honoring the precious goods of human sexuality. In the other vocations of Christian life, genital activity is sacrificed for the sake of the goods which will be harmed and distorted because they cannot truly be realized outside of marriage. In these vocations, a person's sexuality is not denied but lived in different ways. In all the vocations of Christian life, chastity guarantees a life of self-possession in which the demands of following Christ are seen clearly, without the fog of disordered passion. In the subsequent chapters of this book we will see in a more specific way what chastity requires, and why the intelligent love of the followers of Christ makes these seemingly difficult demands.

Chapter Seven
The Requirements of Chastity Within Marriage

God made men and women as sexual beings, and he blessed marriage. Sexual activity in marriage, when it is faithful to the great goods for which marriage was instituted, is very good. It is natural and excellent, and ennobles human life. Thus, "Married love is uniquely expressed and perfected by the exercise of the acts proper to marriage. Hence the acts in marriage by which the intimate and chaste union of the spouses takes place are noble and honorable; the truly human performance of these acts fosters the self-giving they signify and enriches the spouses in joy and gratitude" (*Gaudium et Spes*, no. 49).

By the choice to marry, a man and a woman commit themselves to participate in the goods for which marriage was instituted. In pursuing faithful love and its extension and embodiment in children, spouses pursue goods naturally desired by human persons; in participating in the sacramental good, they take part in the most sublime ends of marriage and marital union. In Chapter 6 we already described the beauty of married life and of marital acts marked by a commitment to the goods of marriage.

But sex, like every good gift of God to man, can be abused. Married persons can engage in sexual activity in unreasonable and sinful ways; they can fail to respect the values that must be honored in sexual activity. Following the guidance of Scripture and Christian tradition, the Church urges the faithful to avoid those kinds of human acts that are irresponsible and wrong. It does so not to focus their attention on sin but to hearten them toward a more faithful and human living of their married vocation. In this chapter we consider ways in which spouses can fail to meet the requirements of chastity, the demands of faithful and life-giving love. First we consider adultery, which fails to honor the good of faithful love. Then we treat contraception, which attacks the procreative good. Finally, we treat other violations of marital chastity.

140

I. Adultery

Adultery was proscribed in the Decalogue, or Ten Commandments (Ex 20:14; Deut 5:18). In a patriarchal society such as existed at the beginning of God's moral revelation there was emphasis on the rights of the husband, and a focus on external deeds.[1] But the Decalogue was concerned with more than the external act and rights externally violated. It explicitly noted the wrongness of *coveting* one's neighbor's wife (Ex 20:17; Deut 5:21), an inner act by which the heart of the sinner is harmed.

The malice of adultery was frequently recalled in the Old Testament. As the revelation given to Israel developed, marriage itself came to be seen as a faithful and loving covenant between man and woman, symbolizing the covenant of grace and fidelity between Yahweh and his people.[2] Implicit in this understanding of marriage is the realization that adultery violates far more than the rights of the husband. It attacks the heart of the marriage covenant itself, and strikes at every person guarded by that covenant. Pope John Paul II, commenting on the significance of the story of human origins in Genesis, properly sums up the teaching of the Old Testament: "Adultery . . . means a breach of the unity by means of which man and woman only as husband and wife can unite so closely as to be 'one flesh.' "[3]

Jesus clearly taught that not only the external deed of adultery is sinful but the desire for it as well (Mt 5:28).[4] Although Jesus forgave the woman caught in adultery, he cautioned her not to sin any more (Jn 8:11). He likewise made it quite clear that adultery violates the rights of both husband and wife, and that it desecrates the covenant of marriage (Mk 10:11-12; Mt 19:9).[5] By adultery he clearly meant sexual union with a person other than one's spouse.[6]

Paul saw sexual union between man and woman in marriage as very good. It is a communion in being, a "one-flesh" unity, symbolizing the intensely personal union between Christ and his bride the Church (Eph 5:25-33).[7] He taught that a Christian becomes one body with Christ in baptism.[8] And he stressed that the body of the Christian — that is, his whole person[9] — is a temple of the Holy Spirit (1 Cor 6:19), a "vessel" to be held in honor as a God-given and sacred reality (1 Thes 4:3-5).[10] Thus, precisely because sexual activity and the body are so meaningful and precious, Paul taught that any act of sexual immorality was an act of desecration, for in such an act the person who had already become one body with Christ, the Holy One of God, was taking something holy — his or her own person now living in Christ — and defiling it. He therefore pleaded with his brothers and sisters in the Lord to "control his own body in holiness and honor" (1 Thes 4:4) and exclaimed: "Do you not know that the unrighteous will not inherit the kingdom of God? Do not be deceived; neither the immoral, nor idolators, nor adulterers, nor homosexuals, nor thieves, nor the greedy, nor drunkards, nor revilers, nor robbers will inherit the kingdom of God" (1 Cor 6:9-10). Adultery is wicked not only because it desecrates the living temple of the Holy Spirit but also because it does violence to a unique and exclusive kind of love, a love divinely intended to signify and partake of the love between Christ and his Church.

This brief summary makes it evident that the New Testament considered adultery — that is, sexual union with a person other than one's spouse — an evil, a desecration completely incompatible with the life of a Christian. Its teaching is admirably summed up in the Letter to the Hebrews: "Let marriage be held in honor among all, and let the marriage bed be undefiled; for God will judge the immoral and adulterous" (Heb 13:4).

The plain sense of this biblical teaching is faithfully proclaimed by the Church. The Fathers and the great medieval moralists, the approved authors of recent centuries, and the magisterium in all cases speak with one voice condemning adultery. In fact, the wrongness of adultery follows so immediately from what is central to the Christian view of marriage and marital relations that it is commonly taken to be obvious.[11] Adultery is therefore considered by many Christians as a clear example of an inherently wrongful act, and it is used as a reference point to elucidate the malice of other sins.[12]

Given the attack on the Christian doctrine of marriage and sexuality in recent decades, it is not surprising that the magisterium has reaffirmed and proclaimed the traditional teaching on adultery. Thus, Pius XI explicitly condemned adultery in *Casti Connubii*;[13] the Fathers of Vatican II stressed its incompatibility with the fidelity demanded by spousal love (*Gaudium et Spes*, no. 49); the American bishops clearly rejected it as gravely sinful in their pastoral on moral values;[14] and John Paul II has branded it as a terrible breach of covenantal love.[15] The *Catechism of the Catholic Church* teaches that the spouse who commits adultery "fails in his commitment . . . does injury to the sign of the covenant which the marriage bond is, transgresses the rights of the other spouse, and undermines the institution of marriage by breaking the covenant on which it is based [and] compromises the good of human generation and the welfare of children who need their parents' stable union" (no. 2381).

This teaching cannot be set aside as culturally conditioned and therefore no longer normative.[16] The living body of the faithful, guided by the Holy Spirit and aware not only of cultural differences but of the unity through time of the Church, knows that every deliberate act of adultery is seriously wrong.

The grounds for this constant teaching of the Church on adultery are readily discernible. Only a brief account of these grounds is necessary here. Adultery is radically inconsistent with the proper pursuit of the goods of human sexuality and of human persons. Although all the goods honored in marriage — the procreative good, the good of friendship between the spouses, and the good of indissoluble unity — are violated by adultery, it is marital friendship which adultery primarily and immediately harms.

The inconsistency between adultery and marital friendship becomes clear if the special character of this friendship — one described in detail in Chapter 6 — is understood. Like many other friendships, marital friendship is a good thing, valued for its own sake. But this friendship differs from other types of friendship in a number of ways. It is rooted in the covenant of irrevocable personal consent, a consent that establishes the man and the woman as irreplaceable and nonsubstitutable spouses, as husband and wife. It is therefore a friendship that is exclusive of others in the sense that husband and wife pledge to be with and for each other fully until death, and aspire to a unity of personal intimacy, to a communion in being.[17] It is a friendship that involves an intimate sharing of life and love, a sharing so complete that it naturally leads to new life.[18] Marital friendship is essentially related to the most basic and intimate of human communities, the family. This friendship, unique among all kinds of human friendships, is the ground of the family and is nourished and expressed in the life of the family.[19] The intimacy of this friendship, so fittingly expressed in the conjugal act,[20] the unity of spouses in a common life, and the open-ended demands of procreating and raising children require that marital friendship be the permanent and exclusive relationship that Christian teaching holds marriage to be.

Adultery obviously inflicts great harm on spouses and on their children. The deep personal hurt and betrayal experienced by the victims of infidelity, the breaking of the bonds of trust and love, the painful effects of divorce — all these evils and many more are the commonly known effects of adultery. These obvious evils do not arise in each and every case of adultery; but evils of this type are the natural consequences of the harm to marital friendship that is necessarily involved in every act of adultery. The unfaithful spouse is ordinarily deceiving himself or herself when he or she thinks the act of adultery will cause no great harm. These evil effects are therefore useful signs of the inherent evil of this desecrating deed.

The argument is sometimes made that adultery can be consistent with the overall values of marriage and of family life if it is a necessary means to avoid great evils or to achieve great goods. Thus, under some circumstances adultery is said to be justified as therapy for sexual dysfunction, or a necessary way of avoiding loneliness and frustration when the spouses are separated, or as a way of gaining favors or avoiding harms — especially where the favors sought or the harms avoided affect one's family or spouse in a profound way. For example, a woman commits adultery with a concentration camp guard so that she will become pregnant and be returned to the family who desperately needs her.[21] Arguments like these, however, are specious. They are essentially consequentialist and assume that the evil immediately brought about by adultery can be balanced by the good an individual hopes to achieve by it. As we saw in Chapter 4, this assumption is false.[22] In this area, as in all areas of life, one's life is disastrously wounded if one is willing to do evil so that good may come about.

Finally, we must consider the argument that sexual intercourse with a person other than one's spouse, if done with the consent of one's spouse, ought not to be called adultery or at any rate ought not to be considered adultery in a morally pejorative sense.[23] This line of reasoning assumes a subtle form of dualism, for it seems to hold that a man and a woman can continue to give themselves (that is, their conscious minds) to each other uniquely and exclusively even as they give their bodies (now regarded as distinct from their "selves") to another. This fallacious Gnostic assumption forgets the unity of the human person and promotes self-deception.

This argument also involves the false assumption that spouses' rights concerning each other's sexual activities are analogous to property rights or to other rights that can be waived. The mutual rights of spouses with respect to each other's sexual activities are not analogous to property rights or to other transferable rights. Rather, these rights are rooted in the marital covenant and in the marriage itself, in the giving and receiving of the *person* of the other. These realities are not subject to manipulation by the spouses; they come into being in the lives of the spouses from their mutual consent to marriage. But once the marriage comes to exist, it is governed by divinely established norms to which married persons must conform. Consensual adultery therefore *is* adultery, as Pope Innocent XI taught long ago.[24]

II. Contraception

The sexual revolution is closely related to the development of contraceptives.[25] At the beginning of this century the common moral position — not simply of Catholics but also of other Christians, of Jews, and of other religious groups and even of nonreligious people — was that sexual activity had to be responsibly related to marital promises and to the obvious purposes of sex. Contraception was viewed as an abuse of sexual activity, shameful and wrong. In it spouses abused each other, and they abused a significant kind of human action by failing to respect one of its obvious and humanly very important purposes. For very many, it still seemed highly desirable to have large families. Even in circumstances in which more children were undesirable, the use of contraception to limit families was judged the use of an evil means.

In recent times many elements of modern life seemed to join together to commend having smaller families. Urbanization was one factor. In city life large families were burdensome in ways in which they had not been in rural life. Medical progress made a difference. When almost all children happily survived birth and infancy, there was not so great a desire to give birth to many children. Social fears of overpopulation arose and were intensely stimulated by those who wished to promote new moral visions — visions, in fact, incompatible with Christianity. Limited social resources as well as limited family resources were presented as urgent reasons to control the family and the general population.

Theoretically this control could have been managed by various kinds of self-discipline and sexual abstinence. But development of natural family-planning methods was slower and was not promoted by the media and family-planning advocates in the way contraception was. Many people of high moral standards who instinctively judged that sex was meaningful and sacred did not see clearly the reasons why contraception was not a humanly satisfactory solution to these problems. When the commercial interests favoring contraception and the moral revolutionaries proposing a new secular ethics portrayed in glowing terms the advantages of contraception, many failed to see the moral and social problems that a contraceptive mentality would create.

Certainly contraception was convenient. It enabled people to reach what had clearly become a desirable end by means that were effective and, moreover, required little self-discipline and no sexual abstinence at all. Everyone could have sex whenever it was desired without the inconvenience of unwanted pregnancies. (Many at first naïvely thought only married couples would take advantage of this.) This convenience led to a rapid progress toward broad social acceptance of what had earlier been recognized as immoral. Even various religious groups came to commend the contraception they had once sharply condemned. The desirability of the end pursued by contraceptionists was so clear that many failed to question sufficiently the morality of this precise means toward that end.

Pressure to change the Catholic teaching on contraception became very great. It became especially intense in the 1960s. Nevertheless, Pope Paul

VI, emphasizing that he was reaffirming the received teaching of the Christian faith on an important question, refused to alter the Church's stand against contraception. He affirmed in very clear language that contraception is seriously wrong. In doing so he was not denying the importance of family planning and responsible parenthood.[26] His concern was with the moral character of the means used to achieve this end.

During his pontificate Pope John Paul II has repeatedly reaffirmed the teaching of Paul VI — and of the entire Catholic tradition and magisterium — on the intrinsic evil of contraception.[27]

Because of the importance of the Church's teaching on contraception and of the difficulties that many experience today in understanding and accepting this teaching, we will treat this matter at some length.

The Meaning of Contraception. Contraception, as the word itself suggests, is action aimed at preventing conception. But it is necessary to begin with a clear definition of "contraception" to make unmistakable the precise nature of the acts to which moral judgments about contraception are intended to apply.

In his encyclical *Humanae Vitae* Paul VI gave an exact account of the nature of contraceptive actions. A contraceptive act is had whenever one does something which is intended precisely to act against the procreative good of an act of coition, i.e., to prevent this good from being realized in and through the act of coition or intercourse. "Every act that intends to impede procreation must be repudiated . . . whether it is done in anticipation of marital intercourse, or during it, or while it is having its natural consequences."[28] Those who contracept, reasonably believing that a freely chosen act of intercourse is the sort of act through which new human life can be given, choose to do something, prior to, during, or subsequent to this freely chosen act precisely *to impede procreation*, i.e., to prevent the conception of the child who might otherwise be conceived in and through this act of intercourse. Thus it is more accurate to speak of "contracepted" intercourse than of "contraceptive" intercourse. Intercourse is the chosen object of one human act, whereas contraception or the impeding of procreation is the chosen object of another human act, namely the contraceptive act.

Thus there are various ways in which intercourse can be contracepted: through the use of various barriers (e.g., condoms or diaphragms), by the use of spermicides or withdrawal, by the use of anovulant pills,[29] by surgical sterilization, and the like. Ordinarily,[30] in contracepted intercourse, a person or couple chooses, first, to engage in sexual intercourse. While choosing to have intercourse, which is known to be essentially related to the procreation of new human life, and precisely because one does not want that act of

146

intercourse to flower into the fruitfulness it can have, one performs the contraceptive act. This act is aimed precisely against the procreative good. The coming-to-be of a new human life (which is in itself a great good, though one may perhaps reasonably desire not to realize it here and now) is treated as an evil, something to be prevented and opposed. The precise point of the contraceptive act, as we shall show more fully below, is to act directly against the great human good of procreation, of human life in its coming to be, and to treat it as if it were here and now an evil, not a good.

Contraception or contracepted intercourse therefore is not identical in meaning with birth control or family planning. Plainly there are other ways to control births and to plan one's family than by engaging in contracepted intercourse. One can control or prevent births by means far worse than contraception — by abortion, for instance. And one can plan one's family by means that are in themselves thoroughly good — that is, by natural family planning.

With this understanding of the meaning of contracepted intercourse (or contraception) in mind, we now propose to examine the Church's teaching on this subject and to develop the basic argument to show that this activity is immoral. Yet before presenting the Church's teaching and our argument, it will first be helpful to note the objections and difficulties raised against this teaching by some Catholic thinkers in recent years. We shall then, in concluding our discussion of contraception, return to these difficulties and objections in order to answer them more adequately.

Objections and Difficulties. A number of recent developments, some sociological and economic, others philosophical and theological, stimulated questioning of the standard Christian teaching on contraception. During the late 1950s and early 1960s, when doubts about the received teaching were raised with increasing force within the Catholic community, a new factor was introduced with the development of oral contraceptives. The pill differed from mechanical contraceptives such as condoms, diaphragms, spermicidal jellies, and so forth in that it did not interfere in any overt way with the sexual act itself. With the pill there seemed to be no behavioral "unnaturalness." Thus, it seemed to some that the pill might prove to be morally acceptable. Possibly the use of the pill as a contraceptive might be accepted without disturbing the fabric of Christian moral life and without having bad effects on the practice of chastity.[31]

These considerations were reinforced by more theoretical criticism of the received teaching. Two such criticisms were especially influential. The first of these claimed that the received teaching was based on an understanding of the natural law that was too physicalistic or legalistic in nature.

147

According to this claim, the natural-law arguments used to support the condemnation of contraception placed excessive emphasis on the biological finality of sexual organs and activity and did not give sufficient attention to the more experiential and psychological dimensions of sexual acts — that is, to their personal significance.[32] The second of these objections was that the Church's received teaching condemning contraception as immoral is derivative and not fundamental, even though it had been constantly taught in the Church. That is to say, the Church was said to have forbidden contraception in the past not because it is in itself wrong but because it was associated with things that really were wrong. In early centuries, it was said, contraception was forbidden because heretics who proposed it believed that life in the flesh is evil. The Church forbade contraception to express her rejection of such outrageous heresy. But, the objection continued, the great values protected then by excluding contraception can now be better protected by other means, without the burdens found in condemning contraception.[33]

The Church's Teaching

Fully aware of these doubts, and, in fact, largely to remove them, Paul VI strongly reaffirmed the received teaching of the Church on contraception. In 1968, after painstakingly deliberating over the matter and taking into account the arguments that had been advanced to support the moral permissibility of contraception, he reaffirmed in his encyclical *Humanae Vitae* the constant teaching of the Church that contraception is intrinsically a serious moral disorder. Although this encyclical met with dissent, and even, at times, contempt, the teaching set forth in it has since been firmly proclaimed by the magisterium. During the spring and summer of 1978 many conferences of bishops used the occasion of the tenth anniversary of *Humanae Vitae's* promulgation as an opportunity to affirm its teaching; similar conferences were held in 1993, on the 25th anniversary of the encyclical.[34] In 1976 the American bishops reaffirmed the traditional teaching in their pastoral *To Live in Christ Jesus*, despite pressures to remain silent on this matter.[35] In 1979 John Paul II commended the U.S. bishops for this statement.[36]

At the 1980 Synod of Bishops, representatives of national hierarchies from around the world addressed the question of contraception once again. After careful consideration, the bishops stated their agreement with the teaching of *Humanae Vitae* and *Gaudium et Spes* on contraception.[37] John Paul II ratified their statement and reflected on the significance of their consideration of the issue. He said: "Consideration in depth of all the aspects of these problems offers a new and stronger confirmation of the importance of the authentic teaching on birth regulation reproposed in the Second Vatican Council and in the encyclical *Humanae Vitae*."[38] It is clear therefore that the pope and the representatives of the bishops of the world have considered very carefully the dissent from the teaching on contraception and have rejected this dissent decisively.

Indeed, time and time again throughout his pontificate John Paul II has vigorously reaffirmed and defended the teaching that contraception is gravely immoral. He has himself developed a strong, personalist argument against contraception by married persons as an act that violates their marital union (this argument will be summarized below). He has, furthermore, emphasized the crucial significance, both moral and anthropological, between the use of contraception and periodic abstinence as ways of meeting parental responsibilities and expressing conjugal love, affirming, indeed, that these two practices are based, ultimately, on "irreconcilable concepts of the human person and of human sexuality."[39] Finally, the *Catechism of the Catholic Church* brands contraception as an "intrinsically evil act" (no. 2370).

The teaching of these recent magisterial statements is always presented as a reaffirmation of the "moral teaching on marriage proposed with constant firmness by the teaching of the Church."[40] And so, indeed, it is. As a leading historian of this question has stated:

> The propositions constituting a condemnation of contraception are, it will be seen, recurrent. Since the first clear mention of contraception by a Christian theologian, when a harsh third-century moralist accused a pope of encouraging it, the articulated judgment has been the same. In the world of the late Empire known to St. Jerome and St. Augustine, in the Ostrogothic Arles of Bishop Caesarius and the Suevian Braga of Bishop Martin, in the Paris of St. Albert and St. Thomas, in the Renaissance Rome of Sixtus V and the Renaissance Milan of St. Charles Borromeo, in the Naples of St. Alphonsus Liguori and the Liège of Charles Billuart, in the Philadelphia of Bishop Kenrick, and in the Bombay of Cardinal Gracias, the teachers of the Church have taught without hesitation or variation that certain acts preventing conception are gravely sinful. No Catholic theologian has ever taught, "contraception is a good act." The teaching on contraception is clear and apparently fixed forever.[41]

149

This teaching has been proclaimed for centuries by bishops and their representatives in every circumstance. Until 1960 there was clearly moral unanimity in the teaching and believing Church. Even today, despite massive pressures of every kind, the unanimity of the teaching Church remains practically intact.[42] Moreover, the teaching has not been proclaimed as a mere rule or order or disciplinary regulation but as an inherently serious matter, closely related to the essentials of Christian morality as revealed in Scripture and tradition. Contraception has always been regarded as seriously wrong — as constituting objectively grave matter. In other words, the following of this teaching has always been taught to be necessary for salvation.

As the First and Second Vatican Councils clearly taught, the bishops of the Church teach infallibly when they propose matters of faith and morals in ways that reveal that they are acting as decisive witnesses to the teaching of the faith.[43] The Church is infallible in its ordinary magisterium, when that teaching has the characteristics noted in *Lumen Gentium*, no. 25.

Distinguished moralists have pointed out that the Church's teaching on contraception seems clearly to have been proposed by the ordinary magisterium in precisely this way.[44] At the very least, these considerations show that the received teaching must be accepted as a practical norm for preachers, confessors, and married people. Moreover, these considerations show that what is at issue is a teaching of the Church concerning morals and not a mere rule or policy. Thus, to "dissent" from this teaching is not simply to disregard commands of prelates but rather it is to attack what the Church presents as confirmed by divine teaching. Most Catholics are not willing to disregard truths closely related to their faith. The apparent disregard of the Church's teaching on contraception by many Catholics shows that the connection between this teaching and Catholic faith needs to be better understood.

It is true that among the faithful much confusion has been generated. There is not now evident the clear and morally unanimous support of the received Catholic teaching which is the desired sign of Catholic unity. But the dissent of the last three decades does nothing to cancel out the testimony of the whole Church, teachers and believers alike, over all the centuries. Some dissenters like to argue that the Holy Spirit is guiding their dissent. But, even though they may have noble intentions, their claim of support from the Holy Spirit is very far from proved. There are many other active forces, not identical with the Holy Spirit, that have led the massive social drive toward contraception; and these motives appear to have influenced some Catholic thinkers too.

It has sometimes been the case that positions which had been deci-

150

sively taught by the Church for a while began to lose their firm hold on many in the Church. Thus, after several centuries of Catholic faith in the divinity of Jesus, and even after the solemn definitions of the Christological councils, worldly influences led to the massive rise of Arianism in the Church. So many began to deny what is the Church's decisive teaching about Christ that St. Jerome did not hesitate to say, "The whole world groaned to find itself Arian." That is, all about them the faithful saw many ceasing to believe that Jesus is literally God. But this failure of some — indeed many — to believe for a while does not erase decisive testimony of the faith over the centuries. Development of doctrine does not mean that the Church could faithfully deny in one age what is affirmed insistently as the word of Christ in another.

Moreover, there is a striking testimony of the faithful in our time in support of the received teaching. Despite the immense propaganda favoring contraception, despite the failure of local teachers of faith to present intelligently and persuasively the position the Catholic faith has always taught, there has been great faithfulness on the part of vast numbers of the faithful. The astonishing growth of the Natural Family Planning (NFP) movement, with its joyful discovery of how valuable the Catholic teaching is, and how it is both livable and able to enrich married life, presages a happy return to a fuller acceptance of Catholic teaching everywhere. The terrible disadvantages of the contraceptive movement are becoming more visible, and it is evident that NFP provides in more human and nobler ways the goods that contraception was seeking to reach.

Theological Argument

The Catholic moral tradition contains a number of arguments against contraception. Catholic certainty in matters of morals is, of course, not dependent simply upon such arguments. The testimony of faith is much firmer, but such moral reflection is important for the family of faith.

Different theological arguments have been advanced to show the truth of the Church's teaching on the intrinsic evil of contraception.[45] Here we will first briefly summarize the argument developed by Pope John Paul II; we will then develop an argument that follows the principled pattern of moral reasoning sketched above in Chapter 4.

John Paul II's major argument to show that it is always gravely immoral for a married couple to contracept is rooted in a profound appreciation for the meaning of the marital act as an act of self-giving love on the part of husband and wife. It is an act fully open to the love-giving, live-giving union of man and woman. Thus, John Paul II writes:

151

When couples, by means of recourse to contraception, separate these two meanings that God the Creator has inscribed in the being of man and woman and in the dynamism of their sexual communion, they act as "arbiters" of the divine plan and "manipulate" and degrade human sexuality — and with it themselves and their married partner — by altering its value of "total" self-giving. Thus the innate language that expresses the total reciprocal self-giving of husband and wife is overlaid, through contraception, by an objectively contradictory language, namely, that of not giving oneself totally to the other. This leads not only to a positive refusal to be open to life but also to a falsification of the inner truth of conjugal love, which is called upon to give itself in personal totality.[46]

The argument we now wish to develop seeks to bring out the anti-life character of contraception — a matter to which John Paul II alludes in the passage cited above ("a positive refusal to be open to life"). In this way we hope to show one way in which the Church's teaching on contraception is an authentic application of the sexual morality rooted in the Scriptures. Like that of Scripture itself, the Church's teaching on contraception is integrally pro-life.[47]

In contracepted intercourse one chooses both to have sexual intercourse and to prevent the act from being procreative. The contraceptive element aimed precisely and directly against the possible coming-to-be of human life. As the American bishops note, such a prevention is a rejection of the "life-giving meaning of intercourse"; and "the wrongness of such an act lies in the rejection of this value."[48]

Three major steps can be noted in the argument to establish this point. First, the procreative good is intrinsically and always good. Second, a contraceptive deed acts directly against this good, and of itself does nothing but assail that good. Third, it is always immoral to so act directly against a basic human good.[49]

Consider the first point: the procreative good is of its very nature always a good. To say this is not, of course, to suggest that in every case it would be wise or right to promote the procreative good. In the concrete conditions of life every kind of real good can be intermingled with serious evils and harms. Truth is a good; but one ought not publish every truth, to the useless harm and embarrassment of others, or in neglect of duties of secrecy. Life itself is good, but one might be wrong to fight simply to sustain another's life (by extraordinary means) when further living cannot be dissociated from excessive pain and humiliation. Similarly, the realization of the procreative good might in a given case involve great dangers to the health of the mother, the stability of the family, or the like. But truth, life, and the procreative good remain in themselves great goods.

The Second Vatican Council and other Church teachings have made clear that Christian teaching honors the procreative good.[50] The teaching of the Church on this matter is clearly based on Scripture, which constantly celebrates the passing on of human life as a great and wonderful thing. To be able to have children is a great good and joy to human persons: a great progeny was among the chief blessings promised to Abraham. Our Lord himself pointed to the great joy that spontaneously follows childbirth; it is good when a child is born into the world.

And what Scripture witnesses is what everyone knows. All who are parents know this quite directly and immediately. Others see it as a desirable possibility — to have a child of one's own would be a good thing. Or if for some special reason they should not have a child, they know that this is not because a child is not a good thing and that having children is not desirable, but because in these circumstances such a good would involve also harms that they wish to avoid.

To acknowledge the intrinsic goodness of procreation is to recognize that human life is good and that its transmission is also good. As Christians, we are able to see reproduction as procreation — that is, as cooperation with God in his act of creating another image of himself, another member of the kingdom, another person called to be an adopted child of God.[51]

We shall weave together our treatment of the next two points: a contraceptive act of its very nature always strikes directly against the procreative good, and such an attack on an intrinsic human good is always wrong in every area of life.

Few Christian moralists have doubted that there is "something wrong" with contraception. Even those who favor contraceptive practices in many circumstances have been aware of the overwhelming Christian testimony against it in tradition. Ordinarily they recognize that reverence for the procreative good must be safeguarded, that a "contraceptive mentality" is difficult to reconcile with Christian values. But some have argued that at times and, indeed, frequently in contemporary circumstances, a greater harm could come from not practicing contraception than from using it. But it is fallacious to argue from a claim that great harms come at times from not practicing contraception to the conclusion that contraception is therefore morally permissible. To do so would be to assume that one may do any kind of act whatsoever — even an act that involves a choice against a basic human good — if that would seem to lead to better consequences in the circumstances. One would be justified, for example, in directly and deliberately killing an entirely innocent person if better consequences would seem to come from so acting than not so acting. Against this view that one may do evil that (a greater) good may come of it we have argued at length in Chapter 4. Here, it is important to point out clearly the structure of what happens in contraceptive acts: one *is* deliberately and directly acting against a great human good — that is, one is doing the evil of assailing the procreative good in the hope that good might come of it.

To do a contraceptive deed is to perform an action that in itself and directly has only one objective: to keep an act of intercourse from being fruitful, to see to it that a new human life does not come to be in and through an act of the kind in which new human life can come to be. The contraceptive act is directly aimed against the realization of the procreative good. One is not simply declining to promote that good; one is taking positive steps directly against it. One is choosing precisely to make the sort of act that, of its very nature, is open to the transmission of new life to be closed to this good.

In Christian tradition there has been concern to recognize that some ways of bringing about good and preventing harm are not permissible. There are some kinds of deeds that a good person simply will not do. And parallel patterns can be seen in diverse kinds of bad acts. The logic and pattern of contraceptive acts is like that of perjury committed for "good reasons." In such perjury one attacks truth in an act (an oath) which of its very nature is ordered to the truth, perhaps on the grounds that by doing so one might prevent a "dangerous truth" from doing harm. This is not like seeking to avoid the harm by remaining silent, for in the latter case one honors the truth by refusing to attack it. Again, contraception is like euthanasia (mercy killing) in its logical structure. In mercy killing one chooses to kill, to act directly against innocent life, for the sake of removing the burdens of a painful or debilitated existence. One chooses against life for the sake of what seems to be noble purposes. The withholding of extraordinary treatments, by way of contrast, is not a choice against life. This decision, like the decision to remain silent, refuses to attack the goods at stake while seeking to deal prudently with the evils present in the situation.

In a contraceptive act, one freely and deliberately chooses to attack a great human good. The motive for this act may be upright; one may wish to avoid for oneself and others the harms that would be inseparable from the untimely realization of that good. But there are many ways in which those harms could be avoided, some good and some evil.

154

Some have sought to avoid the force of this moral principle by saying that in acts like contraception, the evil intended is not the kind of evil one should always avoid but only a premoral or physical evil. The meaning of this objection is that the good of procreation, unlike some other goods, does not include as part of its meaning the morally correct disposition of the human will. Procreation is clearly a good, as are life and knowledge; but these goods can be pursued immorally, and can be realized without any human choice. So, they are not morally defined, and in that sense are "premoral." Such goods can be contrasted with the goods indicated by the virtues; these clearly are morally defined. Justice, for example, is not realized unless the person in question chooses and is disposed to choose justly.

This distinction between kinds of human goods does not, however, provide a way of avoiding the force of the principle that one must not do evil for the sake of good, for while it is the case that life itself or truth or procreation is a premoral good, our free choices bearing on these goods are not simply premoral. And it is precisely these choices that are at issue. In the choice in question, a person chooses against the procreative good, and this choice has a moral deformity, for, as we saw in Chapter 4, one cannot love God and neighbor when one chooses to harm the goods of persons which reflect the infinite goodness of God. Thus, as Paul VI made clear in *Humanae Vitae*, no. 14, the proposal to evaluate actions directed toward premoral goods by the proportionalist principle of the lesser evil does not avoid the inconsistency between proportionalism and the received moral teaching of the Church on the meaning of the principle that the end does not justify the means.

Recall that this same pattern of immoral actions is possible in every aspect of life. One may wish that a truth not be publicized, if that would cause great and unnecessary harm. Hence one legitimately remains silent, or indignantly denies the right of questioners to probe, when one is guarding a legitimate secret. But one must not directly assail the truth, lie, or perjure oneself, or act against one good for the sake of some other good. One may legitimately wish that a life in great pain and near death may come to a peaceful end. One may cease to use extraordinary means to lengthen the life. Fully respecting that life is a good, yet because of the pain and burdens associated with living longer, one might in some circumstances forgo the treatments needed to sustain life. But to treat the good of life, even in its most embattled form, as if it were an evil, and directly to attack it, to kill the dying person — that would be evil.

Similarly with respect to the procreative good, it would sometimes be very unwise for couples to have another child. In some circumstances, the intention not to have a child is appropriate for married couples. But as it is never appropriate or right to do acts that are direct attacks on truth or life or other basic human goods, it is never right to attack directly the procreative good. We are not to do evil so that good may come to be.

In fact, this principle — that one ought not to do evil so that good may come about — is of critical importance in every area of Christian morality. In the early debates over contraception, defenders of received Catholic teaching taught that those who permitted contraception "for good reasons" were adopting a principle that would make any kind of sexual activity (fornication, masturbation, homosexual acts) permissible or good if done for "good reasons." To allow contraception one must deny either that procreation is a good, or assert that it is sometimes permissible to act directly against a basic human good. Either of these is sufficient to justify masturbation, sodomy, and so on. If the procreative good is not a basic good that must always be respected as such, there is no decisive moral barrier to actions like masturbation, sodomy, or adultery. If one can justify acting against a good for overriding reasons, then one can act against the procreative good not only in contraception but in masturbation, sodomy, and so forth.[52]

This argument was denied in the debates of the 1960s by those defending contraception, but the logic of the position they took has now become very clear. Recent history has shown that their original contention was mistaken: contraception could not be accepted while the other prohibitions of Christian sexual morality were maintained. However, many of the revisionists of the 1960s were willing to accept the inherent logic of their position and, in effect, to admit that the original objection to their position was correct. Thus, today the leading moralists who dissented on contraception argue that in given circumstances, when a "greater good" can be served, various sexual acts (such as fornication, adultery, and sodomy) are morally permissible.[53]

They concluded that the whole sexual morality of the Church had been based upon mistaken principles. The development went further. If the argument for contraception is valid, then in other areas of human existence it will be permissible to do evil so that good may come about; and deeds previously judged intrinsically wrong may be justified morally if there is a sufficiently serious motive. One can kill the innocent or commit perjury for noble reasons. Rather than admit that the pro-contraception argument must be erroneous if it leads to such conclusions, some moralists have simply followed the hypothesis wherever it leads. Instead of seeking to justify contraception in terms of principles compatible with Catholic teaching, they drifted into accepting only those aspects of Catholic teaching that could be reconciled with the proportionalist principles justifying contraception.

156

But clearly, if a moral principle leads to such perverse conclusions, then it must be an erroneous principle. At the beginning of the debate every Catholic theologian in the debate would have admitted this.[54]

The account given here shows why the approval of contraception contributes to acceptance of abortion. Contraception is an attempt to prevent the handing on of life, and one who is willing to do an act aimed directly against life as it is passed on is likely to remain ready to act directly against life if, contrary to his or her expectations, the unwanted new life begins.[55] Those who act directly against a good to prevent its realization have only too frequently proved ready to take the next step. If the resolve to prevent a child from coming to be is so strong that one is willing to act deliberately and directly against that good, then one will be more disposed to act directly against the acquired life of the child if its conception is not successfully prevented.[56]

Replies to Objections

We turn now to a consideration of the factors which have given rise to the doubts and the protests on the part of many. With respect to the special character of oral contraceptives, it became clear very quickly that this method did not differ in any essential way from older contraceptive techniques. To think that the use of the pill was different from other contraceptive techniques required a kind of physicalism which is rejected by the Church, and which had been sharply rejected by the dissenters themselves. It is the contraceptive intent of the act itself and not the mere physical form of behavior taken as such that is morally determining.[57] This is confirmed by the fact that the acceptance of the pill has led both in theory and practice to the acceptance of other contraceptives, including sterilization,[58] and to the acceptance of other sexual acts which have been prohibited because they are considered unnatural.

The Church's teaching on contraception is not based on a physicalist sort of natural-law theory. It is the anti-life *intent* together with the anti-covenantal and the anti-sacramental effects, and not the mere biology involved, which are held to be morally determinative. Biology is relevant to the person choosing contraception because his or her beliefs about the connection between coitus and conception lead that person to seek to break that connection in some way. But the goodness of human life and the requirement that one not direct one's intention against that good are not truths derived from biology. The morality involved is that of the requirements of intelligent love.

Of course, the objection that the traditional teaching is physicalist of-

157

ten has another sense, namely that the prohibition of contraceptive inter-course gives undue priority to one of the goods of marriage at the expense of the others.[59] However, to state that procreation is a basic human good is not to say that it is the *only* good or the chief good. If it is *a* basic good, then one should never act directly against it, as one should not directly act against the unitive good in marriage. It is in this sense only that, like other finite goods, it imposes an absolute obligation.[60]

Of course, there are some who will deny that procreation is an intrinsic basic human good. They hold that when procreation is good, it is so only because it is instrumentally valuable. They hold that it is good only when it is assumed into consciousness and freely chosen. Some argue that no bodily goods — goods such as life, health, and procreation — are intrinsic human goods. They cannot be authentic and full human goods because they, as bodily goods, are on a lower level than the conscious, intelligent sphere of what these critics consider properly personal activity and the level of fully human goods. The goods of the human body — bodily life, health, and procreation — are thus set apart from the mind or consciousness, and the human person is identified with the latter.

To propose this, however, is to advance the doctrine of "dualism," a doctrine that considers a human person as a spiritual reality *in* a body rather than as a unified single reality, this living flesh. Dualism neglects not only the experience of personal unity but also the biblical view of the human person as an integral whole.[61] This dualistic view is also contradicted in the teaching of the Church — for example, in *Gaudium et Spes*:

> Man, though made of body and soul, is a unity. Through his very bodily condition he sums up in himself the ele-ments of the material world. Through him they are thus brought to their highest perfection and can raise their voice in praise freely given to the creator. For this reason man may not despise his bodily life. Rather he is obliged to regard his body as good and to hold it in honor since God has created it and will raise it up on the last day.[62]

The passage just cited is explicitly appealed to by John Paul II in his repudiation of dualism in his encyclical *Veritatis Splendor*, where he faced head-on the charge by dissident theologians that the Church's teaching, particularly on matters of sexual morality, was "physicalistic." John Paul II explicitly called attention the dualistic view of the human person underly-ing this charge of "physicalism." Their view, he wrote, "contradicts the

Church's teachings on the unity of the human person," who, "in the unity of body and soul . . . is the subject of his own moral acts." Since the definitive teaching of the Church, the pope continued, maintains that the human person "entails a particular spiritual and bodily structure," it follows that "the primordial moral requirement of loving and respecting the person as an end and never as a mere means also implies, by its very nature, respect for certain fundamental goods," goods such as body life and marital communion.[63]

There are also powerful philosophical arguments against dualism — arguments that are well presented by Thomas Aquinas[64] and that are also forcefully presented by contemporary religious and secular philosophers.[65]

It is, in short, necessary to regard procreation as a basic human good. Although it is true that some people at times have children for ulterior purposes, it is also true that for many people these ulterior purposes do not exhaust their reasons for having children. People often have children simply because they see that it is good to bring human beings into existence. Procreation is constantly portrayed in the Scriptures as a blessing and joy, and this proclamation of Scripture is confirmed by common human experience.

The fact that procreation is an intrinsic basic human good is relevant for answering another important objection, namely the contention that the Church's teaching on contraception, though constant, is merely derivative and instrumental to the protection of other Christian values. As noted already, human life and procreation are intrinsic goods of surpassing value in Christian thought. The obligation not to act directly against this good — or any other intrinsic human good — is also an essential part of the Christian moral tradition. The prohibition against contraception is therefore fundamental and not derivative. The prohibition of contraception is not a dispensable instrument for promoting some other position; it is a necessary requirement of Christian respect for the good of human life. This is confirmed by the consensus over the centuries of the approved modem moralists (until the unjustified dissent of the last two decades), all of who teach that contraceptive intercourse is intrinsically wrong. Moreover, this consensus is based on the consensus of the whole tradition: in different contexts by different arguments and with different emphases teachers of the Catholic Church have concurred in condemning contraception as seriously wrong.[66]

III. Natural Family Planning

We turn now to a consideration of the difference between periodic continence and contraception. The Church has taught that couples may morally regulate the size of their families by methods that do not involve contraceptive acts. These methods have several forms; generically they may be called "natural family planning," or NFP.

Great strides have been made in recent years in perfecting NFP. While earlier forms were less effective, the best contemporary methods are quite reliable, not only for women with regular cycles but for all women. NFP is a genuine, practicable option; it avoids the harmful physical and moral effects of contraception, and it has many important good effects of its own.[67]

Despite Church teaching that contraception is intrinsically wrong and NFP is not, some have insisted that NFP does not differ in morally significant ways from contraception. Some claim that NFP is *natural* "contraception," whereas the use of drugs and mechanical devices is *artificial* "contraception."[68]

Some argue that NFP and contraception have precisely the same purpose (that is, the avoidance of conception) and that therefore they must be morally the same. But this contention involves a fallacy of elementary logic.[69] Two acts — or one act and one deliberate omission — each of which has the same generically stated purpose need not be morally the same. One can get money to feed one's family by acts of stealing or by honest labor. Though they have exactly the same end, these acts are obviously not morally the same. The purpose of one's acts and policies is not the only factor relevant for determining the morality of these acts and policies. *What one does*, as well as one's reason for doing it, is morally relevant.

It is clear that NFP achieves its purpose in a way that is essentially different from contraceptive intercourse. NFP involves no choice to treat the procreative good as an evil and to act directly against it, whereas contraceptive intercourse does.[70] Reflection on the analogies given earlier in this chapter — the difference between perjury and silence in guarding a perilous truth, or the difference between mercy killing and restrained care for the dying — reveals this.[71]

In practicing NFP a couple adopts a policy to have sexual intercourse at infertile times and to refrain from intercourse at fertile times if they have serious reasons to avoid a pregnancy. Refraining from intercourse is not contracepted intercourse, since it is not intercourse at all. Moreover, refraining from intercourse has a different intentional relation to the good of procreation than contracepted intercourse has. In contracepted intercourse one does what one knows to be a potentially procreative act and one also acts to ensure that the procreative potential of that act is not realized. This is acting against the procreative good. In NFP, however, one's intention to

160

avoid a pregnancy is achieved by forgoing the act that one believes will be procreative; one does not act against a good by altogether refraining from acting.[72]

Choosing not to act so as to cause a child to come to be is a different choice than that choosing an act known to be the cause of the child's coming to be, and taking further, contraceptive, steps to prevent that outcome. Thus, the refraining from intercourse which is involved in NFP does not involve the anti-procreative intention of contracepted intercourse. Neither do the acts of intercourse in which a couple engages during infertile periods have this intention. Nothing is done to any of them to render them infertile, since nature itself has made them infertile. The other goods of marriage are quite legitimately pursued in these acts.

Moreover, the whole spirit and style of life promoted by NFP is radically different. As Pope John Paul II has said in *Familiaris Consortio:*

> In the light of the experience of many couples and of the data provided by the different human sciences, theological reflection is able to perceive and is called to study further *the difference, both anthropological and moral*, between contraception and recourse to the rhythm of the cycle: it is a difference which is much wider and deeper than is usually thought, one which involves in the final analysis two irreconcilable concepts of the human person and of human sexuality[73] (emphasis added).

NFP therefore is not contraceptive. Moreover, it not only does not hinder but even promotes the other goods of marriage. The sexual life of the couple using NFP is controlled by chastity. The efforts of self-control must be mutual; thus couples living by NFP are given a motive to unite in a common effort of will. This chaste union obviates the temptation for couples to treat each other as instruments for sexual gratification and allows their sexual expression to be an expression of human communication, of their marital covenant, and of the love of Christ for the Church.[74]

Of course, there will be difficulties in the practice of NFP, just as the Lord has promised us that there would be difficulties of discipleship in other areas of life, for he spoke about carrying the cross daily. Cooperation between spouses in a moderate amount of self-restraint is necessary; but contraception's failure to respect the full meaningfulness of sex, to treat the sexual act as unrelated to the goods that give it its profound meaning, is ultimately destructive. The substitution of easy technological (and immoral) solutions for human ones is a common temptation of our age. But those who persist in finding temperate and human solutions to this problem in NFP testify that this is not only a morally good solution but in many ways enriches the lives of those who follow that path.

IV. Sterilization

Today, partially because of the dangers of the pill and IUD's (intrauterine devices), more and more people are resorting to sterilization as a means of preventing conception. Those who justify contraception as a way of avoiding pregnancy use the same basic moral justification for sterilization. Since sterilization, however, is for all practical purposes irreversible, some hold that a much more serious "proportionate reason" is necessary to justify the choice to sterilize.[75] Frequently sterilization is advocated as the most appropriate way to cope with the problems faced by a couple who are the bearers of a recessive genetic defect of a serious nature, such as Tay-Sachs disease or sickle-cell anemia. For such couples, there is a twenty-five percent chance that any child they conceive will suffer the crippling disease. Sterilization is also recommended at times for women whose health may be seriously threatened were they to become pregnant.[76] It is frequently urged for couples whose families are now judged to be complete.

The Church has constantly taught that contraceptive or direct sterilization is intrinsically immoral.[77] The Church, along with theologians faithful to her teaching, distinguishes between direct or contraceptive sterilization and "indirect" sterilization. Direct or contraceptive sterilization is an act whose sole and immediate purpose is to destroy the procreativity of the person sterilized, whereas indirect sterilization is a medical procedure whose immediate purpose and direct intent is to remove pathological reproductive organs or to inhibit the natural functioning of such organs when such functioning (for example, abnormal hormonal production) aggravates a pathological condition within the person.

The Church condemns direct or contraceptive sterilization for the same reasons that she condemns contraception. The act in question is one that directly attacks a basic human good. One does evil for the sake of some good to come. Moreover, one could achieve the desired ends reasonably through other means, such as NFP. The Church teaches that indirect sterilization is often justifiable. The principle of totality indicates that a person is permitted to undergo a mutilating operation necessary to protect the life and health of the person, even if sterility results as a side effect of the operation.[78]

Some theologians[79] have attempted to claim that the principle of totality can be extended to justify contraceptive sterilization. They have argued that doing so will prevent a future pregnancy that may be hazardous to the life of the mother or that may result in the birth of a child suffering from a genetically induced disability, and in this way contribute to the total well-being of the person thus sterilized and to his or her family.[80] The argument, basically, is that some hoped-for-good-to-come-about can justify the deliberate intention to act directly against a good here and now.

This effort to extend the principle of totality merges, it can be seen, with the attempts of some recent theologians to argue that it is morally permissible to intend to do what they call premoral or nonmoral or ontic evil for the sake of a proportionately greater premoral or nonmoral or ontic good.[81]

Many theologians, as well as decisive Church statements, have vigorously rejected this attempt to justify contraceptive sterilization.[82] The revisionary effort is ultimately based on the belief that we may willingly and directly do evil for the sake of a good-to-come, as long as the good-to-come is "greater" than the good we deliberately and directly repudiate in doing the evil. But, as we have seen, such a position strikes at the heart of Christian morality.

Moreover, the threat of great social evils implicit in such an expanded principle of totality is obvious.[83] There are many who argue that for the good of society as a whole — and indeed for the good of the persons immediately affected — it is right to sterilize the mentally retarded, the indigent, and all those who fail to exercise "responsibility" in begetting.

The temptation to sterilize is perhaps understandable in a technological culture because sterilization appears to be an efficient way of realizing some worthwhile goals. Yet a technically efficient means may not be the morally right means. A sterilizing act performed precisely to remove a pathology or prevent the spread of disease can be morally justifiable; sterilization, substituted for personal control and reasonable self-discipline, cannot be. We are just beginning to recognize the terrible harm that the pill, once hailed as a panacea for the problem of regulating conception,[84] does to women. There are many known serious side effects of sterilization, both for women and for men, and we do not as yet even know the full extent of these side effects. NFP offers realistic and morally good means for avoiding pregnancies when this is necessary. Contraceptive intercourse and contraceptive sterilization seek to provide merely technical solutions to deep human problems; but the solutions they offer also entail morally wrongful choices, the choice to set oneself against a basic human good. As such they are not humanly good solutions.

V. Other Violations of Marital Chastity

The Church's teaching on contracepted intercourse and contraceptive sterilization applies not only to the use of contraceptive devices but also to any acts done with the intention of preventing a complete genital act between spouses from being a potentially life-giving act. Thus, mutual masturbation, oral and anal sex, and similar acts in which orgasms are sought apart from natural intercourse, are gravely wrong. The argument developed in the section against contraception applies very closely to these acts when done with contraceptive intent, as well as to acts of contracepted intercourse in the sense we have defined it.[85]

Moreover, such acts between spouses are not properly ordered to the goods of married life even if they are not done with contraceptive intent. The discussion of masturbation and sodomy, which will be given in the following chapter, will make it clear that the goods of marriage cannot be properly pursued in masturbatory, oral, and anal sexual activity on the part of married couples.[86]

The Church's teaching that natural intercourse open to procreation is the only legitimate form of complete sexual expression, even between spouses, does not imply that mutual genital stimulation other than intercourse is forbidden for spouses as part of the preliminaries to marital intercourse.

Marriage is a mutual commitment in which each side ceases to be autonomous, in various ways and also sexually: the sexual liberty in agreement together is great; here, so long as they are not immoderate so as to become slaves of sensuality, nothing is shameful, if the complete acts — the ones involving ejaculation of the man's seed — that they engage in are true and real marriage acts.[87]

But the qualification in this statement is important. The activities of spouses must be moderate, and the danger of becoming "slaves of sensuality" is real. Pope Pius XII warned against this danger by criticizing an anti-Christian hedonism that encourages "the pursuit of the intensest possible enjoyment" in the preliminaries to marital intercourse and in its consummation, as though in this sphere the moral law enjoined nothing more than that the act itself be accomplished normally, and as though the rest, in whatever manner done, could be justified as being an expression of mutual love which is sanctified by the sacrament of matrimony and deserves praise and reward in the eyes of God and conscience. Unfortunately, the dignity of the human being, the dignity of the Christian, which sets a check on sexual excess, can be left out of account.[88]

Spouses are required to seek the moderation and self-restraint necessary to preserve their lovemaking from becoming the pursuit of the shallow and apparent good of isolated sexual pleasure, rather than the authentic good of human love, sexually expressed in shared joy. There are no hard and fast rules for avoiding the immoderate pursuit of sexual pleasure, given that the life-giving and person-uniting goods of marriage are respected. Nevertheless, there are certain marks of immoderation and certain broad guidelines for marital chastity that spouses and confessors may refer to: a preoccupation with sexual pleasure, succumbing to desire in circumstances in which it would be wise to refrain, and insisting against serious reluctance of one's spouse. One has hardly acquired sufficient self-possession if one could not accept peacefully a few weeks or a few months of abstinence in case of real need.[89]

Spouses should avoid also the danger of insensibility and unjustified abstention. These also can be sins against moderation and can violate the reasonable expectations of the other spouse.[90] Marital intercourse should be a gladly agreed-upon activity, but under certain circumstances one is obliged to accede to the reasonable desires of one's spouse. Unreasonable refusal to have sexual intercourse can harm the person-uniting aim of marriage, and such refusal is often inconsistent with the demands of conjugal justice and charity.

VI. Artificial Insemination and "In Vitro" Fertilization

A basic principle of Christian sexual ethics, as we have seen, is that the goods toward which sexuality is ordered must not be separated from unitive and life-giving acts. There is an "inseparable connection established by God" between the unitive meaning and the procreative meaning of the conjugal act.

This intrinsic connection between the goods of marriage is relevant for understanding many of the contemporary challenges to the Christian ideal of family life. Two such challenges extensively discussed at the present time illustrate the far-reaching character of the Church's teaching on marriage.

The moral issues raised by new technologies for generating human life outside the marital act were faced by Pope Pius XII, who taught that human life, according to God's wise and loving plan, ought to be given only in the marital act because of the inherent relationship between marriage, the marital act, and the begetting of children.[91]

Because of advances made in these new reproductive technologies and

165

the serious problems they raised for married couples naturally desiring to have children of their own and experiencing difficulties in achieving conception, the magisterium, through the Congregation for the Doctrine of the Faith, provided for the faithful and all persons of good will a carefully reasoned study, entitled *Vatican Instruction on Respect for Human Life in Its Origin and on the Dignity of Procreation (Donum Vitae)*. Released in February 1987, this important document offered three major lines of reasoning to show why it is not morally right to generate human life outside the marital act, whether by artificial insemination or by *in vitro* fertilization, whether the gametic cells used were provided by the spouses themselves (called "homologous" insemination and *in vitro* fertilization) or provided by a person or persons other than the spouses ("heterologous" insemination and *in vitro* fertilization).

The first line of reasoning was based on the inseparability of the unitive and procreative meanings of the conjugal act. According to this line of thinking fertilization, is sought rightly only when it is the result of a "conjugal act which is *per se* (of itself) suitable for the generation of children to which marriage is ordered by its nature and by which spouses become one flesh." From the moral point of view, procreation is deprived of its true meaning when is sought, not as the fruit of the conjugal act, the one-flesh unity of the spouses, but as a result of technological procedures.

The second kind of argument was based on the "language of the body." The spouses' one-flesh unity in the conjugal act speaks eloquently of the love-giving, life-giving nature of their marital union. The child is, as it were, the "word" they conceive in giving themselves to each other. This rich meaning is entirely lacking when the origin of new life is no longer linked to the bodily/spiritual union of husband and wife.

The third line of reasoning is rooted in the nature of these technologies of reproduction as forms of "making," of "producing." When a child is "begotten" in the marital act, it comes into being as a gift crowning the gift of husband and wife to one another. It is "begotten," not made. But when a child comes to be by recourse to the new technologies of reproduction, it comes into being as "product" of human artifice. But to treat a human child as a product is to violate its dignity as a person.[92]

Several theologians have developed sound arguments against the artificial reproduction of human persons, some of them seeking to develop the lines of reasoning found in the *Vatican Instruction*.[93]

Thus, artificial insemination and *in vitro* fertilization cannot be proper parts of sacramental marriage nor can they be proper parts of marriage as a natural institution because they leave out the marriage act itself — the act

166

in which the goods of marriage are pursued in their inseparable unity. Human life should come to be only in an act of human love, associated with God's creative act of love. This brief discussion is meant to show that the Church's teaching on marriage is a unified doctrine that directs not only the sexual conduct of individuals and spouses but also the most basic institutions and interpersonal relations of mankind. It is the wisdom of a God who loves us and who wills that we be members of his own Trinitarian family that directs us to be at the same time chaste, loving, and open to new life in our use of the sexual nature the Lord has given us.

Chapter Eight

The Requirements of Chastity Outside the Covenant of Married Love

Chastity is not a virtue for married persons alone, for the goods at stake in human sexuality need to be cherished and reverenced in every person's life. The self-possession of a chaste person is necessary not only within marriage but also within every Christian vocation and, indeed, within every humanly satisfactory life. A proper regard for the human body, a wholesome respect for the handing on of the great good of human life, respect for the real integrity of intimate human relationships — all these are necessary not only for the married but for those who plan marriage, for all who choose the splendor of committed virginity for the sake of the kingdom, and for all whose lives should, however indirectly, support or image marriage and its goods. This includes every person.

Everyone is called to a love that binds persons together in ways that reflect the personal communion of divine love. Single persons exhibit chastity when in the service of human friendship they do not merely behave impulsively; when they do not permit unworthy pursuit of passing gratification to lead them to act in ways that fail to honor goods far more precious than simple pleasure. They pursue chastity when they refuse to depersonalize the human body by using it as though it is but an instrument for gratification. Of course, the lure of pleasure is great and the instincts of selfishness are strong so that the demands of chastity for the unmarried can at times be difficult. But the difficulty is none other than that of truly reverencing persons and the goods of persons in the actual conditions of our life. Like the other difficulties in living well, it can be made light by the grace of Christ.

In the preceding chapter we presented the most central requirements of married love and marital chastity. Here, we present a similar moral analysis of the general requirements of chastity for those who are unmarried. Our special focus will be on those choices and acts which the Church has always taught to be unchaste kinds of acts, for these are acts which must be avoided if the personal and interpersonal fabric of the most basic of human relationships is to be protected from the ravages of lust and selfishness. We will first analyze premarital sex or fornication, then masturbation, followed by homosexual activity. We will conclude this chapter by briefly considering bestiality, rape, incest, and sins of thought. In treating these issues, we draw upon the relevant teaching of Scripture, Christian tradition, and magisterial doctrine. We will note also some of the currently popular objections to, or difficulties with, received Catholic teaching.

I. Premarital Sexual Relations

Christian tradition, as we have seen above in Chapters 1, 2, and 3, has always regarded sexual intercourse between unmarried persons to be seriously wrong. The Church sees this prohibition as part of the natural law. This does not mean that in the turmoil of our sinful world everyone "naturally" grasps the truth of this norm. Nor does it mean that there will not be some who will even regard nonmarital sexual activity as being a good thing, for such actions can be very attractive and even seem to be good. What the Church means in saying that sexual intercourse between unmarried persons violates the natural law is (1) that the malice of this kind of activity follows necessarily from a reflective understanding of the human goods at stake in sexual activity and the requirements of intelligent concern for these goods; and (2) that, as in other areas of human life, persons who fail to observe the requirements of intelligent concern for what truly perfects their human nature, harm themselves and others.

The Church's teaching on the immorality of extramarital intercourse is also based on the conviction that God's revelation, as expressed in Scripture and tradition, unequivocally condemns it. For those who have faith, the word of God is an even surer guide to good living than arguments from the natural law. In making use of Scripture and tradition in this chapter as throughout this entire book, we are avoiding what is called a proof-text approach — that is, using isolated biblical texts as simple proof for a moral or theological belief, doctrine, or principle. Catholic doctrine on matters so long reflected upon and so constantly taught as these is not built upon superficial appeals to isolated fragments of Scripture. Rather, the basis for the Catholic conviction on specific moral questions is the integral vision of human persons and of human sexuality which, with the guidance of the Holy Spirit, is drawn from the word of God as understood, believed, and taught within the family of faith over the centuries. Thus, citation of a given scriptural text or magisterial teaching is meant to highlight statements in which the convictions of the faith are succinctly and powerfully brought to a focus.

169

Scripture. The Old Testament contains the roots of the Christian prohibition of extramarital intercourse, for within the Old Testament the values protected by this prohibition begin to be articulated. This is clearest in the Old Testament insistence on the virginity of women before marriage.[1] This insistence is not equally clear in the case of men — perhaps the patriarchal structure of Israelite society played a part here.[2] Despite this limitation, the Old Testament kept constantly before the eyes of the Chosen People the beauty of monogamous marriage as willed by Yahweh. The Wisdom literature is filled with warnings against sins of lust. Fornication, or *porneia*, is portrayed there as an apostasy from God and a devising of idols.[3]

By the first century A.D., the reflective faith of the Jewish community, instructed by the prophets and the authors of the Wisdom books, came to a remarkably full understanding of the significance of Old Testament teaching on extramarital intercourse. They understood the biblical injunction "Thou shalt not commit adultery" broadly to "prohibit various immoral sexual activities,"[4] and they valued chastity highly. The words of Philo Judaeus, a faithful Jew who lived in apostolic times, are typical of the attitude of first-century Judaism:

> We, the descendants of the Hebrews, have excellent customs and laws. Other nations allow their young men of fourteen years of age to go to prostitutes and to other women who sell their bodies. But according to our laws, all *hetairas* [kept women] are condemned to die. Until there can be legitimate relations, we do not have intercourse with a woman. Both parties enter marriage as virgins, and for us the purpose of marriage is not pleasure but the propagation of children.[5]

What is only pointed to in the Old Testament is clearly affirmed in the New Testament — namely that all sexual intercourse outside of marriage, all fornication, is seriously wrong. This teaching is expressed in the numerous condemnations of *porneia*. This word is usually translated into English as "fornication." Not all of the uses of *porneia* and its cognates in these passages, however, refer directly and clearly to premarital sex. This is not surprising, since "*porneia*" (like the word "fornication" in English) did not refer merely to premarital sex.[6] This term does not simply mean uncleanness but refers to certain kinds of sexual activity which, like fornication in the narrow sense, fail to honor the goods that sexual activity should always respect.

Matthew and Mark report that Jesus includes *porneia* in a list of evil activities which make a person unclean (Mt 15,19; Mk 7:21).[7]

170

These brief indications of the mind of the Lord on this matter were greatly elaborated on in the evangelization and catechesis of pagans by the early Church. The Gentiles did not share the Jewish conviction about the importance of chastity, and so clear teaching was especially needed. Thus, pagan converts were told bluntly that they must abstain from fornication (Acts 15:20, 29; 21:25). The Pauline literature, in particular, not only contains repeated references to fornication as a serious sin but also an explanation of why it is incompatible with Christian life.

The First Letter to the Corinthians contains much of what Paul says about fornication. Paul lists fornicators among those who will not inherit the kingdom of God (1 Cor 6:9). The body, he reminds the Corinthians, is not for fornication but for the Lord (1 Cor 6:13, 14). He then explains why sexual intercourse with prostitutes is wrong for Christians. The bodies of Christians are members of the body of Christ. The Christian who has intercourse with a prostitute joins his body to hers and becomes one flesh with her (1 Cor 6:15-17).

St. Paul goes on to say: "Keep away from fornication. All the other sins are committed outside the body; but to fornicate is to sin against your own body. Your body, you know, is the temple of the Holy Spirit who is in you since you received him from God" (1 Cor 6:18-19).

After proposing virginity as an ideal expression of Christian love, Paul notes that, because of the danger of fornication, in the ordinary case it is good for each man to have his own wife and each woman her own husband (1 Cor 7:2). He goes on to add a comment specifically directed at widows and the unmarried: "It is good for them to stay as they are, like me, but if they cannot control the sexual urges, they should get married, since it is better to be married than to be tortured" (1 Cor 7:8, 9).[8]

Thus, the Church has always understood extramarital sex to be gravely wrong — not only because specific scriptural texts teach this but also because of her understanding of the overall thrust of God's revelation concerning the meaning of love and sex, and of how the goods of sexuality should be honored. Scripture and tradition, as understood and interpreted by the Church, are at one in holding that premarital intercourse or fornication is seriously wrong. The *Catechism of the Catholic Church* sums this up accurately when it says that fornication "is gravely contrary to the dignity of persons and of human sexuality which is ordered to the good of the spouses and the generation and education of children. Moreover, it is a grave scandal when there is corruption of the young" (no. 2353).[9]

171

Why Extramarital Intercourse Is Immoral

The reasons why the Church condemns extramarital intercourse as seriously immoral are clearly set forth by Pope John Paul II in *Familiaris Consortio*. There, referring to "God's plan" for marriage and the family, John Paul II emphasizes that the human meaning of sexual activity is not merely biological, nor is it aimed at mere pursuit of pleasure. It "concerns the innermost being of the human person as such." Sexual intercourse is realized in a truly human way "only if it is an integral part of the love by which a man and a woman commit themselves totally to each other until death." When spouses give themselves humanly and generously to one another in marital intercourse, they signify a will to honor each other and to respect the goods each needs to fulfill his or her life. The self-giving in sexual intercourse is a lie if it fails to be "the sign and fruit" of this total and generous self-giving.

The Holy Father goes on to explain that this total self-giving is possible only within marriage, for marriage is the covenant of conjugal love by which man and woman freely unite their lives into an "intimate community of life and love willed by God himself." Outside of this covenant something is withheld. Instead, one reserves for oneself the possibility that in the future one might decide otherwise than to maintain the community of life and love. Thus, outside of marriage the self-giving is by definition not total. The pope concludes from this analysis that the limitation of sexual activity to marriage is not an unreasonable or arbitrary imposition on people's freedom but an "interior requirement of the covenant of conjugal love."[10]

Pope John Paul's statement draws out the point of the Church's teaching on extramarital intercourse. The Church believes that her absolute prohibition of this kind of activity is reasonable, that it is not simply an inexplicable taboo or ritual requirement for Catholics. The reasons presented by the Church are all related to the fact that extramarital intercourse bruises human persons, their intimate relationships, and their personal integrity. Moreover, since Christians are united with Christ in baptism, the relationships and integrity harmed are not just those of the parties involved but include the body of Christ, which is defiled by such actions.

The failure to respect these goods becomes clear if one carefully considers the different types of extramarital intercourse. Acts of fornication done solely for sexual pleasure obviously trivialize the act of sexual intercourse. In such acts the partners simply use each other and their sexual powers to grasp pleasure for themselves or to give each other pleasure. Such a use of a human person, even if there is mutual consent, is a violation of human dignity,[11] for human love is more meaningful than this. This kind

172

of sexual intercourse totally fails to serve the genuine goods of human sexuality. The procreative good is ignored and the harm to children who might come into being through such relationships is overlooked. Indeed, today many children conceived in extramarital relations are killed within the womb, and many others are raised under deplorable conditions. The good of marital friendship and fidelity is set aside in favor of satisfying a craving for pleasure or to express a much less committed affection. The sacramental significance of sexual activity is ignored or scorned.

When fornication is chosen to promote and to express romantic affection or "love," the trivialization of human sexuality and its goods is not so apparent — but it is present nonetheless. The partners are not, of course, treating each other *merely* as sources of gratification. Still, substantial and necessary goods of human sexuality are ignored and undercut, and this kind of sexual activity abounds in self-deception and mutual exploitation. This becomes clear if one inquires as to the nature of the "love" expressed in "romantic" fornication, for clearly this is not the strong, genuine love of marriage in which spouses decisively commit themselves to each other without reservation.

Fornicators strongly desire to experience of bodily, personal communion, but they can achieve — and they know they can achieve — only the *illusion* of the personally rich communion proper to spouses, a communion made possible by a commitment to the authentic goods of human sexuality: self-giving spousal love and openness to the gift of human life.[12] The human disappointment and suffering that flow from sexual activity without love as complete and lasting as marital love is only too evident in our time.

The affection between fornicators can, no doubt, be deeply felt; but it is deeply flawed. It cannot be the love of Christian marriage. Marital love is in part constituted by an unconditional pledge of fidelity. Those who are not married have not made this commitment. Consequently, their love simply cannot be the intimate love of those who have joined their lives into one life together, who have made themselves "the single subject, as it were, of sexual life."[13] They have not given themselves to each other by an act of irrevocable, unconditional consent. It is profound self-deception for affectionate fornicators to think that their love is like that of married persons for each other.

Thus, the "love" of fornicators just cannot be the love of spouses. Then what sort of love is it? If it is not mere sentiment and affection ungrounded on a real union of lives, it must be some sort of sharing of life; but since it is not marital, it can be no more than a conditional or partial sharing of life. Their act of intercourse does not unite two persons who have made them-

173

selves irreplaceable in each other's life, and united in a common life in the pursuit of all the goods of marriage. Yet this union, this common life, this complete love, is what sexual intercourse is meant to symbolize; it is also what many romantic fornicators wish it to symbolize, even though they know at some level that their refusal to make the commitment of marriage makes this impossible. Thus, the self-deception — the "lie" of which John Paul II spoke.

The love of fornicators is therefore suspect. Authentic human love is a love grounded in full respect for the being of human persons and for the goods needed to fulfill human persons. And where sex is involved, such love demands respect for the good of procreation and for the irreplaceable value of the person to whom one chooses to disclose one's intimate self in coition. But the "love" of fornicators spurns these real goods of human persons and of human existence. Their union is not intended to be fruitful, since no care is taken for possible children — unless it is care not to have them. The conditions for responsible and fruitful love are not met; the commitment necessary for the sharing of a common life is deliberately not made. If the love which was expressed and promoted in such acts were the love it claimed to be, one could pledge oneself with the full love of marital commitment. Willingness to choose the appearances of marital love — the friendship, sexual intimacy, and sharing of life — while rejecting the substance of common commitment to common goals clearly indicates an unwillingness to make serious commitments to human goods. This unwillingness, in turn, is incompatible with the character traits needed to be a faithful partner, responsible parent, and follower of Christ. Thus, the truth as well as deep insight of the Church's teaching that sexual intercourse is a moral and human good only within marriage is based on a realistic appreciation of the meaning of sexual union and the irreplaceable value of human persons.

Objections. There are many today, both in the general culture and within the Christian community, who question this teaching. Many popular objections are based on the conviction that the total prohibition of extramarital intercourse is simply unrealistic. We admit, of course, that morality sometimes requires very difficult things, and that many will choose not to live wisely and well. But, as the discussion of free choice in Chapter 4 makes clear, it is possible for people to choose to do difficult things if they can see the real good to be achieved by the difficult choice. And God is ready to give his saving grace.

A slightly different popular objection is based on a denial that there is any great good at stake in the prohibition of extramarital intercourse. This

174

objection leans toward the view that sexual activity is really trivial, and that recreational sex is not in need of any special justification. Of course, this view is totally at odds with common human experience. It has been one of the main purposes of this book to articulate and focus this experience.

There are, however, more serious objections which have been articulated in the writings of theologians. Three of these are worth discussing in some detail: (1) that sexual intercourse should always be in the context of an interpersonal relationship that involves some affection and commitment but that it need not be limited to the relationship of marriage; (2) that extramarital intercourse always has some ontic deformity but can be morally justified for serious reasons; and (3) that sometimes intercourse between the unmarried really is marital; it is not really premarital but only preceremonial. We will consider these objections in the remainder of this section.

The first objection is that sexual coition does demand a measure of concern and care for the other but does not require the marital covenant.[14] There is, of course, a difference between really exploitative, promiscuous, and commercial sex on the one hand, and, on the other hand, intercourse between unmarried persons who have some feeling and concern for each other. Still, those who make this objection fail to note that extramarital intercourse is always seriously flawed. It always includes some lack of love, some inability or unwillingness to give oneself away in love, some refusal to commit oneself irrevocably to another. This lack of love makes it impossible for their genital embrace to have the meaning that it is meant to have. By enjoying the expression of full love without giving full love itself, they wound each other as well as any child who might come into being as a result of their act. To say that uncommitted love can rightly be expressed by sexual intercourse is to fail to take sexual responsibility seriously enough.[15]

The second objection is that the requirement that sexual activity be limited to marriage is only an ideal which can be set aside if there are sufficiently serious reasons.[16] There are many kinds of sufficient reason according to the objection: for example, the socioeconomic structures of our society are said to impose terrible burdens upon young people today. Many individuals who are deeply committed to each other are, as it were, prevented from marrying. Such unmarried couples may at times rightfully choose to have intercourse: "In this case the union of the partners has much of the personal and human reality of marriage. Often the partners in such intercourse *intend* to marry and will do so if and when their circumstances permit"[17] (emphasis added).

This argument is not sound. First, this position clearly contradicts the teaching of the Church which has been outlined above. Recognition that the Church's position has considerable merit, and that it protects, for, the most part, the human values involved is not acceptance of that teaching. Second, it is clear that this objection is based on the theory of proportionalism; the ontic evil of premarital intercourse is supposedly offset by the other advantages in the forced and unnatural circumstances described. We saw in Chapter 4 that proportionalism is a way of moral thinking that is incoherent on its own terms, inconsistent with the Catholic tradition of moral reasoning, and incompatible with both precepts and basic principles taught insistently by the Church, as John Paul II has insisted in *Veritatis Splendor.* In the case at hand, we have a variation of the proportionalist claim that one may do evil that good may come about. The necessities of uncontrollable external factors do not provide grounds for abandoning Christian principles; if they did, the law of the cross would be nonsense. Remaining faithful to what love requires is essential for guarding human values and the very prospect of true happiness.

The third objection is based on a distinction between *premarital* and *preceremonial* sexual intercourse. This is a distinction between those who are not married — though perhaps they intend to be married — and those who are really married (that is, those who have committed themselves irrevocably to each other as spouses but have not yet gone through the formal exchange of vows). The former — so the argument goes — may not morally have intercourse; the latter, however, since they are — for all intents and purposes — married, may licitly conduct themselves as spouses.[18]

Obviously, this distinction can be easily abused. For example, Anthony Kosnik and his associates call sexual relations between those who have a firm intention to marry but have not committed themselves in the marital covenant, preceremonial and not premarital relations.[19]

The precise question, however, is this: Could two persons who have already exchanged vows of marriage privately, under limited circumstances, licitly engage in the *marital act* and do so precisely because they are *already* married?

In very rare cases, an affirmative answer is appropriate. It has always been the teaching of the Church that it is the consent between the man and the woman that brings marriage into being.[20] Moreover, during much of the Middle Ages the Church recognized the validity of clandestine or secret marriages; but at the Council of Trent she decreed that from that time forward, *for Roman Catholics*, valid matrimonial consent could *not* be given unless this consent were given in the presence of the parish priest (or his duly appointed representative) and two witnesses.[21]

The decision was based on the fact that very great evils occurred because of clandestine or secret marriages, and there is no reason to think that such evils will not occur today if such unions are recognized as marriages. Marriage deserves protection by public safeguards. It is not a private affair between two isolated individuals but a public act of two persons in a society. The family is indeed the most basic and important community within society. The stability and legitimate constitution of the family are obviously important — for spouses, children, and society at large. Thus, the act which constitutes a family is a public act in which all society has a stake. Consequently, the Church may rightly insist, as the state ordinarily does, that the act in which one person marries another be public.[22]

Of course, there could be instances in which two Catholics could validly and rightly exchange vows and make themselves thereby to be married persons without the witness of the priest and two witnesses. For example, if the persons involved lived in an area where no priest could reasonably be expected to be present for a long time, or if the persons were in a concentration camp. But this is not what some contemporary writers are ordinarily talking about when they distinguish between "preceremonial" and "premarital" unions. They tend to blur the central difference between an intent to marry (which is revocable and is proper to engaged persons) and the *actual consent to marriage.* Only the latter creates the reality of marriage; this alone makes man and woman to be husband and wife, and for Catholics it can be done validly only in the presence of the parish priest (or his deputy) and two witnesses, with certain quite rare cases recognized as exceptions by the Church herself.

In conclusion, we have seen here that the logic of love implicit in Scripture and in the teaching of the Church provides substantive reasons to support the Church's centuries-old teaching that extramarital intercourse is an act that simply fails to respect either the reality of sexual intercourse as a life-uniting and life-giving act, or the preciousness of the persons involved in it. When faith insists that every act of fornication is immoral, it is not speaking the language of legalistic restraint. Rather, it is teaching the requirements of authentic love.

II. Masturbation

Masturbation is the deliberate stimulation of the genital organs to the point of orgasm which is not a part of sexual intercourse.[23] Thus understood, masturbation can be done either by a person acting on himself or herself (thus, its frequent description as "self-abuse"), or by one person acting on another. Throughout her history the Church has consistently held

177

that masturbation, when it is a freely chosen act, is seriously wrong, for it always involves a failure to respect the human goods which all sexual activity should take into account. The Fathers of the Church,[24] the medieval Scholastics, and all moral theologians[25] until most recent times have been unanimous in condemning every deliberate act of masturbation as a serious violation of the virtue of chastity.[26] This same teaching has been proposed by the magisterium of the Church from the time when it was discussed by Pope Leo IX in 1054 to the present.[27]

In 1975, responding to the questions that had been raised by some contemporary theologians regarding the malice of masturbation, the Congregation for the Doctrine of the Faith firmly reasserted this teaching of the Church:

> . . . both the Magisterium of the Church — in the course of a constant tradition — and the moral sense of the faithful have declared without hesitation that masturbation is an intrinsically and seriously disordered act. The main reason is that, whatever the motive for acting in this way, the deliberate use of the sexual faculty outside normal conjugal relations essentially contradicts the finality of the faculty. For it lacks the sexual relationship called for by the moral order, namely the relationship which realizes "the full sense of mutual self-giving and human procreation in the context of true love." All deliberate exercise of sexuality must be reserved to this regular relationship.[28]

In reaffirming the constant teaching of the Church that masturbation is "an intrinsically and gravely disordered action," the *Catechism of the Catholic Church* (no. 2352) twice cites this important document from the Congregation for the Doctrine of the Faith.

The Church's certainty that of its very nature masturbation is gravely wrong is first of all rooted in divine revelation. Theologians have frequently cited certain key texts as witnesses to the scriptural condemnation of masturbation — for example, the Onan text in Genesis 38:8-10, or 1 Corinthians 6:9, where St. Paul lists among those who are excluded from the kingdom the *malakoi* or the "soft," or Romans 1:24, where he points out that those who reject God come to dishonor their own bodies.[29]

Contemporary scholarship points out that these texts do not *unambiguously* refer specifically to masturbation.[30] But in condemning irresponsible uses of sex generally, Scripture certainly does include a condemnation of

178

masturbation.[31] As the 1975 *Declaration on Certain Questions Concerning Sexual Ethics* states:"Even if it cannot be proved that Scripture condemns this sin by name [masturbation], the tradition of the Church has rightly understood it to be condemned in the New Testament when the latter speaks of 'impurity,' 'unchasteness,' and other vices contrary to chastity and continence."[32]

The Church has rightly understood Scripture to teach that genital activity should take place only within marriage in ways that rightly express marital love. From St. Paul (1 Thes 4:1-5; 1 Cor 6:15-20) Christians have learned that their bodies are the temples of the Holy Spirit, that their flesh has become one with the flesh of Christ. Our genital organs, Christians have thus rightly concluded, are not playthings or tools that we are to employ simply for pleasure. Rather they are integral to our persons, and our free choice to exercise our genital powers is thus to be in service of human persons and of the goods perfective of human persons. The goods to which sexual activity is ordered, as we have seen throughout this work, include procreation, marital friendship, and chaste self-possession. By respecting these goods when we use our genital powers, we honor the body that has, through baptism, become one body with Christ and a temple of his Spirit. When we do not respect these goods in our genital activity we act immorally, and we desecrate the temple of the Holy Spirit and abuse the body-person who has been purchased at such great price. It is this deeply biblical vision of human sexuality and of the human person that is at the heart of the Church's teaching on the immorality of masturbation.

This vision does not exclude a more purely ethical analysis of the immorality of masturbation, for one who chooses to masturbate exercises his or her genital powers of sexuality in a way that does not take into account the precious human goods that these powers are meant to serve. These are life-uniting and life-giving powers. And in choosing to masturbate we use these meaningful powers in ways which ignore or disdain their life uniting or life-giving meaning. Because they regard their own bodies merely as a means of bringing about a desired conscious state and do not respond as body persons to the real goods making human sexuality meaningful, masturbators violate the body's capacity for self-giving or what John Paul II calls its "nuptial" significance.[33] Psychologists note that there is a sort of narcissism involved in such acts, a turning in on oneself, in the use of powers which should serve one to go beyond oneself. This reason takes on added significance for the Christian, who is to regard himself or herself as a "vessel" consecrated to the Lord and a temple of his Spirit.

Objections. Despite the overwhelming weight of a tradition rooted in of semen for medical examination.) This type of activity could seem to be directed toward a morally upright and nonlustful purpose. It should be noted, first of all, that if this type of act were morally permissible it would be so not because there is an act of masturbation essentially like other acts of masturbation but one which can be morally justified because of its motive. Rather, it would be permissible because the act would be morally speaking a different kind of act — a medical act. Hence, there is in no case any reason for concluding that there are exceptions to the Church's firm judgment that all acts of masturbation are wrong. Still, it is by no means clear that medical masturbation is not in fact an act condemned by the Church's teaching on masturbation, or that, if it is in fact a different kind of act, it is an act which is not also morally wrong.

The designation of medically indicated masturbation as a medical act appears to be a rhetorical redefinition of the act based on the purpose of the masturbation. The inducing of orgasm seems to be of the essence of the act as a moral act — it is by inducing the orgasm that the sperm is procured. Thus, we have, in fact, a disordered sexual act — one directed toward orgasm outside of marital intercourse. The fact that there is a good purpose for such an act does not remove its disorder.[39] Moreover, even if medically indicated masturbation could be shown to be a different sort of act than lustful masturbation — that it is simply an act of obtaining semen for medical purposes and not the performance of a distinctively sexual act — it still does not follow that acts of this type would be permissible. There are, after all, other effective and practical ways to procure sperm. This activity, even if not essentially directed toward sexual pleasure outside of marriage, ordinarily so stimulates such pleasure, and so inclines the agent to delight in sexual pleasure unrelated to the real goods of sexuality, that it may be an unreasonable way to pursue the medical end. Thus, Pope Pius XII's authoritative condemnation of medically indicated masturbation is realistic and well founded.[40]

We turn to the third objection to the Church's teaching on masturbation: that masturbation is objectively a neutral act which *by itself* lacks any moral disorder. There are several versions of this thesis. One is that no *single* act of masturbation can be seriously wrong; if masturbation is wrong it is only because of the larger lifestyle in which it occurs.[41] Another version is that masturbation cannot be seriously wrong because masturbation is natural or normal, an inevitable phase in personal growth.[42]

The first version of this position — that a single act of masturbation cannot be gravely wrong, that only a sustained practice of masturbation as an essential part of one's life could have such gravity — is based on a view of

182

human action we have shown in Chapter 4 to be mistaken, for the primary locus of moral responsibility is in freely chosen actions, not in patterns of behavior. As Pope John Paul II says, "mortal sin . . . exists when a person knowingly and willingly, for whatever reason, chooses something gravely disordered. In fact, such a choice already includes contempt for the divine law, a rejection of God's love for humanity and the whole of creation; the person turns away from God and loses charity. Consequently, the fundamental orientation [of a person's life] can be radically changed by particular acts."[43]

Of course, one can hold that a single act of masturbation cannot be seriously sinful because masturbation is just not the sort of thing that can be seriously sinful — that is, masturbation is not concerned with "grave matter." This is the second version of the view that masturbation is objectively neutral from the moral perspective. Although it is not surprising that many secular writers on sex regard masturbation as innocent or even good, and hold that the only evil associated with it is the mistaken guilt feeling induced by allegedly wrong moral teaching,[44] it is surprising that some Catholic moralists approximate this view. The reason why some Catholic moralists deny that masturbation is concerned with grave matter appears to be their conviction that something so statistically common cannot be seriously wrong.[45]

Now it appears to be the case that masturbation is very common, especially among adolescent males.[46] The moral significance of the statistics in this matter, however, is anything but clear. They report that many people have engaged in this behavior, but they do not indicate the nature of the individual's responsibility for such acts. Nor do they indicate the extent to which those who have masturbated do so frequently, or do so with or without judging their actions to be immoral or shameful, and so on.

Surely, these statistics do not contradict the experience of many confessors over the centuries which shows that those who earnestly desire to turn away from such practices find the resources to do so. It must be remembered that true moral norms state what ought to be the case, not what statistically is the case. A moral norm is not therefore a statistical generalization and cannot be refuted by information about what is statistically common. Thus, it does not follow from the fact that because the normal attitudes of a certain population are racist, the racism of the population is not objectively immoral. Nor would it follow from the fact that because most believers denied their faith during a certain persecution, it is not seriously wrong to deny one's faith. This argument therefore does nothing to undercut the common teaching of the Church that deliberate masturbation, like other sexual sins, is *seriously* wrong. The received teaching of the Church is only too clear. From the perspective of faith, there is no ground to doubt

183

that masturbating is gravely wrong. Christian tradition has taught this constantly,[47] and the reasons for this teaching are integral to the Church's understanding of sexuality, chastity, and human life.

But the statistical information on which this invalid argument is based may suggest that masturbation is often not a fully human act.[48] As we have already indicated, the Church recognizes that even when a person does what is seriously wrong, the agent is not always fully responsible for the act. The act may be compulsive behavior for which the agent bears only indirect responsibility; moreover, an act can be in some measure deliberate and still not be fully free if it proceeds from weakness of the will. Whether or not a given act is truly a human act is determined by an empirical consideration of the circumstances of the act and the agent's state of mind and heart at the time. Nevertheless, the results of behavioral sciences can be very helpful in making these often difficult determinations. Moreover, the knowledge gained from behavioral sciences can be very useful in helping people to deal with compulsive behavior or morally bad habits. It would be a mistake, however, to assume that, in general, individuals or certain types of individuals are not responsible for their sexual behavior: "This would be to misunderstand people's moral capacity."[49]

As John Paul II says, "clearly, situations can occur which are very complex and obscure from a psychological viewpoint, and which influence the sinner's subjective imputability. But from a consideration of the psychological sphere one cannot proceed to create a theological category, which is precisely what 'fundamental option' is, understanding it in such a way that it objectively changes or casts doubt upon the traditional concept of mortal sin."[50]

To sum up: the Church has always taught that masturbation is seriously wrong. Even though the Church recognizes that sins of this type are sometimes not fully imputable, and pastors have shown great gentleness and understanding in helping those who wish to overcome sins of this type, the Church has never qualified her authoritative teaching on the serious wrongness of masturbation. Moreover, the objections to this teaching are based on poor arguments or perspectives contrary to the received teachings of the faith. There is no doubt therefore that the Christian ideal of chastity excludes masturbation, and that it is possible for Christians to acquire the ability to live in accord with this teaching.

III. Incomplete Acts of Lust

The Church has regularly taught in her ordinary teaching that all lustful acts (though not all acts of immodesty) are objectively gravely sinful.

This is true not only of complete acts, acts which aim to complete sexual satisfaction through orgasm, but of all direct and deliberate acts of lust. Thus, solitary acts that would stir up sexual pleasure but not proceed toward complete sexual satisfaction, and acts of fondling or kissing aimed precisely at stirring up sexual arousal in oneself or one's partner even if one does not intend this to lead toward complete external sins — are objectively gravely sinful.[51]

There is always some difficulty in teaching these matters in balanced ways to young people. The sexual practices common even among admired people in our media age and the forms of kissing and fondling that are seen in entertainment by persons presented even as role models may make it seem strange and excessively prudish to suggest that there could be grave immorality in conduct which seems so common. Yet there is a profound inner consistency to the truth the Church teaches in her sexual ethics. Young people conditioned to believe that kisses and caresses of a kind that are intentionally lustful (though they may not fully realize this, and may not be fully culpable if they engage in these), will find it unreasonable to believe that masturbation or premarital sex can really be wrong in somewhat later years.

Care, imagination, intelligence, and sensitivity are always necessary in teaching sexual ethics to the young. They need to realize that excluding deliberately lustful dimensions from the acts in which they show affection in no way means that they cannot be spontaneous and joyful in their expression of real affection. Intelligent teaching of all that the Church has learned of chaste and self-possessed love is liberating and bracing; it does not impoverish human life.

IV. Homosexual Acts

Homosexuality is a complex phenomenon, so much so that the researchers A. Bell and M. Weinberg entitled their massive study *Homosexualities* because they discovered great diversity in lifestyle and personality among the nearly one thousand homosexual men and women interviewed for their work.[52] It is not appropriate, however, to label a person "homosexual," even if he or she has this orientation, because there is something more fundamental about the person. Indeed, the Church, "refuses to consider the person as 'heterosexual' or 'homosexual' and insists that every person has a fundamental identity: the creature of God and, by grace, his child and heir to eternal life."[53] Thus in this section our focus will be on homosexual *acts*.

But before addressing the issue of the morality of homosexual acts some brief remarks concerning the homosexual orientation will be helpful.

185

A person is said to have a homosexual orientation if he or she (1) is attracted physically and erotically by persons of his or her own sex; (2) usually has no similar attraction to the opposite sex; and (3) in many instances has a positive revulsion for sexual acts with a member of the opposite sex. It has traditionally been used to describe a "persistent and predominant attraction of a sexual-genital nature to persons of one's own sex."[54] The attribute common to all homosexuals, however divergent their lifestyles and personalities, is this persistent and predominant erotic attraction to persons of the same sex.[55]

Several consequences of this description of the homosexual condition should be noted. First, one may be homosexually oriented and not engage in homosexual acts,[56] and one may not be so oriented and nonetheless choose to engage in them. Thus, the prisoner or adolescent[57] who engages in homosexual acts is not necessarily a homosexual; and persons with this orientation can, and do, live lives of perfect chastity. Second, as empirical studies show, the description allows for a spectrum of personality types going from a completely heterosexual orientation to a completely homosexual orientation.[58]

Stress on Homosexual Acts. The moral judgment of the Church is directed toward homosexual acts and not toward the homosexual condition. To a large extent this condition is not voluntarily established and is thus outside of direct rational control.[59] The reason for this emphasis on homosexual acts is that morality is concerned with how a person should live one's life, to the extent that living one's life is within one's control, and one's freely chosen acts are the part of one's life that is most fully within one's control.

The homosexual condition may make certain acts appear to be attractive options, but this condition is not itself freely chosen — it is not an act. Nor for many homosexuals is the condition something that can be readily or even significantly altered. However, the claim that the homosexual orientation is irreversible cannot be sustained. There is now abundant evidence, attested to by competent professionals, both secular and religious, to support the "modest conclusion that some persons with a homosexual orientation can acquire a heterosexual one through a process of prayer, group support, and sound therapy. [But] this is not to say that everyone who seeks such a change is able to attain it."[60]

Homosexual acts, however, can be freely chosen and even when done without entirely free choice are frequently in some measure voluntary. These acts therefore are proper objects for moral evaluation; and the homosexual condition is morally relevant as part of the determination of the imputability of homosexual acts.

186

Immorality of Homosexual Acts. The Church's constant teaching on the morality of homosexual acts is unequivocal: such acts are of their very nature seriously wrong. This teaching is clearly based on Scripture and is rooted in the biblical understanding of sexuality. The Bible teaches that the sexual differentiation of the human race into male and female is divinely willed, that male and female complement each other and that marriage, rooted in the irrevocable consent of man and woman to be "one flesh" for life, alone respects the goods of human sexuality. Thus, Scripture teaches that marriage provides the normative condition for genital sexual expression; all other expressions of this kind, whether between man and woman or between members of the same sex, are to be evaluated in the light of this norm.[61]

In addition to this general scriptural account of human sexuality, there are specific biblical passages referring to homosexual acts, and in each of these passages such acts are unambiguously condemned. There are five clear references to male homosexual acts and one to female.[62] The reference in Romans 1:26-27 is in some ways the most telling since homosexual behavior is regarded as a punishment for disbelief: "For this reason God gave them up to dishonorable passions. Their women exchanged natural relations for unnatural, and the men likewise gave up natural relations with women and were consumed with passion for one another, men committing shameless acts with men and receiving in their own persons the due penalty for their error."

Thus, the Church's constant and firm teaching that homosexual acts are seriously wrong is clearly rooted in Scripture. There is no doubt that the Church has taught and believed homosexual acts to be wrong. This is reflected in the writings of the classical theologians and in the approved authors of recent centuries.[63] The *Catechism of the Catholic Church*, speaking of homosexual acts, declares:

> Basing itself on Sacred Scripture, which presents homosexual acts as acts of grave depravity (with references to Gen 19:1-29; Rom 1:24-27; 1 Cor 6:10, and 1 Tim 1:10), tradition has always declared that "homosexual acts are intrinsically disordered" (a citation from the *Vatican Declaration on Certain Questions of Sexual Ethics [Persona Humana]*, no. 8). They are contrary to the natural law. They close the sexual act to the gift of life. They do not proceed from a genuine affective and sexual complementarity. Under no circumstances can they be approved (no. 2387).

187

Both the *Catechism* (no. 2358) and the *Vatican Declaration on Certain Questions of Sexual Ethics* (no.8), which it cites approvingly in the passage quoted above, are careful to stress the distinction between the homosexual *inclination* or orientation and homosexual *acts*, noting that the former is not chosen. But since some persons, in their interpretation of the 1975 *Vatican Declaration* gave an "overly benign interpretation . . . to the homosexual condition itself, some going so far as to call it neutral or even good," the Congregation for the Doctrine of the Faith found it necessary, in 1986, to affirm that the homosexual inclination, "while not a sin, is a more or less strong tendency toward an intrinsic moral evil and thus the inclination itself must be seen as an objective disorder."[64]

But, and this is the critical matter, the *moral* judgment of the Church bears on homosexual *acts*, and, as has been shown, this judgment affirms that such acts are intrinsically evil, firmly condemned by Scripture, and contrary to natural law.

Finally, it is perhaps worth pointing out that the enemies of Christianity have noted the essential connection between Christian ethics and the condemnation of homosexual activity. As James Hitchcock has pointed out:

> Beginning at least as early as Victorian and Edwardian litterateurs like John Addington Symonds and E.M. Forster, intellectualized homosexuality in the modern West has consciously repudiated Christianity as a distorted, inhumane religion which snuffed out the joyous, guilt-free paganism of ancient times. The intent of this homophilia has been to re-create as far as possible the conditions of that ancient paganism, for which the destruction of Christianity as a cultural influence has been seen as an essential prerequisite. Such a view of history, which from the homosexual viewpoint is to a great extent correct, is continued into the present by, among others, Gore Vidal, the admirer of Julian the Apostate, who manifests both the obsessive anti-Christian sentiment and the contempt and hostility toward heterosexual values which seems characteristic of much of the homosexual subculture.[65]

Contemporary Objections to Catholic Teaching. Despite the long-standing teaching of the Church on the objective immorality of homosexual activity, some recent Catholic writers have denied that homosexual activity is always wrong.

These writers argue that (1) the biblical evidence is inconclusive and

188

(2) homosexual activity between homosexually oriented persons (which, they maintain, was not envisioned by the biblical writers) — when this occurs within a relatively stable relationship — is either essentially good and natural, or is at least morally acceptable as the best that can be expected of persons with a homosexual orientation.[66] These writers argue, with respect to the biblical foundation for the teaching, that the story of Sodom and Gomorrah does not involve a condemnation of the homosexual practices of those cities but rather of their inhospitality.[67] Likewise, they claim that the condemnations of homosexual activity in the New Testament are condemnations of idolatrous homosexual acts or of homosexual acts chosen by heterosexuals.[68]

These objections based on the interpretation of Scripture are not well founded. They generally presuppose that the received position on homosexual acts is entirely dependent upon a few isolated proof texts. In fact, however, the Catholic teaching follows necessarily from the whole scriptural vision of what man and woman are, of what sexuality means, and of the nature of morality. If the classical texts on homosexual acts were to be removed altogether from Scripture, the immorality of such acts would still be an obvious implication of the biblical view of sexuality. It should be noted, however, that recent attempts to destroy the force of the classical texts have been shown to be seriously flawed.[69]

Theological Reasons. The basic theological reasons why homosexual acts are always morally wrong, summarized in passage previously cited from the *Catechism of the Catholic Church* (no. 2357), are well presented in the Congregation for the Doctrine of the Faith's *Letter to Bishops of the Catholic Church on the Pastoral Care of the Homosexual Person.* These reasons are based ultimately on God's plan regarding the life-giving and loving union of man and woman in marriage. This entails that "only in the marital relationship [is] the use of the sexual faculty . . . morally good." From this it follows that "to choose someone of the same sex for one's sexual activity is to annul the rich symbolism and meaning, not to mention the goals, of the Creator's sexual design. Homosexual activity is not a complementary union able to transmit life; and so it thwarts the call to a life of that form of self-giving which the Gospel says is the essence of Christian living." Moreover, like every moral disorder, "homosexual activity prevents one's own fulfillment and happiness by acting contrary to the creative wisdom of God."[70]

We have seen that Scripture celebrates sex as life-giving of its very nature. True, not every upright genital act will originate a new life; neither need one intend that it will. There are other worthy goals of sexual activity

189

also. But the life-giving aspect of sexual activity must always be guarded and respected, or sex is trivialized and made inhuman. Genital activity must always be of a kind that does not assail or scorn the procreative good; it must not be structured in ways that rob it of its life-giving thrust. The life-giving meaning of human sexuality is always good and worthy of respect. An awe for this power and a love for the life it can give are essential for the human development of sexuality. But homosexual activity must leave altogether out of consideration this aspect of human sexuality which transcends the activity itself and is essential for its human significance.

Genital activity, moreover, has a life-uniting or person-uniting dimension or meaning. Genital acts serve to join two persons, two lives, by a special kind of love. This is marital love — a love that has an exclusive and enduring quality about it, precisely because it has reference to the life-giving end or meaning of genital sexuality.[71] This is a love which opens those whom it unites to what is other than themselves, to a transcendent goal or good toward which they can commit themselves and their shared lives. But this sort of love is simply incapable of being expressed in homosexual activity. In the homosexual union "the authentic human sense of the other, as nourished by the enriching and complementary otherness of the other sex, is conspicuously absent."[72]

Many forms of homosexual life clearly seek the pleasure of orgasm isolated from any genuinely and authentically satisfying human good.[73] To seek pleasure in good acts, acts that retain their ties to and further real human goods, is not morally wrong. But to organize one's life around the pleasure of orgasms in acts which separate sexual activity from its precious human goods is unreasonable and immoral. Homosexual life is a bitter form of life, for it is founded on actions which pursue not the real goods of human persons but only the mere appearances of these goods. The unhappiness of many homosexuals is a sign that their lives are not properly oriented toward what is truly good.[74]

Many object that not all homosexuality is of this kind. Some homosexual relationships are relatively stable, and at times, perhaps, are as stable as the relationships between some faithful spouses. Homosexuals can love each other, and wish to share and unite their lives.[75]

But even these homosexual relationships, if they involve homosexual actions, are deeply flawed. They do not and cannot have the inner dynamism toward permanence and fidelity which the marriage relationship can have. Homosexual activity is essentially disordered because it cannot be directed toward nor have a proper respect for the goods of human sexuality. Recall that the lovemaking of spouses is directed either toward having chil-

190

dren, or is expressive of a love that essentially includes an orientation toward the fruitfulness of procreation. The love of spouses can and must be enduring because it is essentially related to enduring goods; but homosexual love simply is not ordered to any transcendent good that essentially requires of the partners utter self-giving and faithfulness until death. A marital kind of friendship cannot obtain among homosexuals; their sexual act cannot express a marital kind of love, for they cannot be what spouses are. Their sexual acts cannot be procreative and cannot express a love that is inherently fruitful and procreative.[76]

Some apologists for homosexual activity between partners in a stable relationship which they consider to be the moral equivalent of marriage, argue that although homosexual unions cannot share in the good of procreation, the same is true of the genital union of married men and women who know that they are sterile.[77] This objection, however, is based on the false presupposition that the marriage of man and woman is merely an instrumental good for achieving an end that is intrinsically good, namely, the procreation and education of children. But this understanding of marriage is woefully inadequate. The marital act, which makes the spouses to be literally one body, the "single subject, as it were, of sexual life,"[78] is, of course, the sort of act fit for the gift of new human life. But the procreation of new human life is *not* some good extrinsic to the marriage itself but an intrinsic fulfillment of the good of marriage itself.[79] Children are not "products" that spouses make; rather they are "gifts, which, if all goes well, supervene on their acts of marital union."[80] The whole point of sex in marriage, fertile or not, is the good of marriage itself, considered as a two-in-one-flesh communion of persons consummated and actualized by "marital acts," i.e., acts intrinsically the sort apt to receive the gift of life. The coupling of same sex persons through homosexual acts can in no way be regarded as the consummation and actualization of the marital union of husband and wife.[81]

There are many things homosexual lovers may share and which may form a basis for their life together. However, it is hard to see how their *sexual acts* could express or promote these common goods. To use genital activity, which is essentially ordered to indispensable and distinctive human goods, to serve an affection that cannot minister to such goods — to do these things is to distort radically the finality and sense of these important human acts. That is to say, homosexual acts are of their nature seriously immoral.

Some argue today that true homosexuals can find satisfaction only in homosexual acts, and that there is no reason to believe that all homosexuals are called to the exceptional gift of perfect chastity for the kingdom. Hence, homosexual acts must in some way be permissible for them. But this argument is mistaken, for many people not called to virginal lives (freely undertaken to serve God) find themselves in circumstances in which no sexual activity is licit for them. An example would be a young married person deserted by his or her spouse. Such persons may not have the special graces related to the life of consecrated virginity, but Catholic teaching insists that God makes it possible for them to live as they are required, and that they may not excuse themselves from grave responsibilities because fidelity is, under the circumstances, extremely difficult.

What is the person who finds himself with a homosexual orientation to do? This personal and pastoral question goes far beyond the scope of this study. Nevertheless, homosexual persons can have happy and holy lives, rich in meaning. The fact that they are deeply inclined toward acts of a kind that faith and intelligent reflection show to be immoral is no indication that it might be permissible or even good for them to engage in such acts. There are many persons besides homosexuals who must refrain from the sexual acts toward which they are intensely inclined. Consider the case of spouses whose partners are ill for very long periods, or who are long separated from their partners for any reason. Consider too the case of the heterosexual person who deeply yearns for marriage but never finds someone willing to marry him or her. Such lives, into which the cross of sexual deprivation enters, can still be richly fulfilled lives.

Persons of a homosexual orientation deserve the love and support of the Christian community. They are called to friendship with God and to holiness of life, as are all human persons; and they have distinctive heavy burdens to bear. If, as many homosexuals do, they carry their burdens with generous and chaste fidelity, they support and strengthen all Christians. They become witnesses to the nobility of making great personal sacrifices to guard the great human goods sexuality is ordered to. Should they fall in their human weakness, they should still receive the compassionate concern that all persons long for.

The *Catechism of the Catholic Church* declares that homosexually-oriented men and women "must be accepted with respect, compassion, and sensitivity. Every sign of unjust discrimination in their regard should be avoided. These persons are called to fulfill God's will in their lives and, if they are Christians, to unite to the sacrifice of the Lord's Cross the difficulties they may encounter from their condition" (no. 2358).

Pastoral ministry, rooted in an acceptance and respect for the Church's teaching on homosexual acts, is needed. One of the most helpful of such ministries is "Courage," a group founded by Father John Harvey, O.S.F.S., dedicated to providing persons homosexually oriented with the Christian group support they need to live chaste lives.[82]

The judgment that homosexual acts are wrong does not suggest how one should react to the homosexual-rights movement. Certainly the rights of all persons must be supported. This does not mean that any group has the right to demand that society count as innocent those acts or forms of life that are intrinsically immoral. What it does mean is that the difference in personality structure innocently incurred by some may not be treated as excuses for despising or treating unfairly brothers and sisters in Christ.

V. Bestiality

Bestial acts are those in which a human being copulates with a nonrational animal.[83] Such acts are repulsive to most people and are fairly uncommon.[84] Most people regard bestiality as seriously perverse, and this common opinion is confirmed by Scripture and Church teaching. In the Old Testament, bestiality is condemned as seriously wrong; its punishment was either death or exile.[85] Bestiality is universally condemned by the approved authors as the worst of the unnatural sins against chastity.[86]

The reasons for this severe judgment are readily seen. In bestiality, sex is used in a way that totally thwarts its interpersonal dimensions. Moreover, there is a complete perversion of the order between man and nature intended by God. Sexual activity should express a sublime love for another person and respect for great human goods. To use sexuality to gratify oneself in ways that make personal relationships and shared care for great goods impossible is a gross abuse of one's sexuality.

One might expect that even those moralists who deny that there are absolutes in most areas of sexual morality would clearly acknowledge that bestial behavior is, objectively, always gravely wrong.

But some revisionary Catholic authors cannot bring themselves to condemn even bestiality unequivocally, perhaps because the principles needed to do this would require acknowledging moral absolutes elsewhere as well. It is not enough to acknowledge that "this practice renders impossible the realization of the personal meaning of human sexuality." Concern for the personal growth of those sadly involved in such conduct is good: "Persons so involved need to be gently led to a deeper understanding and appreciation of the full meaning and significance of human sexuality,"[87] for bestial behavior can surely indicate a pathological condition. But moralists should not avoid the duty of providing a moral evaluation of such acts. Bestial acts can be freely chosen; and, if freely chosen, they are always seriously wrong.

193

VI. Rape

The grave immorality of rape seems to be admitted by all.[88] Certainly it is condemned by the Church as a form of lustful behavior that is especially wicked because of the forced and unjust violation of the intimacy of another person.[89]

Rape is the extreme case — perhaps the paradigm case — of treating the person assailed, usually a woman, as a sex object. One of the least controversial objectives of the women's liberation movement has been the protesting of the treatment of women as sex objects, whether in the extreme form of rape, or in pornography, or in the attitude of those who regard women as little more than sources of amusement. The bodies of men and women are not things to be used; men and women are personal in all of their reality. The sexual dimension of a person is properly respected only if it is used in a personal way, in pursuit of a free and personal union.

Rape has become much more frequent in recent years.[90] Many moral factors may be related to this fact. Many in our time consider masturbation morally harmless, and masturbation involves treating one's own body as a "sex object." Pornography is epidemic and recreational sex is widely approved. Both of these phenomena degrade women and treat them not as persons but as objects. Moreover, self-possession in chastity is widely mocked as prudery or as unhealthy repression. Our culture tends to forget that chastity is a necessary requirement for making sexual activity a personal relationship concerned with authentic human goods, and for guarding the world from the barbarism of crimes like rape.

The horror of rape and the trauma it frequently induces in its victims point to the personal and especially intimate depths of human sexuality. Rape is not only an unjust invasion of the person, it is an especially abhorrent invasion. It is altogether more offensive than other violent assaults. Why should this be, if our sexuality were simply another biological function, without inherent ordering to precious values, to be used as people like? The natural abhorrence of rape — even on the part of those who insist that there are no special moral norms in the area of human sexuality — makes clear that sexual activity has a special significance. It is not a routine human activity like taking a walk or eating a snack.[91]

The victim of rape is a victim, not an offender, and deserves sensitive care. Those threatened with rape are not required to offer resistance that is foreseen to be useless or perilous to their lives; but they have the right to resist violently, even if the life of the assailant is endangered. Their own dignity requires that they not cooperate willingly in this assault on their persons. Society has a grave duty to help establish conditions that minimize the occurrence of this crime.

The efforts of a woman to prevent the sperm of her assailant from fertilizing her ovum is not a contraceptive act.[92] To say that it is legitimate for her to seek to prevent conception in this way is not an exception to the universal prohibition of contraception. Contraception occurs when one who freely chooses to have sexual intercourse seeks to prevent the act from having its fruitful outcome.[93] But abortifacient procedures after a rape are morally of a very different nature; they are not defenses against an unjust invasion but attacks on an innocent person — that is, they are acts of abortion[94] and therefore are not permissible.

VII. Incest

Incest is a sin of lust between two persons closely related by blood or affinity. Sexual intercourse or lustful fondling between parent and child or stepchild, or between siblings, would exemplify this sin. We are not here concerned to treat the reasons why marriage between close relatives is forbidden by divine and positive law. What we want to point out here is that there is a twofold malice in incest. It is a sin of lust, an act in which pleasure is irrationally pursued, with gross disregard for the values toward which, of its nature and of divine will, human sexuality is essentially ordered. But it is also ordinarily seen as sin against piety, a failure to give the special honor and love due to those bound together in the close ties of the family.[95]

Sins of incest seem to have become much more common than they once were. At one time the instinctive revulsion against this sin was strong and an effective repressant. But an age that has liberated lust and tended to enslave human persons more deeply to passion has blinded many to the cruelty of this deed, and the grave harm that it so regularly causes. The reasons *why* incest is wrong are parallel to those that explain the malice of other lustful acts, and a culture that fails to recognize the depth and value-relatedness of sexual activity generally needs great help to escape falling into the most inhuman excesses.

VIII. Purity in Thought and Modesty

Realistic moral thinking has always been concerned with purity of heart as well as of external action. The ninth precept of the Decalogue, "You shall not covet your neighbor's wife" (Ex 20:17) is illuminated by the saying of Jesus: "Every one who looks at a woman lustfully has already committed adultery with her in his heart" (Mt 5:28). The inner life of a person — that is, the desires and inclinations freely cultivated in the mind and imagination — is also important in the moral life as it is taught by Catholic faith. Catholic morality is not concerned only with achieving good effects in this world but in guiding men and women toward excellent lives through the free actions of their lives — internal actions as well as external ones.[96]

Obviously self-possession in thought, imagination, and desire has considerable instrumental value for leading a chaste life. One who so controls the inner life will find it much easier to avoid the evils we have been discussing in this chapter and the last. However, the value of internal chastity is not merely instrumental. To have a pure heart and mind is itself an excellent and irreducibly important thing. Without inner self-possession, not only will a person's whole life be in moral disarray but the person's very self is fatally compromised.

Here, we note briefly basic guidelines that illumine the morality of thoughts and desires concerning sexual activity.[97]

(1) Simply thinking about sexual matters is obviously not of itself sinful. To think about sexual activity even of the most sinful kind may be done innocently, even virtuously, when it is done for reasonable motives and with intelligent respect for all the values concerned, including the values of one's own self-possession and integrity. Theologians, moral educators, artists, and many others often have important reasons to reflect on matters that could easily stir up sexual passions. A morally mature person knows ways to make the dangers of falling into sin remote when responsibly reflecting on such matters.

(2) One may, however, entertain sexual thoughts in thoroughly lustful ways as well. This is a matter not simply of "thinking about" such matters but of choosing deliberately to direct the affections in seriously disordered ways, irresponsibly disregarding the goods the heart should cherish. Thus, a certain kind of evil desire is really lustful and seriously wrong — namely the choice or resolve to do deeds that are gravely wrong. Such an inner act is of the kind condemned by the Lord in the Gospel (Mt 5:28). Another kind of inner act is also lustful — namely what might be called "deliberate complacency" in unchaste thoughts. In choosing to take delight in inner representations of things that are lustful, one is choosing in a disordered way, making oneself an unchaste person. Thus, if done with full deliberation, such choices are gravely sinful; when such delight is accepted with less freedom or deliberateness, the measure of guilt will be less, and when the delight is completely nonvoluntary there is no guilt at all.

196

(3) Those who entertain thoughts of a sexual nature that are likely to stir the passions and perhaps lead them to fall into external or internal sins of lust without the good reasons and care suggested in number 1 (above) — but also without the lustful choice noted in number 2 — may be said to be behaving in an *immodest* rather than in a strictly lustful way.

Modesty is a virtue that guards chastity. There are many kinds of actions that can be good or bad: kisses, embraces, forms of dressing and dancing, thoughts of sexual matters and the reading, conversations, forms of entertainment, and the like that stimulate such thoughts. Such actions can be virtuous; kisses and embraces, for example, can be excellent expressions of a right affection, or they can be strictly lustful. For example, when one engages in any of these activities as a prelude to lustful acts, or if they are now engaged in with lustful desires or complacencies.

One behaves immodestly when one's internal or external acts in matters that could lead toward sins of lust are not reasonable. Such acts can be objectively either grave or venial. If one engages in immodest thoughts or behaviors out of curiosity or playfulness — in circumstances in which there is no serious danger of falling into sins of lust, but some risk is present (and there is no reasonable ground for creating that danger) — one's sin is ordinarily venial. Behavior of a kind that ordinarily stimulates sexual passions vehemently, and is a proximate occasion of serious sin, is gravely wrong.

Since in questions of modesty we are not speaking of acts that are intrinsically wrong but of inner and outer acts whose morality is derived from their relationships to other factors, the concrete morality of immodest acts is derived from the circumstances of each case. Obviously what constitutes modesty in dress, language, and the like is highly relative to time and circumstances. But this does not suggest that modesty is merely a matter of opinion; intelligent rules of thumb can be formulated which hold for most cases. It can be clear and certain that, in these given circumstances, to attend a certain obscene motion picture or to read a particular obscene book would be a grave offense against modesty, or even a direct offense against chastity itself.

Parents, confessors, catechists, and other moral teachers need an intelligent grasp of the basic principles of Christian modesty such as they have been given in the ordinary teaching of the Church. Their own education in modesty is not derived merely from study but from the experience of acquiring self-possession and chastity, and from learning the need to guard chastity with intelligently lived modesty. We live in times in which it is difficult to give materially specific directives with clarity. Still, moral teach-

197

ers must seek to give concrete guidance in these matters with sensitive and intelligent care, for a contempt for modesty is evident in much modern entertainment, literature, and advertising. The minds and imaginations of people can be corrupted, and their efforts to achieve self-possession in sexual matters can be undermined, if moral education does not include a bracing education in Christian modesty.

Chapter Nine

Recent Magisterial Teaching and "Catholic Sexual Ethics"

This chapter was first written in 1995, prior to preparing the updated text of *Catholic Sexual Ethics (CSE)*. It now appears in the updated edition, in which we have integrated throughout relevant material from the documents summarized in this chapter. Still this survey of important recent magisterial documents on human sexuality has proved helpful to many. It is thus included in the second edition. Moreover, since this chapter was first written, another very helpful magisterial document has been promulgated, namely, the Pontifical Council for the Family's *The Truth and Meaning of Human Sexuality*. Thus, in revising this chapter we have included a summary of this worthwhile document.

The documents to be summarized are, in chronological order, the following:

(1) *Letter to the Bishops of the Catholic Church on the Pastoral Care of Homosexual Persons*, promulgated by the Congregation for the Doctrine of the Faith on October 1, 1986;

(2) *The Instruction on Respect for Human Life in Its Origin and on the Dignity of Procreation: Replies to Certain Questions of the Day*, promulgated by the Congregation for the Doctrine of the Faith on February 22, 1987;

(3) *The Catechism of the Catholic Church*, promulgated by Pope John Paul II in 1992 (the original text, in French, was officially released on December 8, 1992; the English translation, however, was not published until 1994);

(4) the Holy Father's encyclical *Veritatis Splendor ["The Splendor of Truth"], Addressed to All the Bishops of the Catholic Church Regarding Certain Fundamental Questions of the Church's Moral Teaching*, dated August 6, 1993, and released in October of 1993;

(5) the Holy Father's *Letter to Families*, promulgated on February 2, 1994;

(6) the Holy Father's encyclical *Evangelium Vitae* *["The Gospel of Life"], Addressed to the Bishops, Priests and Deacons, Men and Women Religious, Lay Faithful, and All People of Good Will on the Value and Inviolability of Human Life*, dated March 25, 1995,

(7) *The Truth and Meaning of Human Sexuality: Guidelines for Education within the Family*, issued by the Pontifical Council for the Family, December 8, 1995.

Of these documents, the *Catechism of the Catholic Church* is of the very greatest importance; moreover, it is relevant in some way to everything taken up in *CSE*. It provides an authoritative interpretation of the biblical teaching on sex and marriage (Ch. 2), integrates the understanding of sex in the Catholic tradition (Ch. 3), reaffirms and develops the Church's authoritative teaching on sex and marriage (Ch. 1), sets forth authoritatively the basic principles and norms of Catholic moral life (Ch. 4), discusses the nature and meaning of conscience, the proper way to form a Catholic conscience, and the relationship between personal conscience and the teaching of the Church on moral issues (Ch. 5), and reaffirms and relates to life today the teaching of the Church on chastity, Christian marriage, and virginity (Ch. 6), on the requirements of chastity within marriage (Ch. 7), on the requirements of chastity outside the covenant of married love (Ch. 8), and offers pastoral guidance (Pastoral Conclusion).

The great encyclicals of John Paul II, *Veritatis Splendor* and *Evangelium Vitae*, are also of highest importance. They do not, however, address all the issues taken up in *CSE*. *Veritatis Splendor*, though, is of crucial importance in regard to matters discussed in Chapters 4 and 5 (on patterns of thinking in moral theology and on conscience) and bears on some specific moral issues taken up in *CSE*. *Evangelium Vitae*, a masterful and highly important encyclical, is not directly concerned with the matters taken up in *CSE*. It does, however, speak eloquently of the indispensable role that Christian married couples have to play in developing a culture of life. This is also true of the pope's *Letter to Families*, which develops central truths proclaimed by the Church on marriage and family life.

The two documents of the Congregation for the Doctrine of the Faith (on the pastoral care of homosexual persons and on respect for human life in its origin and the dignity of procreation) are of great importance for some specific matters covered above in the text, namely, homosexual acts and the generation of human life outside the marital embrace.

The Pontifical Council for the Family's document on human sexuality is of particular importance for material considered above in Chapter 6.

200

Procedure

These seven documents will now be examined. They will not, however, be taken up in chronological order. We will first consider the two documents from the Congregation for the Doctrine of the Faith, numbers 1 and 2 above. We will then consider together Pope John Paul II's *Letter to Families* and his encyclical *Evangelium Vitae* in order to show how the teaching in them develops the Catholic understanding of marriage and the mission entrusted to Christian spouses (documents number 5 and number 6 above). Next we will summarize the teaching found in the Pontifical Council for the Family's *The Truth and Meaning of Human Sexuality*. We will end by considering in more detail the significance of the teaching found in Pope John Paul II's encyclical *Veritatis Splendor* and in the *Catechism of the Catholic Church* (documents number 4 and number 3 above), inasmuch as the Holy Father's encyclical provides extensive and precise magisterial teaching on many topics considered in *CSE* and the *Catechism* treats of almost every issue addressed in it.

I. Letter to Bishops of the Catholic Church on the Pastoral Care of Homosexual Persons

The Congregation for the Doctrine of the Faith's *Letter to the Bishops of the Catholic Church on the Pastoral Care of Homosexual Persons* (October 1, 1986) is a very brief, clearly written document, containing eighteen numbered sections. Its contents can be summarized as follows: (1) an introduction setting forth the problem (no. 1); (2) the competence of the Church in this matter (no. 2); (3) contemporary confusion and mistaken interpretations (no. 3); (4) identification of causes of confusion, principally erroneous interpretations of Scripture and correction of these misinterpretations (nos. 4-6); (5) further bases for the Church's teaching (nos. 7-8); (6) pressure groups, civil legislation, proper reaction to crimes against homosexuals (nos. 9-10); (7) critique of one argument to justify homosexual acts (no. 11); (8) vocation of homosexual persons (no. 12); (9) need for correct communication of Church teaching (no. 13); (10) responsibilities of bishops to resist pressure groups (no. 14) and to provide true pastoral care (no. 15); (11) advantages of sound teaching and pastoral programs (no. 16); (12) admonitions to bishops (no. 17); and (13) conclusion (no. 18).

The following points are of most significance with respect to the material on homosexual acts found on pp. 185-193; (1) the competence of the Church; (2) mistaken interpretations of the *Vatican Declaration on Certain Questions of Sexual Ethics* ("*Persona Humana*"); (3) erroneous interpreta-

201

tions of Scripture and their correction; (4) further bases for the Church's teaching; (5) pressure groups, particularly within the Church, and the role of civil legislation; (6) critique of one argument to justify homosexual acts; (7) the homosexual's vocation; (8) responsibilities of bishops.

A. The Competence of the Church. The *Letter* insists that the Catholic moral perspective "finds support in the more secure findings of the natural sciences"; moreover, and more importantly, this viewpoint is "founded upon human reason illumined by faith and is consciously motivated by the desire to do the will of God, our Father" (no. 2). This perspective transcends "the horizons of science," and its more global vision "does greater justice to the rich reality of the human person in his spiritual and physical dimensions created by God and heir, by grace, to eternal life" (no. 2). Here the Congregation is simply reaffirming the truth of Catholic faith that Jesus has not left us orphans and has invested the magisterium of the Church (that is, the Roman pontiff and bishops in union with him) to speak in his name and hand on integrally the saving truths of faith.

B. Mistaken Interpretations of "Persona Humana" (Vatican Declaration on Certain Questions of Sexual Ethics). The document *Persona Humana* or the *Vatican Declaration on Certain Questions Concerning Sexual Ethics* (treated in *CSE* on pp. 178,187, 256, 280; specifically with reference to homosexual acts, pp. 187) had distinguished between the homosexual condition and individual homosexual acts. But this *Letter* points out that later "an overly benign interpretation was given to the homosexual condition itself, some going so far as to call it neutral or even good" (no. 3). To correct this, the *Letter* affirms that the homosexual inclination, while not a sin, "is a more or less strong tendency ordered toward an intrinsic moral evil and thus the inclination itself *must be seen as an objective disorder*" (no. 3; emphasis added).

It is not too difficult to see that this assertion by the Congregation elicited very strong opposition and charges of homophobia. Nonetheless, the Congregation had to speak the truth. Just as concupiscence, which results from original sin, although not itself a sin, is a strong tendency inclining and enticing human persons to sin, and just as the condition of alcoholism, while not itself a sin, nonetheless strongly disposes persons subject to it to abuse alcohol, so too does the homosexual inclination, while not sinful itself, strongly dispose those persons subject to it to abuse the gift of sexuality. In stating this truth the Congregation in no way offers a demeaning judgment about persons who are homosexually oriented. The Congregation's concern is with their pastoral *care*, with helping them to lead chaste lives and to use the means necessary to resist the temptation, at times strongly felt because of their homosexual orientation, to engage in objectively bad sexual acts.

C. *Erroneous Interpretations of Sacred Scripture and Their Correction.* The *Letter* identifies as one of the major causes of current confusion regarding the Church's teaching a "new exegesis of Sacred Scripture which claims variously that Scripture has nothing to say on the subject of homosexuality or that it somehow tacitly approves of it or that all of its moral injunctions are so culture bound that they are no longer applicable to contemporary life" (no. 4). The *Letter* declares that these views are "gravely erroneous" (no. 4).

In correcting these views the document notes that, although many things have changed since the time the Scriptures were written, "there is nonetheless a clear consistency within the Scriptures themselves on the moral issue of homosexual behavior. The Church's doctrine regarding this issue is thus based not on isolated phrases for facile theological argument, but on the solid foundation of a constant biblical testimony." Moreover, "it is essential to recognize that the Scriptures are not properly understood when they are interpreted in a way which contradicts the Church's living tradition. To be correct, the interpretation of Scripture must be in accord with that tradition" (no. 5). The *Letter* then cites an important passage of Vatican II's Dogmatic Constitution on Divine Revelation, *Dei Verbum* (no. 10), affirming that sacred tradition, Sacred Scripture, and the magisterium of the Church are "so connected and associated that one of them cannot stand without the others" (no. 5). *This is a key hermeneutical principle in Catholic theology*, a principle emphasized throughout *Catholic Sexual Ethics*.

The *Letter* then indicates the solid bases, within Scripture, for the Church's teaching: (a) the creation of man as male and female, meant to cooperate with God in giving life to new human persons; (b) the fall and resulting concupiscence; (c) the judgments on homosexual behavior found in the Sodom and Gomorrah story in Genesis 19, Leviticus 18:22 and 20:13, the teaching of Paul in 1 Corinthians 6:9 and Romans 1:18-32, and finally the significance of 1 Timothy 1:10 (no. 6).

D. *Further Bases for the Church's Teaching.* The *Letter* continues by affirming that the Church's teaching on homosexual acts is rooted in God's plan regarding the life-giving and loving union of man and woman in marriage. This entails that "only in the marital relationship [is] the use of the sexual faculty . . . morally good" (no. 7). From this it follows that "to choose someone of the same sex for one's sexual activity is to annul the rich symbolism and meaning, not to mention the goals, of the Creator's sexual design. Homosexual activity is not a complementary union able to transmit

203

life; and so it thwarts the call to a life of that form of self-giving which the Gospel says is the essence of Christian living." Moreover, like every moral disorder, "homosexual activity prevents one's own fulfillment and happiness by acting contrary to the creative wisdom of God" (no. 7).

E. Pressure Groups and the Role of Civil Law. The *Letter* points out that many today, even within the Church, exert pressure to accept the homosexual condition as if it were not disordered and to condone homosexual activity. It observes that those within the Church holding this view often have close ties to people with similar views outside of the Church, people "guided by a vision opposed to the truth about the human person, which is fully disclosed in the mystery of Christ," a vision reflecting, even if not consciously, a "materialistic ideology" (no. 8). The *Letter* insists that the ministers of the Church not allow homosexual persons in their care to be misled by this point of view. It likewise notes that some pressure groups within the Church holding this view falsely seek to create the impression that they speak for all homosexual persons, and it points out that "one tactic used is to protest that any and all criticism of or reservations about homosexual people, their activity and lifestyle are simply diverse forms of unjust discrimination" (nos. 8-9).

Warning about deceitful propaganda, the Congregation urges resistance to legislation that would legitimate the homosexual lifestyle. The Church's position actually defends homosexuals from deceit and is rooted in the clear awareness that "the view that homosexual activity is equivalent to or as acceptable as the sexual expression of conjugal love has a direct impact on society's understanding of the nature and rights of the family and puts them in jeopardy" (no. 9).

While decrying violence in speech or action against homosexual persons, which deserves condemnation, the *Letter* makes it clear that the proper reaction to such crimes "should not be to claim that the homosexual condition is not disordered," and that no one should be surprised that if this claim is accepted, "other distorted notions and practices gain ground and irrational and violent reactions increase" (no. 10).

F. Critique of an Argument Justifying Homosexual Acts. The Congregation then considers one common argument given to justify homosexual acts, namely, that homosexually oriented persons have no other choice than to act in a homosexual way because of their lack of freedom (no. 11). The *Letter* repudiates this position because it is rooted in the "unfounded and demeaning assumption that the sexual behavior of homosexual persons is always and totally compulsive and therefore inculpable" (no. 11). It insists that homosexual persons have the freedom to choose whether or not to engage in homosexual acts; this pertains to the dignity of the homosexual person (no. 6). Here the Congregation in effect affirms the dignity and moral responsibility of homosexually oriented persons. They have the freedom to choose *not* to engage in homosexual acts because they realize that to do so is to determine themselves, by their own free choices, in such a way that they are possessed by their desires and not in possession of them. This argument, alleged to defend the licitness of homosexual acts, is in truth, as the *Letter* makes clear, demeaning to homosexually oriented persons, since it effectively denies their freedom of choice.

G. The Vocation of the Homosexual. The *Letter* maintains that homosexual persons are called "to enact the will of God in their life by joining whatever sufferings and difficulties they experience by virtue of their condition to the sacrifice of the Lord's cross." Self-denial is not pointless; "the cross is a denial of self, but in service to the will of God himself, who makes life come from death and empowers those who trust in him to practice virtue in place of vice" (no. 12).

Homosexual persons, like all of us, are called to chastity (no. 12). See above, pp. 192-193.

H. Responsibilities of Bishops. Bishops must be wary of any programs seeking to pressure the Church to change her teaching (no. 14); they must provide pastoral care in full conformity with the Church's teaching, making it clear that any effort to pass this over in silence or to depart from it is "neither caring nor pastoral" (no. 14). They must choose as persons to care for homosexual persons only those who accept the teaching of the Church and withdraw all support from groups seeking to undermine the Church's teaching (no. 17).

This, in sum, is the teaching of this important *Letter* on the subject of homosexual persons, their pastoral care, and the objectively moral badness of homosexual acts.

II. Instruction on Respect for Human Life in Its Origin and on the Dignity of Procreation ("Donum Vitae")

On February 22, 1987, the Congregation for the Doctrine of the Faith issued this instruction. It is a very remarkable document, covering a great many issues posed by new "reproductive" technologies. These issues were treated on pp. 165-167 above.

The document is divided into an introduction and three principal parts: (I) Respect for Human Embryos; (II) Interventions Upon Human Procreation, subdivided into (A) Heterologous Artificial Fertilization and

(B) Homologous Artificial Fertilization; and (III) Moral and Civil Law, followed by a brief conclusion.

A. Introduction. The Introduction contains five sections. Section 1 is concerned with biomedical research and the teaching of the Church. The purpose of the document is to put "forward the moral teaching corresponding to the dignity of the person and to his integral vocation" with respect to issues posed by contemporary biomedical research. Section 2 deals with the contributions science and technology can make to the human person. But science and technology are not morally indifferent. They require respect for the "fundamental criteria of the moral law," the service of the human person, of his inalienable rights and his integral good according to God's design. Section 3 relates truths about human anthropology to procedures in the biomedical field. Interventions upon the human body affect the human person. This is particularly true in the field of sexuality and procreation where "the fundamental values of life and love are actualized." Biomedical interventions must be given a moral evaluation in reference to the dignity of the human person and his divine vocation. Section 4 proposes two fundamental criteria decisive for moral judgment in this area, namely (1) the inviolability of innocent human life "from the moment of conception until death" and (2) the special character of the transmission of human life, which has been "entrusted by nature to a personal act." Section 5 recalls the teaching of the magisterium, which offers human reason the light of revelation on these two points, holding (1) that human life, from the moment of conception, must be absolutely respected because man is the only creature on earth that God "has wished for himself" and because the spiritual soul of man is "immediately created by God"; and (2) that human procreation requires on the part of the spouses responsible collaboration with the fruitful love of God; it must be realized in marriage through the acts proper and exclusive to spouses.

B. Part I: Respect for Human Embryos. This part contains six major sections. Section 1, on respect due to the human embryo, reminds us that "the human being is to be respected as a person from the first moment of his existence." Modern science recognizes that the biological identity of a new human individual is already constituted in the zygote resulting from fertilization. This scientific conclusion gives a valuable indication for discerning by the use of reason a personal presence at the moment of the first appearance of human life: how could a human individual not be a human person?

The moral condemnation of procured abortion is reaffirmed. "Since the human embryo must be treated as a person, it must also be defended in its integrity, tended and cared for, to the extent possible, in the same way as

206

any other human being." This is the principle determining the answers to the moral questions that will follow.

Section 2 deals with prenatal diagnosis. This is licit if the methods used with the informed consent of parents respect the life and integrity of the embryo and the mother without subjecting them to disproportionate risks. It is gravely immoral when the diagnosis is done with the thought of possibly inducing an abortion depending upon its results. One must deny to the State or any other authority the right to link in any way prenatal diagnosis and procured abortion.

Section 3, concerned with *therapeutic* procedures on human embryos, affirms that such procedures are licit if they respect the embryo's life and integrity and do not involve disproportionate risks. Procedures menacing the life or integrity of human embryos are illicit.

Section 4 takes up medical *research and experimentation* on human embryos. If the research is intended to benefit the embryo, it can be undertaken provided there is certainty that it will not harm the embryo's life or integrity and provided that proper consent has been given. Research and experimentation that is not directly therapeutic is absolutely illicit. Moreover, the corpses of human embryos and fetuses must be respected.

Section 5 affirms that it is absolutely immoral to produce human embryos *in vitro* as research material.

Section 6, which deals with procedures for manipulating human embryos engendered by new reproductive techniques, brands as absolutely immoral efforts to obtain a human being without any connection with human sexuality through "twin fission," cloning, or parthenogenesis. It likewise brands as immoral any and all efforts to make animal-human hybrids or to gestate human embryos in artificial or animal uteruses, as well as the freezing of embryos, efforts to engineer the "sex" of embryos, etc.

C. Part II: Interventions Upon Human Procreation. This part treats of "artificial procreation and insemination," that is, different technical procedures directed toward obtaining a human conception in a manner other than the sexual union of man and woman. It begins by noting the ideological link between procured abortion and *in vitro* fertilization. This deathly dynamic, however, does not exempt us from a further and thorough ethical study of artificial fertilization, whether heterologous or homologous.

a. Heterologous Artificial Fertilization

The term "heterologous" signifies that the gametic cells used to generate human life come from individuals who are not married to each other.

Section 1 deals with the intimate link between marriage and human procreation. From the moral point of view, human procreation must be the

207

fruit of marriage: this is the key principle. Every human being must be accepted as a gift and blessing. The procreation of a new human person must be "the fruit and sign of the mutual self-giving of the spouses." The child has a right to be conceived, carried in the womb, brought into the world, and brought up within marriage. The good of society as well demands this. This is the only way of generating human life that is truly responsible.

Thus Section 2 repudiates heterologous artificial fertilization as immoral because it is contrary to the unity of marriage, to the dignity of the spouses, to the right of the child to be conceived and brought into the world in marriage and from marriage. Moreover, the fertilization of an unmarried or widowed woman by the sperm of any donor whatsoever is not morally justified.

Section 3 rejects "surrogate" motherhood as unacceptable for the same reasons.

b. Homologous Artificial Fertilization

The term "homologous" signifies that the gametic cells used to generate new life come from husband and wife. The key moral principle here is the intimate bond between procreation and the marital act: it is not right, even for husband and wife, to generate human life outside the marital act. Three arguments are then given in Section 4 to support this key principle. The arguments are the following:

1. There is an inseparable connection, willed by God and unlawful for man to break on his own initiative, between the unitive and procreative meanings of the conjugal act. But artificial fertilization and procreation, even if the gametic cells come from husband and wife, severs this bond. Fertilization is licitly sought when it is the result of a "conjugal act which is *per se* suitable for the generation of children to which marriage is ordered by its nature and by which the spouses become one flesh." From the moral point of view, procreation is deprived of its proper perfection when it is not desired as the fruit of the conjugal act, of the one-flesh unity of the spouses.

2. The "language of the body" likewise shows that it is immoral for spouses to generate human life outside of their marital union, an act inseparably corporeal and spiritual. The origin of a new human person should be "linked to the union, not only biological but spiritual," of husband and wife. Their one-flesh bodily union in the marital act signifies (the "language of the body") both their exclusive marital love for one another and the openness of this love to the gift of new human life.

3. Respect for a human person in his origin requires that he not be treated as a product. When a child is begotten through the marital act, he

208

comes to be as a gift from God, a gift crowning their mutual gift of themselves to one another. When a child is "produced" by recourse to artificial insemination or *in vitro* fertilization, it comes to be, not as a gift from God, but as a "product" of human artifice.

Section 5 specifically addresses the morality of homologous *in vitro* fertilization and embryo transfer. Even if we prescind from the ideological link between these procedures and procured abortion, the conclusion must be that these ways of generating human life are immoral. They dissociate the begetting of human life from the conjugal act and in fact establish the dominion of technology over the origin and destiny of the human person. Conception *in vitro* is not achieved or positively willed as the expression and fruit of a specific conjugal act; thus homologous *in vitro* fertilization and embryo transfer objectively deprive the generation of human persons of its proper perfection, namely, that of being the result and fruit of a conjugal act specific to the love of husband and wife. The child so "produced" has not been respected in his origin.

However a child comes into the world, whether as the fruit of a conjugal act or through these technologies, he must be respected as a person and as a gift from God.

Section 6 deals with homologous artificial insemination, that is, when the wife is fertilized outside the marital act by sperm provided by her husband. This is repudiated because it dissociates the two meanings of the conjugal act. The basic principle is this: if the procedure *replaces* or *substitutes* for the conjugal act, it is immoral; if it, however, helps the marital act to achieve its purpose, it may be morally licit. Masturbation is not a morally licit means of obtaining human sperm.

Section 7 treats of the moral criteria for medical intervention in human procreation. The physician is at the service of the person and of human procreation. He does not have the authority to dispose of human persons or to decide their fate. He is to aid the spouses and not, by his technique, substitute for them.

Section 8 is concerned with the suffering of spouses who cannot, by engaging in the marital act, give life to a child or who are afraid of bringing a handicapped child into the world. The desire of spouses for children is natural and legitimate. They do not, however, have a "right" to a child because the child is not an object but a gift from God. Spouses suffering from sterility must bear their cross.

D. Part III: Moral Law and Civil Law. The inviolable right of every innocent human person and the institution of marriage are moral values and constitutive elements of the civil society and its order.

New technological possibilities require the intervention of political authorities and of legislators. Such intervention should be directed to ensuring the common good of the people through respect for their fundamental rights, the promotion of peace and public morality. It furthermore ought to preserve the human community from temptations to selfishness and from discrimination and prejudice.

Among fundamental rights are these: (1) every human being's right to life and physical integrity and (2) the rights of the family and of the child.

Political authority may not approve making human beings through procedures exposing them to the grave risks noted in the document. The recognition by positive law of techniques of artificial transmission of human life would widen the breach already opened by the legalization of abortion. The law cannot tolerate, and in fact must forbid, that human beings, even at the embryonic stage of development, be destroyed, mutilated, or treated as objects of experimentation.

Civil law cannot approve techniques of artificial procreation that, for the benefit of third parties, take away what is a right inherent in the spousal relationship; therefore, civil law cannot legalize donation of gametes between persons who are not united in marriage. Legislation ought also to prohibit embryo banks, postmortem insemination, and surrogate motherhood.

E. Conclusion. In its conclusion the document issues an invitation to all who can do so to exercise a positive influence and ensure that, in family and society, due respect is accorded to human life and love. In particular it addresses an invitation to theologians, above all moralists, to study more deeply and make ever more accessible to the faithful the teaching of the magisterium in the light of a valid anthropology of human sexuality and marriage.

All are invited to act responsibly in the area proper to each and, like the Good Samaritan, to recognize as a neighbor even the littlest among the children of men.

III. Pope John Paul II's "Letter to Families" and His encyclical "Evangelium Vitae"

A. Overview of John Paul II's "Letter to Families." This *Letter*, dated February 2, 1994, was written to commemorate the "Year of the Family." The *Letter* includes an introductory section (nos. 1-5) and two major parts, (1) "The Civilization of Love" (nos. 6-17) and (2) "The Bridegroom Is With You" (nos. 18-23).

In the introductory material John Paul II emphasizes that the family is the first and most important way in which the Church carries out her mission to minister to the needs of human persons, a task that God has entrusted to the Church, The family is the first and most important way because the family is the place where a human person comes into the world and from which he goes in order to realize in a new family his own unique vocation in life (nos. 1-2). The family itself has its origin in the love of God the Father, whose own only begotten Son "entered into human history through the family" (no. 2). The Christian family, moreover, is in truth the "domestic church," entrusted with a unique and indispensable role to play in the redemptive work of the Church (no. 3).

Part I, "The Civilization of Love," is in essence a meditation on the unique and indispensable role that the family, rooted in marriage, has in building up the "civilization of love." This civilization "originates in the revelation of the love of the God who 'is love' (cf. 1 Jn 4:8, 16)" (no. 13), and the family is its very "center and heart" (no. 13). This is so, first of all, because the family built upon the marriage of one man and one woman finds its "primordial model . . . in God himself, in the Trinitarian mystery of his life. The divine 'We' is the eternal pattern of the human 'we,' especially of that 'we' formed by the man and the woman created in the divine image and likeness" (no. 6).

The family is the heart and center of the civilization of love, secondly, because marriage, which can be considered as the "rock" on which the family is built, is a covenant of faithful and indissoluble spousal love, entrusted by God with the mission of cooperating with him by welcoming the gift of new human life lovingly and by educating new human life — new human persons — to his service and the love and service of all human persons: to building up the "civilization of love" and in this way making an utterly indispensable contribution to the wider human community, which has the obligation to recognize and respect the inviolable rights of spouses and the dignity of marriage (cf. nos. 6-17).

In Part II, "The Bridegroom Is With You," the pope is at pains to show that the civilization of love is not a utopia (this truth had been affirmed in Part I, but it is developed in Part II). It is not a utopia because the requirements of spousal love — which is at the heart and center of the "civilization of love" — while demanding and seemingly impossible when viewed in a merely human way, *can be* faithfully carried out in union with Jesus. For Jesus, the Bridegroom, is with Christian husbands and wives, whose marriage he has raised to the dignity of a sacrament both signifying and capable of making efficaciously present within the world the love-giving, life-giving, grace-giving bridal union between him and his Church. He has made Christian husbands and wives "new beings" by virtue of their union

211

with him through baptism, and he nourishes them with the Eucharist, his own body and blood. Moreover, he has entrusted them — and their mission to develop the "civilization of love" — to his Mother, the Mother of fairest love. If they welcome him into their hearts, he, the Bridegroom, will abide with them to strengthen them inwardly and give them the help they need in order to carry out the mission entrusted to them and to their families as the "domestic church" (cf. nos. 18-23).

B. Overview of Pope John Paul II's Encyclical "Evangelium Vitae." This encyclical, dated March 25, 1995, is an impassioned defense of the incomparable dignity, indeed sanctity, of human life. In the encyclical's Introduction the Holy Father affirms the incomparable worth of the human person, briefly enumerates the new and terrible threats menacing innocent human life today (in particular the lives of the unborn, the weak, the elderly, and the widespread social acceptance of a culture of death), and emphasizes that the encyclical was written only after consulting bishops throughout the world for advice (cf. nos. 2-6).

The first chapter, entitled "Present-Day Threats to Human Life," is an in-depth examination of these threats — particularly abortion, euthanasia, and barbaric experimentations on human persons — and of the root causes of them. Here John Paul II, mincing no words, declares that today we are confronted by "a culture which denies solidarity and in many cases takes the form of a veritable 'culture of death,' " a culture "actively fostered by powerful cultural, economic and political currents which encourage an idea of society excessively concerned with efficiency," with the result that we can in truth speak of a "war of the powerful against the weak" and a "conspiracy against life" (no. 12).

The Roman pontiff sees this culture of death rooted in a distorted notion of subjectivity, a false understanding of freedom conceived as completely autonomous, utterly individualistic, and bound by no moral norms. This culture of death has led to the "eclipse of the sense of God and of man" and the emergence of secularistic humanism, with the result that man "no longer considers life as a splendid gift of God, something 'sacred' entrusted to his responsibility and thus also to his loving care and 'veneration' " (cf. nos. 19-22). Despite these terribly negative signs of the time, the Holy Father discerns some significant "signs of hope," among them the many married couples who generously accept children as the supreme gift of marriage, families willing to serve life and give themselves to the least of their brothers and sisters, people who generously volunteer hospitality and a supportive environment for the weak, and similar movements and initiatives (cf. nos. 26-28). In concluding this chapter John Paul II points out that "the unconditional choice for life reaches its full religious and moral meaning when it flows from, is formed by, and nourished by *faith in Christ*" (no. 28).

Chapter Two, "The Christian Message Concerning Life," begins by focusing attention on Jesus Christ, "the Word of Life" (1 Jn 1:1), who by his death "reveals all the splendor and value of life, inasmuch as his self-oblation on the Cross becomes the source of a new life for all people (cf. Jn 12:32)" (no. 33). The pope goes on to emphasize that human life is surpassingly good because, unlike the life of other living creatures, it manifests God in the world and is "a sign of his presence, a trace of his glory (cf. Gen 1:26-27; Ps 8:6)" (no. 34). Moreover, as Jesus reveals to us, God wills that human persons, in and through union with Jesus, become literally his very own children, members of the divine family. Thus human life becomes the " 'place' where God manifests himself, where we meet him and enter into communion with him" (no. 39). The life of every human being is sacred and inviolable because God personally treasures and cares for it; his commandment that we are not to kill is rooted in the love and reverence due to the life that he has given and confided to our trust (nos. 38-41).

So deeply does he love and trust us that God allows us to share in his lordship by taking responsibility for human life. Husbands and wives, in particular, are privileged to be his partners in raising up new human life and giving it a home where it can take root and grow; but the mission to serve life, particularly when it is at its weakest, involves everyone (no. 43), and human life is most vulnerable when it comes into the world as a precious gift from God, when it suffers, and when it draws near to death (nos. 44-47). God's command not to kill "is a specific command intended to protect the dignity and sanctity of human life," and it finds its fulfillment in Jesus, who shows us the authentic meaning of human life, namely, that of "being a *gift which is fully realized in the giving of self*," in the "gift of self in love for one's brothers and sisters" (no. 49). This "Gospel of Life" is ultimately fulfilled on the tree of the Cross, for from the pierced side of the Redeemer we have give to us "the very life of God." Jesus "proclaims that *life finds its center, its meaning, and its fulfillment when it is given up*" in love (no. 51).

This, then, is the Christian message concerning human life, God's precious gift.

Evangelium Vitae's Chapter Three, "God's Holy Law," is devoted to the intimate link between the Gospel of Life and the commandment, grounded in self-giving love, that we are not to kill. This chapter, which draws heavily both on the teaching set forth in the *Catechism of the Catholic Church* and

213

on what the Holy Father had said in *Veritatis Splendor* on the truth of moral absolutes (cf. below), develops the idea that "in giving life to man God *demands* that he love, respect, and promote life. The *gift* thus becomes a *commandment*, and the *commandment is itself a gift*" (no. 52).

Because it is God's gift and is thus sacred and inviolable, human life, particularly when weak and helpless, has God as its "goel," that is, its "defender" (no. 53). The negative commandment "You shall not kill" simply indicates an extreme that can never be exceeded; implicitly it encourages a positive attitude toward life, an attitude immeasurably deepened and enriched by the command that we are to love our neighbor as ourselves (nos. 53-54).

Since human life is precious, it ought to be protected and defended by acts of legitimate defense. John Paul II notes that "unfortunately it happens that the need to render the aggressor incapable of causing harm sometimes involves taking his life." He continues by saying that "in this case, the fatal outcome is attributable to the aggressor whose action brought it about, even though he may not be morally responsible because of a lack of the use of reason" (no. 55). Although legitimate defense of human life and appropriate punishment of evildoers in principle justify the death penalty, John Paul II declares that in contemporary society cases when the death penalty is in fact justified are "very rare, if not practically non-existent" (no. 56).

But the command "You shall not kill" is absolute, that is, without any exceptions, when it refers to the killing of innocent human life, and "all the more so in the case of weak and defenseless human beings, who find their ultimate defense against the arrogance and caprice of others only in the absolute binding force of God's commandment" (no. 57). In fact, the Roman pontiff continues, the absolute inviolability of innocent human life is a moral truth clearly taught by Scripture, the Church's tradition, and the magisterium. He thus invokes the "authority which Christ conferred upon Peter and his Successors," and "in communion with the Bishops of the Catholic Church" he confirms "that the direct and voluntary killing of an innocent human being is always gravely immoral," and he continues by saying: "This doctrine, based upon the unwritten law which man, in the light of reason, finds in his own heart (cf. Rom 2:14-15), is reaffirmed by Sacred Scripture, transmitted by the Tradition of the Church and taught by the ordinary and universal Magisterium" (no. 57).

Later on he relates this teaching to the absolute inviolability of unborn human life. Again invoking the authority that Christ conferred on Peter and his successors in communion with the bishops, he writes: "*I declare that direct abortion, that is, abortion willed as an end or as a means, always constitutes a grave moral disorder*, since it is the deliberate killing of an innocent human being," and he affirms that this doctrine too is "based upon the natural law and upon the written Word of God, is transmitted by the Church's Tradition and taught by the ordinary and universal Magisterium" (emphasis added) (no. 62). Still later the Holy Father confirms that "*euthanasia is a grave violation of the law of God*, since it is the deliberate and morally unacceptable killing of a human person," and that this doctrine, too, "is based upon the natural law and upon the written Word of God, is transmitted by the Church's Tradition and taught by the ordinary and universal Magisterium" (emphasis added) (no. 65).[1]

Chapter Four, entitled "For a New Culture of Human Life," is an appeal to proclaim the good news of the "Gospel of Life" and to carry out the work of evangelization, "an all-embracing, progressive activity through which the Church participates in the prophetic, priestly, and royal mission of the Lord Jesus" (no. 78). What the pope calls the "new culture of human life" in this encyclical corresponds to what he had called the "civilization of love" in his *Letter to Families*.

To celebrate the "Gospel of Life" and to develop a new culture of human life is an integral part of our human vocation and central to our everyday life. Our mission is to provide the context in which "heroic actions . . . are born," actions proclaiming the Gospel of Life "*by the total gift of self.*" John Paul II declares that such heroism is reflected quietly in the lives of brave mothers "who devote themselves to their own families without reserve, who suffer in giving birth to their children, and who are ready to make any effort, to face any sacrifice, in order to pass on to them the best of themselves" (no. 86).

To develop the new culture of life a tremendous educational effort must be expended, including the development of centers for natural methods of regulating fertility, for preparing couples for marriage and supporting them in their marriage, for assisting unwed mothers to welcome new life and care for it. Needed too are communities to help treat those suffering from drug addiction, from AIDS, and for all who are disabled. The elderly and the terminally ill must be given the support necessary to sustain them in their final days; it requires a reconsideration of the role of hospitals, clinics, and convalescent homes, which must be "places where suffering, pain and death are acknowledged and understood in their human and specifically Christian meaning" (no. 88).

Unique responsibilities for proclaiming the Gospel of Life belong to health-care personnel, those engaged in political and civic affairs, and legislators, who must seek especially to support families and motherhood. In fact, "a family policy must be the basis and driving force of all social policies" (no. 90).

John Paul II notes in particular, as he had in his *Letter to Families*, the decisive responsibility of the family in developing a new culture of life, affirming that "this responsibility flows from its very nature as a community of life and love, founded on marriage, and from its mission to 'guard, reveal, and communicate love.' " The family, he insists, is the "true sanctuary of life." It is the "domestic church," summoned to proclaim, celebrate, and serve the Gospel of Life. Married couples are called upon to be givers of life; they must recognize that procreation is "a unique event which clearly reveals that *human life is a gift received in order then to be given as a gift*," and they must raise their children in the love and service of God and neighbor, praying daily, practicing solidarity within the home, and extending hospitality and solidarity to others (nos. 92-93). Consequently, the family urgently needs to be helped and supported (no. 94).

To build a new culture of life the first and foremost step is to form consciences rightly about the incomparable and inviolable worth of every human life and to reestablish the essential link between life and freedom and between freedom and truth. Men must acknowledge that they are God's creatures; otherwise the dignity of the human person and the inviolability of human life will be rejected or compromised (nos. 95-96).

Human life will not be revered, John Paul II emphasizes, unless young people learn to value their sexuality and come to see the intimate bond between sexuality and authentic human love. Education in sexuality is education in chastity, a virtue enabling human persons to respect the "spousal" meaning of the body and the responsibility of married couples to respect the beauty of human procreation and to be open to the gift of life by respecting their fertility and by using only natural methods to regulate it (no. 97).

To develop a new culture of life we must have the courage to "adopt a new life-style," one based on a correct scale of values: "the primacy of being over having, of the person over things" (no. 98). Everyone has a role to play in developing this culture, but an indispensable one belongs to intellectuals, in particular Catholic intellectuals and the institutions in which they work. Women are called upon to bear witness to the meaning of genuine love, especially of love for human life at its inception. Women who have had abortions should remember that the "Father of mercies is ready to give [them] forgiveness and peace" and enable them to recommit themselves to the service of life (no. 99).

We need to remember that, in developing the new culture of life, our greatest friend and helper is God himself; we need to ask his help in prayer and fasting so that "the power from on high will break down the walls of lies and deceit" (no. 100). The Gospel of Life — the new culture of life — is not meant for believers alone, but for everyone, because the value at stake, the value of human life, "is one which every human being can grasp by the light of reason." To be actively pro-life is "to contribute to the renewal of society through the promotion of the common good"; no genuine democracy can exist "without a recognition of every person's dignity and without respect for his or her rights."

In the Conclusion to the encyclical John Paul II turns to gaze on Mary, the Virgin Mother so closely associated with the Gospel of Life. She helps us "realize that life is always at the center of a great struggle between good and evil, between light and darkness." She helps us understand that "it is precisely in the 'flesh' of every person that Christ continues to reveal himself and to enter into fellowship with us, so that rejection of human life . . . is really a rejection of Christ." She helps us face our mission of proclaiming life, for like her we are not "to be afraid," for "with God nothing is impossible (Lk 1:30, 37)" (nos. 102-105).

C. Significance of the "Letter to Families" and "Evangelium Vitae" for "Catholic Sexual Ethics." These two documents of Pope John Paul II are of particular significance for their teaching on marriage and the role of the Christian family in the world today. As the summary of his *Letter to Families* makes clear, John Paul II forcefully reaffirms the teaching of the Church on marriage as summarized above in Chapter 1, in particular pages 22-29, and on chastity, Christian marriage, and spousal love as summarized in Chapter 6, pages 122-137. Similarly, in this *Letter* the Roman pontiff reaffirms, in number 16, the Church's teaching on chastity and the life of consecrated virginity, considered above on pages 137-139. Thus in the *Letter* John Paul II underlines the truths that God is the author of marriage, that it comes to be only through the free personal consent of the man and the woman to be husband and wife, that it is by its nature ordered to the procreation and education of children, that it has been raised to the dignity of a sacrament by Jesus, that it is a vocation to holiness, etc.

But the Holy Father not only reaffirms these truths in his *Letter to Families*; he deepens and develops the Church's understanding of marriage in many ways. He does so by rooting the ultimate source of marriage and marital love in the inner triune life of God himself. As he did in his apostolic exhortation *Familiaris Consortio* (which has been summarized in previous chapters), he devotes considerable energy to showing that the voca-

217

tion to marriage is the ordinary way in which men and women carry out the mission entrusted to them: to *give themselves away in love* and to form a *communion of persons*, modeled on the communion of persons in the Trinity. Similarly, he is at pains to help Christian spouses realize more deeply how their marital union is not only a sign or symbol of the life-giving, love-giving, grace-giving bridal union of Christ with his bride the Church, but truly makes this bridal union efficaciously present in the world today. And it is this crucially important truth that he also develops in the final chapter of *Evangelium Vitae*, when he focuses attention on the absolutely paramount role that marriage and family life have to play in developing the new culture of life, in furthering the "civilization of love."

But one of the most significant contributions John Paul II makes to deepening the Catholic understanding of marriage and the indispensable role that Christian spouses and the family they form have to play in the drama of redemption is to show that the Church's teaching on marriage (and with it, the Church's teaching on chastity and sexual morality) is intimately and indissolubly linked to the Church's teaching on social, economic, and political morality. The major purpose of the *Letter to Families* is to make it clear to everyone that the "civilization of love," the civilization that finds its ultimate source in the self-giving love of the triune God, can only come into being and flourish if the beauty and dignity of marriage and family life is respected and recognized and only if Christian spouses and their families *become what they are*, the sanctuaries of life and love, ready and willing to *serve* society and the human community. This crucial theme is once again taken up in the final chapter, as we have seen, of *Evangelium Vitae*.

Perhaps the point can be put this way: the "culture of death," which John Paul II analyzes in depth in Chapter One of *Evangelium Vitae*, is rooted in an individualistic subjectivism characterized by a spurious understanding of human freedom. This culture of death has spawned the widespread social acceptance of contraception and abortion (and now of euthanasia and other attacks on human life). The slogan dear to the hearts of those who champion contraception and abortion as ways of solving human problems is that "no unwanted child ought ever to be born," and the way to prevent this tragedy from coming to pass is to allow men and women (even adolescent young men and women) to engage in sex whenever they feel like it and ward off its evil consequences — in particular, the birth of "unwanted children" — by the use of contraceptives and, should they fail, abortion. John Paul II devotes all his energy to oppose this demeaning understanding of human sexuality and of human life. In its place he proclaims the truth, rooted in the Gospel of Life, that "no person — including unborn children, the weak, the elderly, the crippled — ought to be unwanted," and the only way to develop a society, a culture, a civilization in which *all* human persons are indeed wanted and loved as God wants them to be wanted and loved, is to respect the goods of human sexuality, that is, the goods of new human life and of faithful spousal love.

This is the way the Holy Father deepens and develops the Church's teaching on human sexuality, marriage, and family life.

IV. The Truth and Meaning of Human Sexuality: Guidelines for Education Within the Family

This document issued by the Pontifical Council for the Family contains an introduction (nos. 1-7) and eight roman-numbered parts: (I) Called to True Love (nos. 9-15); (II) True Love and Chastity (nos. 16-25); (III) In the Light of Vocation (nos. 26-36); (IV) Father and Mother as Educators (nos. 37-47); (V) Paths of Formation Within the Family (nos. 48-63); (VI) Learning Stages (nos. 64-111); (VII) Practical Guidelines (nos. 112-144); and (VIII) Conclusion (nos. 145-150).

Here we will summarize its teaching on (1) the nature and meaning of human sexuality; (2) the meaning of love and the virtue of chastity; (3) the vocation to marriage and the vocation to virginity/celibacy, inasmuch as these are the issues most centrally related to topics taken up in the book.

A. The Nature and Meaning of Human Sexuality. The document discusses human sexuality within the context provided by its presentation of love as self-giving (see below). It stresses that man is called to love and self-giving in the "unity of body and spirit," that "femininity and masculinity are complementary gifts through which human sexuality is an integrating part of the concrete capacity for love which God has inscribed in man and woman" (no. 10). Citing John Paul II's *Letter to Families*, it says that "sexuality is a fundamental component of personality, one of its modes of being, of manifestation, of communicating with others, of feeling, of expressing and of living human love" (no. 10). The capacity to love as self-giving is "incarnated" in the *"nuptial meaning of the body"* which bears the imprint of the person's masculinity and femininity" (no. 10). Moreover, this time citing an audience given by John Paul II on Jan. 16, 1980, the document emphasizes that human sexuality is both procreative and unitive or self-giving: "The human body, with its sex, and its masculinity and femininity, seen in the very mystery of creation, is not only a source of fruitfulness and procreation, as in the whole natural order, but includes right 'from

219

the beginning' the 'nuptial' attribute, that is, *the capacity of expressing love: that love precisely in which the man-person becomes a gift* and — by means of this gift — fulfils the very meaning of his being and existence" (no. 10).

Human sexuality, "insofar as it is a way of relating and being open to others," "has love as its intrinsic end, more precisely, love as donation and acceptance, love as giving and receiving. . . . When such love exists in marriage, self-giving expresses, through the body, the complementarity and totality of the gift" (no. 11).

But human life, as John Paul II says in *Evangelium Vitae* (no. 92) "is a gift received in order then to be given as a gift." This gift of life is realized in marriage (and in the vocation to celibacy or virginity), and this gift includes the whole person, body as well as soul (nos. 12-13). Married love indeed surpasses friendship, and "to this love alone belongs sexual giving, 'realized in a truly human way only if it is an integral part of the love by which a man and a woman commit themselves totally to one another until death' " (no. 14, citing John Paul II's *Familiaris Consortio*, no. 11). But married love is not authentic unless it is open to the gift of new life (no. 15, with an internal citation from *Familiaris Consortio*, no. 14). In short, human sexuality is something that permeates the human body/person, manifests the complementarity of male and female, is appropriately expressed genitally only in marriage, a reality vivified by married love, a love open to the gift of life.

B. The Meaning of Love and the Virtue of Chastity. God is love and has made man for love. Human persons are called to love as friendship and self-giving. Love is true only " 'when it creates the good of persons and of communities; it creates that good and gives it to others' " (no. 9, citing John Paul II's *Letter to Families*, no. 14).

In it only in the light of love understood in this way that human sexuality can be properly understood (see preceding section).

Chastity and true love are intimately interrelated. Indeed, this document declares that "*Chastity is the spiritual power which frees love from selfishness and aggression*" (no. 16). Chastity is the "joyous affirmation of someone who knows how to live self-giving, free from any form of self-centered slavery. This presupposes that the person has learned how to accept other people, to relate with them, while respecting their dignity in diversity" (no. 17). Chastity, as the *Catechism of the Catholic Church* (no. 2339) reminds us, "includes an apprenticeship in self-mastery which is a training in human freedom. The alternative is clear: either man governs his passions and finds peace, or he lets himself be dominated by them and becomes unhappy" (no. 18).

Human beings can fulfill their vocation to be holy as God is holy only by cultivating the virtue of chastity (no. 19). Marital chastity is "the most valid premise for educating children in chaste love and in holiness of life" (no. 20). Chastity is an indispensable expression of charity (no. 20).

    C. The Vocation to Marriage and the Vocation to Virginity/Celibacy. Vatican Council II emphasized the role of the Christian family in cultivating and fostering vocations — vocations to marriage and to a life of virginity or celibacy undertaken in response to the requirements of God's reign (cf. *Lumen Gentium*, no. 11, no. 26). In educating their children in human love and sexuality, parents need to help them see that marriage itself is a divine vocation, whose "true nature and nobility," as Paul VI said in *Humanae Vitae*, no. 8, is revealed "when it [marriage] is considered in its supreme origin, God, who is love, the Father 'from whom every family in heaven and on earth is named' (Eph 3:15)" (cited in no. 28). Marriage, in short, is not the end product of evolution but is "the wise institution of the Creator to realize in mankind his design of love" (no. 28, citing *Humanae Vitae*, no. 8).

    Married love is characterized by being "human (i.e., both physical and spiritual), total, faithful, and fruitful" (no. 29; cf. *Humanae Vitae,* no. 9). This love is sanctified in Christian marriage, which is a true sacrament of the new law, giving divine, sanctifying grace and enabling husbands and wives to live as loving spouses who welcome the gift of life (no. 30).

    In addition to the vocation to marriage, Christian revelation presents the vocation to virginity. Today we face a crisis in vocations to the priesthood and religious life; this crisis is connected with the crisis facing marriage today, for when the vocation to marriage is properly cherished, the vocation to the life of virginity is too. Indeed, the Christian family, rooted in marriage, ought to be the seedbed for vocations to the virginal life (nos. 34-36).

    Moreover, a truly Christian family can help "communicate an understanding of the value of celibacy to unmarried children or to those who are incapable of marriage for reasons apart from their own will" (no. 36).

V. Pope John Paul II's Encyclical "Veritatis Splendor"

    This document is of paramount importance for matters taken up in Chapters 4 and 5 of *CSE*. Here its teaching on the following issues considered in these chapters will be set forth and related to what was said in the text: (A) freedom of choice; (B) the "law" of love, the human good, and moral norms; (C) proportionalism and moral absolutes; and (D) conscience and its formation.

A. Freedom of Choice. In *Veritatis Splendor* John Paul II emphasizes, as does our text (cf. pp. 69-70), that human persons are gifted with freedom of choice and that human persons determine their lives as moral beings in and through the choices that they freely make. Thus he says that our freely chosen acts "do not produce a change merely in the state of affairs outside of man but, to the extent that they are deliberate choices, they give moral definition to the very person who performs them, determining his *profound spiritual traits*" (no. 71). Moreover, while rejecting "fundamental option" theories, which *relocate* self-determination from the free choices one makes every day and places it in an allegedly more profound exercise of "basic freedom" distinct from any particular free choice (see *Veritatis Splendor*, nos. 65-67), he likewise insists, as we did above (cf. pp. 94-95), that it is proper to speak of a fundamental commitment or choice shaping one's entire moral life, and that for the Christian this is the "decision of faith, of the *obedience of faith* (cf. Rom 16:26) . . . by which man makes a total and free self-commitment to God, offering 'the full submission of intellect and will to God as he reveals' " (no. 66). Finally, he teaches that this free commitment or fundamental choice "*is always brought into play through conscious and free decisions. Precisely for this reason, it is revoked when man engages his freedom in conscious decisions to the contrary, with regard to morally grave matter*" (no. 67).

B. The "Law" of Love, the Human Good, and Moral Norms. The material set forth above on pp. 71-95 on the law of love, the human good, and moral norms is in full conformity with the teaching proclaimed by the Holy Father in *Veritatis Splendor*. In company with Scripture and the entire Catholic tradition he affirms that the basic principle of morality is formulated in the twofold command to love God and neighbor, and he is at pains to show the intimate relationship between the precepts of the Decalogue and this twofold law of love. He notes that Jesus himself, in his dialogue with the rich young man (Matthew 19:16-21), makes clear "the close connection . . . *between eternal life and obedience to God's commandments* [which] . . . show man the path of life and lead to it" (no. 12). The first three commandments of the Decalogue call us "to acknowledge God as the one Lord of all and to worship him alone for his infinite goodness" (no. 11). When the young man demands to know "which commandments" he must observe to gain eternal life he is, the Roman pontiff says, asking "what he must do in life in order to show that he acknowledges God's holiness" (no. 13). And in response Jesus reminds him of the Decalogue's precepts concerning our neighbor. "From the very lips of Jesus," the Holy Father then observes, "man is once more given the commandments of the Decalogue" (no. 12), commandments rooted in the commandment that we are to love our neighbor as ourselves, a commandment expressing *the singular dignity of the human person*, 'the only creature that God has wanted for its own sake' " (no. 13).

At this point John Paul II then develops a matter of crucial importance for understanding the relationship between the primordial command to love our neighbor as ourselves and the specific moral precepts of the second tablet of the Decalogue. His point is that we can love our neighbor and respect his dignity as a person only by cherishing the real goods perfective of him and by refusing to damage, destroy, or impede these goods. Appealing to Jesus' words, the pope insists that "the different commandments of the Decalogue are really only so many reflections on the one commandment about the good of the person, at the level of the many different goods which characterize his identity as a spiritual and bodily being in relationship with God, with his neighbor, and with the material world. . . . The commandments of which Jesus reminds the young man are meant to safeguard the *good* of the person, the image of God, by protecting his *goods*" (no. 13), goods such as life itself, the marital communion, and other goods of this kind.

C. Proportionalism and Moral Absolutes. The proportionalist method of making moral judgments, considered and rejected above on pages 80-90, is also rejected by John Paul II, along with what he calls "consequentialism." The pope distinguishes between what he calls "teleology" and "teleologism." He affirms that the moral life has an essentially "*teleological character*, since it consists in the deliberate ordering of human acts to God, the supreme good and ultimate end *(telos)* of man" (no. 73). But he contrasts teleology with "teleologism," declaring: "Certain *ethical theories*, called '*teleological,*' claim to be concerned for the conformity of human acts with the ends pursued by the agent and with the values intended by him. The criteria for evaluating the moral rightness of an action are drawn from the *weighing of the nonmoral or premoral goods* to be gained and the corresponding nonmoral or premoral values to be respected. For some, concrete behavior would be right or wrong according to whether or not it is capable of producing a better state of affairs for all concerned. Right conduct would be the one capable of 'maximizing' goods and 'minimizing' evils" (no. 74).

One type of "teleologism" is "consequentialism," which, John Paul II says, "claims to draw the criteria of the rightness or wrongness of a given

223

way of acting solely from a calculation of foreseeable consequences stemming from a given choice." Another variant, "proportionalism," seeks to do so "by weighing the various values and goods being sought," and "focuses rather on the proportion acknowledged between the good and bad effects of that choice, with a view to the 'greater good' or 'lesser evil' actually possible in a particular situation" (no. 75). Proponents of these theories assert that it is impossible to determine whether an act traditionally regarded as intrinsically evil would really be morally evil until one has considered, in the concrete situation, the "premoral" good and evil state of affairs it is likely to cause. They conclude that the foreseen proportions of "premoral" goods to evils in the alternatives available can at times justify exceptions to precepts traditionally regarded as absolute (cf. no. 75).

The Holy Father firmly repudiates these theories, declaring that they are "not faithful to the Church's teaching" on intrinsically evil acts and moral absolutes (no. 76). He then states that these ways of evaluating human acts are inadequate because "everyone recognizes the difficulty, or rather the impossibility, of evaluating all the good and evil consequences and effects — defined as premoral — of one's own acts" (no. 77). He insists that human acts are morally specified precisely by the "object" of one's free and deliberate choice. This object, as he rightly observes, "is in fact a freely chosen kind of behavior . . . the proximate end of a deliberate decision which determines the act of willing on the part of the acting person" (no. 78). With this understanding of the "object" of a human act in mind, it is easy to grasp the Roman pontiff's argument, namely, that "reason attests that there are objects of the human act which are by their nature 'incapable of being ordered' to God because they radically contradict the good of the person made in his image" (no. 80). In short, some sorts of human acts, specified by the object deliberately and freely chosen, are intrinsically evil — killing an innocent human person, directly intended abortion, contraception, committing adultery, and the like. The moral norms proscribing such acts are moral absolutes.

In fact, John Paul II declares that the "teaching representing the central theme" of his encyclical, the teaching being reaffirmed "with the authority of the Successor of St. Peter," is the teaching concerning "*the universality and immutability of the moral commandments*, particularly those which prohibit always and without exception *intrinsically evil acts*" (no. 115).

D. Conscience and Its Formation. A brief but incisive treatment of conscience and its formation (on this see Ch. 5 above) is provided by John Paul II in numbers 54-64 of *Veritatis Splendor*. In his consideration of conscience the pope focuses on its meaning as a *practical judgment* "which makes known what man must do or not do, or which assesses an act already performed by him" (no. 59). He vigorously rejects as utterly incompatible with Catholic faith the view that makes conscience "autonomous," that is, a law unto itself. Rather he insists that the dignity of conscience lies in its capacity to disclose the *truth* about moral good and evil, the truth "indicated by the 'divine law,' *the universal and objective norm of morality*" (no. 60; cf. no. 63). He repudiates the claim, subjectivistic in nature, that separates or even opposes "the teaching of the precept [for example, the precept not to commit adultery] . . . and the norm of the individual conscience, which would in fact make the final decision about what is good and what is evil" (no. 56), precisely because this erroneous claim seeks "to legitimize so-called 'pastoral solutions' contrary to the teaching of the Magisterium, and to justify a 'creative' hermeneutic according to which the moral conscience is in no way obliged, in every case, by a particular negative precept" (no. 56).

It is necessary for persons to educate, that is, to form their conscience, sincerely seeking the *truth*, and seeking it where they can be confident it can be found. Moreover, because the Catholic Church, as Vatican II reminds us in a passage cited by John Paul II (*Dignitatis Humanae*, no. 14), "is by the will of Christ the teacher of truth," whose duty it is "to declare and confirm by her authority the principles of the moral order which spring from human nature itself," "it follows that the authority of the Church, when she pronounces on moral questions, in no way undermines the freedom of conscience of Christians. This is so not only because freedom of conscience is never freedom 'from' the truth but always and only freedom 'in' the truth, but also because the Magisterium does not bring to the Christian conscience truths which are extraneous to it; rather it brings to light the truths which it ought already to possess, developing them from the starting point of the primordial act of faith. The Church puts herself always and only at the *service of conscience*, helping it . . . especially in more difficult questions, to attain the truth with certainty and to abide in it" (no. 64).

VI. The "Catechism of the Catholic Church"

The *Catechism of the Catholic Church* was proposed by the bishops at the extraordinary synod of bishops held in 1985 to commemorate the twentieth anniversary of the close of Vatican Council II to provide a "compendium of all Catholic doctrine regarding both faith and morals," offering "sound doctrine suited to the present life of Christians."[2] Pope John Paul II wholeheartedly made the desire of the synod bishops his own and entrusted a commission of twelve cardinals and bishops under the presidency of Cardinal Ratzinger and assisted by an editorial committee of seven diocesan bishops, experts in theology and catechesis, to prepare this *Catechism*. After working intensely for six years and revising drafts nine times, this commission finally produced the text published in 1992.

This *Catechism*, or compendium of Catholic faith and life, will, as John Paul II says, "make a very important contribution to that work of renewing the whole life of the Church, as desired and begun by the Second Vatican Council."[3] It is divided into four major parts: (1) The Profession of Faith, concerned with the truths of the Catholic faith; (2) The Celebration of the Christian Mystery, concerned with the liturgical and sacramental life of the Church and of Christians; (3) Life in Christ, devoted to articulating the way the Christian life, rooted in faith, is to be lived; and (4) Christian Prayer, concerned with the prayer life of Christians.

The sections of the *Catechism* of principal concern to issues taken up in *Catholic Sexual Ethics* are the whole of Part Three, on the Christian moral life, and Chapter Three of Section Two of Part Two, devoted to a consideration of Christian marriage, or the sacrament of matrimony. Here the material found in Part Three will be summarized. The *Catechism's* treatment of the sacrament of matrimony in Part Two is in essence a recapitulation of the developed teaching of the Church on marriage as set forth in the documents of Vatican Council II and John Paul II's apostolic exhortation *Familiaris Consortio*, and summarized above in Chapter 1.

The "Catechism" and the Christian Moral Life

The material included in this part of the *Catechism* (Part Three), as already noted, is important for issues taken up above in Chapters 4, 5, 7, and 8. The basic teaching of this part can be summarized by considering the following: (1) the Christian moral life is essentially an endeavor on the part of human persons, helped by God's grace, to answer God's invitation to eternal life in personal union with him; (2) the Church is by God's will our Mother and Teacher; (3) in order to attain our vocation we must be willing to shape our choices and acts in accordance with the truth.

1. The Christian Moral Life as an Endeavor to Answer God's Invitation to Life Eternal. Chapter One of Section One of Part Three of the *Catechism* emphasizes the dignity of the human person, and in its very first article develops the theme that man is indeed the image of the all-holy God. The first paragraph of this article (no. 1701) begins by citing the beautiful passage from Vatican Council II's *Gaudium et Spes* (no. 22), in which the Council Fathers remind us that "Christ . . . in the very revelation of the

226

mystery of the Father and of his love, makes man fully manifest to himself and brings to light his exalted vocation" (no. 1701; cf. no. 1710).

Article one of this chapter then affirms the truths that man, made in God's image, is endowed with reason, whereby he can come to know the truth, including moral truth, and with free will, which enables him to determine his own life by directing himself toward his true good (nos. 1704-1706, 1711-1713). In addition, it reminds us that because of original sin we are inclined toward evil and subject to error (nos. 1707, 1714), but that God, in his great mercy, has sent us his only-begotten Son to redeem us from sin and to enable us to become truly God's children, capable of acting rightly and of doing good (nos. 1709, 1715).

Article two centers attention on our vocation to beatitude and on the beatitudes proclaimed by Jesus that express the Christian's vocation, illumine the actions and attitudes meant to characterize Christian life, and herald the blessings and rewards in store for Christ's faithful (nos. 1716-1717, 1725-1726). Along with the Decalogue the beatitudes of our Lord's Sermon on the Mount describe for us the path leading to God's eternal kingdom (nos. 1724, 1728-1729).

Article three then develops in more depth the meaning of man's freedom or his capacity to determine himself by his own free choices, his responsibility to choose rightly and to avoid freely choosing evil, and his need for God's grace, which in no way opposes human freedom but rather enables it to be exercised rightly (nos. 1730-1748).

Man's need for God's never-failing grace in order to fulfill his vocation and to live as God wants him to is developed more fully in article two of Chapter Three, Section One of Part Three. This article emphasizes that we do not justify ourselves, but that God takes the initiative in reconciling sinful men and women with himself by the grace of the Holy Spirit, poured into the hearts of those who have, through baptism, died to sin and have risen to new life in Christ (cf. nos. 1996ff). Grace, a sharing in God's own divine life, is infused by the power of the Holy Spirit into our being so that we are sanctified, made holy, and enabled to live worthily as God's children (nos. 1996-2000; cf. nos. 2017-2027). Since we are now children of God, who share in his divine nature, we are called to a life of perfection and of holiness, which cannot be achieved unless we are willing to bear our cross and to mortify ourselves (nos. 2012-2015; 2028-2029).

2. The Church Is, by God's Will, Our Mother and Teacher. Article three of Chapter Three, Section One, Part Three, is devoted to this issue. The *Catechism* begins this subject by noting that it is *in* the Church, the communion of all the baptized, that Christians fulfill their vocation and that the

Christian moral life must be considered a spiritual worship because it is a life that finds its source and summit in the Eucharistic sacrifice (nos. 2030-2031). It then affirms, following the teaching of Vatican Council II, that the magisterium of the Church, invested in the college of bishops under the headship of the Roman pontiff, has the God-given authority and responsibility to teach in Christ's name the saving truth of faith and morals (nos. 2033-2034). It goes on to say that the gift of infallibility extends to those elements of Christian doctrine, including morals, without which the saving truths of the faith cannot be safeguarded, faithfully presented, or observed (no. 2035). In fact, the *Catechism* insists that the authority of the magisterium extends to *specific* precepts of natural law insofar as their observance is required by our Creator and is necessary for our salvation (no. 2036). The magisterium has a prophetic role to play in reminding men of the requirements of the natural moral law, and the faithful have a right to be properly instructed and the duty to observe the moral teaching proposed by the magisterium (nos. 2036-2037). Thus the faithful ought not to regard the teaching of the magisterium as an imposition from without but rather ought to accept its teaching as a child accepts the teaching of a loving mother (cf. no. 2040).

3. Shaping Choices and Acts in Accord With the Truth. Under this heading is included the *Catechism's* teaching on the morality of human acts, the role of conscience, and the moral law, matters central to issues taken up in *Catholic Sexual Ethics.*

A. The Morality of Human Acts. This subject is treated in article four, Chapter Three, Section One of Part Three. The *Catechism* teaches that the sources for the morality of human acts are the object chosen (what one freely chooses to do), the end for whose sake the object is chosen, and the circumstances in which the action takes place (nos. 1750ff). It emphasizes that *all* these elements must be morally good if the whole human act is to be morally good (no. 1755). It clearly identifies the object as the subject matter freely chosen and willed by the agent, and it teaches that the object so identified specifies the morality of the act insofar as reason can determine whether or not this object is in conformity or not to objective norms of morality (no. 1751). It insists that a good intention, understood as the intention of the *end* for whose sake an object is chosen, cannot justify the means if this means is morally evil by reason of its object (no. 1753). It clearly affirms that there are definite kinds of human acts, specified by their objects, that are always wrong for one to choose because choosing them entails a disordered will or moral evil, and it gives fornication as an example of such an intrinsically evil act (no. 1755). In short, the *Catechism* firmly holds that there are some kinds of human acts, specified by the objects freely chosen, that are intrinsically evil and that, corresponding to such intrinsically evil acts, are moral absolutes or exceptionless moral norms.

B. Conscience. This subject is taken up in article six, Chapter One, Section One, Part Three. The *Catechism's* teaching, like that of the Holy Father's in *Veritatis Splendor*, focuses on the meaning of conscience as a practical judgment about the morality of human acts either antecedent to their performance or subsequent to their doing. It insists that the judgment of conscience is not infallible but can be mistaken, that men have the obligation to form or educate their conscience by sincerely seeking the truth, and that moral conscience is properly formed only if persons are open to God's truth, seek it in prayer, and let themselves be guided by the authoritative teaching of the Church (nos. 1776-1802).

C. The Moral Law. Article one, Chapter Three, Section One of Part Three is devoted to this subject. Here the *Catechism*, following Vatican Council II and the entire Catholic tradition, insists that God's divine and eternal law, his wise and loving plan for human existence, is the highest norm of human life and action (no. 1950; cf. no. 1975). God, moreover, has enabled his rational creature, man, to participate in this wise and loving plan through the natural law (no. 1954; cf. no. 1978). The natural law is universal and immutable (nos. 1956, 1958). While varying in its application (no. 1957), the natural law nonetheless unites human persons and imposes upon them common moral principles and norms that always retain their validity (no. 1958). Because it is sometimes difficult to grasp the moral truths of the natural law, particularly as a result of sin, God's grace and revelation are needed for sinful human persons to come to know the truths required to live an upright human life (cf. no. 1960).

The moral teaching of the Old Law given to the Chosen People is summarized in the precepts of the Decalogue. The Old Law is a preparation for the law of the Gospel, or the law of love, which brings the natural law and the Old Law to fulfillment and perfection. Far from abolishing the moral requirements of the natural law and of the Decalogue, the new law of love deepens and fulfills them by summoning human persons to be as perfect as the heavenly Father is perfect and to shape their lives in accordance with the Sermon on the Mount and its Beatitudes (nos. 1961-1986).

The *Catechism* provides details on the requirements of the moral law in Section Two of Part Three, devoted to a consideration of the ten precepts of the Decalogue, or the Ten Commandments. Of particular relevance to *Catholic Sexual Ethics*, obviously, is the teaching of the *Catechism* regarding the sixth and ninth precepts of the Decalogue, those prohibiting adultery and the coveting of one's neighbor's wife.

In its treatment of the sixth commandment the *Catechism* first reaffirms the Church's teaching, rooted in the Scriptures, on the goodness of human sexuality as created by God and on the sexual complementarity of man and woman whose very nature inclines them to the goods of marriage and family (nos. 2331-2332). It stresses that the union of man and woman *in marriage* is a way of imitating in the flesh God's generosity and fecundity (no. 2335).

The *Catechism* then reminds us of our vocation to chastity, a virtue pertaining to the cardinal virtue of temperance. Chastity enables men and women to come into possession of themselves as sexual beings and of their sexual desires so that they are able to *give* themselves away to others, either in the covenant of marital love or in virginity (nos. 2337-2350). It then considers offenses against chastity. Among these it lists lust, masturbation, fornication, pornography, prostitution, and rape (nos. 2351-2356). It then takes up the issue of homosexuality, reaffirming the Church's teaching that homosexual acts are intrinsically disordered, contrary to natural law and in no way to be approved (no. 2357), and encouraging homosexually-inclined persons to cultivate the virtue of chastity (no. 2359).

In its discussion of the sixth commandment and its requirements the *Catechism* then addresses husbands and wives and their relationship. It speaks of the beauty of faithful spousal love, which is expressed fittingly in the marital act (nos. 2360-2362), observing that the union of husband and wife in the conjugal act fosters the good of the spouses themselves and the transmission of human life, meanings or values of marriage that are inherently interrelated and can never be deliberately separated without jeopardizing the couple's spiritual life and compromising the goods of marriage (no. 2363). Addressing the fecundity of marriage and the marital act, the *Catechism* reaffirms the teaching that every marital act must be open to the transmission of life, speaks approvingly of periodic continence as the morally proper way of exercising parenthood responsibly, and unequivocally repudiates contraception, defined as any action that, either in anticipation of the marital act, in its accomplishment, or in the development of its natural consequences, proposes either as an end or means to impede procreation (nos. 2366-2372). It concludes this section with paragraphs emphasizing that children are precious gifts from God, expresses special praise for couples who generously welcome the gift of new human life, and offers solace for couples involuntarily sterile (nos. 2373-2379).

The *Catechism* then condemns in no uncertain terms grave offenses against the dignity of marriage, including adultery, divorce, incest, so-called free-love unions, and trial marriages (nos. 2380-2391).

In its consideration of the ninth commandment the *Catechism* challenges Christians to overcome covetousness by purifying their hearts and cultivating the virtues of chastity and modesty by recourse to prayer (nos. 2514-2527).

Pastoral Conclusion

Sexual morality must be taught in the Church in the spirit in which Christ taught.[1] In the preceding chapters we have spoken of "the biblical foundations, the ethical grounds, and the personalistic reasons" that underlie Catholic teaching in sexual ethics.[2] We have pointed out that the Church's insistent teachings in sexual morality are entirely faithful to Gospel teaching, are true and good, and that they liberate the human spirit by guiding us to live in ways that are truly good.

But this splendid and saving teaching must be proclaimed in a very flawed world in which cultural conditions can make it very difficult to follow even necessary precepts. It must be presented to people who are very weak. It must be spoken to contemporary men and women who frequently find acceptance of Catholic doctrine in this area difficult because of the pervasive pressures of the world, and even because of the halfhearted support of — or in some cases, dissent from — this teaching on the part of many in the Church herself.

The aim of pastoral theology, and the purpose of pastoral labors, is to help the faithful actually live their lives in accordance with the teachings of faith, and so to grow in love and in the grace of God. By no means is pastoral theology concerned with replacing the excellent and necessary teachings of the Gospel with more lenient maxims, which undermine essential respect for human values and weaken personal resolve to live in accord with the authentic requirements of love.

In this concluding part of the book, we can only sketch the most basic elements of a pastoral stance that flows from Catholic teaching. We stress the following points:

(1) The importance of teaching Catholic sexual morality faithfully, intelligently, and attractively;

(2) The need to make clear the objective truth of Catholic moral teaching in sexual ethics, its seriousness, and also the reasons why those who perform acts that are objectively gravely sinful are often not guilty of grave sin;

(3) Finding ways to give the faithful practical assistance in living in accord with the excellent standards of Catholic faith;

(4) Helping all see how Christ assists his people to bear the burdens of chaste living without excessive stress.

I. Teaching Sexual Ethics Faithfully, Intelligently, Attractively

Teaching Faithfully. Catholic teachers — bishops, priests, parents, religious educators — have the privilege and the duty of teaching faithfully and clearly the Catholic vision of sexuality and its authentic moral teachings. They must not excuse themselves on the pretext that in our time Catholic teachings on chastity are too difficult, or that people of our time have rejected what faith teaches in this area. For Catholics have a right to Catholic teaching in this very important matter, and they need the light of the Gospel to come to appreciate the truth and goodness of what faith teaches about chaste love.[3]

We must teach the precepts that guard pure love persistently. For the faithful are daily battered by the voices of the world, with its teachings about sexuality that are incompatible with Christian life. They will suffer great harm if they are not fortified by the saving teaching of the Gospels.

Teaching as Jesus Taught. Jesus strengthened and heartened the people to whom he preached by speaking with authority (Mt 7:29). He spoke as one who knew with certainty what is true and truly good. And he spoke out of a life of such excellence that his hearers realized that he was in fact teaching the truth their hearts long for and needed.[4] Even when he taught difficult precepts, he enabled his hearers to realize that he spoke in defense of their lives and of their greatest good.

Over the centuries the Church has spoken with authority in the name of Jesus on questions of sexual morality, as she has in all essential areas of moral life. The Church has spoken with a bracing authority, because in a bewildered and suffering world, she has know with certainty important and saving truths, and has recognized that forceful teaching is necessary to support persons in their weakness (cf. 1 Cor 14:8).

Our Times Require Excellent Teaching. Even in the midst of the spiritual confusion of our time, the pastoral leader must teach the sexual ethics of the Church with the merciful firmness of Christ. The duty to teach the doctrine of the Church in this area is certain,[5] and the harm done to the faithful when this doctrine is not faithfully proclaimed is all too clear. Public opinion surveys reveal that many Catholics do not accept the sure teachings of the Church in this area. As a result, many tend to live in ways that assail the most precious values, and fail to respect the human goods that must be honored if we are to have a fulfilled and happy life on earth, and live in the love of God with a secure hope for eternal life.

Though a life of self-possession and of disciplined love is ultimately

233

far happier than a life wounded by lust, the young and the weak do not know this through their own experience. In many ways the world around them [and sometimes even Catholic educators] tends to deceive them, by telling them that the excellent ways of Christ are too difficult, or that what seems so attractive to the flesh must be right for them. Consequently, if pastoral leaders within the Church seem uncertain whether the sexual morality always proclaimed by the Church is true they undermine whatever resolve the weak and the young can muster.

Teaching With One Voice. Recent popes have regularly reminded scholars and pastoral leaders of their duty to teach with one voice the truth about marriage and sexual morality which has constantly been taught in the family of faith.[6] The fact that there has been an unprecedented outburst of illegitimate dissent from this teaching in our time, the fact that the modern media induce many of the faithful to accept the unhappy ethics of shallow hedonism, the fact that those who proclaim the teaching of the Church on these matters can be subjected to a measure of ridicule and loss of popularity — all these things do not remove the duty to proclaim faithfully the teaching of the Church on sexual morality.[7] For the faithful have a right to receive all the authentic teaching of the Church.[8]

The faithful are not receiving the teaching of the Church about sexual morality unless they are given that teaching in a fully Catholic way. Thus, they must not simply be told that the Church "officially" teaches this or that. For to say simply that does not help the faithful realize that the Church teaching is true and good, that it proposes the way the Lord wills us to live, and that, consequently, they have a grave duty to believe it and live by it. Only the sound conviction that the Church's teachings are true and that they can be lived gladly with the help of God's grace will provide the strength needed by one who is tempted to commit fornication or to enter an invalid marriage. Those who speak for the Lord must do all they can to provide this strength, and to do this they must speak his truth as what it is — the way to live in Christ.

II. Teaching Compassionately and Truthfully

Pastoral care must seek to be honest and charitable in its assessment of the measure of subjective guilt incurred by those who lapse into behavior that objectively is mortally sinful. Catholic faith teaches that sins of lust are objectively so gravely disordered that those who perform them freely and with a sufficient understanding of their malice do commit mortal sins. They tragically separate themselves from the love of Christ and endanger their eternal salvation. Moreover, the Church teaches that, while passion and

234

ignorance frequently lessen or take away the personal guilt of sexual sins, people can and do commit mortal sin by lustful thoughts and actions. It is useful to list here some of the considerations essential for a balanced pastoral approach to this question.

1. *Activities That Are Objectively Gravely Wrong Are Not Always Subjectively So.* To say that lustful actions, such as acts of fornication or masturbation, are objectively gravely sinful is certainly not to say that every person who engages in behavior of these kinds necessarily incurs personally the guilt of grave sin.[9] Ignorance and antecedent passion can lessen or remove such guilt. The lives of many are lived in such difficult conditions, subject to utter poverty and grave injustices, and in the midst of gravely scandalous provocations, that it can be very difficult for them to grasp the serious nature of sins of lust. Psychological impediments (for example, in the case of compulsive actions) may remove responsibility considerably — or, in some cases, entirely — from lustful behavior. Those who are told by trusted teachers and advisers that it is permissible to do kinds of actions that faith has regularly condemned as always objectively gravely wrong may at times follow this bad advice with some real measure of good faith. Those who are deeply troubled by bad actions they have performed — while influenced by scandal, injustice, false teaching, or compulsions of which they were victims — deserve gentle, strong, and competent pastoral care.

2. *Sexual Sins Are Often Subjectively Grave Sins.* In some individual cases a spiritual guide may have specific reasons for judging that a particular person has not sinned by indulging in sexual acts which are objectively gravely immoral. This may be true, for example, if the action in question seems compulsive to the point that it is not within the person's control. But there is no reason whatever for assuming that people who engage in such behavior virtually always escape the guilt of personal mortal sin. People can and do commit mortal sins by lustful deeds and by deliberately indulging in lustful desire.[10] Nor it is right to suggest that a person who wishes to live his or her life generally in ways pleasing to God, but engages occasionally in lustful deeds of a kind common enough in worldly society, would retain a fundamental stance of faithfulness to God — that one does not lose grace or endanger eternal salvation by deliberately engaging in such acts.[11] Single gravely wrong acts (normally preceded by less grave sins) can be formal mortal sins, for if one is prepared to do, and chooses to do, an action that is gravely evil and known to be opposed to the demanding will of God (or does not know this precisely because of a gravely culpable unwillingness to learn the truth), then one does not maintain a faithful love of God. Rather, one thus expresses the spirit of one

who does not in fact love God in even the minimum measure required to live in his grace (cf. Jn 14:15).[12]

3. *Ignorance and the Gravity of Sins.* The fact that one does not know or believe that it is mortally sinful to engage deliberately in a particular lustful act is very relevant. But it does not always indicate that one has not incurred personally the guilt of formal mortal sin,[13] for ignorance in this matter can itself be deliberate and gravely sinful. Self-deception is only too easy for us human beings. One who culpably maintains ignorance of truths that God has made very accessible (by the gift of public revelation and by the graces that make the assent of faith possible) can sin mortally without honestly acknowledging any responsibility. In fact, those who commit mortal sins in any area are only too ready to seek to persuade themselves that what they choose to do is reasonable and right for them. Thus, they add to their sin by acting against the truth that has been made accessible to them.

4. *Passion and the Gravity of Sins.* Antecedent passion and the reality of human weakness are important considerations in assessing subjective guilt. But the fact than an objectively grave act was done out of weakness and with some influence of passion is no certain sign that mortal sin was not committed. As long as the person maintains substantial freedom, knows that a proposed action is gravely wrong (or is gravely culpable in his ignorance of that fact), and in choosing to act or not act retains essential self-mastery, one is capable of grave sin, and of meritorious fidelity to God.[14] Christians are bound to be faithful to God, and to lead morally good lives, even when it is difficult to do so. God's grace make faithfulness very possible.

5. *Principles for Spiritual Guidance.* In evaluating subjective guilt, the role of those who have any kind of teaching or advising role is different from that of casual acquaintances and friends. Ordinarily, it is quite proper to have a generous interpretation of other people's conduct. It is inappropriate to judge that our friends and acquaintances have in fact formally sinned, even if it is manifest that some of their conduct exhibits behavior of a kind that the Church teaches to be gravely wrong.

But teachers and advisers have special duties; frequently, they have the duty to help others escape self-deceit. Thus, any general presumption that those who are doing things which the Catholic faith teaches to be gravely wrong should be assured that they are in good faith is a serious mistake. False assurances of this kind can be extremely harmful. They can support forms of malice that directly imperil the salvation of the one advised, and they can imperil also the salvation of the adviser.

In giving spiritual direction, an adviser must have profound concern for the truth. When one is morally certain that grave sin has been committed, or that it has not, his advice should follow his considered judgment. When it is far from clear whether of not mortal sin has been committed (in forming judgments in these matters, the guidance of those moralists and spiritual authors whose work has faithfully mirrored received Catholic positions is to be followed), advice must reflect the uncertainty of the situation. Grace is a most precious gift; mortal sin is a terrible evil. One who may have committed a mortal sin, or may yet be entangled in a practice or actions that are objectively mortally sinful, needs the help of his advisers to find his way toward a better state.

6. *Witnesses to What Is Truly Good.* In certain rare cases and for special reasons it may be right for confessors or spiritual directors to be silent about the objective immorality of actions that a penitent or someone whom they advise has engaged in. Divine revelation, however, was given to the Church concerning moral matters because it is good for us to know the truth about how we should live to gain eternal life. Hence Catholic pastoral leaders would fail gravely in their duties if they did not make publicly known the full malice of sexual sins. When, moved by grace, a person asks about the morality of sinful behavior that he or she has engaged in or proposes to engage in, that person is to be answered truthfully; and one must not routinely suppose that even habitual sinners or very weak persons will be unable or unwilling to respond to the calls of grace. Human lives are made far better when the light of truth and the many supports of faith are made richly accessible. To be quiet about Catholic teachings concerning sexual morality in order to escape conflicts with those who brazenly deny these teachings, or out of a fear of mockery from worldly forces, or because of a mistaken judgment that the less the faithful know about the truth God has reveal the less likely they are to commit sins — this is not the stance of pastoral love. Rather, "to diminish in no way the saving teaching of Christ constitutes an eminent form of charity for souls."[15]

7. *Sinful Kinds of Acts Do Harm Even When Innocently Done.* Pastoral care is, of course, concerned with more than subjective guilt or innocence in this matter. Catholic moral teaching about sex speaks the truth about basic human goods and is concerned about what really is good for human persons. Lustful actions are really bad for human beings, They are not merely "forbidden." They harm those who engage in them, even if they do not know that they are evil acts, and even when these acts are not morally imputable to the one performing them. Hence the pastoral teacher and adviser must be concerned to help people know what is good in these matters, and assist them to walk in ways that really serve their human fulfillment and their salvation.

8. *The Power of God's Grace.* The remembrance that human beings can and do commit mortal sins should not lead to despair or excessive sadness. All teaching and guidance in sexual ethics is to be carried out in a spirit of faith and with trust in divine mercy. Difficult and excellent things are commanded in the New Law. Human weakness could be inclined to fear that what faith teaches is too difficult. But it is a commonplace in Catholic teaching that the accessibility of God's grace must be remembered here. Indeed, the entire fulfillment of the moral law would be impossible for fallen humankind without the assistance of the grace and mercy of God. Advisers who have experienced how true it is that God enables very weak persons to do what he has required of them can speak with realistic encouragement to even the weakest sinners.

III. Giving Practical Assistance for Living the Truth

The Christian teacher must not only teach the excellence of the ways in which the Lord would have his people walk. He is also called upon to give the many forms of practical assistance which they need to live as they are called to live.

Instilling a Desire for Holiness and a Love of Chastity. The Second Vatican Council stressed at length the essential need in the Church for stirring up a hunger for holiness. To lead good lives we must seek to grow in faith, hope, and love, and in living with entire faithfulness to the demands of love. Thus, pastoral leaders must seek to help the faithful to live in those excellent ways which make this life happy in the midst of trials, and which make the people of God worthy of eternal life. Holiness of life is not the special goal of a certain elite within the Church. Each one of God's people is called to holiness and can fulfill his or her vocation only by pursuing generous love faithfully. Education in chastity must be carried on in the context of this duty to pursue holiness. Thus, chastity is not to be taught in abstraction from other virtues. It is to be grasped as a necessary ingredient in a holy, free, and good life.

Revealing the Goodness and Attractiveness of Chaste Love. In the confusion of our time, pastoral leaders must see to it that the faithful are taught well the meaning of chastity. Chastity is not an irrational form of repression. It is an essential part of temperance and self-possession, for it gives to the emotions, affections, and passions themselves an orderly direction, so that the human desire for sexual pleasure is itself wisely directed only toward pleasures which are properly related to authentic human goods. Thus, the chaste person finds it easy to forgo pleasure which it would not be wise or good to pursue. The full realization of chastity is different, therefore,

238

from that type of continence in which many people struggle more or less constantly against serious sexual temptation. They genuinely want to be chaste, but they have not succeeded in fully integrating their personalities and sexual desires around their morally good choices. They have not been assisted to the generous acquisition of a full possession of the virtue of chastity — which makes living chastely much easier and much more satisfying. Those who, through faithful concern to act chastely, and through prayer and the help afforded in the sacraments, come to a solid possession of the virtue of chastity acquire with it peace and self-possession, and escape from the burden of constant struggle and temptation.

Profound Importance of Chastity. It is true that chastity is far from the greatest of virtues. St. Thomas Aquinas — along with much of Catholic tradition — teaches that chastity is a form of temperance, which is the least excellent of the cardinal virtues.[16] Nevertheless, Catholic tradition has also emphasized the indispensable importance of this lowly virtue. For the self-control and tranquility it provides are necessary conditions for the full development of the more exalted virtues. The moral tradition of the Church often pointed out how disastrous are the spiritual fruits of unchastity. The "offspring of lust," that is, the bitter fruits which the tradition perceived as flowing from lives lived unchastely, are indeed formidable. The tradition lists them as: "blindness of mind, lack of balanced consideration, inconstancy, precipitation, love of self, hatred of God, excessive clinging to the present world, and horror or despair of the world to come." These are the bitter and disastrous fruits of a life that lacks self-possession and the will to live chastely.[17]

Pastoral leaders must then take very seriously the problems created when a culture tends to lead great numbers of the faithful into sins of impurity. Experience shows how those who fall into sins of lust begin to find faith and the practice of faith uninteresting. In any place where the pastors do not seriously seek to guard chastity, we must expect to see a corresponding decline in faith and in efforts to live a life of charity.

Formation for Teachers of Chastity. Pastoral leaders must see to it that those who educate the young in chastity have themselves not merely learned the ways of Christ theoretically but are themselves seeking to lead chaste and good lives. They must have tasted for themselves how true it is that temperance and chastity can be achieved even in a sinful world. They must be persons who firmly and fully believe the truth of Catholic teaching about marriage and sexual morality, and who have tasted in their lives the joy and freedom of living chastely. Those who have experienced the ways in which self-possession is happily achieved can give heart and encouragement to beginners in the school of Christ.

Chastity and Freedom. Central to their efforts, as Pope John Paul II has pointed out, must be education in the true sense of freedom.[18] True sexual liberation is not achieved by pretending that each person may without fear do any kind of act toward which he or she is actually inclined, whether it serves real human goods and the authentic fulfillment of life or not. It is not achieved in the life of one dominated by one's passions, without faith-enlightened concern for what is required by love of oneself and of others. It is achieved when one's passions are mastered: that is, not repressed, but governed by generous love. Then one can freely choose to live as one needs to live to acquire in joy what a person must possess to achieve his or her entire fulfillment, and to serving the common good of one's friends in the family of God.[19]

Removing the Impediments That Make Chastity Difficult. Pastoral care must not only make clear the excellence of chastity but also assist in removing the impediments to chaste living and in providing the natural and supernatural supports needed to make chastity flourish in the Christian community.

Social Conditions and Chastity. Many people in the world "lack both the means necessary for survival, such as food, work, housing, and medicine, and the most elementary freedoms." In wealthier countries "excessive prosperity and the consumer mentality, paradoxically joined to a certain anguish and uncertainty about the future," deprive the faithful of the courage and generosity needed to pursue holiness and self-possession.[20] People everywhere are wounded by the invasion's of the mass media, which bring into every home solicitations to live lives patterned on ways of thinking entirely alien to the Gospel. Realistic education in chastity cannot be carried out without awareness of these evils, and without serious efforts to overcome them as far as possible.

It is not necessary, however, to overcome every social evil before inviting the faithful to holiness of life. Still, the faithful are heartened when they see that their leaders are aware of the burdens under which they labor to serve Christ, and when they can see that pastoral leaders are earnestly helping them in visible and realistic ways.

Strong Christian community life must be built up to assist the faithful in countering social pressures toward accepting the many forms of lust that appeal to fallen man. It is essential to avoid that despair which judges that in the circumstances of our time young people will fall into fixed practices of masturbation or fornication, that the married will adopt a contraceptive mentality and practice, and that adultery will be commonplace. For this kind of despair leads to compromising sound pastoral practice and even to rejecting Catholic teaching. Since on this view pastoral practice can really do nothing to guard people from the inevitable triumph of sexual immorality, there is a temptation to downplay the importance of sexual sins and to seek a Christianity that accepts gravely sinful practices as a normal part of a good Christian life. From the time of the Church's birth Christians have known that these counsels of despair are entirely wrong. The fire of the early Christians, love, their pursuit of perfection despite their weaknesses and the corruptive influences of the life of the Roman Empire, enabled them to build communities in which chastity flourished. Certainly grave sin did not leave these communities entirely, as they will not leave ours; but Christian communities whose members cherish and nourish chastity make it possible for all those willing to respond to God's grace to grow in the freedom and strength of virtue.

Specific Alternatives to Sinful Practices. Many Catholic people today engage in behavior that is objectively mortally sinful because they have difficult problems and are not aware of realistic and not excessively burdensome ways of resolving them. Many Catholic spouses practice contraception, even in ways that are times in fact abortifacient,[21] or choose the gravely sinful alternative of sterilization, because they do not know any effective and morally acceptable ways of limiting family size. Often this decision leads them to resentment of the Church and to a kind of despair.

Making Natural Family Planning Accessible. But much of this sorry condition could be removed if pastoral leaders carried out their duties in the way John Paul II has pointed out. A virtuous decision concerning a difficult problem can be made much easier if pastoral leaders see to it that contemporary forms of natural family planning — which are secure and safe, and which are strong supports for marital love — were really made accessible to all Catholic people in every place. The faithful are helped when excellent preaching makes it clear why the use of natural family planning and the use of contraception manifest radically different philosophies of life, and involve "in the final analysis two irreconcilable concepts of the human person and of human sexuality."[22] In this matter the Church *must*, Pope John Paul II points out, offer "practical help." "Every effort must be made to render such knowledge [of natural family planning] accessible to all married people and also to young adults before marriage, through clear, timely, and serious instruction."[23]

The Practical Importance of Supernatural Helps. Faith calls us to live in the ways of love — which does often make great demands. But it is necessary to walk in these ways for life to become human and happy. Divorce is bitterly painful to both spouses and children; yet to live in faithful love of one partner until death, in shared love of the goods that can make life together happy, requires serious efforts not likely to be sustained without the assistance of grace. The distinctive gift of Christ, our teacher, is that he gives those who believe in him not only knowledge of what is good but also "power to become children of God" (Jn 1:12). Things that would be beyond human power are possible to those who seek assistance from the Lord in confident prayer and in devout use of the sacraments, especially the sacrament of reconciliation and the Eucharist. Those turning aside from bad habits, or seeking in young years to acquire self-possession and chastity benefit greatly by finding a confessor whose spiritual assistance will give them light and encouragement, and who can strengthen their resolve to acquire that purity of heart which supports faithful and generous love.

Pastoral Care for the Family. The family itself is the "little church," the first school of virtue for the young, the community in which love and the requirements of love must first be learned. But the Christian family is assaulted in many ways by the materialistic and hedonistic forces that are so powerful in our culture, and so pervasive in their influence through the mass media. The many forms of care which the Church owes to the family were pointed out by the Synod of Bishops in 1980, and summarized by John Paul II in his apostolic exhortation *Familiaris Consortio.* All these need to be put into effect to help the family of our time to be the school of human values. No other group can replace the family in doing its proper and indispensable tasks. Unless the family flourishes, both civil society and the Church suffer deeply, and the healthy personal growth of young people is deeply endangered. When families seem to be too weak to carry out their proper roles, one should not have immediate recourse to other social structures to achieve what is desired. Rather, every effort must be made to strengthen the family itself, and enable the family to become what it must be. For nothing can replace the family. "Parents are the first and most important educators of their children, and they also possess a fundamental competency in this area: they are educators because they are parents."[24]

Pastoral leaders should be familiar with the many recent Church documents which make it clear that support of the family must be the central focus of pastoral efforts today. Many families today are deeply wounded, and need strong help; and the pastoral life of the Church generally cannot flourish without the presence of strong families given freedom and the resources to carry out their indispensable role. It must be the primary pastoral care of the Church to aid parents and families, for the Church herself cannot prosper if families do not prosper. Families can flourish in grace and become holy even in times like our own; and unless they are helped to do so, the Church herself cannot flourish.[25]

Preparation for Marriage. If education in Catholic faith and in Christian living is to flourish, homes must be strong and parents must be enabled to carry out their indispensable tasks in the face of all the obstacles our culture creates.

Many young couples who approach the Church with the intention of marrying in the Church, and of establishing families, have been deeply wounded by the circumstances of the times. Many of them are not practicing Catholics. Often they know their faith only poorly, and do not have possession of good reasons for believing what faith teaches. It is especially important at this time for the Church to provide a really excellent immediate preparation for the Sacrament of Marriage.

Fortunately, the Holy See has prepared an excellent set of guidelines to govern preparation for marriage in our time.[26] Surely we ought not fall into discouragement, or believe that in our time people simply cannot prepare suitably for Christian marriage. The time of immediate preparation for marriage is a time of grace. The young people are ordinarily in love, and this gift of sincere human love, with its great hopes, can itself prove a singular blessing. Those about to marry have earnest hopes that their marriages will endure. Their experience of honest love can help them realize that the cynical and selfish spirit of the world ought not dominate their spirits. They are often prepared to learn freshly of Christ, and of the great love to which he calls all, and the special love he has for those entering marriage.

We can expect much of marriage preparation programs, if the leaders and instructors in the program approach it wisely. Certainly, as the *Instruction* urges, they must have a great love for the young people they are assisting. They must also have a good doctrinal and personal formation, so that they reveal to the young the full Catholic vision of marriage and marital love, and permit them to see how earnestly they love all that faith teaches, and how earnestly they themselves are seeking to live their lives in Christ. There must be a strong evangelizing element in marriage preparation. The engaged couples must be taught the meaning of marriage, the greatness of this vocation, the Catholic understanding of marital love, and the goodness and wisdom of its moral requirements. Many kinds of assistance musts be offered to each couple: helps toward communicating well and learning generosity in their new life, and helps to understand why natural family planning liberates couples from the bitter burdens of contraception, and the deeply flawed understanding of love that it serves.

243

Pastoral Care for Young People. In the world today it can be very difficult for young people to grow up enjoying a profound personal possession of their Catholic faith, and with a sound understanding of the goodness of Catholic moral teaching. The education in chastity given to the young must be intelligently and faithfully shaped. Since parents are the first and most indispensable teachers of pure love for their children, the Church owes them assistance to become able to carry out their responsibilities. From earliest years children must be helped to experience the greatness of love, to desire to have generous love, and to acquire that self-possession that is needed to grow in love. They must be helped to experience the joy of overcoming that selfishness which is the enemy of true love, and to feel the freedom of being liberated from overwhelming needs to act as immediate pleasure suggests.[27]

Other realistic helps must be given to the young if the Christian community seriously wishes to make chastity a reality for many of them. They must be educated in ways of critically evaluating what the mass media and modern forms of entertainment make popular, so that they may appreciate and enjoy those aspects of popular culture that are suitable and learn not to be harmed by those elements that are harmful. The community must also assist them to find forms of creative play and experiences of beauty which are in full harmony with their Christian vision of life.

Education of Young People in Chastity. Education in the Christian vision of sexuality and in chaste living for the young is primarily the responsibility of parents. They are uniquely qualified to give such instruction, because of their close knowledge of their own children, and their special love for them. If in some respects and under certain circumstances, others assist parents in this matter, education in the Catholic vision of sexuality and in chaste love must still be carried out under the attentive guidance of parents. And these programs must be penetrated with the spirit of pure love that shines in the Gospel.[28]

Many secular forms of sex education assume that most young people will adopt the lustful practices so common in our society — masturbation, fornication, and the like; and they seek not so much to guide people away from immoral activity and the great harm that does to their inner lives, as to protect them from the most visible effects of immoral activity: sexually transmitted diseases and unwanted pregnancies. Often these programs assume the hedonistic attitudes of our time, and consequently set up sexual education programs so as to help people realize for themselves and others as much pleasure as possible, in ways that do not "hurt" others. But reflection on the harm that is done by separating interest in sexual activity from the indispensable human goods toward which that activity should be essentially ordered tends to be entirely neglected in such programs.

Pastoral leaders have the duty to see to it that no inappropriate forms of sexual education are tolerated in Catholic contexts, and the duty to assist parents who rightly wish to protect their children from such programs when they are thrust upon their children in public schools or in other public contexts. They must see to it also that only excellent programs in teaching chaste love are permitted in Catholic contexts, and that those who direct or teach in Catholic programs sincerely believe Catholic teaching in the whole area of sexuality, so that they may genuinely help the young to grow in the love of chastity.

Chastity, Justice, and Peace. Christian life cannot be taught in fragmented segments; it is a living whole, and neglect of any essential elements redounds to the harm of every part. In recent years some groups of Catholics have stressed too exclusively the importance of the social teaching of the Church with its concern for justice and peace, and others have stressed too exclusively the importance of personal holiness, or guarding life and attending to purity of mind and body. Different stresses can, of course, be acceptable, for it is not possible for everyone to focus energies on all things. But there must be real respect on everyone's part for all the essential goods which fulfill human life. All must be concerned both with matters of social justice, matters of personal morality, and holiness of life.

It would be fatal to a Catholic pursuit of justice and peace to count it unimportant if the faithful should reject Catholic teaching on chaste love. For the fruits of lust — as we have seen above — lead to disorder in every moral area. They lead to a contempt for that love and concern for others' rights that may interfere with the satisfaction of one's own undisciplined desires. Chastity is far from being the greatest virtue, but the greatest virtues, such as justice, are not possible without chastity. Nor may those who struggle to support personal holiness of life minimize the importance of caring for a just social order. For one who promotes chastity — but not the social conditions that favor it and flow from it — fails to appreciate the essentially social character of the entire fabric of Christian life. Self-possession without love for others is not the Christian virtue of chastity.

IV. Making the Burdens of Chastity Light

The Christian teacher wishes to share the gladness of living in Christ with his beloved students and friends. He should have a special desire to assist those who fear that the ways of chaste and generous love may be too difficult to follow. The leaders of the Church have sought to show great concern and compassion for such people. The bishops taking part in the 1980 Synod on marriage took great care to make clear that they understood well how the circumstances of life today make faithfulness to the teachings of faith on contraception, divorce and remarriage, and fidelity within marriage so difficult for many people. And in his apostolic exhortation on the family, summing up the work of the synod, Pope John Paul II spoke with great gentleness on the pastoral care of the family in very difficult cases.[29]

Compassion and Faithfulness to Principle. The Church's sensitivity to these difficulties should not be understood as an acceptance of what are in fact counsels of despair. One must compassionately understand what leads many into invalid marriages, into habitual fornication, toward practices of contraception or to sterilization. But proper compassion for persons should not lead to an approval of sin, however reluctant. For when men and women — pressed by hard circumstances — solve their problems in ways that are objectively gravely evil, they are doing deeds that deepen the wounds and sorrows of their lives.

They are creating disorder and pain in the world in which they live. For sexual sins are not simply violations of arbitrary precepts. They are, rather, attacks on the basic human values that are indispensable for authentically human lives. Deeds that are in fact base and sinful are never reasonable solutions even to tragic problems.

False "Pastoral" Solutions. That is why the Church has always rejected allegedly "pastoral solutions" which in fact involve approval of kinds of actions that the Church knows always to be immoral. When John Paul II presented the received Catholic teaching concerning persons who are living as spouses in invalid marriages, contracted after civil divorces, he revealed a sensitive understanding of the difficulty of their position. But he did not pretend for a moment that it could be good to tell such people that if they "really think" that it is good for them to perform within invalid marriages actions that are in fact adulterous, then these are good acts for them. He insisted (as the received teaching of the Church always has) that persons who are living in unions that are in fact adulterous many not be told that it is permissible for them to receive the Eucharist.

He readily understands (as every compassionate person would) how extremely difficult it is to be faithful to Catholic teaching in some circumstances. Consider the case of a woman who has been abandoned by her husband and who has several children. She is suffering from loneliness and poverty, and has the opportunity to "marry" an attractive man who is deeply devoted to her and her children. But the Church, illumined by the Gospel, teaches that she ought not attempt marriage again in such circumstances. To attempt to marry anew while the one to whom she is yet bound in marriage is alive is in itself a bad kind of action. The prohibition may seem at first a brutal exercise in legalism. Some may be tempted to find a "pastoral solution," that is, to tell her that in this case to enter into a union which the Church knows to be in fact adulterous would be permissible.

The Holy Father presents a much different answer. There is a pastoral duty to help the woman understand that it is not shallow legalism but concern for faithful love and for spouses and children everywhere that requires faithfulness to the teaching of Christ. She must be helped to see that her pain is not meaningless and cruel, and that she is able to transform the loneliness and suffering into a generous witnessing of the importance of faithful love, even when we have ourselves been treated badly. Her heroic decision not to enter an invalid marriage becomes a reminder to everyone of the duty to be faithful to the values that serve every home and every family. Such faithfulness is a support of spousal love and of children everywhere. Meanwhile the community has great duties to her, and should assist her in bearing the burdens she carries for the sake of all.

Not Doing Evil to Achieve Good. Pastoral love does not propose solutions that are opposed to the true and healing teachings of faith. For when one commends evil kinds of deeds in hopes of achieving a better life, one enters into a hopeless path. If the revelation of God together with the faith of the Catholic Church is true, objectively evil deeds wound both the world and the inner lives of those who perform them. It is often only by difficult ways that one can save one's life, maintain its integrity, and ultimately its blessedness.

Grace and Love Make Light and Easy What Otherwise Would Be Too Burdensome. Christ never hid from his disciples the excellence and the difficulty of his teaching concerning marriage and sexual morality. The Gospels portray him as not at all surprised when the apostles themselves found his teaching on divorce difficult to believe (see Mt 19:10). He assured them, however, that this excellent but sometimes seemingly harsh teaching (in fact indispensable for guarding faithful love and the procreative good in this broken world) would indeed be made bearable by the gift of God. Even more, Christ insisted that the whole burden of his teaching was an easy burden, that the yoke he imposes on his own (for their sake) would be a light one for those who draw near to him (cf. Mt 11:30).

There are many paradoxes in Christian morality. By dying we come to life. By the cross we come to joy. The hard way is easy but walking the easy

247

path leads to unbearable sorrow. To come to the viewpoint and to the experience of faith is not an easy task. But the conversion of heart this requires is indispensable for the saving of both human a divine goods in our lives.

Those who wish to live chaste lives, faithfully respecting every human value in their choices, will experience trials and stress but also great comfort and consolation. Contemporary literature and experience reveal that those who deliberately engage in lustful deeds in the hope of escaping pain and stress tend to fall into even greater anxieties and strains. The ways of living taught by faith work. The paths of intelligent love are often difficult, but to abandon these paths always proves tragic.

St. Thomas Aquinas asks pointedly whether the New Law, with its sublime and demanding moral teaching, might not in fact be more difficult to observe than the Old Law itself. He responds, with the voice of tradition and the experience of Christianity, that it is not.[30] He acknowledges that in one sense the new law is more difficult than the old. It requires a form of life that is intrinsically more demanding because it is more excellent. Yet it is made easy in a number of ways. Those who with devoted hearts accept the graces that invite them to life in Christ receive from the Holy Spirit gifts that make bearable, even light and pleasant what otherwise would certainly have been too difficult and even unsupportable. God's great mercy, and his grace, make the best ways of living also light and easy. To walk the ways of intelligent love is to choose a life surrounded with countless blessings and great peace.

Notes

Introduction

1. Perry London, "Sexual Behavior," in *Encyclopedia of Bioethics*, vol. 4, ed. Warren Reich (New York: Macmillan, 1978), p. 1567.
2. Ibid.
3. Ibid., p. 1569.
4. See Louis Janssens, "Considerations on *Humanae Vitae*," *Louvain Studies*, 2 (1969), 249. Janssens is a prominent Catholic moralist.
5. See Ashley Montagu, *Sex, Man, and Society* (New York: Putnam's, 1969), pp. 22-23.
6. See Philip S. Keane, S.S., *Sexual Morality: A Catholic Perspective* (New York: Paulist Press, 1977), pp. 100-110; Anthony Kosnik et al., *Human Sexuality: New Directions in American Catholic Thought* (New York: Paulist Press, 1977), pp. 148-149, 152-169.
7. See Daniel C. Maguire, "The Freedom to Die," in *The New Theology, No. 10*, ed. Martin E. Marty (New York: Macmillan, 1973), p. 189. See also Keane, *Sexual Morality*, pp. 109-110, for a justification of the use of contraceptives by nonmarried persons.
8. See Charles E. Curran, "Dialogue with the Homophile Movement," in his *Catholic Moral Theology in Dialogue* (Notre Dame, Ind.: Fides, 1972), pp. 184-219. See also John McNeill, S.J., *The Church and the Homosexual* (Kansas City, Mo.: Andrews and McMeel, 1976).
9. John Paul II, *Familiaris Consortio*, no. 31. [*NOTE*: Besides *Vatican Council II: The Conciliar and Post Conciliar Documents and Vatican Council II: More Post Conciliar Documents*, ed. Austin Flannery, O.P., excerpts from the conciliar and post-conciliar documents (such as *Familiaris Consortio*) can be found in a number of other sources, including *The Pope Speaks* and *NC Documentary Service*.]

Notes for Chapter One

1. See St. Thomas Aquinas, *Summa Theologiae*, 1, q. 1, a. 1.
2. See Germain Grisez, *The Way of the Lord Jesus*, vol. 1, *Christian Moral Principles*, ch. 35, qq. F and G for a brief, clear, and accurate account

of the assent due to teachings of this kind. See also William E. May, *An Introduction to Moral Theology* (rev. ed.: Huntington, Ind: Our Sunday Visitor, 1994), pp. 236-248.

The Congregation for the Doctrine of the Faith's 1990 *Instruction on the Ecclesial Vocation of the Theologian* discusses this issue in some detail, providing a helpful commentary on the nature of the "religious submission" that the Fathers of Vatican Council II said is to be given to such authoritative but noninfallibly proposed magisterial teachings. It clearly distinguishes between *questions* that can be raised about such teachings (nos. 24-31) and *dissent* from such teachings (nos. 32-41). It holds that questioning can be compatible with the "religious assent" required, but it firmly and decisively repudiates dissent from these teachings as incompatible with this required religious assent. It recognizes that one might, in a given instance, *suspend* or *withhold* assent, so long as this is accompanied by a willingness to submit one's questions to the magisterium and to accept the magisterium's judgment about these questions. But dissent is not compatible with this "religious submission."

Pope John Paul II rightly points out that "no damage must be done to the *harmony between faith and life: the unity of the Church* is damaged not only by Christians who reject or distort the truths of faith but also by those who disregard the moral obligations to which they are called by the Gospel (cf. 1 Cor 5:9-13)" (*Veritatis Splendor*, no. 26). He emphasizes that "*dissent . . . is opposed to ecclesial communion and to a correct understanding of the hierarchical constitution of the People of God"* (no. 113).

3.   Vatican Council II, *Lumen Gentium*, no. 25: "Although the bishops, taken individually, do not enjoy the privilege of infallibility, they do, however, proclaim the doctrine of Christ infallibly on the following conditions: namely, when, even though dispersed throughout the entire world but preserving for all that amongst themselves and with Peter's successor the bond of communion, in their authoritative teaching concerning matters of faith or *morals*, they are in agreement that a particular teaching is to be held definitively and absolutely" (emphasis added; cf. Vatican Council I, *Dei Filius*, DS 3011 [DS refers to *Enchiridion Symbolorum Definitionum et Declarationum de Rebus Fidei et Morum*, ed. Henricus Denzinger and Adolphus Schönmetzer, 36th ed. (Freiburg: Herder, 1976). Hereafter this volume will be referred to as DS followed by the paragraph number or numbers — in this case, for example, DS 3011.]

Some theologians today contend that no specific moral teachings of the Church have been infallibly proposed. In fact, some claim that the Church *cannot* propose specific moral norms infallibly. From this claim they draw the conclusion that one may reject moral teachings of the Church, such as those relating to sexual ethics, which have been universally proposed as necessary for salvation if one judges he has good reasons to do so. This question is examined in Chapter 5. Representative statements of this position can be found in the following sources: Francis Sullivan, S.J., *Magisterium: Teaching Authority in the Church* (New York: Paulist, 1983), ch. 6; Charles E. Curran et al., *Dissent in and for the Church* (New York: Sheed and Ward, 1969); and Daniel Maguire, "Moral Absolutes and the Magisterium," pp. 57-107 of *Absolutes in Moral Theology?*, ed. Charles E. Curran (Washington, D.C.: Corpus, 1968). This radical and spurious claim completely fails to take into consideration the infallibility of the ordinary and universal magisterium as exercised by the bishops of the entire world, teaching in union with the pope that specific matters of the moral life must be held definitively (cf. *Lumen Gentium*, no. 25). For detailed expositions of the serious deficiencies in the reasoning of these theologians see the following: Germain Grisez, *The Way of the Lord Jesus*, vol. 1, *Christian Moral Principles* (Chicago: Franciscan Herald Press, 1983), ch. 35; William E. May, *An Introduction to Moral Theology* (revised ed.; Huntington, Ind: Our Sunday Visitor, 1995), pp. 228-236. For an explanation of the background and theological context of *Lumen Gentium*, no. 25, see John C. Ford, S.J., and Germain Grisez, "Contraception and the Infallibility of the Ordinary Magisterium," *Theological Studies*, 39 (1978), 263-267. On the competency of the magisterium in matters of morals see Ronald D. Lawler, O.F.M. Cap., "The Magisterium and Catholic Moral Teaching," in *Persona, Verità e Morale: Atti del Congresso Internazionale di Teologia Morale (Roma, 7-12 aprile 1986)* (Rome: Città Nuova Editrice, 1987), pp. 217-233; T. Lopez, " 'Fides et Mores' en Trento," *Scripta theologica* 5 (1973), 175-221; Jacques Marie Aubert, "Le Magistère Morale de l'Église," *La foi et les temps* (August, 1981), 311-333.

Moreover, the *Instruction on the Ecclesial Vocation of the Theologian*, issued by the Congregation for the Doctrine of the Faith on May 24, 1990, explicitly taught that "Revelation also contains moral teachings which *per se* could be known by natural reason. Access to them, however, is made difficult by man's sinful condition. *It is a doctrine of faith that these moral norms can be infallibly taught by the Magisterium*" (no. 16, with reference to Vatican Council I, Dogmatic Constitution *Dei Filius*, ch. 2, DS 3005).

251

Finally, in his 1995 encyclical *Evangelium Vitae* Pope John Paul II, invoking his papal authority and after consulting with all the bishops of the world, authoritatively reaffirmed as Catholic teaching the truth that all intentional killing of innocent human beings, all directly procured abortions, and all acts of mercy killing or euthanasia are gravely immoral, and each time he referred explicitly to the teaching of *Lumen Gentium*, no. 25, concerning the infallibility of the *universal and ordinary magisterium of the Church*. He clearly taught that these specific moral norms have been and are infallibly proposed by the magisterium (see *Evangelium Vitae*, nos. 57, 62, 65).

4. St. Thomas Aquinas, *Quodlibetum* IX, q. 8.

5. An exceptionally valuable source for magisterial teaching on marriage and family and sexual issues is provided by the six-volume work *Enchiridion Familiae: Textos del Magistero Pontificio y Conciliar sobre el Matrimonio y la Familia (Siglos I a XX)*. This work, edited by Augusto Sarmiento and Javier Escriva-Ivars, was published jointly in 1992 by the Instituto de Ciencias para la Familia of the University of Navarre and the Istituto Giovanni Paolo II per Studi su Matrimonio e Famiglia. This multi-volume work provides texts on marriage and family found in the papal and conciliar magisterium from the time of Pope Clement of Rome in 97 A.D. until 1988 during the pontificate of Pope John Paul II. Volume 1 includes material from Clement of Rome (97) up to and including Pius XI (1939); volume 2 incorporates texts from Pius XII (1939-1958) and John XXIII (1958-1963); volume 3 has texts from Paul VI (1963-1978), John Paul I (1978), and John Paul II (1978-1980); volume 4 provides texts from John Paul II (1981-1982); and volume 5 texts from John Paul II (1983-1988). Volume 6 is a masterful index to the previous five volumes. The texts of the magisterium are given in their original language (Latin, Italian, French, Spanish, English, etc.) in the bottom half of the page and in a Spanish translation the first half of each page.

The finest single-volume study of marriage and family in the documents of the magisterium is that of Ramon Garcia de Haro, *Marriage and the Family in the Documents of the Magisterium: A Course in the Theology of Marriage* (2nd ed.: San Francisco: Ignatius Press, 1993), tr. William E. May.

6. See *Enchiridion Familiae* [hereafter *EF*], 1.

7. See Lateran Council II, March 4, 1139, canon 23 (DS 718; *EF* 1.104) Lateran Council IV, February 4, 1215, canon 1 (DS 802; *EF* 1.125), "Not only virgins and the continent but also the married, pleasing to

God by true faith and good action, will be judged worthy of attaining eternal beatitude."

8. Innocent III, "Letter to the Archbishop of Terragona," December 18, 1208, *Ejus Exemplo* (DS 795; *EF* 1.124).

9. Among other documents affirming the same truth are the following: First Council of Toledo, October 400, canon 236 (DS 206; *EF* 1. 16); Council of Braga, May 1, 563, canons 11 to 13 (DS 461-463; *EF* 1.41); Council of Florence, *Decree Pro Jacobitis*, February 4, 1442 (DS 1353; *EF* 1.139-140).

10. On this see Edward Schillebeeckx, *Marriage: Human Reality and Saving Mystery*, tr. N. D. Smith (New York: Sheed and Ward, 1965), esp. pp. 244-260. See also the masterful study of G. Baldanza, "La grazia sacamentale matrimoniale al Concilio di Trento. Contributo per uno studio storico-critico," *Ephemerides Liturgicae* 98 (1983), 89-140.

11. Council of Florence, bull *Exultate*, November 22, 1439 (DS 1327; *EF* 1.139).

12. See Council of Trent, Session 24, 1563; DS 1797-1812; *EF* 1.141-146. In the canons following this dogmatic decree Trent solemnly proclaimed the indissolubility of marriage — not even adultery can sever the bond between husband and wife — its sacramental character, and the Church's God-given authority over marriage. See ibid. An excellent analysis of the teaching of the Council of Trent on marriage is given by Garcia de Haro, *Marriage and Family in the Documents of the Church*, pp. 64-79.

13. Pope Leo XIII, encyclical, *Arcanum Divinae Sapientiae*, in *Official Catholic Teachings: Love and Sexuality*, ed. Odile M. Liebard (Wilmington, N.C.: McGrath, 1978), nos. 3, 5, 6, pp. 2-3, 4-5. [*NOTE*: Hereafter *Official Catholic Teachings: Love and Sexuality* will be referred to as Liebard's *Love and Sexuality*.] See also *EF* 1.147-153.

14. A fine summary and analysis of *Casti Connubii* is given by Garcia de Haro, *Marriage and Family in the Documents of the Magisterium*, pp. 107-145. The text of *Casti Connubii* is found in Liebard's *Love and Sexuality*, pp., and in *EF* 1.709-794).

15. Garcia de Haro, *Marriage and Family in the Documents of the Magisterium*, pp. 147-194, provides a detailed analysis of the teaching of Pope Pius XII on marriage.

16. It should be noted that the Council Fathers refer in a footnote at this point in the text to the threefold good of marriage originally articulated by St. Augustine and long since appropriated by the magisterium.

17. Garcia de Haro offers an exceptionally comprehensive account and

analysis of the teaching of Vatican Council II on marriage in his *Marriage and Family in the Documents of the Magisterium*, pp. 211-282.

18. See Garcia de Haro, *Marriage and Family in the Documents of the Magisterium*, pp. 283-332 for a detailed analysis of the teaching of Paul VI on marriage and marital sexual morality.

19. In 1960, while still a professor of moral philosophy at the University of Lublin, he wrote a very probing study of human sexuality, sexual morality, marriage, and the family, *Love and Responsibility*. This book, translated by H. Willetts, was published in English in 1980 by Farrar, Straus, Giroux, and has since been republished by Ignatius Press.

20. These addresses have been published in four volumes in English translation: *The Original Unity of Man and Woman: Catechesis on Genesis* (Boston: St. Paul Editions, 1981), *Blessed Are the Pure of Heart: Catechesis on the Sermon on the Mount and the Writing St. Paul* (Boston: St. Paul Editions, 1982), *Reflections on Humanae Vitae* (Boston: St. Paul Editions, 1983), *Theology of Marriage and Celibacy* (Boston: St. Paul Editions, 1984). There is now a one-volume edition of these addresses, *The Theology of the Body: Human Love in the Divine Plan* (Boston: Pauline Books and Media, 1997), referred to hereafter as *TB*.

21. Here it is worth noting that of the 5127 pages of text found in *Enchiridion Familiae,* more than 2600 provide magisterial documents from the pontificate of John Paul II, and this series concludes with the year 1988.

22. Pope John Paul II, Address of December 22, 1981, in which John Paul II presented his new apostolic exhortation. Text in *EF*, 14.3415f.

23. Part one is entitled, "Bright Spots and Shadows for the Family Today," and offers both an analysis of the contemporary situation facing the family and presents anew the most important moral principles necessary for an adequate solution to modern problems. Part two is called "The Plan of God for Marriage and the Family" and discusses the meaning of marriage and its fundamental structure as designed by God and integrated into the economy of grace by Jesus. Part three, the longest of the document, is called "The Role of the Christian Family," and takes up in great depth the indispensable and necessary role that the Christian family plays in (1) forming a community of love, (2) serving life, (3) serving the wider human community, and (4) participating in the redemptive mission of the Church. The final part, Part Four, called "Pastoral Care of the Family: Stages, Structures, Agents and Situations," gives explicit attention to situations of greater difficulty confronting marriage and family life today.

24. See Garcia de Haro, *Marriage and Family in the Documents of the*

Magisterium, pp. 333-408, for an analysis of the teaching of John Paul II on marriage and family.

25. John Paul II makes the connection between these two goods of marriage in an especially compelling way: "In its most profound reality, love is essentially a gift; and conjugal love, while leading the spouses to the reciprocal 'knowledge' which makes them 'one flesh,' does not end with the couple, because it makes them capable of the greatest possible gift, the gift by which they become cooperators with God for giving life to a new human person" (*Familiaris Consortio*, no. 14).

26. Pius XI, *Casti Connubii*, in Liebard's *Love and Sexuality*, no. 84, p. 42.

27. The condemned view is that there is no fault whatsoever in seeking marital intercourse "solely for the sake of pleasure" — that is, without considering the goods to which marriage is ordered. For the condemnation, see Decree of the Holy Office," March 2, 1679; DS 2109.

28. Pius XII, "Address to Midwives," October 29, 1951; in Liebard's *Love and Sexuality*, p. 119.

29. Ibid., pp. 119-120.

30. Paul VI, *Humanae Vitae*, nos. 12-13.

31. See John Paul II, *Familiaris Consortio*, nos. 28-32; the new *Code of Canon Law*, Canon 1061, no. 1, states that an act which consummates marriage must be one open both to the transmission of life and to the fostering of love. The new code was approved by John Paul II on January 25, 1983.

32. Thus the *Catechism of the Catholic Church* declares: "Sexuality is ordered to the conjugal love of man and woman. In marriage the physical intimacy of the spouses becomes a sign and pledge of spiritual communion. . . . The spouses' union achieves the twofold end of marriage: the good of the spouses themselves and the transmission of life. These two meanings or values of marriage cannot be separated without altering the couple's spiritual life and compromising the goods of marriage and the future of the family. The conjugal love of man and woman thus stands under the twofold obligation of fidelity and fecundity" (nos. 2360, 2363).

33. Pius XII, "Address to Midwives," in Liebard's *Love and Sexuality*, p. 121.

34. Pope John Paul II, Apostolic Constitution *Fidei Depositum*, On the Publication of the *Catechism of the Catholic Church*, prepared following the Second Vatican Ecumenical Council, no. 3.

35. *Catechismus Romanus*, p. 3, c. 7.

36. See St. Leo IX, "Letter to St. Peter Damian," 1054; DS 687-688; "Decree of the Holy Office," March 2, 1679; DS 2109. Congregation for

the Doctrine of the Faith, "Declaration on Certain Questions of Sexual Morality," December, 1975.

Notes for Chapter Two

1. Pope John Paul II, "A Fundamental Disquietude in All Human Existence," General Audience of May 28, 1980, in *Blessed Are the Pure of Heart: Catechesis on the Sermon on the Mount and the Writings of St. Paul* (Boston: St. Paul Editions, 1983), pp. 48-54 (*TB,* pp. 114-117).

2. See Manuel Miguens, "Biblical Thoughts on 'Human Sexuality,' " in *Human Sexuality in Our Time: What the Church Teaches*, ed. George A. Kelly (Boston: St. Paul Editions, 1979), pp. 102-118, especially pp. 103-107.

3. John L. McKenzie, "Aspects of Old Testament Thought," *New Jerome Biblical Commentary*, eds. Raymond E. Brown, S.S., Joseph Fitzmyer, S.J., and Roland E. Murphy, O. Carm. (Englewood Cliffs, N.J.: Prentice-Hall, Inc., 1990), p. 1305, no. 123.

4. See Pope John Paul II, "Nuptial Meaning of the Body," General Audience of January 9, 1980, in *Original Unity of Man and Woman: Catechesis on the Book of Genesis* (Boston: St. Paul Editions, 1981), p. 108 *(TB,* p.61). In this text Pope John Paul II is explicitly concerned with the account in Genesis 2, but the expression "beatifying beginning" can also be applied to the narrative in Genesis 1.

5. See John L. McKenzie's masterful account of the Baal myth and its attendant fertility cult in *The Two-Edged Sword: An Interpretation of the Old Testament* (New York: Doubleday Image, 1966), ch. 3: "The Gods of the Semites." On pp. 76-77 McKenzie "translates" this ancient myth into language understandable today: "the supreme good, the good life, consists in the satisfaction of human material needs. This is all we ask of the gods, and this is all they can give us. They bless us in full when they satisfy these needs not only in the minimum necessary for survival, but in abundance, so that we enjoy not only the simple life, but also the material comforts of life. . . . The highest of all pleasures is the pleasure of sex; life offers nothing finer, nothing which so raises a man to the level of the divine. Consequently, the difference of the sexes exists only that the male may have this supreme satisfaction; woman is his possession, and her noblest function is to satisfy his sexual appetite. When she does this, she is a goddess; otherwise, she is a high-grade domestic animal, a drudge, not fully a human being." He concludes by saying: "One suspects that many modern Europeans and Americans, if transported suddenly into the Babylon of the sec-

ond millennium, after an initial adjustment to inconveniences in such things as language, travel, and plumbing, would find themselves spiritually at home. They would never feel at ease with the ancient Hebrews" (p. 77). The accounts of human origins and of human sexuality in Genesis 1 and 2 are deliberately framed to repudiate this understanding of these realities.

6. The relevant text from Genesis 1 reads as follows: "Then God said, 'Let us make man [`adam] in our image, after our likeness; and let them have dominion over the fish of the sea, and over the birds of the air, and over the cattle, and over all the earth, and over every creeping thing that creeps upon the earth.' So God created man [`adam] in his own image, in the image of God he created him, male and female he created them. And God blessed them and said to them, 'Be fruitful and multiply, and fill the earth and subdue it; and have dominion over the fish of the sea and over the birds of the air and over every living thing that moves upon the earth' "(Gen 1:26-28).

7. On this see, for example, Francis Martin, "Male and Female He Created Them: A Summary of the Teaching of Genesis Chapter One," *Communio* 10 (Summer, 1993), 257, 259-260.

8. See ibid., pp. 254-255: "The first function of the description of `adam as male and female is to place sexual differentiation and sexuality itself within a world created by God and seen by him as good. Sex is not a means of cultivating cosmic powers, as in the fertility cults, nor is it an expression of an hubris that degrades it to the level of self-assertion and power and thus despises its modest but true place as something properly human. It is one expression of the way in which humans image God. As God creates in his image and likeness, Adam begets in his likeness and image, and Eve acquires a man-child with the help of Yhwh (see Gen. 4:1)."

9. Edward Schillebeeckx, *Marriage: Human Reality and Saving Mystery* (New York: Sheed and Ward, Inc. 1965), p. 16.

10. On this see, for example, Raymond F. Collins, *Christian Morality: Biblical Foundations* (Notre Dame, Ind: University of Notre Dame Press, 1986), p. 163.

11. The relevant text follows: "then the LORD God formed man [`adam] of dust from the ground, and breathed into his nostrils the breath of life; and man [`adam] became a living being. . . . Then the LORD God said, 'It is not good that the man [`adam] should be alone; I will make him a helper fit for him.' . . . So the LORD God caused a deep sleep to fall upon the man [`adam], and while he slept took one of his ribs and

257

closed up its place with flesh; and the rib which the LORD God had taken from the man [`adam`] he made into a woman [*ishshah*] and brought her to the man [`adam`]. Then the man [`adam`] said, 'This at last is bone of my bones and flesh of my flesh; she shall be called Woman [*ishshah*], because she was taken out of Man [*ish*].' Therefore a man [*ish*] leaves his father and his mother and cleaves to his wife [*ishshah*], and they become one flesh. And the man and his wife were both naked, and were not ashamed" (Gen 2:7, 18, 21-25).

12. Pope John Paul II has reflected deeply on the meaning of man's "original solitude." See his "Meaning of Man's Original Solitude," General Audience of October 10, 1979, in *Original Unity of Man and Woman*, pp. 43-47 *(TB,* pp. 35-37). Commenting on Genesis 2:18 and its context, John Paul II shows that this text dramatically discloses the uniqueness — the solitude — of man in the created universe. None of the other animals, over whom the man exercises authority (signified by his being given by God the power to "name" them; cf. Gen 2:19-20), is his equal. He thus "becomes aware of his own superiority, that he cannot be considered on the same footing as any other species of living beings on earth. . . . Man is alone because he is 'different' from the visible world, from the world of living beings. Analyzing the text of the Book of Genesis we are, in a way, witnesses of how man 'distinguishes himself' before God-Yahweh from the whole world of living beings (*animalia*) with his first act of self-consciousness, and of how, therefore, he reveals himself to himself and at the same time asserts himself as a 'person' in the visible world" (pp. 46, 48).

13. Commenting on Genesis 2:23 ("This at last is bone of my bones and flesh of my flesh"), John Paul II says that the first man, "exclaiming in this way," "seems to say: here is *a body that expresses the 'person.' "* See his "Nuptial Meaning of the Body," General Audience of January 9, 1980, *Original Unity of Man and Woman*, p. 109 *(TB,* p. 61).

14. Several biblical scholars have noted the covenantal significance of the words "flesh" and "bone" in this text. See, for instance, Walter Brueggemann, "Of the Same Flesh and Bone (Gn 2:23a)," *Catholic Biblical Quarterly* 32 (1970), 532-542.

15. Collins, *Christian Morality*, p. 159.

16. Pope John Paul II, "Marriage Is One and Indissoluble in the First Chapters of Genesis," General Audience of November 11, 1979, *Original Unity of Man and Woman*, pp. 81-82 *(TB,* p. 50).

17. Perhaps the most probing analysis of the significance of original nakedness is provided by Pope John Paul II. See in particular the follow-

ing addresses, all found in *Original Unity of Man and Woman:* (1) "Meaning of Original Human Experiences," General Audience of December 12, 1979 (pp. 85-91, *TB,* pp.51-54); (2) "Fullness of Interpersonal Communication," General Audience of December 19, 1979 (pp. 92-98, *TB*, pp. 54-57); (3) "Creation as Fundamental and Original Gift," General Audience of January 2, 1980 (pp. 99-105, *TB*, pp.57-60). The biblical scholar Francis Martin explicitly calls attention to the great significance of the theological anthropology developed by John Paul III in his reflections on Genesis 1-3 in his "Male and female he created them. . . ."

18. On this see in particular Pope John Paul II's "Nuptial Meaning of the Body," General Audience of January 9, 1980; "The Man-Person Becomes a Gift in the Freedom of Love," General Audience of January 16, 1980; "The Mystery of Man's Original Innocence," General Audience of January 30, 1980; "Man and Woman: A Mutual Gift for Each Other," in *Original Unity of Man and Woman*, pp. 106-134 (*TB*, pp.60-72).

   Richard M. Hogan ably summarizes John Paul II's notion of the nuptial meaning of the body in his essay, "A Theology of the Body: A commentary on the audiences of Pope John Paul II from September 5, 1979 to May 6, 1981," *Fidelity* 1.1 (December, 1981), 10-15, 24-27, at 12.

19. Such freedom from shame is, in the Old Testament, an eschatological promise linked to freedom from sin and the experience of God's saving power (cf. Is 45:17; Zeph 3:11).

20. Johannes Bauer, "Marriage," in *Sacramentum Verbi: An Encyclopedia of the Bible*, ed. Johannes Bauer (New York: Herder & Herder, 1985), 3.551. On this also see Schillebeeckx, *Marriage: Human Reality and Saving Mystery*, pp. 21-22.

21. Steven Clark, *Man and Woman in Christ: An Examination of the Roles of Men and Women in the Light of Scripture and the Social Sciences* (Ann Arbor, Mich: Servant Books, 1980), p. 22. See also Pierre Grelot, *Man and Wife in Scripture* (New York: Herder & Herder, 1965), pp. 37-38.

22. Karol Wojtyla (Pope John Paul II), *Love and Responsibility*, tr. H. T. Willetts (New York: Farrar, Straus, Giroux, 1981), p. 190.

23. Pope John Paul II analyzes in depth the devastating effect of concupiscence on human sexuality and the nuptial meaning of the body, particularly in the following addresses: "A Fundamental Disquietude in All Human Existence," General Audience of May 28, 1980; "Relationship of Lust to Communion of Persons," General Audience of June

4, 1980; "Dominion over the Other in the Interpersonal Relation," General Audience of June 18, 1980; "Lust Limits Nuptial Meaning of the Body," General Audience of June 25, 1980; and "The 'Heart' — A Battlefield Between Love and Lust," General Audience of July 23, 1980. These addresses are found in *Blessed Are the Pure of Heart*, pp. 48-78 (*TB*, pp. 114-128). Because of Adam's sin and the entrance of concupiscence into the human heart, the "nuptial meaning" of the body is, as it were, "veiled." The Pope says that because of this "the human body in its masculinity-femininity has *almost* lost the capacity of expressing this [nuptial, marital, self-giving] love" (p. 74, emphasis added). Commenting on his own use of "almost" here, John Paul II goes on to say that he added "almost" "because of the dimension of the gift — namely, the capacity of expressing love with which man, by means of femininity or masculinity, becomes a gift for the other — has continued to some extent to permeate and mold the love that is born in the human heart. The nuptial meaning of the body has not become completely suffocated by concupiscence, but only habitually threatened" (p. 75, *TB*, p. 126). Through his redemptive act, Jesus enables us to "recover" the "nuptial meaning" of the body and to overcome concupiscence.

24. A good discussion of this is found in Clark, *Man and Woman in Christ*, pp. 31-36.

25. A brief but excellent commentary by a biblical scholar on Genesis 3 (the Fall) and Genesis 4 (its effects on family life) is given by Michael Duggan, *The Consuming Fire: A Christian Introduction to the Old Testament* (San Francisco: Ignatius Press, 1991), pp. 76-79.

26. Schillebeeckx, *Marriage: Human Reality and Saving Mystery*, p. 33.

27. See Elaine Adler Goodfriend, "Adultery," in *The Anchor Bible Dictionary*, ed. David Noel Freedman et al. (New York: Doubleday, 1992), 1:82-86.

28. See ibid., 82.

29. Joseph Jensen, O.S.B., "The Relevance of the Old Testament," in *Dimensions of Human Sexuality*, ed. Dennis Doherty (Garden City, N.Y.: Doubleday, 1979), pp. 1-8, at 6-7.

30. Roland E. Murphy, O.Carm., "Wisdom and Eros in Proverbs 1-9," *Catholic Biblical Quarterly* 50 (1988), 600-603, at 603.

31. Schillebeeckx, *Marriage: Human Reality and Saving Mystery*, pp. 42-43.

32. On this see Thomas McCreesch, "Wisdom as Wife: Proverbs 31:10-31," *Revue Biblique* 92 (1985), 25-46; see also the study by Claudia V. Camp,

Wisdom and the Feminine in the Book of Proverbs, ed. David M. Gunn, Vol. 11, Bible and Literature Series (Decatur, Ga: Scholars Press, 1985).

33. As noted in the text, scholars differ in their interpretation of the story of Sodom and Gomorrah, with some holding that the sin of the men of Sodom was not homosexuality but inhospitality (e.g., Collins, *Christian Morality*, pp. 172-173; Richard B. Hayes, *The Moral Vision of the New Testament* [San Francisco: Harper Collins, 1996], p. 381), whereas others (e.g., Miguens, "Biblical Thoughts on 'Human Sexuality,' " pp. 116-117) argue that it definitely was the sin of homosexuality. Richard J. Clifford suggests that the Sodomites were guilty of a twofold crime, that of inhospitality and that of forbidden sex — and by referring here to Lv 18:22 Clifford makes it clear that the forbidden sex in question is homosexual activity. See his "Genesis," in *New Jerome Biblical Commentary*, p. 23, no. 30. On this question also see Jensen, "The Relevance of the Old Testament," p. 8. An excellent discussion of Old Testament teaching on the malice of homosexual acts is given by Maurice Gilbert, "La Bible et l'homosexualité," *Nouveau Revue Théologique* 109 (1987), 78-95.

34. See, for example, Collins, *Christian Morality*, pp. 176-177.

35. On this see Miguens, "Biblical Thoughts on 'Human Sexuality,' " pp. 114-115.

36. Schillebeeckx develops these ideas briefly and well in his *Marriage: Human Reality and Saving Mystery*, pp. 108-109, 125-140, 155-176. See also Manuel Miguens, "On Being a Christian and the Moral Life: Pauline Perspectives," in *Principles of Catholic Morality*, ed. William E. May (Chicago: Franciscan Herald Press, 1980); Germain Grisez, *The Way of the Lord Jesus*, vol. 1, *Christian Moral Principles* (Chicago: Franciscan Herald Press), pp. 551-682; Servais Pinckaers, *The Sources of Christian Ethics* (Washington: The Catholic University of America Press, 1996), pp. 104-132.

37. This is a Mishnaic text quoted by Collins, *Christian Morality*, p. 184.

38. This is the view taken by Anthony Kosnik et al. in *Human Sexuality: New Directions in American Catholic Thought* (New York: Paulist, 1977), p. 26.

39. On this see Quentin Quesnell, "Made Themselves Eunuchs for the Kingdom of Heaven," *Catholic Biblical Quarterly* 30 (1968) 335-358.

40. Schillebeeckx, *Marriage: Human Reality and Saving Mystery*, pp. 127, 131.

41. Long ago St. Augustine called our Lord's Sermon on the Mount the magna carta of the Christian life, indeed, the "*perfect pattern of the Chris-*

tian life" (see his *The Lord's Sermon on the Mount*, tr. John J. Jepson, S.S., in *Ancient Christian Writers*, no. 5 [Westminster, Md: Newman Press, 1948], p. 11). St. Thomas declared that the Lord's Sermon on the Mount "contains completely the information needed for the Christian life. In it the inner movements of the person are perfectly ordered" (*Summa Theologiae*, 1-2, 108, 3). Pope John Paul II says that in the Sermon on the Mount "Jesus brings the commandments to fulfillment . . . by interiorizing their demands and by bringing out their fullest meaning" (*Veritatis Splendor*, no. 15). The Holy Father says elsewhere ("Christ Calls Us to Rediscover the Living Forms of the New Man," General Audience of December 3, 1980, in *Blessed Are the Pure of Heart* [Boston: St. Paul Editions, 1983], pp. 193-194, *TB*, p. 175) that our Lord calls man "to rediscover — on the foundation of the perennial and, so to speak, indestructible meanings of what is 'human' — the living forms of the 'new man.' . . . He leads the intellect and the heart of his listeners to that 'fullness of justice' willed by God. . . . Christ clearly indicates that the way to attain this must be the way of temperance and the mastery of desires, that is, at the very root, already in the purely interior sphere ('Everyone who looks at a woman lustfully. . .'). The ethos of redemption contains in every area — and directly in the sphere of the lust of the flesh — the imperative of self-control, the necessity of immediate continence and of habitual temperance."

42. Matthew 19:3-12: "And Pharisees came up to him and tested him by asking, 'Is it lawful to divorce one's wife for any cause?' He answered, 'Have you not read that he who made them from the beginning made them male and female [cf. Gen 1:28] and said, "For this reason a man shall leave his father and mother and be joined to his wife, and the two shall become one?" [cf. Gen 2:24]. So they are no longer two but one. What therefore God has joined together, let no man put asunder.' They said to him, 'Why then did Moses command one to give a certificate of divorce, and to put her away?' He said to them 'For your hardness of heart Moses allowed you to divorce your wives, but from the beginning it was not so. And I say to you: whoever divorces his wife, except for unchastity [lewd conduct (*porneia*) is a separate case], and marries another, commits adultery; and he who marries a divorced woman, commits adultery.' The disciples said to him, 'If such is the case of a man with his wife, it is not expedient to marry.' But he said to them, 'Not all men can receive this precept, but only those to whom it is given. For there are eunuchs who have been so from birth, and there are eunuchs who have been made eunuchs by men, and there are eunuchs who have

made themselves eunuchs for the sake of the kingdom of heaven. He who is able to receive this, let him receive it.' "

Mark 10:2-12: "And Pharisees came up and in order to test him asked 'is it lawful for a man to divorce his wife?' He answered them 'What did Moses command you?' They said, 'Moses allowed a man to write a certificate of divorce, and to put her away.' But Jesus said to them: 'For your hardness of heart he wrote you this commandment. But from the beginning of creation, "God made them male and female" [cf. Gen 1:27]. "For this reason a man shall leave his father and mother and be joined to his wife, and the two shall become one. So they are no longer two but one" [cf. Gen 2:24]. What therefore God has joined together, let no man put asunder.' And in the house the disciples asked him again about this matter. And he said to them, 'Whoever divorces his wife and marries another commits adultery against her; and if she divorces her husband and marries another, she commits adultery.' "

Luke 16:18: " 'Everyone who divorces his wife and marries another commits adultery, and he who marries a woman divorced from her husband commits adultery.' "

43. See Schillebeeckx, *Marriage: Human Reality and Saving Mystery*, p. 154ff; Grelot, *Man and Wife*, pp. 86-90.

44. Schillebeeckx, *Marriage, Human Reality and Saving Mystery*, p. 154.

45. See John J. O'Rourke, "Divorce in the New Testament," *Dimension: Journal of Pastoral Concern 1* (1969), 138-146.

46. J. Bauer, "Marriage," *Sacramentum Verbi* 2.552. See also Joseph Fitzmyer, S.J., "The Matthean Divorce Texts and Some New Palestinian Evidence," *Theological Studies* 37 (1977), 197-226 (reprinted in Fitzmyer's *To Advance the Gospel: New Testament Studies* [New York: Crossroad, 1981], pp. 79-111) and also Schillebeeckx's analysis of the Matthean text in *Marriage: Human Reality and Saving Mystery*, pp 141-154.

47. On this see Silverio Zedda, *Relativo e assoluto nella morale del San Paolo* (Brescia: Paideia, 1984), ch. 5. See also Joseph Jensen, O.S.B., "Does *Porneia* Mean Fornication? A Critique of Bruce Melina," *Novum Testamentum* 20 (1978), 161-184.

48. See Schillebeeckx, *Marriage: Human Reality and Saving Mystery*, pp. 160-162.

49. This is the source for what came to be known as the "Pauline Privilege," the dissolution of a nonsacramental marriage by the Church if the non-believing partner refuses to remain with the partner who has become a Christian. On this see Schillebeeckx, *Marriage: Human Reality and Saving Mystery*, pp. 159-163.

50. Pierre Benoit, O.P., "Christian Marriage according to Saint Paul," *Clergy Review* 65 (1980), 314.
51. Today the Pauline authorship of this letter is denied by many, although some exegetes maintain Pauline authorship, at least indirectly (on this, cf. Benoit, work cited in previous note, p. 315f).
52. For comment, see Peter Elliott, *"What God Has Joined"*: *The Sacramentality of Marriage* (New York: Alba House, 1990), pp. 46-72.
53. The full text of 1 Cor 6:15-20 reads: "Do you not know that your bodies are members of Christ? Shall I therefore take the members of Christ and make them the members of a prostitute? Never! Do you not know that he who joins himself to a prostitute becomes one body with her? For as it is written, 'The two shall become one.' But he who is united to the Lord becomes one spirit with him. Shun immorality [*porneia*]. Every other sin which a man commits is outside the body, but the immoral man [*ho porneuon*] sins against his own body. Do you not know that your body is a temple of the Holy Spirit, within you, which you have from God? You are not your own; you were bought with a price. So glorify God in your body."
54. 1 Thes 4:3-6 reads as follows: "For this is the will of God, your sanctification: that you abstain from immorality [*porneia*]; that each one of you know how to control his own body [member (wife?) *skeuos*] in holiness and honor, not in the passion of lust like heathen who do not know God; that no man transgress, and wrong his brother in this manner, because the Lord is an avenger in all these things, as we solemnly forewarned you."

The Greek work *skeuos* in v. 4 literally means "vessel" or "dish." Some biblical scholars provide cogent arguments to hold that in this text the term refers to one's "wife." On this see, for instance, the arguments given by O. Larry Yarbrough, *Not Like the Gentiles: Marriage Rules in the Letters of Paul* (Atlanta, Ga: Scholars Press, 1985; Dissertation Series No. 80), pp. 68-76. Others, however, offer good reasons for translating it as "member" or one's own "body." See, for instance, Silverio Zedda, S.J., *Relativo e assoluto nella morale di San Paolo*, pp. 61-64. No matter what the translation, scholars agree that this is a key text giving Paul's teaching on sexual morality.
55. One of the most careful and penetrating studies of this matter is given by Zedda in his *Assoluto e relativo nella morale di San Paolo*, ch. 5. See also John J. O'Rourke, "Does the New Testament Condemn Sexual Intercourse Outside of Marriage?" *Theological Studies* 37 (1976) 478-479; Joseph Jensen, O.S.B., "Does *Porneia* Mean Fornication? A

Critique of Bruce Malina," *Novum Testamentum* 20 (1978) 161-184.
56. The basic norm of Christian life, as summarized in the text, is the way Zedda proposes it in his study of Paul's thought. See his *Relativo e assoluto nella morale di San Paolo,* pp. 34-35. He then shows, massively, that sexual immorality (*porneia*), which includes all non-marital sexual acts, violates this norm. Cf. ibid., ch. 5, pp. 63-85. On this see also Yarbrough, *Not Like the Gentiles,* pp. 123-127. Yarbrough uses somewhat different language, but his principal conclusion after studying St. Paul's texts very minutely, is that sexual immorality (non-marital sex) violates God's will for the Christian.

Notes for Chapter Three

1. Several works can be noted here, but none can be recommended without qualification, and none, of course, is an attempt at a systematic history of the Catholic theological treatment of human sexuality or sexual morality: see Derrick S. Bailey, *The Male-Female Relationship in Christian Thought* (New York: Harper and Row, 1968); John T. Noonan, Jr., *Contraception: A History of Its Treatment by Catholic Theologians and Canonists* (Cambridge, Mass.: Harvard University Press, 1965); Joseph Kern, *The Theology of Marriage: The Historical Development of Christian Attitudes Toward Sex and Sanctity in Marriage* (New York: Sheed and Ward, 1964). In addition to these works there are a number of works on the theological study of sexuality by various saints and doctors of the Church. Some of these will be cited in this chapter. There is a wealth of useful material in the relevant articles in the *Dictionnaire de Théologie Catholique,* ed. A. Vacant, E. Manganot, and A. Amann (Paris: Librairie Letouzey et Ane, 1902-1950), 15 vols.
2. See Noonan, *Contraception,* pp. 56-106; Arno Karlen, *Sexuality and Homosexuality* (New York: Morrow, 1972); F. Van der Meer, *Augustine the Bishop: The Life and Work of a Father of the Church* (New York: Sheed and Ward, 1962), ch. 1.
3. See Noonan, *Contraception,* pp. 57-70, for an account of Gnosticism.
4. Irenaeus, *Adversus Haereses,* I.28 (PG 7.690). [*NOTE*: In referring to the writings of the Fathers of the Church, the title of work will first be given, followed by book and chapter number (in this instance, I.28), or book, chapter, and section number (for some Fathers). Reference will then be given to the pertinent volume and column, in the famous collection of patristic sources provided by J.P. Migne. Migne collected the works of the Greek-writing Fathers into 161 volumes, published in a town near Paris between 1857-1866. In this collection he provided the

Greek text with a Latin translation in parallel columns. The reference is to the volume of this collection and to the column containing the Greek text. Thus the text of Irenaeus to which reference is made is found in Migne's *Patrologiae Cursus Completus: Series Graeca* (hereafter PG), vol. 7, col. 690. Migne likewise collected the writings of the Fathers who wrote in Latin into 221 volumes, which he published originally between 1844 and 1855. These volumes, called *Patrologiae Cursus Completus: Series Latina* (hereafter PL), provide the Latin texts of the Fathers in pages made up of two columns, and the reference is to the volume of this collection and the column or columns concerned. Thus a reference such as PL 34.394 in Note 10 below means vol. 34 of Migne's collection of Latin texts, col. 394.]

5. Clement of Alexandria, *Stromata*, 3, 12.83 (PG 8.1176).
6. Justin Martyr, *Apologia*, 1.29 (PG 6.373).
7. Athenagoras of Athens, *Legatio*, 33 (PG 6.965, 968).
8. See Noonan, *Contraception*, p. 75; here, the appeals to nature by these Fathers are said to be a way of reinforcing positions held on other grounds.
9. See Clement of Alexandria, *Stromata*, 3.12.84 (PG 8.1177, on procreation and marriage); 7.12.70 (PG 9.497, on marital virtue).
10. See L. Godefroy, "Le Marriage au Temps des Pères," *Dictionnaire de Théologie Catholique*, 9.2, cots. 2077-2123.
11. See Theodoret, *Quaestiones in Genesi*, c. 3, q. 37 (PG 80.136); Augustine, *De Genesi ad Litteram*, 9.3 (PL 34.394); John Damascene, *De Fide Orthodoxa*, 2.30 (PG 94.976).
12. See Kern, *Theology of Marriage*, pp. 41-60.
13. Gregory of Nyssa, *De Opificio Hominis*, 17 (PG 44.187); John Chrysostom, *De Virginitate*, 17 (PG 48.546); *Homilia in Genesi*, 18 (PG 53.153); Theodoret, *Quaestiones in Genesi*, c. 3, q. 37 (PG 80.136); Damascene, *De Fide Orthodoxa*, 2.30 (PG 94.976).
14. Clement of Alexandria, *Stromata*, 3.7 (PG 8.1162).
15. Lactantius, *Divinarum Institutionum*, 6.23 (PL 6.715f): "Whoever cannot control his affections, let him keep them within the confines of the marriage bed." Chrysostom, *De Verbis Illis Apostoli, "Propter Fornicationem"* (PG 51.210): "There are two reasons why marriage was instituted, that we may live chastely and that we may become parents."
16. On this see St. John Chrysostom, *On Marriage and Family Life*, trs. Catherine P. Roth and David Anderson (Crestwood, N.Y.: St. Vladimir's Seminary Press, 1986). This small work contains short but beautiful

texts of Chrysostom on the goodness of marriage and family life: Homily 19 on 1 Corinthians 7; Homily 20 on Ephesians 5:22-33; Homily 21 on Ephesians 6:1-4; Homily 12 on Colossians 4:18; Sermon on Marriage; and How to Choose a Wife.

17. Developing Catholic doctrine has made it clear that the procreative good is not the only good at stake in marriage; but this development has in no way suggested that this good is not essential. See *Gaudium et Spes*, nos. 48, 50.

18. Among Augustine's explicit treatments of marriage are *De Bono Conjugale* (PL 40.373-394), *De Nuptiis et Concupiscentia* (PL 44.413-474), and *De Conjugiis Adulterinis* (PL 40.451-486).

19. For criticisms of these misrepresentations of Augustine, see John Hugo, *St. Augustine on Nature, Sex, and Marriage* (Chicago: Scepter Press, 1969). See also Eugene Portalié, *A Guide to the Thought of St. Augustine* (Chicago: Henry Regnery, 1960). D. Paul, "Saint Augustine on Marriage," *Augustinus* 12 (1967), 165-180; Joseph Thonnard, "La morale conjugale selon saint Augustin," *Revue des Etudes Augustiniennes* 15 (1969) 113-131.

20. On this see the very excellent study of Philip Lyndon Reynolds, *Marriage in the Western Church: The Christianization of Marriage During the Patristic and Early Medieval Periods*, vol. 24 of Supplements to *Vigiliae Christianae*, Texts and Studies of Early Christian Life and Language (Leiden/New York/Cologne: E. J. Brill, 1994), pp. 241-251, where he shows that in his early writing *De Genesis contra Manichaeos* Augustine was attracted to this position, although in his more mature writings (e.g., *De civitate Dei*) he definitively rejected this notion.

21. *Opus Imperfectum Contra Julianum*, 6.30 (PL 45.1582).

22. See, for example, Louis Dupré, *Contraception and Catholics* (Baltimore: Helicon, 1964), pp. 26-27.

23. See Portalié, *A Guide to the Thought of St. Augustine*, pp. 297-313; Hugo, *St. Augustine on Nature, Sex, and Marriage*, pp. 52-67.

24. See Ibid.

25. *Contra Julianum*, 6.15.47 (PL 44.849).

26. *De Nuptiis et Concupiscentia*, 1.25 (PL 44.429-430).

27. For Augustine, sin as such is only in the will; see *Confessions*, 8, chs. 5, 9-10; *The City of God*, 22, ch. 24.

28. Perhaps the best study of St. Augustine's understanding of concupiscence is provided by F. -J. Thonnard, "La notion de concupiscence en philosophie augustinienne," *Recherches Augustiniennes* 3 (1965), 90-99.

29. See *De Natura et Gratia*, 43.50 (PL 44.271): "God does not command the impossible, but by commanding He admonishes you that you should do what you can and beg Him for what you cannot." This text is cited by the Council of Trent (DS 1536).

30. For the Augustinian distinction between use and enjoyment and its application in articulating the proper attitude toward God and earthly things, see *De Vera Religione*, 24.45 (PL 34.165-166) and *De Doctrina Christiana*, 1.35.39 (PL 34:42).

31. See *De Bono Conjugali, De Nuptiis et Concupiscentia*, passim. On the permanent value of Augustine's understanding of the goods of marriage see Augustine Reagan, C.Ss.R., "The Perennial Value of Augustine's Theology of the Goods of Marriage," *Studia Moralia* (1981), 351-377.

32. *De Bono Coniugali*, c. 16, no. 18 (PL 40, 385): "and neither [nourishment nor generation] can take place without carnal pleasure, which, however, when moderated and used naturally, cannot be the same as concupiscence."

33. *Sermo* 159, c. 2, no. 2 (PL 38, 868-869): "Conjugal embraces give delight; so too do the embraces of prostitutes. But the former are legitimate, the latter not."

34. On this whole question see the helpful essay of Cormac Burke, "St. Augustine and Conjugal Chastity," *Communio* 17, 1990, 545-565.

35. *De Bono Conjugali*, 16.18 (PL 40.385-386).

36. *Contra Julianum*, 5.9 (PL 44.806).

37. *De Genesi ad Litteram*, 9.7 (PL 34.397).

38. *De Bono Conjugali*, 6 (PL 40.377-378).

39. *De Conjugiis Adulterinis*, 1.12 (PL 40.459); *De Nuptiis et Concupiscentia*, 1.17 (PL 44.424-425); *De Bono Conjugali*, 6 (PL 40.377-378).

40. *Enarratio in Psalmos*, 50.7 (PL 36.591-592). The complete text says: "It is not therefore because it is sin to have to do with wives that men are conceived in iniquity. . . . This chaste operation (*opus hoc castum*) in a married person hath not sin, but the origin of sin draweth with it condign punishment."

41. *De Gratia Christi et Peccato Originali*, 2.43 (PL 44.407-408); see *De Nuptiis et Concupiscentia*, 1.16 (PL 44.424).

42. *De Bono Conjugali*, 6 (PL 40.377-378).

43. Ibid., 9 (PL 40.380). Augustine follows this point by noting the connection between marital friendship and procreation: "For from these come the propagation of the human race in which friendly association is a great good."

268

44. On this see Reynolds, *Marriage in the Western Church*, ch. 12.
45. *In Johannis Evangelium*, 9.2 (PL 31.1458-1459).
46. *De Bono Conjugali*, 24.32 (PL 40.394-395).
47. Ibid.
48. See Edward Schillebeeckx, *Marriage: Human Reality and Saving Mystery* (New York: Sheed and Ward, 1965), p. 286.
49. Ibid., p. 283.
50. Vatican Council II, for example, makes use of Augustine's teaching on the three goods of marriage; see *Gaudium et Spes*, no. 48.
51. See John T. McNeill and Helena Gamer, "Records of Civilization," in *Medieval Handbooks of Penance: A Translation of the Principal Libri Poenitentiales*, vol. 29 (New York: Columbia University Press, 1938). See also John T. McNeill, *The Celtic Penitentials and Their Influence on Continental Christianity* (Paris: 1938). Noonan, *Contraception*, pp. 152-170, provides an account of the penitential materials relevant to sexual morality.
52. These proscriptions were rooted in the belief that the corruption of the sexual appetites by original sin required abstinence from sexual activity to show the proper respect for God within the worship of the Church. Thus, it is unlikely that these proscriptions are the result of Stoic or Manichean influences on the authors of the penitentials, but rather arise from their reading of Scripture.
53. See Noonan, *Contraception*, pp. 179-193, for an account of medieval Gnosticism, the ideal of romantic love, and their connection.
54. Peter Lombard, *Libri IV Sententiarum*, III, d. 37, c. iv: "Non moechaberis, 'id est, ne cuilibet miscearis, excepto foedere matrimonii. A parte enim totum intelligitur. Nomine igitur *moechiae* omnis concubitus illicitus illorumque membrorum non legitimus usus prohibitus debet intelligi.' " The internal quote is from Augustine, *Quaestiones in Exodi*, q. 71, no. 4, PL 31.622.
55. Peter Lombard, Ibid., IV, d. 28, c. ii.
56. See, for example, Bonaventure, *In IV Sententiarum*, d. 33, a. 1, qq. 1, 2; *Summa Fratris Alexandri*, P. III, q. 35, m. 4; P. II, q. 147, m. 2; Albert the Great, *In IV Sententiarium*, d. 33, a. 5; Thomas Aquinas, *In IV Sententiarum*, d. 33, q. 1, aa. 1-3 (=*Summa Theologiae*, Supplement, q. 65, aa. 1-5).
57. It was the unanimous opinion of the medieval theologians that the distinction of humankind into man and woman was for the sake of procreation. This point was made by Peter Lombard, *Liber Sententiarum*, II, d. 18, c. 1; the commentaries on this text reinforce the point. See, for

example, Aquinas, *In II Sententiarum*, d. 20, q. 1, a. 1; *Summa Theologiae*, I, q. 98, a.2, sed contra.

58. *De Malo*, q. 15, a. 1: "Finis autem usus genitalium membrorum est generatio et educatio prolis; et ideo omnis usus praedictorum membrorum qui non est proportionatus generationi prolis et debitae ejus educationi, est secundum se inordinatus." See also *Summa Theologiae*, II-II, q. 153, a. 2; *Summa Contra Gentiles*, bk. III, ch. 122.

59. Bonaventure, *In IV Sententiarum*, d. 33, a. 1: "In matrimonio est quidam amor singularis, in quo non communicet alienus: unde naturaliter omnis vir zelet uxorem quantum ad hoc, ut nullum alium diligat, ut diligat ipsum in actu illo: et omnis uxor similiter zelet virum ad hoc. . . . Caritate adveniente, quae facit omnia communia, numquam facit uxorem communem propter privatum amorem qui debet esse in matrimonio." See Sister Paula Jean Miller, F.S.E., *Marriage: The Sacrament of the Divine-Human Communion*, vol. 1, *A Commentary on St. Bonaventure's Breviloquium* (Quincy, Ill.: Franciscan Press, 1996).

60. See Note 80 below on the authorship of this work.

61. See Lombard, *Liber Sententiarum*, II, d. 31, c. 2, and the commentaries on this text. See also Aquinas, *Summa Theologiae*, I-II, q. 83, a. 4; *De Veritate*, q. 25, a. 6.

62. Lombard, *Libri IV Sententiarum*, II, d. 31, c. 4; IV, d. 26, cc. 2-4; Bonaventure, *In II Sententiarum*, d. 31, a. 1, q. 3.

63. See ibid.

64. The medieval theologians often spoke of the goods of marriage as "excusing" marital intercourse, but they regarded these goods as intrinsic perfections of marriage. Aquinas, for example, says the following: "Ista bona, quae matrimonium honestant, sunt de ratione matrimonii; et ideo non indiget eis quasi exterioribus quibusdam ad honestandum, sed quasi causantibus in ipso honestatem, quae ei secundum se competit." *In IV Sententiarum*, d. 31, q. 1, a. 2, ad 2 (=*Summa Theologiae*, Supplement, q. 49, a. 1, ad 2).

65. See Bonaventure, *In IV Sententiarum*, d. 31, a. 2, ad 1, 2, 3.

66. See Hugh of St. Victor, *De Sacramentis*, II, P. XI (PL 176.479-520). See Schillebeeckx, *Marriage*, pp. 320-324, for a summary.

67. Hugh of St. Victor, *Summa Sententiarum*, tr. 7, c. 2, PL 176.155. This is cited by Lombard, *Libri IV Sententiarum*, IV, d. 26, c. 5.

68. See Fabian Parmisano, O.P., "Love and Marriage in the Middle Ages I," *New Blackfriars*, 50 (1969), 604. For an analysis of Thomas Aquinas's discussion of this matter, see Germain Grisez, "Marriage: Reflections Based on St. Thomas and Vatican II," *Catholic Mind*, 64 (1966), 4-19.

69. The doctrine that marriage was one of the seven sacraments developed during the Middle Ages; Aquinas, following Lombard, held that it was one of the sacraments; see *Summa Theologiae*, Supplement, q. 42, a. 3; *Summa Contra Gentiles,* bk. 4, ch. 78. For an account of the development toward Aquinas's position, see Schillebeeckx, *Marriage*, pp. 328-343.

70. See Schillebeeckx, Ibid.; Innocent III, for example, clearly affirmed the sacramentality of marriage in 1208.

71. The medieval theologians realized, of course, that not all couples could have children because of sterility. But they held that sterile spouses need not repudiate the good of offspring. Such an intention in the exchange of marriage vows would vitiate the marital consent.

72. See Parmisano, "Love and Marriage in the Middle Ages II," *New Blackfriars*, 50 (1969), 649-660.

73. See Aquinas, *In IV Sententiarum*, d. 26, q. 1, aa. 3, 4 (=*Summa Theologiae*, Supplement, q. 41, aa. 3,4); Bonaventure, *In IV Sententiarum*, d. 26, q. 1, a. 3; d. 31, a. 2, q. 1.

74. See, for example, Lombard, *Libri IV Sententiarum*, IV, d. 31, c. 5; Bonaventure, *In IV Sententiarum*, d. 31, a. 2, q. 2; Aquinas, *In IV Sententiarum*, d. 31, q. 2, a. 3 (=*Summa Theologiae*, Supplement, q. 49, a. 6).

75. See texts cited above in Note 73.

76. See *In IV Sententiarum*, d. 32, q. 1, a. 1 (=*Summa Theologiae*, Supplement, q. 64, a. 2).

77. *In IV Sententiarum*, d. 31, q. 2, a. 2 (=*Summa Theologiae*, Supplement, q. 49, a. 4); it should be noted that in the very next article Aquinas states that the third good of marriage — the indissoluble bond — pertains to the essence of marriage and not to its use, and therefore makes marriage to be upright but not the act of marriage.

78. See *In IV Sententiarum*, d. 26, q. 1, a. 4 (=*Summa Theologiae*, Supplement, q. 64, a. 2).

79. See *Summa Theologiae*, II-II, q. 26, a. 11. In *Summa Contra Gentiles*, bk. 3, ch. 123, Aquinas says: "Inter virum et uxorem maxima amicitia esse videtur; adunantur enim non solum in actu camalis copulae, quae inter bestias quamdam suavem amicitiam facit, sed ad totius domesticae conversationis consortium." In ch. 125, he writes of the great union between spouses which leads them to love each other more fervently. For an account of the various kinds of friendship in Aquinas, and the particular form found in marriage, see Guy Durand, *Anthropologie*

Sexuelle et Marriage Chez Thomas d'Aquin (Lyon: Université de Lyon, 1966-1967), pp. 150-172.

80. Étienne Gilson, *A History of Christian Philosophy in the Middle Ages* (New York: Random House, 1955), p. 327.

81. See Alexander of Hales, *Summa Theologica* (= *Summa Fratris Alexandri*), II, 1, Inq. IV, tr. II, Sect. II, q. 2; see Parmisano, "Love and Marriage in the Middle Ages II," 684-685.

82. Ibid.

83. See *In IV Sententiarum*, d. 31, q. 2, a. 3 (=*Summa Theologiae*, Supplement, q. 49, a. 6). The view Aquinas rejects here is that of William of Auxerre, *Summa Aurea*, IV, tract. *De Matrimonio*, q. Utrum bona matrimonii excusent. . . (folio 287r of the Paris edition of 1500).

84. *Summa Theologiae*, I-II, q. 31, aa. 1, 2; q. 33, a. 4; q. 34, a. 4; see also Durand, *Anthropologie Sexuelle*, pp. 176-183.

85. John C. Ford, S.J., and Germain Grisez, "Contraception and the Infallibility of the Ordinary Magisterium," *Theological Studies*, 39 (1978), 258-312, at 277-286.

86. The universality of the condemnation of contraception is demonstrated by Noonan, *Contraception*, p. 6.

87. See "The Question Is Not Closed: The Liberals Reply" and "On Responsible Parenthood," in *The Birth Control Debate*, ed. Robert G. Hoyt (Kansas City, Mo.: *National Catholic Reporter*, 1969).

88. "The Question Is Not Closed," p. 76.

89. Michael Valente, *Sex: The Radical View of a Catholic Theologian* (New York: Bruce-Macmillan, 1970).

90. Anthony Kosnik et al., *Human Sexuality: New Directions in American Catholic Thought* (New York: Paulist Press, 1977).

91. Charles E. Curran, "Divorce in the Light of the Revised Moral Theology," in his *Ongoing Revision: Studies in Moral Theology* (Notre Dame, Ind.: Fides, 1975), pp. 77-78; Curran favors the change in Catholic teaching on contraception and proposes that the logical consequences for other areas of sexual morality be frankly admitted.

92. Noonan, *Contraception*, mistakenly supposes that the medieval theologians required procreative intent as a condition for marital intercourse to be wholly good. He praises the position of Martin Le Maistre, a fifteenth-century writer who held that there was no prohibition of intercourse on the part of a husband who is "scarcely master of himself because of the vehemence of the desire of lust." His wife is "given to him for the sake of solace and remedy." This sexist position is clearly

opposed to the realistic and balanced position of the medievals who taught that marital relations thus motivated were venially sinful.

93. Parmisano, "Love and Marriage in the Middle Ages I," 603.

94. See J.B. Gury, S.J., *Compendium Theologiae Moralis* (Turin: M.D. Autia, 1852), no. 688. This is an early edition of one of the most reedited and influential manuals of moral theology. Gury taught that spouses may rightly seek marital intercourse out of "the desire of fostering or bringing about decent friendship." See also Dietrich von Hildebrand, *In Defense of Purity* (New York: Sheed and Ward, 1935). For a careful summary and evaluation of Hildebrand's position and that of other influential authors of the twentieth century, see John C. Ford, S.J., and Gerald Kelly, S.J., *Contemporary Moral Theology*, vol. 1, *Marriage Questions* (Westminster, Md: The Newman Press, 1963). This volume makes clear that it had become the common teaching of theologians prior to Vatican II that marital intercourse was morally legitimate insofar as it expressed marital love.

95. Cajetan, *Commentarium in II-II*, q. 153, a. 2: "Unde non debet persona de hujusmodi delectatione recepta dolere, sed potius Deo gratias agere." See Louis Vereecke, C.Ss.R., "L'éthique Sexuelle des Moralistes Post-Trindentins," *Studia Moralia*, 13 (1975), 175-196, at 178-181.

96. See Vereecke, "L'éthique Sexuelle," 182-185.

Notes for Chapter Four

1. See Thomas Aquinas, *Summa Theologiae*, I-II, q. 106, a. 1.

2. See Rudolph Schnackenburg, *The Moral Teaching of the New Testament*, tr. J. Holland-Smith and W.J. O'Hare (New York: Herder and Herder, 1971), pp. 15-89.

3. See Germain Grisez, *The Way of the Lord Jesus*, vol. 1, *Christian Moral Principles* (Chicago: Franciscan Herald Press, 1983), for a systematic treatment of the foundations of Christian ethics, which incorporates the teaching of Vatican Council II.

4. See Joseph M. Boyle, Jr., Germain Grisez, and Olaf Tollefsen, *Free Choice: A Self-Referential Argument* (Notre Dame, Ind.: University of Notre Dame Press, 1976), pp. 8-10.

5. See ibid., pp. 11-12.

6. See DS 1521, 1554, 1939, 1941, and 1966; see also Grisez, *Christian Moral Principles*, ch. 2, q. B, and app. 1, for a fuller account of Church teaching on free choice.

7. *Summa Theologiae*, I, q. 83, a. 1.

8. Pope John Paul II, *Veritatis Splendor,* no. 71. Later in this number the Pope cites a beautiful passage from St. Gregory of Nyssa's *De Vita Moysis* (II, 2-3): "All things subject to change and to becoming never remain constant, but continually pass from one state to another, for better or worse. . . . Now human life is always subject to change; it needs to be born ever anew. . . . But here birth does not come about by a foreign intervention, as is the case with bodily beings . . . it is the result of a free choice. Thus we *are* in a certain way our own parents, creating ourselves as we will, by our decisions."

9. See *Catechism of the Catholic Church,* no. 1731.

10. On this see John Paul II, *Veritatis Splendor,* nos. 35-53.

11. The view that morality is an expression of an arbitrary divine will is called "the divine command theory," or "theological voluntarism." This view is rejected by the great teachers of the Church. Aquinas makes the classical rebuttal in *De Veritate,* 23, 6; for a modern discussion, see William K. Frankena, *Ethics,* 2nd ed. (Englewood Cliffs, N.J.: Prentice-Hall, 1973), pp. 28-30.

12. The view that human choices create the goodness of things can be called "existentialism." This view is associated with the writings of the French philosopher Jean Paul Sartre; a somewhat similar position is developed in the work of English philosopher R.M. Hare. For critiques, see Alvin Plantinga, "An Existentialist's Ethics," in *The Review of Metaphysics,* 12 (1958), 235-256; Henry B. Veatch, *For an Ontology of Morals* (Evanston, Ill.: Northwestern University Press, 1971), pp. 19-84.

13. Aristotle, *Nicomachean Ethics,* 1, ch. 7, provides the classical formulation of the perfectionist account of goodness. Aquinas developed Aristotle's idea; throughout his ethical writing he defines the good as "fullness of being" and as perfection; see *Summa Theologiae,* I-II, q. 18, a. 1. See also Grisez, *Christian Moral Principles,* ch. 5, q. A.

14. The internal quote is from the Preface of the Mass of the Solemnity of Christ the King.

15. See Xavier Léon-Dufour, *Dictionary of Biblical Theology,* 2nd ed. (New York: Desclée, 1973), entries on Justice, Love, and Peace.

16. See *Gaudium et Spes,* ch. 2, and the social encyclicals of the last century, for authoritative teaching on justice and related goods.

17. See Léon-Dufour, *Dictionary of Biblical Theology,* entries on Peace, Truth, and Wisdom.

18. The cowardly, imprudent, or intemperate person does establish a kind of relationship between the various elements of the self. These relations are unstable and profoundly unsatisfactory even by the standards

a non-virtuous person might set. This is so because not every kind of self-integration truly contributes to one's perfection as a human being.

19. In Scripture, truth is primarily a matter of trustworthiness; knowledge a matter of intimate experience and fellowship; and wisdom a matter of practical reasonableness or prudence; see Léon-Dufour, *Dictionary of Biblical Theology*, entries on Truth, Knowledge, and Wisdom. Still, knowledge as the grasping of truth, and wisdom as the understanding of reality, are valued in the Scriptures, especially in the Wisdom literature. Until recently the value of theoretical understanding has been expressed more in the life of the Church than in its explicit teaching — for example, in the honor given to thinkers like Augustine and Aquinas, and implicitly to the vocation of the intellectual life they pursued. For recent, explicit endorsements of the pursuit of truth, see *Gaudium et Spes*, no. 15; *Dignitatis Humanae*, nos. 1-2.

20. See Léon-Dufour, *Dictionary of Biblical Theology*, entry on Life.

21. Our listing of human goods is inspired by the list given by Aquinas, *Summa Theologiae*, I-II, q. 94, a. 2. See also Grisez, *Christian Moral Principles*, ch. 5, q. D. In *The Way of the Lord Jesus* vol. 2, *Living a Christian Life*, (Quincy, Ill.: Franciscan Press, 1993), Grisez argues that marriage must be regarded a distinct basic human good (pp. 555-569). This development would alter some of the arguments we make later in this book. His thesis, which he himself roots in the teaching of the contemporary magisterium on marriage, strengthens the Church's teaching on sexual and marital morality.

22. See John Finnis, *Natural Law and Natural Rights* (New York: Oxford University Press, 1980), pp. 95-97, for a development of this point. The critique of hedonism is as old as Western philosophy; see Plato, *Philebus*, 20e-22e, 27d, 60a-61b, 67a; Aristotle, *Nicomachean Ethics*, X, 1172b, 10-25.

23. This point is overlooked by many popular criticisms of the Church's teaching on sexual morality; see, for example, the parody of the traditional teaching on sexual pleasure in Anthony Kosnik et al., *Human Sexuality: New Directions in American Catholic Thought* (New York: Paulist Press, 1977), pp. 24-25, 34, 40.

24. See Aristotle, *Nicomachean Ethics*, X, 1174b, 14-1175a, 10.

25. See Aquinas, *Summa Contra Gentiles*, bk. 3, ch. 26, for a statement of the dependence of pleasure on the thing which the pleasure accompanies.

26. See Grisez, *Christian Moral Principles*, ch. 1, qs. D and E, and the literature cited there, for the shortcomings of what Grisez calls "classical moral theololgy."

27. Pope John Paul II, *Veritatis Splendor*, no. 13.
28. On the meaning of the object of a human act that specifies it see ibid., no. 78. See also St. Thomas Aquinas, *Summa Theologiae*, 1-2, q. 18.
29. *Veritatis Splendor*, no. 80.
30. See ibid., nos. 80, 81.
31. Ibid., no. 115.
32. Ibid., no. 79.
33. Ibid., no. 74.
34. Thus Richard A. McCormick, S.J., in reviewing essays by Joseph Fuchs and Bruno Schueller written in the early 1970's, emphasized that the common theme of both these moralists (and of some others too) was a movement toward a "morality of consequences." Again and again in this essay McCormick singled out "the key part played by consequences in the development of norms." With Schueller he agrees that the moral assessment of an act "must be made 'teleologically,' i.e., from consequences," and he observed that Fuchs "has obviously taken a rather giant step in the direction of a consequentialist methodology . . . [indeed] the very 'meaning' of an action can only be gathered when all aspects of the action, especially its consequences, have been weighed as far as possible." See McCormick, "Notes on Moral Theology 1972," reprinted in *Notes on Moral Theology 1965-1980* (Washington: University Press of America, 1980), pp. 352, 359, 371.
35. On this see ibid., "Notes on Moral Theology, 1975," p. 521 ff.
36. See Garth Hallett, *Christian Moral Reasoning. An Analytical Guide* (Notre Dame, Ind.: University of Notre Dame Press, 1983), p. 46; Timothy E. O'Connell, *Principles for a Catholic Morality* (New York: Seabury, 1978), p. 153; Richard A. McCormick, *Notes on Moral Theology: 1965 Through 1980* (Washington, D.C.: University Press of America, 1981), pp. 354-355; Louis Janssens, "Norms and Priorities in a Love Ethic," *Louvain Studies*, 6 (1977), 214; for a handy collection of proportionalist thought, see *Readings in Moral Theology No. 1: Moral Norms and Catholic Tradition*, ed. Charles E. Curran and Richard A. McCormick (New York: Paulist Press, 1978).
37. See Richard A. McCormick, *How Brave a New World? Dilemmas in Bioethics* (New York: Doubleday, 1981), p. 5; here, McCormick makes clear that he accepts a nuanced account of the human good like the one set out in Part II of this chapter.
38. See Lisa Sowle Cahill, "Contemporary Challenges to Exceptionless Moral Norms," in *Moral Theology Today: Certitudes and Doubts* (St. Louis: The Pope John Center, 1984), pp. 121-135, for a clear, recent

statement of the restrictions on the use of the proportionalist method by one who is sympathetic to it.

39. On practical absolutes, see Daniel Maguire, *Death by Choice* (New York: Doubleday, 1974), p. 99; on virtually exceptionless norms, see Richard A. McCormick, *Ambiguity in Moral Choice* (Milwaukee: Marquette University Press, 1973), p. 73.

40. McCormick, *Ambiguity in Moral Choice*, pp. 78-79.

41. See John Paul II, *Veritatis Splendor*, no. 75.

42. See, for example, John Paul II's apostolic exhortation *Reconciliatio et Poenitentia*, no. 17; Congregation for the Clergy, *General Catechetical Directory* (April 11, 1971), no. 63. The importance of moral absolutes for Christian morality is apparent to its opponents; see, for example, the influential article of Jonathan Bennett, "Whatever the Consequences," *Analysis* 26 (1966), 83-102.

43. John Paul II, *Veritatis Splendor,* nos. 80, 115.

44. See *Catechism of the Catholic Church*, nos. 2268-2283 (on intentional killing of innocent, abortion, euthanasia, suicide); 2381 (on adultery).

45. Arguments for dissent from authoritative Church teaching are characteristic of the proportionalist movement. These arguments — involving more than appeals to the method of proportionalism — also involve views on conscience, authority, and ecclesiology. These matters will be discussed in detail in Chapter 5 of this book.

46. See McCormick, *Ambiguity in Moral Choice*, pp. 78-79.

47. The most serious attempts by proportionalists to find this mode of moral reasoning in St. Thomas are those of John Milhaven, John Dedek, and Louis Janssens. See Milhaven's "Moral Absolutes in Thomas Aquinas," in *Absolutes in Moral Theology?*, ed. Charles E. Curran (Washington: Corpus, 1968), 154-185, reprinted in Milhaven's *Toward a New Catholic Morality* (New York: Doubleday, 1972), pp. 135-167, 228-236; Dedek's "Intrinsically Evil Acts: An Historical Study of the Mind of St. Thomas," *The Thomist*, 43 (1979), 385-413; Janssens' "Ontic Evil and Moral Evil," *Louvain Studies*, 4 (1972), 115-156, reprinted in *Readings in Moral Theology No. 1: Norms and the Catholic Tradition*, ed. Charles E. Curran and Richard A. McCormick (New York: Paulist Press, 1979), pp. 40-93, as well as Janssens' "Norms and Priorities in a Love Ethic," *Louvain Studies*, 6 (1977), 207-238, and "St. Thomas Aquinas and the Question of Proportionality," *Louvain Studies*, 9 (1982), 26-46. For a critique of the interpretation of Aquinas given by Dedek and Milhaven, see Patrick Lee, "Permanence of the Ten Commandments: St. Thomas and His Commentators," *Theological Studies*, 42 (1981),

277

422-433. For a critique of Janssens' interpretation of Aquinas, see William E. May, "Aquinas and Janssens on the Moral Meaning of Human Acts," *The Thomist*, 48 (1984), 566-606. For attempts to find proportionalism in past Catholic thought, particularly in the just-war theory, see O'Connell, *Principles for a Catholic Morality*, p. 153.

48. John Paul II, *Veritatis Splendor,* no. 77.
49. This argument has been developed extensively by Germain Grisez in a number of his works; for a recent summary of the argument along with relevant references to earlier analyses, see his *Christian Moral Principles*, ch. 6, q. F; see also Finnis, *Natural Law and Natural Rights*, p. 115.
50. See Alan Donagan, *The Theory of Morality* (Chicago: University of Chicago Press, 1977), pp. 199-209.
51. See Dan W. Brock, "Recent Work on Utilitarianism," *American Philosophical Quarterly*, 10 (1973), 241-276; Bernard Williams, *Morality: An Introduction to Ethics* (New York: Doubleday, 1972), pp. 89-107; and Bernard Williams and J.J.C. Smart, in "A Critique of Utilitarianism," *Utilitarianism: For and Against* (Cambridge, England: Cambridge University Press, 1973), pp. 172-209.
52. Richard A. McCormick, "A Commentary on the Commentaries," in *Doing Evil to Achieve Good*, ed. Richard McCormick and Paul Ramsey (Chicago: Loyola University Press, 1978), p. 277. This volume contains McCormick's *Ambiguity in Moral Choice*, already referred to above, along with responses by several moralists, including an important critical essay by Paul Ramsey and McCormick's responses to the essays.
53. See Grisez, *Christian Moral Principles*, ch. 6, q. E, for an account of various meanings of "greater good" compatible with common sense and the Catholic moral tradition. See also John Paul II, *Veritatis Splendor*, no. 80.
54. See Grisez, *Christian Moral Principles*, ch. 6, q. D, for a development of this rejoinder.
55. See John Paul II, *Veritatis Splendor*, nos. 75-76.
56. See Williams, *Morality*, pp. 104-105: ". . . . A utilitarian is always justified in doing the least bad thing which is necessary to prevent the worst thing that would otherwise happen in the circumstances (including of course, the worst thing that someone else may do) — and what he is thus justified in doing may often be something which, taken in itself, is fairly nasty. The preemptive act is built into utilitarian conceptions, and certain notions of negative responsibility (that you are re-

sponsible for what you fail to prevent, as much as for what you do) are by the same token characteristic of it. This being so, it is empirically probable that an escalation of preemptive activity may be expected: and the total consequences of this, *by utilitarian standards themselves*, will be worse than if it had never started."

57. John Paul II, *Veritatis Splendor*, nos. 96, 97.

58. See John Paul II, *Veritatis Splendor*, no. 12; *Catechism of the Catholic Church*, nos. 1954-1960.

59. On this see William E. May, *An Introduction to Moral Theology* (rev. ed., Huntington, Ind: Our Sunday Visitor, 1994), pp. 87-89, 103-105.

60. This statement of the first moral principle is adapted from Grisez, *Christian Moral Principles*, ch. 7, q. F; for a different formulation, compatible with the one stated here, see Karol Wojtyla (John Paul II), *Love and Responsibility*, tr. H.T. Willetts (New York: Farrar, Straus, and Giroux, 1981), p. 41; Wojtyla calls the basic principle "the personalistic norm" and explicates its meaning by contrasting it with utilitarianism and relating it to the love commandments. "The norm, in its negative aspect, states that the person is the kind of good that does not admit of use and cannot be treated as an object of use and as such the means to an end. In its positive form the personalistic norm confirms this: the person is a good towards which the only proper and adequate attitude is love. The positive content of the personalistic norm is precisely what the commandment to love teaches."

61. John Paul II, *Veritatis Splendor*, nos. 90-95.

62. Ibid., nos. 95-98; see also John Paul II, *Evangelium Vitae*, nos. 57-58.

63. See *Summa Theologiae*, I-II, q. 18, a. 4, ad 3; this principle was adopted by later moral theologians and stated in the following pithy formula, which is almost impossible to render meaningfully in a literal translation: "Bonum ex integra causa; malum ex quocumque defectu."

64. *Catechism of the Catholic Church,* nos. 1650-1761; *Veritatis Splendor*, nos. 75, 77-78.

65. See John Paul II, *Veritatis Splendor*, no. 71; cf no. 80.

66. See Joseph M. Boyle, Jr., "Toward Understanding the Principle of Double Effect," *Ethics*, 90 (1980), 527-538; and "The Principle of Double Effect: Good Actions Entangled in Evil," in *Moral Theology Today*, pp. 243-260.

67. For a discussion of this denial, see McCormick, *Ambiguity in Moral Choice*, pp. 72-83.

68. See *Veritatis Splendor*, nos. 76, 78.

69. See, for example, Josef Fuchs, S.J., "Basic Freedom and Morality," in

279

his *Human Values and Christian Morality* (Dublin: Gill, 1970), pp. 92-111. For references to other statements of fundamental-option theory along with a critical analysis, see Joseph M. Boyle, Jr., "Freedom, the Human Person, and Human Action," in *Principles of Catholic Moral Life*, ed. William E. May (Chicago: Franciscan Herald Press, 1981), pp. 237-266. The articles by Ronald Lawler, O.F.M. Cap., and John R. Connery, S.J., in this volume provide further discussion and references on this matter. See also the remarks on this matter by John Paul II in *Reconciliatio et Poenitentia* (December 2, 1984), no. 17.

70. John Paul II, *Veritatis Splendor*, nos. 65-68. The pope's particular concern is using the idea of fundamental option to excuse the deliberate choice of gravely evil actions. This, he teaches, is contrary to Scripture and Tradition.

71. John Paul II, *Veritatis Splendor*, no. 71. In his philosophical writings John Paul II developed at length the self-determining character of a person's choices. See Karol Wojtyla (John Paul II), *The Acting Person* (Dordrecht, Boston, and London: D. Reidel, 1979), pp. 105-186, especially pp. 149-151.

72. See Grisez, *Christian Moral Principles*, ch. 2, q. I.

73. See Sacred Congregation for the Doctrine of the Faith, *Declaration on Certain Questions Concerning Sexual Ethics* (Washington, D.C.: U.S. Catholic Conference, 1976), pp. 10-12.

Notes for Chapter Five

1. Major documents of the universal magisterium concerned with conscience are the following: Vatican Council II, *Gaudium et Spes*, nos. 16-17; Vatican Council II, *Dignitatis Humanae*, nos. 2-3, 14; *Catechism of the Catholic Church*, Part 3, Section 1, Chapter 1, Article 6, nos. 1776-1802; Pope John Paul II, *Veritatis Splendor*, Chapter Two, Section II, nos. 54-64. In its treatment of conscience the *Catechism of the Catholic Church* considers (I) the judgment of conscience, (II) the formation of conscience, (III) to choose in accord with conscience, and (IV) erroneous conscience.

Other relevant magisterial documents include: Sacred Congregation of the Holy Office, Instruction on "Situation Ethics": *Contra Doctrinam* (February 2, 1956); Canadian Catholic Conference, *Statement on the Formation of Conscience* December 1, 1973 (available in pamphlet form from the Daughters of St. Paul, St. Paul Publications, Boston, 1974); Irish Episcopal Conference, *Conscience and Morality: A Doctrinal Statement of the Irish Episcopal Conference*, February 22,

1980 (also available in pamphlet form from the Daughters of St. Paul, St. Paul Publications, 1980).

Useful theological literature on conscience includes: Philippe Delhaye, *The Christian Conscience* (New York: Desclee, 1968); *Conscience: Its Freedom and Limitations*, ed. William C. Bier, S.J. (New York: Fordham University Press, 1971); William B. Smith, "The Meaning of Conscience," in *Principles of Catholic Moral Life*, ed. William E. May (Chicago: Franciscan Herald Press, 1981), pp. 361-382, Germain Grisez, "The Duty and Right to Follow One's Judgement of Conscience," in *"Humanae Vitae": 20 Anni Dopo: Atti del II Congresso Internazionale di Teologia Morale* (Milan: Edizioni Ares, 1989), pp. 211-222.

2. See John Macquarrie, *Three Issues in Ethics* (New York: Harper and Row, 1970), pp. 113-114.

3. The use of "conscience" in the New Testament was apparently limited to the judgment of one's own past acts. See James C. Turro, "Conscience in the Bible," in *Conscience: Its Freedom and Limitations*, ed. W.C. Bier, pp. 3-8; but see Eric D'Arcy, *Conscience and Its Right to Freedom* (New York: Sheed and Ward, 1961), pp. 8-12, for an interesting argument by a philosopher that St. Paul has a directive or legislative sense of conscience as well.

4. See Thomas Aquinas, *Summa Theologiae*, I, q. 79, a. 13; Canadian Catholic Conference, *Statement on the Formation of Conscience*, no. 6; Irish Episcopal Conference, *Conscience and Morality*, no. 2; National Conference of Catholic Bishops, *To Live in Christ Jesus: A Pastoral Reflection on the Moral Life* (Washington, D.C.: U.S. Catholic Conference, 1976), p. 10.

5. *Catechism of the Catholic Church*, no. 1778.

6. Pope John Paul II, *Veritatis Splendor*, no. 59.

7. See Charles E. Curran, *Themes in Fundamental Moral Theology* (Notre Dame, Ind.: University of Notre Dame Press, 1977), p. 211; Curran mistakenly argues that the traditional view of conscience cannot account for the legitimate role of affectivity in conscience. For a more adequate account, see Germain Grisez, *The Way of the Lord Jesus*, vol. 1, *Christian Moral Principles* (Chicago: Franciscan Herald Press, 1983), ch. 10, q. D; ch. 31, q. E.

8. This is the common teaching of the tradition. See Aquinas, *De Veritate*, q. 17, a. 3; D'Arcy, *Conscience and Its Right to Freedom*, pp. 87-112, provides a commentary.

9. Conscience in this sense is called "*synderesis*" by Aquinas and much of the subsequent tradition; see *Summa Theologiae*, I, q. 79, a. 12.

10. See also *Catechism of the Catholic Church*, no. 1780: "Conscience includes the perception of the principles of morality (synderesis), their application in the given circumstances by practical discernment of reasons and goods, and finally judgment about concrete acts yet to be performed or already performed."
11. See *Summa Theologiae*, I-II, q. 100, aa. 1, 3, ad 1.
12. *Summa Theologiae*, I-II, q. 100, a. 1.
13. The Abbott translation of *Gaudium et Spes* mistakenly translates "voice of the law" as "voice of conscience."
14. *Gaudium et Spes*, no. 16.
15. Pope John Paul II, *Veritatis Splendor*, no. 62.
16. Walter E. Conn, *Conscience: Development and Self-Transcendence* (Birmingham, Ala.: Religious Education Press, 1981), p. 205.
17. See John M. Finnis, "Natural Law, Objective Morality, and Vatican Council II," in *Principles of Catholic Moral Life*, ed. William E. May, pp. 113-150, especially pp. 114-121, for an explanation of the teaching of Vatican II on conscience; see also William E. May, "Conscience, the Natural Law and Developmental Psychology," *Communio*, 2.1 (1975).
18. Macquarrie, *Three Issues in Ethics*, p. 114.
19. Ibid.
20. Pius XII, "Radio Message on Rightly Forming Conscience in Christian Youth," March 23, 1952, *Acta Apostolica Sedis*, 44 (1952), 271. [*NOTE:* Hereafter *Acta Apostolica Sedis* will be referred to as AAS followed by volume and page numbers — in this case, for example, AAS 44.271.]
21. *Gaudium et Spes*, no. 16; John Paul II, *Veritatis Splendor,* no. 58.
22. Conn, *Conscience*, p. 205.
23. Ibid., p. 213.
24. See ibid., p. 209f. Conn develops an analogy between ethics and esthetics. He says: "Because the ethical analyst realizes that decisions are made in particular situations according to the subject's best *creative* understanding of the complex concreteness of the situation, he or she does not regard interpretations of general problem areas like abortion as applicable in a *deductive* way to particular cases, any more than a literary critic pretends to offer the author a formula on how to compose a fine poem or a first-rate novel." In response, it should be noted first that creativity does have a proper role in the moral thinking of a mature and conscientious person; such a person will seek to find ways to carry out all his or her responsibilities so as to best serve human goods and the often conflicting requirements of common life.

282

However, such creativity as is clearly a part of moral life does not exclude rigorous application of moral principles to cases in such a way as to absolutely exclude some kinds of acts. It is a parody of this application, which finds its formal development in casuistry, to say that it is deductive in the sense that it takes no real thinking or creative understanding.

25. John Paul II, *Veritatis Splendor*, no. 60.

26. For the theological tradition, see the sources cited above in Note 8; for magisterial teaching, see *Gaudium et Spes*, no. 16; *Dignitatis Humanae*, no. 2; *Catechism of the Catholic Church*, no. 1778; Pope John Paul II, *Veritatis Splendor*, no. 60.

27. Sometimes we arrive at a doubtful judgment of conscience; since it is wrong to be willing to do what might be wrong, one must not follow a doubtful conscience but must instead seek to resolve the doubt. The traditional "moral systems" provide a reflexive device for doing this. In this context, "doubtful" means having a real question as to whether an action is morally good or bad. Its opposite is moral certainty which is not the certainty of strict proof. See Delhaye, *The Christian Conscience*, pp. 213-242, for a summary of the traditional discussion of doubtful conscience.

28. See Timothy E. O'Connell, *Principles for a Catholic Morality* (New York: Seabury, 1978), pp. 91-92; O'Connell says that one's conscience is infallible. This confuses the absolute obligation to follow a certain conscience with the truth status of that judgment. One must follow one's conscience, but that does not imply that its judgment is beyond criticism. Moreover, if one's conscience is in error, and it is one's fault that it is, one is culpable for the error. Thus, one may have an obligation to follow an erroneous conscience and commit sin in so doing, not because one follows conscience but because one has not taken proper care to form one's conscience adequately. One reason why some mistakenly suppose that conscience is infallible is that they misunderstand the teaching that God speaks to persons in the depths of their conscience. The correct sense of this teaching does not imply that what God reveals to people in this way has the infallibility of faith itself, for God thus speaks to us through the natural and fallible resources of our hearts and minds.

29. Thus, in *Veritatis Splendor*, no. 62, Pope John Paul II, recapitulating Catholic tradition, writes: "Conscience *is not an infallible judge*; it can make mistakes."

30. See *De Veritate*, q. 17, a. 4; *Summa Theologiae*, I-II, q. 19, a. 5.

31. Pope John II, *Veritatis Splendor*, no. 63.

32. See *Summa Theologiae*, I-II, q. 19, a. 6.

33. *To Live in Christ Jesus*, p. 10.

34. See *Summa Theologiae*, I-II, q. 100, a. 3.

35. *Dignitatis Humanae*, no. 14. The *Catechism of the Catholic Church* puts it this way: "In forming our conscience we are assisted by the gifts of the Holy Spirit, aided by the witness or advice of others, and guided by the authoritative teaching of the Church" (no. 1785). See also nos. 2030-2051 on "The Church, Mother and Teacher."

36. John Paul II, *Veritatis Splendor*, no. 64.

37. See *Summa Theologiae*, I-II, q. 91, a. 2; for Aquinas the natural law is a participation in the eternal law by which God providentially guides the universe. The divine law is the law of God made known by revelation. This also includes the natural law, which is included within both the Mosaic law and the new covenant of Jesus. See also *Dignitatis Humanae*, no. 3.

38. John Henry Newman, *Letter to the Duke of Norfolk*, cited in the Irish Episcopal Conference's *Conscience and Morality*, no. 20.

39. *Conscience and Morality*, no. 11.

40. *Catechism of the Catholic Church*, no. 2039.

41. See Charles E. Curran, *Ongoing Revision: Studies in Moral Theology* (Notre Dame, Ind.: Fides, 1975), pp. 76-87; Curran argues that contraception is now recognized as morally good by married persons themselves, even though officially condemned by the Church. He goes on to apply this same line of reasoning to the indissolubility of marriage.

42. For an analysis of moral dilemmas of this kind, see Germain Grisez, *The Way of the Lord Jesus* vol. 2, *Living a Christian Life*, (Quincy, IL: Franciscan Press, 1993), ch. 5.

43. See *Gaudium et Spes*, nos. 27, 51.

44. *To Live in Christ Jesus*, p. 12.

45. *Catechism of the Catholic Church*, no. 2037.

46. Some specific moral teachings have been defined. The Council of Trent's condemnation of polygamy is a clear case (DS 1802). This Council's affirmation of the indissolubility of marriage also seems to be a solemn definition of a specific moral precept (DS 1805, 1807).

47. Pope John Paul II, *Evangelium Vitae*, nos. 57, 62, and 65.

48. See Grisez, *Christian Moral Principles*, ch. 35, qs. D and E, for an explanation of this point.

49. See John C. Ford, S.J., and Germain Grisez, "Contraception and the Infallibility of the Ordinary Magisterium," *Theological Studies*, 39

(1978), 258-312; Marcellinus Zalba, S.J., "Infallibilità del Magistero Ordinario e Contraccezione," *Renovatio*, 14 (1979), 79-90.

50. See Francis A. Sullivan, S.J., *Magisterium: Teaching Authority in the Catholic Church* (New York: Paulist Press, 1983), pp. 148-152, for a recent summary of this position by one who accepts it.

51. As we have seen, John Paul II, explicitly referring to *Lumen Gentium*, no. 15, clearly taught in that encyclical that the teaching of the Church on the absolute inviolability of innocent human life from direct attack and on the intrinsic evil of every intentional act of abortion and euthanasia has been infallibly proposed by the ordinary and universal magisterium of the Church.

52. Sullivan, *Magisterium*, pp. 148-152, 227-228, does not explicitly accept proportionalism. However, most of the moralists he cites are proportionalists; the list contains well-known dissenters from Church teaching on sexual morality, and no theologians known for support of the magisterium on these matters. For a typical account by a proportionalist, see Philip S. Keane, S.S., *Sexual Morality: A Catholic Perspective* (New York: Paulist Press, 1977), p. 54: "If we accept the notion that the ultimate morality of an action comes from the action in its total concreteness, the Church can never catch up with this total concreteness in such a way as to make infallible or fully absolute decisions on all aspects of concrete or specific moral cases." This argument fails to distinguish between the concreteness of an individual act and the specificity of a kind of act. Every individual act is some kind of act, and some kinds of acts have been taught by the Church to be wrong. Thus, the phrase "ultimate morality of an action" is ambiguous. In some sense, of course, a decisive evaluation of an act requires a consideration of all the concrete circumstances of the act. One who wishes to evaluate fully the entire goodness or badness of an action must take into account not only the kind of act but also the intentions with which it was done as well as all the morally relevant circumstances. But it is not true that one must consider all these features before making *any* decisive judgment about the act. If one knows that a given act was an act of rape or of abortion or a contraceptive act, one knows that this is objectively a gravely evil kind of act and that every concrete act that would be an exemplification of this kind of act is objectively wrong and ought not be done. Such a judgment is not final in the sense of taking into full account every morally relevant aspect of the case. But that does not prevent the judgment from being decisive. Proportionalists, as we saw in Chapter 4, do not accept the traditional teaching that acts of certain kinds are always wrong.

285

53. See Sullivan, *Magisterium*, pp. 143-145. Here, Sullivan disputes what he supposes to be Ford's and Grisez' effort to demonstrate that the received teaching on contraception is part of the secondary object of infallible teaching. What he says here could easily be applied to other areas of the Church's teaching on sexual morality. On this, see John Paul II, *Reconciliatio et Poenitentia* (December 2, 1984), no. 17.
54. See Germain Grisez, "Infallibility and Specific Moral Norms: A Reply to Francis A. Sullivan, S.J.," *The Thomist*, 49 (1985).
55. *Catechism of the Catholic Church*, no. 2036.
56. Charles E. Curran et al., *Dissent in and for the Church* (New York: Sheed and Ward, 1969), p. 26; in "Ten Years Later," *Commonweal*, 105 (1978), 429, Curran affirmed the more general thesis that dissent can be legitimate with respect to any specific moral teaching.
57. See J.R. Lerch, "Teaching Authority of the Church (Magisterium)," *New Catholic Encyclopedia*, 13.965; Francisco A. Sullivan, S.J., *De Ecclesia*, vol. 1, *Quaestiones Theologiae Fundamentalis* (Rome: Gregorian University Press, 1963), p. 354; I. Salaverri, S.J., *Sacrae Theologiae Summa*, vol. 1, *Theologiae Fundamentalis*, 5th ed. (Madrid: Biblioteca de Autores Cristianos, 1952), p. 708, no. 699; L. Lercher, *Institutiones Theologiae Dogmaticae*, vol. 1, 5th ed. (Innsbruck: Rauch, 1951), p. 297.
58. Sullivan, *Magisterium*, p. 167, one of those who claim that the standard position of the approved authors is to allow dissent from authoritative but noninfallible teaching, cites Lercher, *Institutiones*, p. 297, in support of dissent. What Lercher actually says is this: "If the Roman Pontiff, using his authority but not to its highest degree, obliges all to give their assent to something as true (whether as revealed or as connected with revelation), it does not seem that in principle he is infallible, nor must we say that the Holy Spirit will never permit him to issue an erroneous decree. Certainly, the Holy Spirit will never permit it to happen that by such a decree the Church would be led into error. The way in which the error would be excluded more probably consists in the assistance of the Holy Spirit given to the head of the Church, by which such an erroneous decree would be prevented. However, it is not unthinkable that an error should be excluded by the Holy Spirit in this way: that the subjects recognize the decree to be erroneous and cease to give their assent to it." This is hardly a rationale for public dissent.
59. See Congregation for the Doctrine of the Faith, *Instruction on the Ecclesial Vocation of the Theologian*, nos. 21-41.

286

60. *Lumen Gentium*, no. 25. Sullivan, *Magisterium*, pp. 155-156, provides a recent example of the kind of argumentation to which we refer here. He argues that, because one of the schemata preparatory to *Lumen Gentium* was dropped from consideration by the Council, there is evidence that the Council meant to weaken restrictions on dissent. The schema in question referred to Pius XII's strong rejection of theological dissent in the encyclical *Humani Generis* (DS 3885). However, the very text of Pius XII which Sullivan supposes the Council meant to reject is explicitly referred to in *Optatam Totius*, no. 16. As Avery Dulles, *A Church to Believe In* (New York: Seabury, 1982), p. 124, has said: "The position of Pius XII to this effect [that the decisive judgment of a pontiff ends theological debate] in *Humani Generis* (DS 3885), even though not explicitly repeated by Vatican II, still seems to stand as official teaching, especially in view of its reaffirmation by Paul VI."

61. Richard A. McCormick, S.J., *Notes On Moral Theology: 1965 Through 1980* (Washington D.C.: University Press of America, 1981), p. 667.

62. In *Vertatis Splendor*, no. 113, Pope John Paul II emphasized that "*dissent . . . is opposed to ecclesial communion and to a correct understanding of the hierarchical constitution of the People of God.* Opposition to the teaching of the Church's Pastors cannot be seen as a legitimate expression either of Christian freedom or of the diversity of the Spirit's gifts." See also John Paul II, *Familiaris Consortio*, no. 73; *Code of Canon Law* (1983), canons 752-754, 823, 1371.

63. Daniel C. Maguire, "The Freedom to Die," in *The New Theology No. 10,* ed. Martin E. Marty and Dean Peerman (New York: Macmillan, 1973), p. 18. Charles Curran argues this position in many of his writings on sexual morality; see *Themes in Fundamental Moral Theology,* pp. 27-80, especially pp. 64-69; *Issues in Sexual and Medical Ethics* (Notre Dame, Ind.: University of Notre Dame Press, 1978), pp. 38-39.

64. See Germain Grisez, *Contraception and the Natural Law* (Milwaukee: Bruce, 1964), pp. 47-53.

65. Pope John Paul II, *Veritatis Splendor*, nos. 48-49.

66. See Keane, *Sexual Morality*, pp. 52-54; O'Connell, *Principles for a Catholic Morality*, pp. 91-92.

67. See *Gaudium et Spes*, no. 16; see Finnis's commentary cited above in Note 17.

68. Curran uses the terms "hierarchical" and "papal" to describe the Church's magisterium; he calls the teaching office of professional theologians the "doctrinal magisterium," and maintains for theologians a

source of teaching authority independent of the papal and episcopal magisterium; see *Ongoing Revision*, pp. 45-48, 75-87.

69. See Grisez, *Christian Moral Principles*, ch. 35, q. A, for a positive account of the sense of the faithful.

70. See Richard McCormick, *Notes on Moral Theology*, pp. 784-786; Avery Dulles, S.J., is the theologian perhaps best-known for the position of the twofold magisterium. However, Dulles's remarks are guarded. He rightly emphasizes that the theologians have a teaching office, and certainly never draws the conclusion which we are disputing. See his *Survival of Dogma* (New York: Doubleday, 1973), pp. 98-108; "The Theologian and the Magisterium," *Catholic Theological Society of America: Proceedings of the Thirty-First Annual Convention*, 31 (1976), 335-346; *A Church to Believe In*, pp. 110-111, and especially his more cautious remarks on the twofold magisterium, pp. 118-132.

71. Maguire, "Of Sex and Ethical Methodology," in *Dimensions of Human Sexuality*, ed. Dennis Doherty (New York: Doubleday, 1979), pp. 139-140. Richard Roach, S.J., provides a critique of Maguire's misuse of probabilism in his review of this volume in *Fidelity*, 2.8 (1983), 23-25. Probabilism was never used to justify dissent from magisterial teaching but was a basis for preferring one from a number of theological opinions on matters not settled by the magisterium.

72. This is implicitly admitted by McCormick in his lament in "Notes On Moral Theology: 1983," *Theological Studies*, 45 (1984), 84, that many theologians have rejected the position of dissent and instead follow the magisterium.

73. See Yves Congar, O.P., "Pour Une Histoire Semantique du Terme 'Magisterium,'" *Revue des Sciences Philosophiques et Théologiques*, 60 (1976), 85-98.

74. Aquinas, *Quodlibetum*, IX, q. 8, corp.

Notes for Chapter Six

1. See Germain Grisez, *The Way of the Lord Jesus*, vol. 1, *Christian Moral Principles* (Chicago: Franciscan Herald Press, 1983), ch. 23, for an explanation of the concept of personal vocation and its role in Christian moral life.

2. John Paul II, *Familiaris Consortio*, no. 11.

3. Congregation for Catholic Education, *Educational Guidance in Human Love* (November 1, 1983), p. 5.

4. Pope John Paul II, "The Human Person Becomes a Gift in the Freedom of Love," General Audience of January 16, 1980, in *Original Unity of*

Man and Woman: Catechesis on the Book of Genesis (Boston: St. Paul Editions, 1981), pp. 113-114 (*TB*, p. 63).

5. On the nature of the complementarity between males and females see the following: Pope John Paul II, *Original Unity of Man and Woman*, especially pp. 85-126 (*TB*, pp. 51-69); Robert E. Joyce, *Human Sexual Ecology* (Washington, D.C.: University Publications of America, 1980), especially chapter 5, pp. 63-87; David L. Schindler, "Catholic theology, gender, and the future of Western civilization," *Communio* 20 (1993) 200-239; William E. May, *Marriage: The Rock on Which the Family Is Built* (San Francisco: Ignatius Press, 1995), ch. 2, "Marriage and the Complementarity of Male and Female."

6. Karol Wojtyla, *Love and Responsibility*, pp. 45-54 (New York: Farrar, Straus, Giroux, 1981).

7. On sensuality and concupiscence and the difference between them, see ibid., pp. 147-160.

8. On sentiment and sentimentality, see ibid., pp. 151-153.

9. Pontifical Council for the Family, *The Truth and Meaning of Human Sexuality: Guidelines for Education Within the Family* (December 8, 1995), no. 16.

10. The *Catechism of the Catholic Church* affirms that virtues "are firm attitudes, stable dispositions, habitual perfections . . . that govern our actions, order our passions, and guide our conduct according to reason and faith. They make possible ease, self-mastery, and joy in leading a morally good life. The virtuous man is he who freely practices the good" (no. 1804).

11. Albert Plé, *Chastity and the Affective Life* (New York: Herder and Herder, 1965), p. 117.

12. Thomas Aquinas, *Summa Theologiae*, II-II, q. 32, a. 1, ad 1.

13. Romanus Cesario, *Moral Virtues and Theological Ethics* (Notre Dame, Ind: University of Notre Dame Press, 1991), pp. 52-57. See also Plé, *Chastity*, pp. 118-119.

14. Plé, *Chastity*, pp. 117-119.

15. Aquinas, *Summa Theologiae*, II-II, q. 141, c.1, ad 1; see also q. 151, aa. 1, 2. See also Wojtyla, *Love and Responsibility*, pp. 147-159, 200-210.

16. See Aquinas, *Summa Theologiae*, II-II, q. 142, a. 1; see also Plé, *Chastity*, p. 125.

17. See Aquinas, *De Virtutibus in Communi*, q. 4. a. 4, ad 15; see also Plé, *Chastity*, pp. 125-126.

18. See Wojtyla, *Love and Responsibility*, p. 171.

19. See ibid., 170.

20. Plé, *Chastity*, pp. 126-127.

21. *Catechism of the Catholic Church*, no. 2347.

22. Ibid., no. 2334.

23. Pius XI, *Casti Connubii*, in Liebard's *Love and Sexuality*, p. 24. For other magisterial teaching, see DS 1797-1800, for Trent; *Gaudium et Spes*, nos. 47-52; Paul VI, *Humanae Vitae*, nos. 4, 6-8; John Paul II, *Familiaris Consortio*, nos. 11-16.

24. See *Gaudium et Spes*, no. 48; *Codex Juris Canonici* (Vatican City: Libreria Editrice Vaticana, 1983), Canon 1055.

25. The Church has constantly taught that the free consent of the man and woman to live together is what makes their union a marriage. See Edward Schillebeeckx, *Marriage: Human Reality and Saving Mystery* (New York: Sheed and Ward, 1965), pp. 287-302, for a history of this teaching. The Council of Florence taught that "the efficient cause of marriage is the mutual consent duly expressed in words relating to the present" (DS 1327). Pius XI in *Casti Connubii* taught that "each individual marriage . . . arises only from the free consent of each of the spouses; and this free act of the will, by which each party hands over and accepts those rights proper to the state of marriage, is so necessary to constitute the marriage that it cannot be supplied by any human power" (Liebard's *Love and Sexuality*, p. 24). See also Vatican Council II, *Gaudium et Spes*, no. 48. *Codex Iuris Canonici*, Canon 1057.

26. See Walter Brueggemann, "Of the Same Flesh and Bone (Gn 2.23a)," *Catholic Biblical Quarterly*, 32 (1970), 532-542; Brueggemann shows that the formula used in Genesis is a covenantal formula common in the Old Testament. Thus, it has strong connotations of fidelity.

27. John Paul II, *Original Unity of Man and Woman: Catechesis on the Book of Genesis* (Boston: Daughters of St. Paul, 1981), pp. 81-82 (*TB*, p. 50).

28. See John L. McKenzie, "Toward a Biblical Theology of the Word," in his *Myths and Realities: Studies in Old Testament Theology* (Milwaukee: Bruce, 1963), for a discussion of the "word" in biblical thought.

29. See Aquinas, *Summa Theologiae*, Supplement, q. 48, a. 1, for an account of how marital consent implicitly contains consent to the marital act.

30. The teaching of Augustine on this point is detailed in Chapter 3 of this work. Pius XI, *Casti Connubii*, in Liebard's *Love and Sexuality*, pp. 26-31, says that in Augustine's teaching on the goods of marriage "is contained a splendid summary of the whole doctrine of marriage." *Gaudium et Spes*, no. 48, cites Pius XI and Augustine. Leo XIII, *Arcanum Divinae Sapientiae*, in Liebard's *Love and Sexuality*, p. 9,

emphasizes that even the marriages of the unbaptized participate in the goods of marriage and can be called the sacrament of marriage. See also Augustine Reagan, C.Ss.R., "The Perrenial Value of St. Augustine's Theology of the Goods of Marriage," *Studia Moralia* (1981) 351-377.

31. See Aquinas, *Summa Theologiae*, Supplement, q. 49, a. 3, for an account of the good of the sacrament as the most essential of the goods of marriage.

32. See Augustine, *De Nuptiis Adulterinis*; also Schillebeeckx, *Marriage*, pp. 218-287.

33. See Schillebeeckx, *Marriage*, pp. 141-142, for an account of the biblical roots of the patristic and medieval teaching on the indissolubility of marriage. See also John Lucas, "The *Vinculum Conjugale*: A Moral Reality," *Theology*, 78 (1975), 225-230, for an account of the indissolubility of marriage by a non-Catholic.

34. See *Gaudium et Spes*, no. 48. It should be noted that the Church does "dissolve" the marriages of some non-Christians when one partner becomes a Christian and the other refuses to allow the first to carry out the obligations of the conversion, and it dissolves some nonconsummated marriages. In both cases the dissolution is done with the authority of God himself, and by no human authority. In the former case there is no implication that marriage is not naturally indissoluble. Likewise in the latter, for the dissolution is possible only because the marriage is not, as it were, fully completed by consummation. See Schillebeeckx, *Marriage*, pp. 155-168, 287-302.

35. See Council of Trent, Session 7, March 3, 1547, "Decree on the Sacraments, Canons on the Sacraments in General" (DS 1601-1608).

36. See Leo XIII, *Arcanum Divinae Sapientiae*, in Liebard's *Love and Sexuality*, p. 5; *Gaudium et Spes*, no. 48.

37. See Schillebeeckx, *Marriage*, pp. 133-140.

38. See ibid., p. 137: "Experience of marriage 'in the Lord' does not imply any extrinsic addition to secular; that is, the making Christian . . . of marriage, of its natural and human interrelationships . . . is an entirely intrinsic process."

39. John Paul II, *Familiaris Consortio*, no. 13; see also Schillebeeckx, *Marriage*, pp. 167-170.

40. *Gaudium et Spes*, no. 48; see also John Paul II, *Familiaris Consortio*, nos. 13, 49-64. See Michael F. McAuliffe, *Catholic Moral Teaching on the Nature and Object of Conjugal Love* (Washington, D.C.: Catholic University Press, 1954), for a survey of Catholic teaching on this matter.

41. International Theological Commission, *Thèses de Doctrina Matrimonii Christiani*, in *Gregorianum*, 3.4 (1978), 453-464, at 450; English translation in *Origins: NC Documentary Service*, 8.12 (1975).
42. See John Paul II, *Familiaris Consortio*, no. 11.
43. *Gaudium et Spes*, no. 50; see also Germain Grisez, "Marriage: Reflections Based on St. Thomas and Vatican II," *The Catholic Mind*, 64 (1966), 5-19.
44. See Aquinas, *Summa Theologiae*, Supplement, q. 49, a. 5, ad 1.
45. See Pius XI, *Castii Connubii*, in Liebard's *Love and Sexuality*, p. 30: "This conjugal faith, which is most aptly called by St. Augustine the 'faith of chastity,' blooms more freely, more beautifully, and more nobly, when it is rooted in that more excellent soil, the love of husband and wife which pervades all the duties of the married life and holds pride of place in Christian marriage. For matrimonial faith demands that husband and wife be joined in an especially holy and pure love . . . as Christ loved the Church."
46. *Gaudium et Spes*, no. 49. See also Paul VI, *Humanae Vitae*, no. 9; John Paul II, *Familiaris Consortio*, nos. 11-14, 20-21, 28.
47. *Gaudium et Spes*, no. 49.
48. See St. Thomas Aquinas, *Summa Theologiae*, Supplement to Third Part, q. 49, a. 4. On the truth that the marital act is not simply an act between persons who merely "happen" to be married but is rather an act participating in and open to the goods of marriage, see William E. May, *Marriage: The Rock on Which the Family Is Built* (San Francisco: Ignatius Press, 1995), pp. 26-28, 48-50, 69-71.
49. See John Paul II, "Analysis of Knowledge and Procreation," in *Original Unity of Man and Woman*, pp. 146-152 (*TB*, pp. 77-80).
50. See John Kippley, *Birth Control and the Marriage Covenant* (Collegeville, Minn.: The Liturgical Press, 1976), pp. 105-113; Dietrich von Hildebrand, *In Defense of Purity* (New York: Sheed and Ward, 1935), pp. 54-76; Mary R. Joyce, *Love Responds to Life* (Kenosha, Wis.: Prow Press, 1970), pp. 8-26.
51. Paul VI, *Humanae Vitae*, no. 13. On this see Germain Grisez, Joseph Boyle, John Finnis, and William E. May, " 'Every Marital Act Ought to Be Open to New Life': Toward a Clearer Understanding," *The Thomist* 52 (1988) 390-399.
52. *Lumen Gentium*, no. 11; *Apostolicam Actuositatem*, no. 11.
53. Pope John Paul II, *Familiaris Consortio*, no. 50.
54. Pope John Paul II, *Evangelium Vitae*, no. 92. See Pope John Paul II, *Centesimus Annus*, no. 39.

55. Among the documents of the Church dealing with the rights and duties of parents as educators are the following: Pope Pius XI, *Divini Illius Magistri;* Vatican Council II, *Gravissimum Educationis; The Charter for Families.*

56. *Gaudium et Spes*, no. 49. See also *Catechism of the Catholic Church*, no. 1632.

57. Pope John Paul II, *Familiaris Consortio*, no. 37. See also Pontifical Council for the Family, *The Truth and Meaning of Human Sexuality: Guidelines for Education within the Family* (December 8, 1995); Pontifical Council for the Family, *Preparation for the Sacrament of Marriage* (May 13, 1996).

58. John Paul II, *Familiaris Consortio*, no. 16.

59. See Schillebeeckx, *Marriage*, pp. 105-110, 123.

60. Ibid., p. 131.

61. *Catechism of the Catholic Church,* no. 2231.

62. See Roger Balducelli, O.S.F.S., "The Decision for Celibacy," *Theological Studies*, 36 (1975), 219-242.

63. *Catechism of the Catholic Church,* no. 2338.

Notes for Chapter Seven

1. For the exegesis of these Old Testament passages, see Friedrich Hauck, "Moicheuo, ktl.," in *Theological Dictionary of the New Testament*, ed. Gerhard Kittel, tr. Geoffrey W. Bromiley (Grand Rapids, Mich.: Eerdmans, 1967) 4.730-731. See Elaine Adler Goodfriend, "Adultery," *Anchor Bible Dictionary*, ed. David Noel Freedman et al. (New York: Doubleday, 1992), 1.82-86; John L. McKenzie, "Adultery," *Dictionary of the Bible* (Milwaukee: Bruce, 1965).

2. On this see Gordon Paul Hugenberger, *Marriage as a Covenant: A Study of Biblical Law and Ethics Governing Marriage Developed from the Perspective of Malachi. Supplements to Vetus Testamentum*, 52 (Leiden: Brill, 1994); F. C. Fensham, "The Marriage Metaphor in Hosea for the Covenant Relationship Between the Lord and His People (Hos 1:2-9)," *Journal of Northwest Semitic Languages* 12 (1984) 71-78; see also Edward Schillebeeckx, *Marriage: Human Reality and Saving Mystery* (New York: Sheed and Ward, 1965), pp. 31-63, 89-91.

3. John Paul II, "Ethical, Anthropological Content of 'Do Not Commit Adultery!' " (address of April 23, 1980), in *Blessed Are the Pure of Heart* (Boston: Daughters of St. Paul, 1983), pp. 26-32 (*TB*, p. 107). On this matter the observations of Schillebeeckx, *Marriage*, pp. 52-54, 61-62, 89-91, are helpful.

4. An excellent commentary on the significance of lustful desire as a rupturing of the covenant with God and the introduction of the "world" opposed to God spoken of by John (1 Jn 2:15-16) in place of the "world" of Genesis 1 and 2 that was "good" in the sight of God is provided by John Paul II in his address of April 30, 1980, "Lust, A Rupture of the First Covenant With God," in *Blessed Are the Pure of Heart*, pp. 33-40 (*TB*, pp. 108-111).
5. On this, see Schillebeeckx, *Marriage*, pp. 141-155. See also Hauck, "Moicheuo, ktl."
6. This is evident from the fact that Jesus considered as adulterous the union of a person who divorced and remarried. This indeed is the sense in which the term *adultery* is understood by users of ordinary language. Yet it seems necessary to make this point explicit inasmuch as some contemporary moralists (for example, Richard A. McCormick, S.J., in his "Notes on Moral Theology," *Theological Studies*, 39 [1978], 93) use the term to describe coition with the "wrong" person, leaving open for further judgment whether the "wrong" person is someone who is not one's spouse.
7. Contemporary scholars debate whether Ephesians was written by Paul or not. Even those who believe it to be the work of another writer agree that the teaching in it on the significance of sexual union is Pauline, for it is in conformity with the teaching of 1 Corinthians 6. On the deep significance of Ephesians 5, see Schillebeeckx, *Marriage*, pp. 111-119. See also Hans Urs von Balthasar, "Ephesians 5:21-33 and *Humanae Vitae*: A Meditation," in *Christian Married Love*, ed. Raymond Dennehy (San Francisco: Ignatius Press, 1981), pp. 55-74.
8. See, for instance, 1 Corinthians 6. For an excellent commentary on this central theme in Pauline theology, see George T. Montague, S.M., *Maturing in Christ: St. Paul's Program for Growing in Christ* (Milwaukee: Bruce, 1964). See also Manuel Miguens, O.F.M., "Being a Christian and the Moral Life: Pauline Perspectives," in *Principles of Catholic Moral Life*, ed. William E. May (Chicago: Franciscan Herald Press, 1981), pp. 89-111. See also the excellent study of O. Larry Yarbrough, *Not Like the Gentiles: Marriage Rules in the Letters of Paul*, Society of Biblical Literature Dissertation Series 80 (Atlanta, Ga: Scholars Press, 1985), pp. 89-121.
9. For the meaning of *body* in Paul, see John A.T. Robinson, *The Body: A Study in Pauline Theology* (London and Naperville, Ill.: SCM Press and A.J. Allen, 1961).
10. The meaning of the term *skeuos* in 1 Thessalonians 4:4 has been dis-

puted. Literally it means "vessel," "container," or "dish." Some exegetes believe that in this passage it means "wife," whereas others hold that it means one's own "body." Among those who hold that it means "body" are J. Terence Forestell, C.S.B., "The Letter to the Thessalonians," *The Jerome Biblical Commentary*, ed. Raymond E. Brown, S.S., Joseph Fitzmyer, S.J., and Roland E. Murphy, O. Carm. (1st ed. Englewood Cliffs, N.J., 1968), 48.23. Other scholars hold that it means "wife," among them O. Larry Yarbrough, *Not Like the Gentiles: Marriage Rules in the Letters of Paul*, p. 68ff. Some others hold that it refers to the male organ; see Yarbrough for a discussion of the different interpretations.

11. Thus, the reference to adultery in the condemnations of laxism by Innocent XI in 1679 assumes the serious wrongness of adultery and makes clear that the consent of one's spouse does not make an extramarital sexual act nonadulterous. See DS 2150.

12. See Cyprian (*De Ecclesiae Catholicae Unitate*), PL 4.507, who compares the embracing of false doctrine to adultery.

13. Pius XI, *Casti Connubii* (Washington, D.C.: U.S. Catholic Conference, 1969), p. 25.

14. National Conference of Catholic Bishops, *To Live in Christ Jesus: A Pastoral Reflection on the Moral Life* (Washington, D.C.: U.S. Catholic Conference, 1976), p. 19.

15. See text cited above in Note 3.

16. The view that the condemnation of adultery in Scripture, Christian tradition, and by the magisterium is culturally conditioned is advanced by Anthony Kosnik et al., *Human Sexuality: New Directions in American Catholic Thought* (New York: Paulist Press, 1977), pp. 17-29.

17. See the addresses of John Paul II for November 14 and November 21, 1979 ("By the Communion of Persons Man Becomes the Image of God" and "Marriage: One and Indissoluble in Genesis"). The text of these addresses is found in John Paul II, *Original Unity of Man and Woman: Catechesis on the Book of Genesis* (Boston: Daughters of St. Paul, 1981), pp. 70-84; (*TB*, pp. 48-51); see also the comments of Dietrich von Hildebrand, *Man and Woman* (Chicago: Franciscan Herald Press, 1965), p. 18.

18. *Gaudium et Spes*, no. 50: ". . . It must be said that true married love and the whole structure of family life which results from it is directed to disposing the spouses to cooperate valiantly with the love of the Creator and Saviour, who through them will increase and enrich his family from day to day."

19. John Paul II has written profoundly on the relationship between spousal friendship and the giving of new life within the family. See, in particular, his addresses of January 2, 1980 ("Creation as Fundamental and Original Gift") and of March 5, 1980 ("Analysis of Knowledge and of Procreation"); texts in *Original Unity of Man and Woman*, pp. 99-105, 146-152 (*TB*, pp. 57-60, 77-80); see also his analysis in *Love and Responsibility*, tr. H.T. Willetts (New York: Farrar, Straus, and Giroux, 1981), pp. 224-237.

20. *Gaudium et Spes*, no. 49.

21. This case was made famous by Joseph Fletcher, *Situation Ethics: The New Morality* (Philadelphia: Westminster, 1966), pp. 164-165.

22. See Paul Ramsey, *Deeds and Rules in Christian Ethics* (New York: Scribner's, 1967), pp. 145-225, for a detailed critique of Fletcher's consequentialism.

23. This seems to be the view of such writers as Robert and Anna Francoeur and Nona and George O'Neill. See the Francoeurs' *Hot Sex — Cool Sex* (New York: Harcourt Brace Jovanovich, 1974) and the O'Neills' *Open Marriage* (Philadelphia: Lippincott, 1972).

24. For the teaching of Innocent XI, see DS 2150; for John Paul II, see *Love and Responsibility*, pp. 221-222.

25. On this, see, for instance, Herant A. Katchadourian and Donald T. Lunde, *Fundamentals of Human Sexuality*, 3rd ed. (New York: Holt, Rinehart, and Winston, 1980), pp. 486-487; Ashley Montagu, *Sex, Man, and Society* (New York: Putnam's, 1969), ch. 1.

26. Paul VI, *Humanae Vitae*, no. 10; AAS 60.487-488.

27. John Paul II has explicitly taken up the issue of contraception, each time reaffirming vigorously the teaching that it is intrinsically immoral, in many places. Among the more important sources for his teaching are the following (listed chronologically): (1) his apostolic exhortation *Familiaris Consortio* (November, 1981), no. 32; (2) his series of 15 addresses from July 11 to November 28, 1984, devoted to the teaching of *Humanae Vitae* and published under the title *Reflections on Humanae Vitae: Conjugal Morality and Spirituality* (Boston: St. Paul Editions, 1984, *TB*, pp. 386-423); (3) his "Address to the II International Congress of Moral Theology," November 12, 1988, in *"Humanae Vitae": 20 Anni Dopo. Atti del II Congresso Internazionale di Teologia Morale* (Milano: Edizioni Ares, 1989), pp. 12-18; and (4) his encyclical *Evangelium Vitae*, no. 13.

28. Paul VI, *Humanae Vitae*, no. 14.

29. It should be noted that the anovulant pills now marketed in the United

States may well be abortifacient in addition to being contraceptive. These pills first seek to prevent conception by inhibiting ovulation. Should ovulation, however, still occur, they seek to prevent conception by rendering the mucus of the cervix hostile to sperm. Should some sperm, however, survive and should one fertilize the ovum, these pills then act abortifaciently by changing the lining of the uterine wall, making it reject the developing embryo. On this issue, see Thomas Hilgers, M.D., "The New Technologies of Birth," in *New Technologies of Birth and Death*, ed. Donald McCarthy (St. Louis: The Pope John Center, 1981), pp. 29-55. See also Pope John Paul II, *Evangelium Vitae*, no. 13.

30. We say "ordinarily" here because it is possible that one who is not choosing sexual intercourse can choose to make another's act of intercourse infertile. For instance, a young couple may live, for financial reason's, in the wife's family home. They are themselves totally opposed to contraception, would never choose to contracept their marital union, and are in fact anxious to have a child. But the young woman's father, who thinks that they ought not have a child, puts some sterilizing agent into his daugther's food precisely to impede procreation. Whether this should be called "contraception" is perhaps disputed, but it surely shares the moral malice of any couple's choosing to make their own sexual intercourse contracepted. Such possibilities make clear the sense in which contraception is not itself a sexual act but an action taken in relationship to one's own or another's sexual acts. On this see Germain Grisez, Joseph Boyle, John Finnis, and William E. May, " 'Every Marital Act Ought to Be Open to New Life': Toward a Clearer Understanding," *The Thomist* 52 (1988), 365-426, at 369-370.

31. For an account of this situation, see G.E.M. Anscombe, *Contraception and Chastity* (London: Catholic Truth Society, 1977), pp. 15-17.

32. See Philip S. Keane, S.S., *Sexual Morality: A Catholic Perspective* (New York: Paulist Press, 1977), pp. 43-46, and the literature cited there. One of the best-known statements of this objection is given by Charles E. Curran, in his *Themes in Fundamental Moral Theology* (Notre Dame, Ind.: University of Notre Dame Press, 1977), pp. 27-80.

33. This was suggested by John T. Noonan, Jr., *Contraception: A History of Its Treatment by Catholic Theologians and Canonists* (Cambridge, Mass.: Harvard University Press, 1965), pp. 508-533.

34. Among the many episcopal statements made during this period, the following are representative: Karol Wojtyla (John Paul II), *Fruitful and Responsible Love* (New York: Seabury, 1979), pp. 13-35 (this was an address he gave in Milan in June, 1978, at an international symposium

on the anniversary of *Humanae Vitae*); the Bishops of India, *"Humanae Vitae*: Ten Years Later" (a statement of January 17, 1978), *The Pope Speaks*, 23 (1978), 183-187; Cardinal Terence Cooke, "Address to Symposium on Natural Family Planning," New York, May 23, 1978, published in *L'Osservatore Romano* (English edition) (June 27, 1978), 3. In 1993 more than 3000 people participated in a week-long celebration of the 25th anniversary of the encyclical, entitlted "Love and Life," in Omaha, Neb. This conference, attended by more than 50 US bishops along with Alfonso Cardinal Lopez Trujillo, President of the Pontifical Council for the Family, was sponsored by the Pope Paul VI Center under the direction of Thomas Hilgers, M.D. Similar celebrations were held around the world.

35. *To Live in Christ Jesus*, p. 18.
36. John Paul II, "An Address to the U.S. Bishops," October 5, 1979, *Origins: NC Documentary Service*, 9.18 (October 18, 1979), 289.
37. See John Paul II, *Familiaris Consortio*, no. 29.
38. Ibid., no. 31.
39. Ibid., no. 32.
40. Paul VI, *Humanae Vitae*, no. 6; AAS 60.484-485.
41. Noonan, *Contraception*, p. 6.
42. It is important to recognize in this connection that the highly publicized statements of various national conferences of bishops which were issued in 1968 and 1969 after the publication of *Humanae Vitae* do not contradict the received teaching on contraception. Some of them do suggest that it is possible responsibly to dissent from this teaching, but they go no further than that; they do not deny the teaching or propose a new teaching. See John Ford, S.J., and Germain Grisez, "Contraception and the Infallibility of the Ordinary Magisterium," *Theological Studies*, 39 (1978), 308-311, for an analysis of these episcopal statements. This is not to deny, of course, that there is considerable dissent among theologians, clergy, and faithful. Although this dissent is very confusing and troubling to many Catholics, it is important to emphasize that it has no normative status. See the analysis in Grisez, *Christian Moral Principles*, ch. 36. q. B.
43. For the first Vatican Council's teaching on the infallibility of the ordinary magisterium, see Session IV (July 18, 1870), Constitution *Pastor Aeternus*, c.4, "De Romani Pontificis Infallibili Magisterio." See, in particular, DS 3069. For the Second Vatican Council's teaching on the infallibility of the pope and of the bishops united with the pope in the ordinary exercise of their teaching office, see *Lumen Gentium*, no. 25.

44. See Ford and Grisez, "Contraception and the Infallibility of the Ordinary Magisterium," 258-312.

45. In her book *Humanae Vitae: A Generation Later* (Washington, D.C.: The Catholic University of America, 1991), pp. 98-129, Janet Smith provides an account of many of these arguments. In *Contraception and Chastity*, Elizabeth Anscombe argues that contraception is not a proper act of intercourse because it is not an act that is the sort of act open to the transmission of life. Thus, it cannot be a true marital act, and sex acts that are not true marital acts are either mere lasciviousness or an inauthentic substitute for marital union. John Kippley, *Sex and the Marriage Covenant: A Basis for Morality* (Cincinnati: Couple to Couple League, 1991 — a revision of his older *Birth Control and the Marriage Covenant*), pp. 50-76, argues that contraception is inconsistent with the marriage covenant. Arguments emphasizing that contraception by married persons sever the bond between the unitive and procreative meanings of the conjugal act are developed by Mary R. Joyce, *The Meaning of Contraception* (Collegeville, Minn: The Liturgical Press, 1969) and Dietrich von Hildebrand, *The Encyclical Humanae Vitae: A Sign of Contradiction* (Chicago: Franciscan Herald Press, 1969). In *Love and Responsibility*, pp. 224-237, Karol Wojtyla argues that unless those who engage in sexual intercourse are willing and able to accept fatherhood and motherhood they are violating the personalist norm. In *Contraception and the Natural Law* (Milwaukee: Bruce, 1964) and in "A New Formulation of a Natural Law Argument Against Contraception," *The Thomist* 30 (1966), 343-361, Germain Grisez developed an argument against contraception on the ground that it attacked the good of procreation, an argument developed by John Finnis, "Natural Law and Unnatural Acts," *Heythrop Journal* 11 (1970) 379-387. Grisez and Finnis, along with Joseph Boyle and William E. May, have developed, clarified, and strengthened this argument in " 'Every Marital Act Out to Be Open to New Life': Toward a Clearer Understanding." See note 30 above.

46. John Paul II, *Familiaris Consortio*, no. 32. John Paul II's thought on this matter, briefly set forth in the text cited and developed by him in many writings, has been well synthesized and presented by Janet Smith, *Humanae Vitae: A Generation Later*, pp. 230-265.

47. In what follows we will summarize the argument developed by Grisez et al. in " 'Every Marital Act Ought to Be Open to New Life': Toward a Clearer Understanding." In *Humanae Vitae: A Generation Later*, pp. 340-370, Smith claims that this argument, emphasizing the anti-life character of contraception, while essentially true, is "inadequate" chiefly

because, she claims, it shifts attention from the objective act of contraception to subjective intentions. Smith, unfortunately, seriously misunderstands the argument and ignores totally the sixteen pages of the essay devoted to showing why the choice to contracept is always wrong because it is contrary to *objective* norms of natural law. For an appreciative but critical assessment of Smith's study, see William E. May's review of her work in *The Thomist* 52 (1992) 155-161.

48. *To Live in Christ Jesus*, p. 18.

49. For a development of these points, see Grisez et al., "Every Marital Act Ought to Be Open to New Life."

50. *Gaudium et Spes*, nos. 49, 50; *To Live in Christ Jesus*, p. 18; John Paul II, "An Address to the U.S. Bishops," 289, and " 'Stand Up' for Human Life," his homily on the Capital Mall, Washington, D.C., October 7, 1979, in *Origins: NC Documentary Service*, 9.18 (October 18, 1979), 291.

51. On this, see John Paul II, address of January 2, 1980, "Creation as Fundamental and Original Gift," and address of March 5, 1980, "Analysis of Knowledge and of Procreation," in *Original Unity of Man and Woman*, pp. 99-105, 146-152 (*TB*, pp. 57-60, 77-80).

52. See Anscombe, *Contraception and Chastity*, pp. 18-19.

53. Thus, Kosnik et al., in *Human Sexuality*, point out that fornication in some circumstances can be all right, that "creative adultery" is conceivable, and that homosexual acts between homosexually oriented persons in a stable relationship are also morally permissible. These authors even indicate that bestiality may be permissible when no other sexual "outlets" are available. See pp. 148-149 (adultery), 153ff. (fornication), 186-218 (homosexuality), and 229-230 (bestiality). In his essay, "Divorce from the Perspective of a Revised Moral Theology," Charles E. Curran, in his *Ongoing Revision: Studies in Moral Theology* (Notre Dame, Ind.: Fides, 1976), pp. 77-78, admits that those were correct who thought, during the debates over contraception, that if contraception were morally permissible, then other forms of sexual activity were justifiable. He, of course, agrees that premarital sex, masturbation, and homosexual activity can at times be morally permissible.

54. See "The Question Is Not Closed: The Liberals Reply," in *The Birth Control Debate*, ed. Robert G. Hoyt (Kansas City, Mo.: *National Catholic Reporter*, 1969), pp. 74-85. This is one of the documents from the Papal Commission on birth regulation.

55. That contraception leads to abortion hardly needs further proof. In fact, many of the most widely used "contraceptives," especially the IUD

(intrauterine device) are not really contraceptive but abortifacient. The pill at times acts in a contraceptive way and at times as an abortifacient. See Note 29 above.

56. Here, it is instructive to note that frequently abortion is described as "post-conceptive" birth control. Moreover, some ethicists — among them David H. Smith ("The Abortion of Defective Fetuses: Some Moral Considerations," in *No Rush to Judgment: Essays in Medical Ethics* [Bloomington, Ind.: The Poynter Center, 1978], pp. 144-148) — argue that if people "responsibly" seek to prevent conception by the use of contraceptives which subsequently "fail," then abortion is morally justifiable. See also Judith Jarvis Thompson's influential and widely reprinted defense of abortion, "A Defense of Abortion," *Philosophy and Public Affairs* 1 (1972), 1-27.

57. On this, see Grisez et al., " 'Every Marital Act Ought to Be Open to New Life,' " 369-384. On intent see Pope John Paul II, *Veritatis Splendor*, no. 78.

58. For the connection between the pill and sterilization, see Charles E. Curran, "Sterilization: Exposition, Critique, and Refutation of Past Teaching," in *New Perspectives of Moral Theology* (Notre Dame, Ind.: University of Notre Dame Press, 1976), pp. 207-211. For a critique of Curran, see William E. May, "Sterilization: Catholic Teaching and Catholic Practice," *Homiletic and Pastoral Review*, 72.12 (1976), 9-29.

59. See Curran, "Natural Law," *Themes in Fundamental Moral Theology*, pp. 39-40.

60. It is perhaps worth noting here that *Gaudium et Spes* deliberately refrained from using the traditional terminology of the primary and secondary ends of marriage. This does not mean that Vatican II denied the proposition affirmed in the tradition that procreation is the primary end of marriage; nor do we intend to deny this in affirming that procreation is only one good. The Commission sponsoring *Gaudium et Spes* responded to the requests of "many Fathers" that certain changes be made in the wording of the statements on the origin and properties of marriage. The Commission noted that in a pastoral text there was no need for an enumeration of the juridical elements of marriage. It also noted that the hierarchy of goods within marriage had already been sufficiently stated many times in Church tradition and by the magisterium. The Commission went on to observe that it is possible to look at the hierarchy of goods from a different point of view and then said: "Moreover, in the text of *Gaudium et Spes*, which speaks to the world in a direct and pastoral style, very technical terminology (e.g.,

the hierarchy of ends) is clearly avoided. In any case the primordial importance of procreation and education is mentioned at least 10 times in the text, as it often speaks of sacramentality, and fidelity and indissolubility are emphasized at least 7 times in the text" *Acta Synodolia Sacrosancti Oecumenici Vaticani Secundi*, vol. 4, (Rome: Typis Polyglottis Vaticanis, 1978), pp. 476-477. The primacy of the procreative good within marriage is not a primacy of value but of definition; the procreative good is what defines marriage as the kind of community and institution it is and distinguishes it from other forms of friendship. This does not imply that procreation is primary in the intentions of spouses or that it is more valuable than the good of marital love or fidelity. Surely, it does not absolutize the value of procreation as compared with other values in and out of marriage.

61. See Wulstan Mork, O.S.B., *The Biblical Meaning of Man* (Milwaukee: Bruce, 1967), pp. 14-32; Albert Gelin, S.S., *The Concept of Man in the Bible*, tr. David Murphy (Staten Island, N.Y.: Alba House, 1967), pp. 13-24.

62. *Gaudium et Spes*, no. 14.

63. Pope John Paul II, *Veritatis Splendor*, no. 48.

64. See *Summa Theologiae*, 1, qq. 75-76; see also Germain Grisez, "Dualism and the New Morality," *Atti del Congresso Internazionale Tommaso D'Aguino nel Suo Settimo Centenario*, vol. 5, *L'Agir Morale* (Naples: Edizione Domenicane, 1977), pp. 323-330.

65. For good critique of dualism see Patrick Lee, *Abortion and Unborn Human Life* (Washington, D.C.: The Catholic University of America Press, 1996), pp. 31-37; David Braine, *The Human Person: Animal and Spirit* (Notre Dame, Ind: University of Notre Dame Press, 1992), pp. 290-341.

66. For a more detailed critique of this objection, see Ford and Grisez, "Contraception and the Infallibility of the Ordinary Magisterium," 291-299.

67. On the benefits and effectiveness of natural family planning see the following: Hanna Klaus, M.D., "Fact Sheet: Action, Effectiveness, and Medical Side-Effects of Common Methods of Family Planning," *Current Medical Research* (Washington, D.C.: National Conference of Catholic Bishops, 1993); R. T. Kambie, "NFP Use Effectiveness and Continuation," *Obstetrics and Gynecology* 165.6 (1991) 2041-2047; A. D. Nolasco, "Can Natural Family Planning Really Work?" *Population Forum* (1989) 1.13-16; Barbara Barnett, "Fertility Awareness Benefits Couples," *Network: Family Health International* 17.16 (1996),

302

1-20; Mary Shivanandan, "The How and the Why of Natural Family Planning," *Catholic Update*, ed. Fr. Jack Wintz, O.F.M. (Cincinnati: St. Anthony Messenger Press, 1995).

68. This is the contention, for instance, of Kosnik et al., *Human Sexuality*, pp. 114, 292-295.

69. Formally this is the fallacy of drawing an affirmative conclusion in a Figure II syllogism; the conclusion does not follow, as the following example shows:

From	All crows are birds.
and	All eagles are birds.
it does not follow that	All eagles are crows.
Thus, from	All contraceptive acts are for avoiding pregnancy.
and	All use of NFP is for avoiding pregnancy.
One cannot validly conclude	All use of NFP is contraceptive.

70. This is not to suggest that the only way one violates the good of procreation is by acting against it in contraceptive intercourse. Married couples ordinarily have an obligation to have some children if they can, because marriage is of its nature ordered to the procreation and education of children. To refuse to fulfill this obligation — even by use of NFP throughout one's fertile years — is ordinarily a violation of the procreative good. See Anscombe, *Contraception and Chastity*, p. 19, and William E. May, "Contraception, Abstinence, and Responsible Parenthood," *Faith and Reason*, 3.1 (1977), 46-49; Karol Wojtyla (John Paul II), *Love and Responsibility*, pp. 224-237.

71. For a development of relevant analogies, see Mary R. Joyce, *The Meaning of Contraception*, p. 41; and Anscombe, *Contraception and Chastity*, p. 20. Anscombe asks us to consider two types of protest by industrial workers who have a legitimate complaint against their employer. In one type of protest the workers act violently — for example, by destroying machinery in the factory. In the other they "work to rule," by doing their job at a slow pace within the limits of minimal justice. Clearly there is a moral difference between the cases. If the protest is justified in the first place, the latter strategy is clearly justified but not the former. The use of contraception is analogous to the use of violent protest.

72. It has been objected that the *timing* of these acts functions so as to render them infertile, and thus in reality such acts are acts of contra-

ceptive intercourse. Perhaps this objection is based on simply ignoring the distinction between *anti*-procreative acts and *non*-procreative acts. But this objection may be the claim that the timing of the acts of intercourse is just another contraceptive measure, like withdrawal, for example, which puts space between sperm and ovum. This version of the objection fails because it does not analyze carefully enough precisely how the timing of the act affects the agents' understanding and intention. If a couple chooses to have intercourse at times when they are not fertile, they cannot be choosing to engage in procreative activity; they believe that they are incapable of procreating at that time. They cannot have an anti-procreative intention nor can they have a procreative intention, given what they know about their own fertility. The procreative good is not, as it were, engaged or at issue in these acts. They cannot be acting against the procreative good when they are convinced that the act of intercourse cannot in this instance be procreative. Thus, they act for the other goods of marriage and they do not act against the good of procreation. In other words, the timing of an act of intercourse cannot be understood as an accidental feature that can be used to distort an essentially procreative activity. The use of contraceptives, by contrast, does involve such a distortion since they are used *only* to prevent what one believes to be a procreative act from being open to the gift of life. (We admit that it is possible for couples to use NFP for selfish reasons in order to exclude children from their lives. Such use of NFP is morally wrong, but it is not wrong because it is contraceptive — which it is *not*. It should be noted too that couples can use NFP to increase the chances of pregnancy when they seek to pursue the procreative good.)

73. John Paul II, *Familiaris Consortio*, no. 32. On this see William E. May, "Irreconcilable Concepts of the Human Person and Human Sexuality," in *The Catholic Faith* 3.1(January-February 1997), 38-43; "A Profoundly Different Understanding," in Ibid. 3.2 (March-April 1997), 25-29.

74. See Janet Smith, *Humanae Vitae: A Generation Later,* pp. 118-128; Germain Grisez, "Natural Family Planning Is Not Contraception," *International Review of Natural Family Planning*, 1 (1977), 123-126; and Joseph Boyle, "Contraception and Natural Family Planning," in *Why Humanae Vitae Was Right*, pp. 407-418.

75. On this, see Charles E. Curran, "Sterilization: Exposition, Critique, and Refutation of Past Teaching," pp. 207-211; John Dedek, *Contemporary Medical Ethics* (New York: Sheed and Ward, Inc., 1975), pp. 113-120.

76. See, for instance, Bernard Häring, *Medical Ethics* (Notre Dame, Ind.: Fides, 1972), pp. 90-91.
77. See, for example, Paul VI, *Humanae Vitae*, no. 14; National Conference of Catholic Bishops, *Ethical and Religious Directives for Catholic Health Care Services* (Washington, D.C.: U.S. Catholic Conference, 1995), no. 53. See also the July 9, 1980 "Statement on Tubal Ligation" of the National Conference of Catholic Bishops, *Hospital Progress*, 61.9 (1980), 39.
78. A good presentation of magisterial documents and theological analysis of this matter is given by Gerald A. Kelly, *Medical-Moral Problems* (St. Louis: Catholic Hospital Association, 1955).
79. For example, Häring, *Medical Ethics*, pp. 90-91; John Boyle, *The Sterilization Controversy* (New York: Paulist Press, 1977).
80. Martin Nolan, "The Principle of Totality," in *Absolutes in Moral Theology?* ed. Charles E. Curran (Washington, D.C.: Corpus, 1968). For an incisive critique of this effort to extend the principle of totality, see Paul Ramsey, *The Patient as Person* (New Haven, Conn.: Yale University Press, 1971), pp. 178-181.
81. John Boyle, who agrees that contraceptive sterilization is justifiable on the grounds that it promotes the greater good, provides a good history of this position in *The Sterilization Controversy.*
82. The effort to justify contraceptive sterilization on the grounds of the principle of totality was explicitly rejected by the National Conference of Catholic Bishops in their "Statement on Tubal Ligation."
83. Pius XII, "Address to the Delegates of the Eighth Congress of the World Medical Association," September 30, 1954, AAS 46.587-598.
84. For a typical statement hailing the pill as a revolutionary and liberating discovery, comparable to the discovery of fire and the invention of the wheel, see the rhapsodic hymn to the pill given by Ashley Montagu in his *Sex, Man, and Society*, ch. 1.
85. Thus, Paul VI says in *Humanae Vitae* that any use of marriage must remain open (*per se destinalus*) to procreation. Anscombe (*Contraception and Chastity*) pp. 18-21, makes very clear the conceptual link between contraception and such acts as masturbation and sodomy. Her argument is that if contraception is permissible, then so are such acts.
86. See Pius XII, "Address to the Second World Congress on Fertility and Sterility," May 19, 1956; AAS 48.473. The English is from John C. Ford, S.J., and Gerald A. Kelly, S.J., *Contemporary Moral Theology*, vol. 2, *Marriage Questions* (Westminster, Md.: The Newman Press, 1964), p. 212. Ford and Kelly discuss this and other relevant texts, pp. 188-234.

87. Anscombe, *Contraception and Chastity*, pp. 21-22; see Ford and Kelly, *Marriage Questions*, pp. 224-234, for a judicious discussion of the dangers of hedonism in this area.

88. See Pius XII, "Address to the Midwives," October 29, 1951; AAS 43.835-854.

89. Anscombe, *Contraception and Chastity*, p. 26; Ford and Kelly, *Marriage Questions*, pp. 228-230, suggest three principles for evaluating sexual behavior between spouses: conjugal justice, conjugal chastity, and Christian self-restraint. They make clear how prudent application of these principles helps not only in the avoidance of lustful immoderation but also in the efforts of mutual sanctification.

90. Anscombe, *Contraception and Chastity*, p. 26. See also Grisez et al., "Every Marital Act Ought to Be Open to New Life," 390-399.

91. See Pius XII, "Address to the Fourth International Congress of Catholic Doctors," September 29, 1949, AAS 41.557-561; "Address to Midwives," October 29, 1951, AAS 43.835-854; "Address to the Second World Congress on Fertility and Sterility," May 19, 1956, AAS 48.467-474. English translations of the latter two addresses are available in Liebard's *Love and Sexuality*, pp. 101-122, 173-179.

92. Congregation for the Doctrine of the Faith, *Instruction on Respect for Human Life in Its Origin and on the Dignity of Procreation*. See also *Catechism of the Catholic Church*, nos. 2373-2379.

93. See William E. May, "*Donum Vitae*: Catholic Teaching Concerning Homologous *In Vitro* Fertilization," in *Infertility: A Crossroad of Faith, Medicine, and Technology*, ed. Kevin Wm. Wildes, S.J., vol. 53 of Philosophy and Medicine (Dordrecht/Boston/London: Kluwer Academic Publishers, 1997), pp. 73-92; see May, *Marriage: The Rock on Which the Family Is Built* (San Francisco: Ignatius Press, 1995), pp. 85-100; Donald DeMarco, *Biotechnology and the Assault on Parenthood* (San Francisco: Ignatius Press, 1991); Paul Ramsey, *Fabricated Man* (New Haven, CT: Yale University Press, 1970), pp. 104-160, and "Shall We 'Reproduce'?" *Journal of the American Medical Association* 220 (1972), 1346-1350, 1480-1485. The words of Pius XII in his "Address to Midwives" (translation from Liebard's *Love and Sexuality*, pp. 117-118) are instructive: "To consider unworthily the cohabitation of husband and wife, and the marital act as a simple organic function for the transmission of seed, would be the same as to convert the domestic hearth, which is the family sanctuary, into a mere biological laboratory. . . . There is much more than the union of two life germs, which can be brought about even artificially, that is, without the cooperation of hus-

306

band and wife. The marital act, in the order of, and by nature's design, consists of personal cooperation which the husband and wife exchange as a right when they marry."

Notes for Chapter Eight

1. Friedrich Hauck and Siegfried Schulz, "Porne," in *Theological Dictionary of the New Testament*, vol. 6, ed. Gerhard Kittel, tr. Geoffrey W. Bromiley (Grand Rapids, Mich.: Eerdmans, 1968), pp. 585-586.
2. Ibid., p. 585.
3. Ibid., pp. 586, 587-588.
4. Raymond F. Collins, *Christian Morality: Biblical Foundations* (Notre Dame, Ind: University of Notre Dame Press, 1986), pp. 184-186.
5. Philo, *De Josepho*, 9.
6. One of the best studies of the meaning of *porneia* in the New Testament and, in particular, in the thought of St. Paul is provided by Silverio Zedda, S.J., in his book *Relativo e Assoluto nella morale di San Paolo* (Brescia: Paideia Editrice, 1984), ch. 5. Zedda provides abundant evidence to show that this term, while having as some of its specific meanings "prostitution" and "incest," was used to designate any kind of sexual shamelessness, including intercourse outside of marriage and simple "fornication," or consensual coition by persons who are not married. See also Manuel Miguens, O.F.M., "Christ's Members and Sex," *The Thomist*, 39 (1975), 24-48; Joseph Jensen, "Does *Porneia* Mean Fornication? A Critique of Bruce Malina," *Novum Testamentum*, 20 (1978), 161-184, and especially 179-181.
7. The only other mention of *porneia* in the Gospels is in the Matthean divorce texts (Matthew 5:32, 19:9). Current biblical scholars tend to hold that the term *porneia* in these Matthean texts refers to incestuous kinds of relationships, termed *zenut* in Hebrew. See Joseph Fitzmyer, S.J., *To Advance the Gospel: New Testament Studies* (New York: Crossroad, 1981), pp. 79-111.
8. John J. O'Rourke, "Does the New Testament Condemn Sexual Intercourse Outside of Marriage?" *Theological Studies*, 37 (1976), 478-479, makes it clear that Paul is referring here to extramarital intercourse: "Obviously the Apostle is not speaking of idolatry, nor of marriages prohibited by law, nor of evil in general. He is not speaking of sacred prostitutes, an institution which at one time had flourished in Corinth, but which was most likely nonexistent in a Roman *colonia*. Surely he is not speaking of commercial prostitution. He is not saying that it is

307

likely that a girl who remains unmarried and does not have the special gift which he possesses (see 1 Cor 7:7b) will become a whore, because the reason that he gives for both a man and a woman is the same: *dia tes porneias*. Thus the only possible understanding in context of *porneia* is illicit sexual intercourse (see also 1 Cor 7:9, where Paul says of the 'unmarried' [agamoi] and the widows, 'if they cannot exercise self-control, let them marry' [ei de ouk egkateuontai gamesatosan])." See also Jensen, "Does *Porneia* Mean Fornication?" pp. 181-182. In addition to the study by Zedda referred to in note 6 above, see also the excellent treatment of St. Paul's sexual ethics (which unequivocally repudiated any extramarital genital sex as incompatible with the Christian life) provided by O. Larry Yarbrough, *Not Like the Gentiles: Marriage Rules in the Letters of Paul*. Society of Biblical Literature Dissertation Series No. 80 (Atlanta, Ga: Scholars Press), pp. 89-121.

9. See also Innocent IV, *Sub Catholica Professione*, March 6, 1254, in DS 835; Decrees of the Holy Office (September 24, 1665, DS 2045; March 2, 1679, DS 2148); Pius XI, *Casti Connubii*, December 31, 1930, AAS 22.558-559; Sacred Congregation for the Doctrine of the Faith, *Declaration on Certain Questions Concerning Sexual Ethics* (Washington, D.C.: U.S. Catholic Conference, 1976), no. 7.

10. John Paul II, *Familiaris Consortio*, no. 11.

11. See Karol Wojtyla (John Paul II), *Love and Responsibility*, tr. H.T. Willetts (New York: Farrar, Straus, and Giroux, 1981), p. 41, for a discussion of what he calls the "personalist principle": "This norm, in its negative aspect, states that the person is the kind of good which does not admit of use and cannot be treated as an object of use and as such the means to an end. In its positive aspect the personalist norm confirms this: the person is a good towards which the only proper and adequate attitude is love."

12. The argument briefly summed up here is cogently developed by Germain Grisez, *The Way of the Lord Jesus*, vol. 2, *Living a Christian Life,* (Quincy, Ill.: Franciscan Press, 1993), pp. 651-653.

13. Wojtyla, *Love and Responsibility*, p. 30.

14. See *Toward a Quaker View of Sex* (London: Friends Homes Service Committee, 1963); *Sex and Morality: A Report Presented to the British Council of Churches* (Philadelphia: Fortress Press, 1966); United Church of Christ, *Human Sexuality: A Preliminary Study* (New York: United Church Press, 1977). See also Joseph Fletcher, *Situation Ethics: The New Morality* (Philadelphia: Westminster, 1966); John A.T. Robinson, *Honest to God* (Philadelphia: Westminster, 1963).

15. On this, see Paul Ramsey, *Deeds and Rules in Christian Ethics* (New York: Scribner's, 1967), ch. 1.
16. See, for example, Philip S. Keane, S.S., *Sexual Morality: A Catholic Perspective* (New York: Paulist Press, 1977), pp. 92-113.
17. Ibid., p. 107. The principal point is that Keane is here arguing that coition between persons definitely not married (for they only *intend* to marry) can be and is under some circumstances morally good.
18. See Paul Ramsey, "A Christian Approach to the Question of Sexual Relations Outside of Marriage," *Journal of Religion*, 45 (1965), 100-118, at 112. Ramsey places careful qualification on his view in an updated version of the above article in *One Flesh: A Christian View of Sex Within, Outside, and Before Marriage* (Bramcote, Notts, England: Grove Books, 1975).
19. See Anthony Kosnik et al., *Human Sexuality: New Directions in American Catholic Thought* (New York: Paulist Press, 1977), pp. 155-165, for an example of this abuse.
20. On this, see Edward Schillebeeckx, *Marriage: Human Reality and Saving Mystery* (New York: Sheed and Ward, 1965), pp. 37-102.
21. Council of Trent, Session 24, November 11, 1563; DS 1813-1816. The requirement of a canonical form was later incorporated into the 1917 *Codex Juris Canonici*, Canon 1098. In the 1983 revised *Codex* the relevant canon is Canon 1108. Canon 1116 spells out circumstances in which this form is not required. A new canon in the 1983 *Codex*, Canon 1117, declares that Roman Catholics who have by a formal act repudiated their Roman Catholicism may marry validly without this canonical form.
22. The essentially public character of marriage is clearly set forth in *Familiaris Consortio*, no. 11.
23. See Joseph J. Farraher, S.J., "Masturbation," *New Catholic Encyclopedia* (New York: McGraw-Hill, 1965), 9.438, for a general discussion; for a more thorough discussion with several classical definitions, see *Dictionnaire de Théologie Catholique*, ed. A. Vacant, E. Manganot, and A. Amann (Paris: Librairie Letouzy et Ane, 1902-1905), 15 vols., 9.1346-1347. See also Marcellinus Zalba, S.J., *Theologiae Moralis Compendium*, vol. 1, (Madrid: Biblioteca de Autores Cristianos, 1958), pp. 771-775, for a modern definition and discussion. Zalba defines pollution as the complete, separate use of the generative faculty. By *complete* he means to orgasm, by *separate* he means outside of sexual intercourse. He goes on to argue that all directly and perfectly voluntary pollution is intrinsically a grave sin.

309

24. See, for instance, Augustine, *Opus Imperfectum Contra Julianum*, 4, 11, 10 (PL 44.74) il 3, 20, 38 (PL 44.72) and *De Nuptiis et Concupiscentia*, 2, 26, 42 (PL 44.460). The penitentials in use from the sixth through ninth centuries strongly condemned masturbation. See, for example, *Paenitentiale Aquilonale* (Canon 2) and *Luci Victoriae* (Canon 8), cited in Josef Fuchs, S.J., *De Castitate et Ordine Sexuali*, 2nd ed. (Rome: Gregorian University, 1960), p. 49. See also the references in John T. Noonan, Jr., *Contraception: A History of Its Treatment by Catholic Theologians and Canonists* (Cambridge, Mass.: Harvard University Press, 1965), pp. 70-77, for a discussion of patristic and Jewish views on masturbation.

25. For medieval thought, see, for instance, Thomas Aquinas, *Summa Theologie*, II-II, q. 154, a. 5. Zalba and Fuchs, cited above in Notes 23 and 24, are representatives of the manualist tradition.

26. It should be noted that not only in the Catholic theological tradition has masturbation been regarded as seriously immoral but also in the whole Christian tradition until relatively modern times. For Protestant thought on this subject, see references given by Derrick S. Bailey, *The Male-Female Relationship in Christian Tradition* (New York: Harper and Row, 1968).

27. See Leo IX, Epistola "Ad Splendidum Nitentis" ad Petrum Damiani, 1054, DS 687-688; Alexander VII, "Errores Doctrinae Moralis Laxioris," September 14, 1665, DS 2044; Innocent XI, "Errores Doctrinae Moralis Laxioris," March 2, 1679, DS 2149; Pius XI, "Decree of Holy Office on Masturbation," July 24, 1929, DS 3684; addresses of Pius XII, October 8, 1953, AAS 45.677-678; May 19, 1956, AAS 48.472-473; Sacred Congregation for the Doctrine of the Faith, *Declaration on Certain Questions Concerning Sexual Ethics*, no. 9; Sacred Congregation for Catholic Education, "Educational Guidance in Human Love," November 1, 1983, no. 98.

28. *Declaration on Certain Questions Concerning Sexual Ethics*, no. 9.

29. On the use of the Onan texts, see the discussions in Noonan, *Contraception*, under Onan in the index.

30. See Fuchs, *De Castitate et Ordine Sexuali*, pp. 47-48; John L. McKenzie, "Onan," in his *Dictionary of the Bible* (Milwaukee: Bruce, 1965).

31. In *Relativo e Assoluto nella morale di San Paolo*, pp. 115-119, Zedda argues that relevant Pauline texts (e.g., 1 Thes 4:4, 1 Cor 7:2-9, 2 Cor 7:1), especially if read in the light of the Greek text of Sirach 23:17, which speaks of the "man who lusts after his own body" (*anthropos pornos en somati sarkos autou*), surely support the conclusion that au-

310

toeroticism is among the vices on which St. Paul pronounces, as a teacher of the faith, a judgment of reproval.

32. *Declaration on Certain Questions Concerning Sexual Ethics*, no. 9.
33. On this see Grisez, *Living a Christian Life*, pp. 649-651.
34. See, for example, Michael Valente, *Sex: the Radical View of a Catholic Theologian* (New York: Bruce-Macmillan, 1970).
35. See John C. Ford, S.J., and Germain Grisez, "Contraception and the Infallibility of the Ordinary Magisterium," *Theological Studies*, 39 (1978), 263-277, for an exposition of the conditions under which the ordinary magisterium teaches infallibly; these conditions are set out in *Lumen Gentium*, no. 25. In the remainder of this article Ford and Grisez apply these conditions to the teaching on contraception; some of this material is directly relevant to the teaching on the morality of masturbation; their analysis suggests that a similar argument can be made concerning the received teaching on masturbation.
36. See Germain Grisez, "Dualism and the New Morality," *Atti del Congressa Internazionale Tommaso D'Aquino nel Suo Settimo Centario*, vol. 5, *L'Agir Morale*, (Naples: Edizione Domenicane, 1977), pp. 323-330.
37. See *Dictionnaire de Théologie Catholique*, "Luxure: Especes," 9.1347-1349, for a critical summary of the theological arguments against masturbation. Plainly these arguments do not assume that procreation is the only legitimate goal of sexual activity.
38. See Kosnik et al., *Human Sexuality*, pp. 219-229.
39. See "Decree of the Holy Office, August 2, 1929," DS 3684; Henry Davis, S.J., *Pastoral and Moral Theology*, vol. 2, *Commandments of God: Precepts of the Church*, 8th ed. (New York: Sheed and Ward, 1959), p. 259.
40. See references to Pius XII, in Note 27 above.
41. See Kosnik et al., *Human Sexuality*, pp. 227-229; Charles E Curran, "Masturbation: An Objectively Grave Matter?" in *A New Look at Christian Morality* (Notre Dame, Ind.: Fides, 1968), pp. 200-221.
42. See Charles E. Curran, *Contemporary Problems in Moral Theology* (Notre Dame, Ind.: University of Notre Dame Press, 1970), pp. 159-188; Keane, *Sexual Morality*, pp. 62-68.
43. Pope John Paul II, *Veritatis Splendor*, no. 70, citing from his own *Reconciliatio et Poenitentia*, no. 17. Congregation for the Doctrine of the Faith, *Declaration on Certain Questions Concerning Sexual Ethics*, no. 10: "According to the Church's teaching, mortal sin, which is opposed to God, does not consist only in formal and direct resistance to the commandment of charity. It is equally to be found in this opposi-

tion to authentic love which is included in every deliberate transgression, in serious matter, of each of the moral laws."

44. Among the authors taking this perspective are: Albert Ellis, *Sex Without Guilt* (New York: Grove Press, 1965), pp. 10-19; Eleanor Hamilton, *Sex Before Marriage* (New York: Bantam Books, 1970), pp. 6-7, 13-16; James L. McCary, *Human Sexuality*, 2nd ed. (New York: Van Nostrand, 1979), pp. 183-184; Herant A. Katchadourian and Donald T. Lunde, *Fundamentals of Human Sexuality*, 3rd ed. (New York: Holt, Rinehart, and Winston, 1980), pp. 291-308. It is not surprising that these authors regard masturbation in such a casual way because they have adopted an extremely separatist view of human sexuality. They regard its procreative meaning merely as a biological function, and regard sex as simply one way for a lonely individual to break out of his or her prison of loneliness.

45. See the works of Curran and Keane cited above in Note 42, and that of Kosnik et al., previously cited so frequently in these pages.

46. See Farraher, "Masturbation," 438.

47. See *Dictionnaire de Théologie Catholique*, "Luxure: Gravité," 9.1340-1345, for a survey of biblical, theological, and magisterial discussions of the gravity of sexual sin.

48. For a sound, complete discussion on these points, see John C. Ford, S.J., and Gerald Kelly, S.J., *Contemporary Moral Theology*, vol. 1 (Westminster, Md.: The Newman Press, 1969), pp. 174-247.

49. See *Declaration on Certain Questions Concerning Sexual Ethics*, no. 9: "On the subject of masturbation modern psychology provides much valid and useful information for formulating a more equitable judgment on moral responsibility and for orienting pastoral action. Psychology helps one to see how the immaturity of adolescence (which can sometimes persist after that age), psychological imbalance or habit can influence behavior, diminishing the deliberate character of the act and bringing about a situation whereby subjectively there may not always be serious fault. But in general, the absence of serious responsibility must not be presumed; this would be to misunderstand people's moral capacity."

50. Pope John Paul II, *Veritatis Splendor*, no. 70, citing his own *Reconciliatio et Poenitentia*, no. 17.

51. See *Summa Theologiae*, II-II, q. 154, a. 4; this is the standard reference for the common teaching of the manuals.

52. A. Bell and M. Weinberg, *Homosexualities* (New York: Simon and Schuster, 1978).

53. Congregation for the Doctrine of the Faith, *Letter to Bishops of the Catholic Church on the Pastoral Care of the Homosexual Person*, October 1, 1986, no. 16.
54. See John Harvey, O.S.F.S., *The Homosexual Person: New Thinking in Pastoral Care* (San Francisco: Ignatius Press, 1987), p. 27. Harvey adds that he uses the term *"predominant* to indicate that there may be a lesser degree of erotic interest in the other sex," and the term "persistent to indicate that these erotic feelings toward someone of the same sex have persisted beyond the adolescent phase." In subsequent pages Harvey judiciously reviews and discusses the descriptions of homosexuality provided by contemporary researchers, in particular Dr. Gerald van den Aardweg and Dr. Elizabeth Moberly.
55. It is very necessary to distinguish between "*transitory homosexuality*, which may be a phase of development, especially during adolescence, and *chronic homosexuality*, the latter being the type of homosexuality that is generally meant when one uses the term" (Gerald van den Aardweg, *On the Origins and Treatment of Homosexuality* [New York: Praeger, 1986], p. 1, cited by Harvey, *The Homosexual Person*, p. 27).
56. As van den Aardweg puts it, "the criterion lies in one's feelings, not in one's manifest behavior." Ibid.
57. On this see Ruth Tiffany Barnhouse, *Homosexuality: A Symbolic Confusion* (New York: Seabury, 1977), p. 22. See also above, note 55.
58. Other distinctions among types of homosexuality are those between *compulsive, symptomatic*, and *episodic* homosexuality. On this see Jeffrey Keefe, O.F.M. Conv., "Key Aspects of Homosexuality," in John F. Harvey, O.S.F.S., *The Truth About Homosexuality: The Cry of the Faithful* (San Francisco: Ignatius Press, 1996), pp. 54-61.
59. There is a debate regarding the factors contributing to the development of the homosexual orientation. Although some studies — frequently sensationalized in the press — have indicated some genetic basis for the orientation, these studies have never been successfully reduplicated. As a result, the vast preponderance of evidence leads to the conclusion that the orientation is brought about principally because of environmental factors affecting psychosexual development, although there may well be, at least in some cases, some *predispositions* of a genetic origin. A judicious review of relevant research on this question is given by Jeffrey Keefe, "Key Aspects of Homosexuality," pp. 32-54.
60. John F. Harvey, *The Truth About Homosexuality*, p. 114. This statement appears at the end of a chapter (pp. 69-114) dealing with the possibility of changing a homosexual orientation to a heterosexual one. In his

survey of relevant literature, Harvey first reviewed and noted both the limitations of the empirical data in and a priori assumptions governing the work of authors claiming that such a change is not possible (C. A. Tripp, Robert Bidwell, Richard Green, and Laura Reiter). He then turned to the clinical psychologists and psychiatrists (Gerald van den Aardweg, E. Mansel, Myrna Loy Pattison, George Rekers, Charles Socarides, Ismond Rosen, Lawrence Hatterer) and religious counselors with professional knowledge and experience (Elizabeth Moberly, Leanne Payne, Andy Comiskey, William Consiglio, Joe Dallas, Bob Davies, Lori Rentzel, and Frank Worthen) who testify to the possibility of such a change. Concluding, Harvey says: "All these professional men and women present evidence that their counselees have been able to make the journey from homosexuality to heterosexuality. [Indeed] some of these counselors . . . were homosexual in orientation themselves. . . . They make it clear that they were able to make the transition by the help of God's grace" (p. 114).

61. This is the Church's constant understanding of the relevant teaching of the Scripture on this subject. See Pierre Grelot, *Man and Wife in Scripture* (New York: Herder and Herder, 1965), pp. 34-37, and Edward Schillebeeckx, *Marriage*, pp. 14-16, 20-21. See also John L. McKenzie, "Human Origins," in *The Two-Edged Sword: An Interpretation of the Old Testament* (New York: Doubleday, 1966), where McKenzie makes the point that Genesis 1 and, in particular, Genesis 2 — the story of the creation of mankind as male and female and of marriage — is also the story of the creation of marriage. See also the article on sex in *The Interpreter's Dictionary of the Bible* (Nashville, Tenn.: Abingdon, 1966). See also Roger Shinn, "Homosexuality, Christian Conviction, and Enquiry," *The Same Sex*, ed. Ralph Weltge (Philadelphia: Pilgrim Press, 1969), p. 26: "The Christian tradition over the centuries has affirmed the heterosexual, monogamous faithful marital union as normative for the divinely given meaning of the intimate sexual relationship." Even Charles E. Curran ("Dialogue with the Homophile Movement" in his *Catholic Moral Theology in Dialogue* [Notre Dame, Ind.: Fides, 1972]), who attempts to justify homosexual relations between homosexually constituted persons within a stable relationship on the grounds of a "theology of compromise," acknowledges that this is the normative tradition. This is also acknowledged by Keane, *Sexual Morality*, pp. 87-88.

62. On male homosexuality, see Leviticus 18:22, 20:13; Romans 1:27; 1 Corinthians 6:9-10; 1 Timothy 1:9-10; on female homosexuality, Romans 1:26-27.

63. See *Summa Theologiae*, II-II, q. 154, aa. 11-12; Salmanticenses, tr. XXVI, C.VII, 109; Zalba, 1, pp. 780-781.

64. Congregation for the Doctrine of the Faith, *Letter to Bishops of the Catholic Church on the Pastoral Care of the Homosexual Person*, no. 3.

65. James Hitchcock, *Catholicism and Modernity: Confrontation or Capitulation?* (New York: Seabury, 1979), p. 207.

66. See, for example, John McNeill, S.J., *The Church and the Homosexual* (Kansas City, Mo.: Andrews and McMeel, 1976); Kosnik et al., *Human Sexuality*, pp. 186-218.

67. See McNeill, *The Church and the Homosexual*, pp. 42-53. See also Kosnik et al., *Human Sexuality*, pp. 191-192. For a counterargument that this story definitely includes a reference to homosexuality, see Manuel Miguens, O.F.M., "Biblical Thoughts on 'Human Sexuality,' " in *Human Sexuality in Our Time*, ed. George A. Kelly (Boston: Daughters of St. Paul, 1979), pp. 112-115. It is important in this connection to note that the Epistle of Jude (v. 7) refers to Sodom and Gomorrah, and indicates their sin as unnatural vice.

68. McNeill, *The Church and the Homosexual*, pp. 53-56. Several authors, including Kosnik et al. and McNeill, champion the view, promulgated widely by the influential book of John Boswell, *Christianity, Social Tolerance, and Homosexuality* (New Haven: Yale University Press, 1990) that the strong condemnation of homosexual acts in the book of Leviticus is motivated, not by the nature of these acts themselves, but rather by the role they played in pagan cult. An excellent critique of this view is given by the biblical scholar George Montague: "Sexual morality is often connected with the cult, but this does not prove that sexual sins, such as homosexual acts and bestiality, were condemned only because they were part of the Canaanite worship. While the book of Leviticus does have a cultic framework, the legislation of Leviticus does not give idolatry as the reason for avoiding the sexual practices of the Canaanites. Quite the contrary. The reason given why the Lord is driving the nations out of the land is not their worship of false gods, but their abominable sexual practices (Lev 18:24-30; 20:28). . . . To say that the concern of Leviticus is not ethical but cultic (or in Boswell, 'ritual impurity') is a gross oversimplification and even more misleading is the statement [made by Kosnik et al.], 'the condemnation of homosexual activity in Leviticus is not an ethical judgment.' " See Montague, "A Scriptural Response to the Report on Human Sexuality," *America*, Oct. 1977, 284-285.

315

69. See Barnhouse, *Homosexuality: A Symbolic Confusion*, p. 180. See also Miguens, article cited above in Note 67. Joseph Jensen, "The Relevance of the Old Testament," in *Dimensions of Human Sexuality*, ed. Dennis Doherty (New York: Doubleday, 1979), p. 8, points out the failure of biblical writers to distinguish between homosexual activity and homosexual orientation. Still, he notes that this provides no suggestion that the biblical condemnation of the former is based on anything beyond "the nature of the act itself."

70. *Declaration on Certain Questions Concerning Sexual Ethics*, no. 8.

71. On this, see John M. Finnis, "Natural Law and Unnatural Acts," *Heythrop Journal*, 11 (1970), 384-385. (See also Chapter 6 of this book.)

72. Guindon, *The Sexual Language*, 339.

73. See Paul Cameron, "A Case Against Homosexuality," *The Human Life Review*, 4.3 (1978), 17-49. Cameron is a psychologist and argues effectively on the basis of the empirical data that homosexual activity undercuts the values required for stable family life and society because of its direction to immediate sexual gratification. See also Samuel McCracken, "Are Homosexuals Gay?" *Commentary* (January 1979), 19-29, for further convincing documentation of the almost exclusive orientation toward pleasure on the part of most homosexuals, and of their consequent irresponsibility; two quotes from homosexuals are most revealing: "... Gay people have more fun than your average married guy in a home with two or three kids. You have more time and money. You don't have the responsibilities. ... I can lavish ... presents ... on my nephews and take them to the zoo and have a great old time. When they get tired and cranky I take them back to mommy and dad — you know, dad has just finished paying two hundred bucks for their teeth." "... It's so hard to be a straight man, harder than to be a faggot, because the rewards are so stupid — the rewards that you are told you can have. Whereas if you're a faggot, I guess you can make up your own rewards. ... It's more fun to be a faggot because nobody expects anything of us."

74. McCracken, "Are Homosexuals Gay?" 20-21, shows convincingly by a critical analysis of data published in pro-homosexual books that the claim that homosexuals are as happy as other people has not been established; in particular, he points to data which show that suicide attempts are significantly higher among homosexuals than among others — for example, 3% for white non-homosexual males, 18% for white homosexual males.

75. Ibid., 22, cites the following statistics: 14% of homosexual males studied and 38% of females lived in an equivalent of a "happy marriage."

But 84% of the males studied "cruised" at least once a month, 42% at least once a week. Half the males in the study cited had at least five hundred sexual partners.

76. Ibid., 27: "The fact is that homosexuality generally entails a renunciation of responsibility for the continuance of the human race and of a voice in the dialogue of the generations. This is a renunciation made also by some heterosexuals and indeed by some married heterosexuals. There is, however, a still greater renunciation made by homosexuals, and that is of the intricate, complicated, and challenging process of adjusting one's life to someone so different from oneself as to be in a different sex entirely."

77. See Stephen Macedo, "Homosexuality and the Conservative Mind," *Georgetown University Law Journal* 84 (1995), 261ff.

78. Karol Wojtyla, *Love and Responsibility*, p. 30.

79. This truth is developed at length by Germain Grisez in *Living a Christian Life*, pp. 555-584. In developing this truth he shows that the magisterium of the Church, particularly in the teaching of Vatican Council II and in the many writings of John Paul II on marriage, clearly holds that marriage is something good in itself and not merely good as an instrument for generating life.

80. This idea is brought out at length and beautifully by the document, *In Vitro Fertilization and Public Policy, Evidence Submitted to the Government Committee of Inquiry into Human Fertilization and Embyology by the Catholic Bishops' Joint Committee on Bio-Ethical Issues, On Behalf of the Catholic Bishops of Great Britain* (May, 1983). See also John Finnis, "Law, Morality, and 'Sexual Orientation,' " *Notre Dame Law Review* 69 (1994) 1049-1076; Robert George and Gerard V. Bradley, "Marriage and the Liberal Imagination," *The Georgetown Law Journal* 84 (1995) 301-320.

81. For a further development of the ideas briefly set forth in this paragraph see the studies of Finnis and George/Bradley identified in note 80. Here it is well worth noting that in his encyclical *Humanae Vitae* Pope Paul VI made it very clear that the marital act "renders spouses *fit*" to receive new life (no. 10). The Latin text is very precise because it says that the marital act *"eos [the spouses] idoneos [fitting] facit."* Unfortunately, the common English translation says that the marital act "make the spouses *capable*" of receiving the gift of life, but Paul's Latin text is much more precise. For a commentary on the significance of this passage from *Humanae Vitae* see William E. May, *Marriage: The Rock on Which the Family Is Built* (San Francisco: Ignatius Press, 1995), chapter 4.

82. The purpose, nature, and history of "Courage" is set forth in some detail by Harvey in his *The Truth About Homosexuality*, pp. 19-30.

83. See *Dictionnaire de Théologie Catholique*, 14, 4.1350, for an elaboration and explanation of this definition.

84. See A.C. Kinsey et al., *Sexual Behavior in the Human Male* (Philadelphia: Saunders, 1948), pp. 667-673; *Sexual Behavior in the Human Female* (Philadelphia: Saunders, 1953), pp. 502-509.

85. See Leviticus 18:23, 29; 20:15-16; Exodus 22:19. See the commentary on these passages in *The Jerome Biblical Commentary*, ed. Raymond Brown, S.S., Joseph A. Fitzmyer, S.J., and Roland E. Murphy, O. Carm. (Englewood Cliffs, N.J.: Prentice-Hall, 1968), pp. 60, 78-79.

86. See *Summa Theologiae*, II-II, q. 154, a. 12, ad 4; Marcellinus Zalba, S.J., *Theologiae Moralis Compendium*, vol. 1, pp. 781-782.

87. Kosnik et al., *Human Sexuality*, pp. 229-230.

88. For a standard statement of the Catholic position, see Zalba, *Theologiae Moralis Compendium*, vol. 1, pp. 765-766.

89. See Ibid., and Bernard Häring, *The Law of Christ*, vol. 3, (Westminster, Md.: The Newman Press, 1966), p. 300.

90. See Sharon L. McCombie et al., "Development of a Medical Center Rape Crisis Intervention Program," *American Journal of Psychiatry*, 133.4 (1976), 418-421, at 418: "It is the fastest rising violent crime in the United States: the FBI reported a 68% increase in rape (from 31,000 to 51,000 cases) between 1968 and 1973, and police records in Boston show a 43.5% increase between 1972 and 1973." It is common knowledge also that many cases of rape are not reported. See L.S. McGuire et al., "Survey of Incidence of and Physicians' Attitude Toward Sexual Assault," *Public Health Report*, 91.2 (1976), 103-109.

91. Here the words of Dietrich von Hildebrand, *In Defense of Purity* (New York: Sheed and Ward, 1935), pp. 12-14, are instructive: "Sex . . . as contrasted with other departments of bodily experience is *essentially* deep. Every manifestation of sex produces an effect which transcends the physical sphere and, in a fashion quite unlike the other bodily desires, involves the soul deeply in its passion. . . . It is characteristic of sex that in virtue of its very significance and nature it tends to become incorporated with experiences of a higher order, purely psychological and spiritual. Nothing in the domain of sex is so self-contained as the other bodily experiences, e.g., eating and drinking. The unique profundity of sex . . . is sufficiently shown by the simple fact that a man's attitude toward it is of incomparably greater moral significance than his attitude to the other bodily appetites. Surrender to sexual desire for

its own sake defiles a man in a way that gluttony, for example, can never do. It wounds him to the core of his being. . . . Sex occupies a central position in the personality. . . . Sex can indeed keep silence, but when it speaks it is no *obiter dictum*, but a voice from the depths, the utterance of something central and of utmost significance. In and with sex man, in a special way, gives himself."

92. For a well argued defense of this position see Grisez, *Living a Christian Life*, p. 512.

93. See National Conference of Catholic Bishops, *Ethical and Religious Directives for Catholic Health Care Services* (Washington, D.C., United States Catholic Conference, 1995), Directive 36. For an accessible discussion of some of the contemporary issues and literature on this point, see Benedict Ashley, O.P., and Kevin O'Rourke, O.P., *Health Care Ethics: A Theological Analysis* (4th ed. Washington, D.C., Georgetown University Press, 1997), pp. 303-305.

94. See Ashley and O'Rourke, *Health Care Ethics*, pp. 303-305.

95. See *Summa Theologiae*, II-II, q. 154, a. 9.

96. Keane (*Sexual Morality*), pp. 58-59, misses this important point. He says, ". . . It can thus be said that in most cases sexual thoughts and fantasies do not deeply involve the average person; they are not very significant as an area of moral concern." This statement is ambiguous; he may be saying that most sexual thoughts are such that they never become an object of choice. This is contrary to common experiences; sex is important, and when a person is self-consciously dealing with sexual matters deliberation is triggered and choice is required. Keane may, of course, simply mean that sexual thoughts are not a morally serious matter. We have argued otherwise, and his position is simply inconsistent with the common teaching of the Church and with ordinary common sense.

97. For a fuller account, see *Dictionnaire de Théologie Catholique*, 9.4, "Luxure," 1352-1354, for the standard classification. See also Zalba, *Theologiae Moralis Compendium*, vol. 1, pp. 786-789. For an account in English, see Henry Davis, S.J., *Pastoral and Moral Theology*, pp. 218-221.

Notes for Chapter Nine

1. In these passages Pope John Paul II is *not* solemnly defining the truth that innocent human life is absolutely inviolable and that the direct and voluntary killing of an innocent human being, direct abortion, and euthanasia are always gravely immoral. He is not, in other words, making

an *ex cathedra* pronouncement. Nonetheless, the Holy Father concludes each of these passages by explicitly referring to Vatican Council II's Dogmatic Constitution on the Church, *Lumen Gentium*, no. 25. In the passage to which he refers, the Council Fathers declare the following: "Although the bishops, taken individually, do not enjoy the privilege of infallibility, they do, however, *proclaim the doctrine of the Church infallibly on the following conditions: namely, when, even though dispersed throughout the entire world but preserving for all that amongst themselves and with Peter's successor the bond of communion, in their authoritative teaching concerning matters of faith or morals, they are in agreement that a particular teaching is to be held definitively and absolutely*" (emphasis added). Since John Paul II makes explicit reference to this key text of *Lumen Gentium*, and since he is also at pains to point out, in each of these passages, that there is agreement among the bishops in communion with the pope regarding the absolute inviolability of innocent human life and the grave evil of the direct and voluntary killing of innocent human beings, of direct abortion, and of euthanasia, it is evident that in these passages John Paul II is affirming that these truths *are infallibly taught by the ordinary and universal magisterium of the Church.* On this matter see the following: Angel Rodriguez Luño, "La legge divina del 'non uccidere,' " a commentary on Chapter Three of *Evangelium Vitae*, in *Studi Cattolici*, 29 (1995), 435-445, and William E. May, "Pope John Paul II's encyclical *Evangelium Vitae* ('The Gospel of Life'): A Synopsis," *The Catholic Faith*, 1.1 (September 1995).

2. *Final Report of the Extraordinary Synod of Bishops*, December 7, 1985, *Enchiridion Vaticanum*, vol. 9, II, B, a, no. 4: p. 1758, no. 1797; cited by Pope John Paul II in his *Apostolic Constitution "Fidei Depositum," on the Publication of the "Catechism of the Catholic Church" Prepared Following the Second Vatican Ecumenical Council*, in *The Catechism of the Catholic Church*, p. 3.

3. John Paul II, *Apostolic Constitution "Fidei Depositum,"* in the *Catechism of the Catholic Church*, p. 3.

Notes for Pastoral Conclusion

1. The fundamental principles of pastoral theology are exemplified in the pastoral visits John Paul II has regularly made to many nations. Pastoral theology has an integrative and immediately practical thrust: in sincere charity it seeks to understand the situation of those to whom the Gospel is taught; it offers encouragement and assistance; it is compassionate in

320

the face of weakness but firm in its concern to proclaim the saving truth in its fullness, and to hearten the faithful to follow Christ generously. The American bishops outlined the fundamental principles of a pastoral approach to moral questions in two pastorals: *To Teach as Jesus Taught* and *To Live in Christ Jesus: A Pastoral Reflection on the Moral Life* (Washington, D.C.: U.S. Catholic Conference, 1975 and 1976).

2. John Paul II, *Familiaris Consortio*, no. 31.

3. Thus, John Paul II stresses how important it is to offer practical assistance in observing the moral precepts that express the requirements of love in *Familiaris Consortio*, no. 35, and in his concern to help pastoral leaders to see how great are the problems they must help the faithful to overcome (see Parts I and IV of *Familiaris Consortio*).

4. The Church insists that her teachings on morality are not merely authoritative declarations or rulings but express the truth entrusted to the Church by God; see Vatican Council II, *Dei Verbum*, ch. 1; John Paul II, *Redemptor Hominis*, no. 12. In his apostolic exhortation *Reconciliatio et Poenitentia* (December 2, 1984), John Paul II speaks of the duty of all teachers in the Church to avoid subjective views and seek to proclaim in moral matters the truth found in the word of God as interpreted by the magisterium (cf. no. 25). See also his encyclical *Veritatis Splendor* (August 6, 1993), esp. nos. 114-117.

5. The primacy of the duty of teaching the faith, including its moral aspects, is clear in the recent teaching of the Church. See Vatican Council II, *Lumen Gentium*, no. 25; *Christus Dominus*, nos. 12-13; on the right of the faithful to have the whole of the faith proclaimed to them, see John Paul II, "Address at Catholic University to Presidents of Catholic Universities and Colleges," October 7, 1979, in *Pilgrim of Peace* (Washington, D.C.: U.S. Catholic Conference, 1979), pp. 166-167. See also *Code of Canon Law* (1983), Canons 747, 760. See also *Veritatis Splendor*, nos. 114-117.

6. See the moving appeal of John Paul II to theologians in *Familiaris Consortio*, no. 31. See also Paul VI, *Humanae Vitae*, nos. 28-30.

7. John Paul II reminded American bishops that this duty remains foremost for bishops, even when it becomes painful: "The bishop must announce to the young and the old, to the rich and the poor, to the powerful and weak the fullness of truth, which sometimes offends, even if it always liberates. . . . Precisely because he cannot renounce the preaching of the Cross, the bishop will be called upon over and over *to accept criticism*, and to admit failure in obtaining a consensus of doctrine acceptable to everyone." See "The Bishop — A Living Sign of

Jesus Christ," September 5, 1983, in *Ad Limina Addresses: April 15-December 3, 1983* (Washington, D.C.: U.S. Catholic Conference, 1984), p. 18.

8. This is an insistent theme in contemporary Church documents in catechesis and pastoral theology, confronting tendencies to be silent about authentic teachings that some scholars reject, or to present a vision of the faith that fails to proclaim the excellent and saving but demanding requirements of the Gospel. See Paul VI, *Humanae Vitae*, no. 29; *Evangelization in the Modern World* (December 8, 1975), no. 78.

9. See Sacred Congregation for the Doctrine of the Faith, *Declaration on Certain Questions Concerning Sexual Ethics*, nos. 9-10.

10. See Pius XII, "Address to Psychotherapists," AAS 45.278-286; see also *Declaration on Certain Questions Concerning Sexual Ethics*, no. 10.

11. On grave inadequacies in some forms of fundamental option theory, see Pope John Paul II, *Encyclical Letter: Veritatis Splendor (The Splendor of Truth)*, (1993), nos. 65-68.

12. See *Declaration on Certain Questions Concerning Sexual Ethics*, no. 10. For a presentation of "fundamental option" theories in accord with authentic Catholic teaching, and a critique of extreme views, see Ronald Lawler, O.F.M. Cap., "The Love of God and Mortal Sin," and Joseph M. Boyle, Jr., "Freedom, the Human Person, and Human Action," in *Principles of Catholic Moral Life*, ed. William E. May (Chicago: Franciscan Herald Press, 1981), pp. 205-215, 237-266. See also Germain Grisez, *The Way of the Lord Jesus*, vol. 1, *Christian Moral Principles* (Chicago: Franciscan Herald Press, 1983), ch. 16, qs. B through E.

13. See Grisez, *Christian Moral Principles*, ch. 17, q. A.

14. See ibid., ch. 17, qs. C through F.

15. John Paul II in *Familiaris Consortio*, no. 33, quotes this passage from Paul VI, *Humanae Vitae*, no. 29.

16. Thomas Aquinas, *Summa Theologiae*, II-II, q. 141, a. 8.

17. See Ibid., II-II, q. 153, a. 5.

18. Pope John Paul II commends contemporary concern for freedom, and notes the importance of understanding freedom in authentically human and Gospel ways in *Veritatis Splendor*, nos. 31-34.

19. See John Paul II, *Familiaris Consortio*, no. 37.

20. Ibid., no. 6.

21. That some of the most popular forms of birth control, notably IUD's and most contemporary forms of the birth control pill, permit conception (and so the coming-to-be of a new human being) and then cause the destruction of that person is well known. See Kevin Hume, "Latest

322

Research Findings: The Pill and the I.U.D.," *Proceedings of the First International Congress for the Family* (Madras: Office of the Congress, 1983), pp. 86-95. For a theological reflection on these facts, see Germain Grisez, *Abortion: The Myths, the Arguments, and the Realities* (Washington, D.C.: Corpus, 1970), p. 344.

22. John Paul II, *Familiaris Consortio*, no. 32.

23. Ibid., no. 35.

24. Pope John Paul II, *Letter to Families (Gratissimam Sane)* [1994], no. 16.

25. Pope John Paul II's *Familiaris Consortio* is the basic document. Also to be noted are the Holy See's *Charter of Rights for the Family* (1967) and Pope John Paul II, *Letter to Families* (1994). See also: Pontifical Council for the Family, *The Truth and Meaning of Human Sexuality* (1995). See especially, Pontifical Council for the Family, *Instruction: Preparation for Marriage* (1996).

26. Ibid.

27. Ibid.

28. On providing a suitable education for young people in the Christian vision of love and sexuality, see *Familiaris Consortio,* no. 37; Pontifical Council for the Family, *The Truth and Meaning of Human Sexuality* (1995); Congregation for Christian Education, *Educational Guidance in Human Love* (1983). A number of programs have been prepared for education in chastity for the young in the spirit of these documents, for example, *The Catholic Vision of Love* [Huntington, Ind.: Our Sunday Visitor Publishing, Inc., 1996], prepared by the Diocese of Pittsburgh.

29. See *Familiaris Consortio,* nos. 77-85.

30. Aquinas, *Summa Theologiae*, I-II, q. 107, a. 4.

Index

A

Aardweg, Gerald van den, homosexuality, 313-314
abortion, link to contraception, 300-302
Albert the Great, 59, 269
Alexander VII, masturbation, 310
Alphonsus Liguori, marital act, 66, 149
Amann, A., 265, 309
American bishops, adultery, 104, 295; binding norms, 110; conscience, 104; contraception, 148, 298; sterilization, 305; treatment of rape victims, 319
American Bishops, 152, 321
anal and oral sex, 164
Anscombe, G.E.M. (Elizabeth), 297, 299, 300, 303, 305, 306
Apostolicam Actuositatem, 292
Aquinas, Thomas, see Thomas Aquinas
Aristotle, critique of hedonism, 275; nature of good, 274; pleasure, 63
artificial insemination/fertilization, 165-166, 207-209
Ashley, Benedict, treatment of rape victims, 319
Athanasius, 48
Athenagoras of Athens, 48, 266
Aubert, Jacques Marie, 251
Augustine, 50, 57, 149; concupiscence, 51, 267-269; goods of marriage, 52-55, 60-61, 131, 253, 265-269, 290-292; goods of marriage and marital act, 53-55, 265-269; masturbation, 310; Sermon on the Mount, 261-262

B

Bailey, Derrick S., 265, 310
Baldanza, G., 253
Balducelli, Roger, 293
Barnhouse, Ruth, 313, 316
Bauer, Johannes, divorce in NT, 42, 263; marriage in the NT, 36, 259
Bell, A., 185, 312
Bennett, Jonathan, 277
Benoit, Pierre, 44, 264
bestiality, 39, 58, 64, 169, 193, 300, 315
Bonaventure, marital love, 59, 61-62, 269-271; marriage and marital act

61-62; marriage as remedy, 59, 270; sexual sins, 59, 61-62, 270

Boswell, John, 315

Boyle, Joseph, contraception, 297, 299; free choice, 279-280, 322; NFP, not contraceptive, 304; principle of double effect, 273

Boyle, John, 305

Bradley, Gerard V., 317

Braga, Council of, goodness of marriage, 253

Burke, Cormac, pleasure in St. Augustine, 268

C

Cahill, Lisa S., proportionalist, 276

Cajetan, Thomas Cardinal, 66, 273

Camp, Claudia, 260

Canadian Bishops, conscience, 280, 281

Catechism of the Catholic Church, 111, 306, 320; absolute norms, 82, 277; celibacy, 138, 293: chastity, 128, 220; conscience, 98, 107, 228-229, 280, 290; contraception, 29, 149; fornication, 171; homosexual acts, 187, 189; immorality of extramarital sexual acts, 30; love for homosexually inclined persons, 192; magisterium and specific natural law precepts, 114, 286; marriage, 26; masturbation, 178; moral law, 229; morality of human acts, 228-229; nature of Christian moral life 225-231; principle of completeness, 92; purpose of sexuality, 255; sexual ethics, 229-231; task of magisterium, 21; virtues, 289

Cesario, Romanus, 289

Charter for Families, 293

Christus Dominus, duty to teach Catholic faith and morals, 321

Clement of Alexandria, goodness of marriage, 48-49, 266; marital continence, 49, 266

Clark, Steven, 259, 260

Clifford, Richard, Sodom and Gomorrah story, 261

Collins, Raymond, biblical teaching on sex, 257, 261, 307

complementarity of sexes, 289

Congar, Yves, 288

Congregation for Catholic Education, 288, 310

Congregation for the Doctrine of the Faith, *Instruction on the Ecclesial Vocation of the Theologian*, 116, 250-251, 286; *Instruction on Respect for Human Life in Its Origin and on the Dignity of Human Procreation ("Donum Vitae")*, 166, 205-210, 306; *Letter to the Bishops of the Catholic Church on the Pastoral Care of Homosexual Persons*, 188-189, 201-

205, 313, 315; *Vatican Declaration on Certain Questions of Sexual Ethics ("Persona Humana")*, 178, 187, 188, 255-256, 280, 308, 310, 311, 322

Conn, Walter, transcendental conscience, 100, 282

Connery, John, 280

conscience, 96-121; dignity of, 99, 119; duty to follow, 102-105; formation of Catholic, 105-111; meaning of, 94-100

contraception, 144-157; basic argument against, 152-157; constancy of Church's teaching, 148-151; defined 146-147; John Paul II and, 151-152, 299; link to abortion, 300-302; replies to objections against basic argument, 157-159; not NFP, 159-162

Curran, Charles, E., conscience, 281; contraception and other sexual acts, 65, 272; dissent, 115, 286; homosexuality, 249, 314; masturbation, 182, 311; physicalism, 297; sterilization, 300, 301, 304, 305

Cyprian, 295

D

D'Arcy, Eric, conscience, 281

Davis, Henry, 311, 319

Dedek, John, 277, 304

Dei Verbum, 19, 20, 32, 119, 203, 321

Delhaye, Philippe, conscience, 281, 283

DeMarco, Donald, reproductive techniques, 306

Dignitatis Humanae, conscience and God's law, 98, 101, 275, 280; dignity of conscience, 119, formation of Catholic conscience, 105, 225, 283-284; task of magisterium, 21

dissent, 113-121, 277

Donagan, Alan, 278

Dulles, Avery, 287, 288

Duggan, Michael, OT sexual teaching, 260

Dupré, Louis, 267

Durand, Guy, 271

E

Elliott, Peter, 264

Evangelium Vitae, absolute norms protecting innocent human life infallibly proposed by ordinary magisterium, 112-113, 252, 284; Christian family, "sanctuary of life," 292; overview of, 212-218; relevance for sexual ethics 217-219

F

G

Grelot, Pierre, 259, 263, 314
Gregory Nazianzus, 48
Gregory of Nyssa, 49; free choice and self-determination, 274
Grisez, Germain, 64, 249, 251, 261, 270, 272, 273, 284, 287, 298, 308, 317, 319, 323; conscience, 281, 284; contraception, 281, 292, 297, 299, 300, 301; critque of dualism, 203, 302, 311; formulation of first principle of morality, 279; free choice, 273, 279, 283; human goods, 275; human goods, incommensurable, 84, 278; infallibility, 251, 277, 286; moral dilemmas, 284; mortal sin and fundamental option 322; NFP not contraceptive, 304; personal vocation, 288; sense of the faithful, 288
Gury, J.B., 273

H

Häring, Bernard, 305,
Hallett, Garth, proportionalism, 276
Hamilton, Eleanor, 312
Hare, R.M., 274
Harvey, John, homosexuality and homosexual acts, 313, 318
Hauck, Friedrich, 293, 294, 307
Hayes, Richard B., Sodom and Gomorrah story, 261
Hildebrand, Dietrich von, 66, 273, 292, 295, 299; depth of sex, 318
Hilgers, Thomas, 297, 298
Hitchcock, James, 188, 315
Hogan, Richard M., synthesis of John Paul II's thought, 259
Holy Office, 308, 310, 311;instruction on "Situation Ethics," 280
homosexual acts, biblical teaching 39, 45, 315; moral analysis of, 185-193, 201-205
homosexual persons, *Letter to Catholic Bishops on Pastoral Care of*, 201-205
Hugo, John, 267
Hugh of St. Victor, 60; marriage, 270
Hugenberger, Gordon Paul, marriage in OT, 293
Human goodness and human goods, 72-78

I

incest, 195
infallibly proposed teachings, 19-22; specific moral norms, 111-115

328

Innocent III, 22; marriage, 253, 271
Innocent IV, fornication, 308
Innocent XI, 308, consentual adultery, 144, 296
Instruction on Respect for Human Life in Its Origin and on the Dignity of Procreation ("Donum Vitae"), 166-167, 205-210, 306
International Theological Commission, 292
in vitro fertilization, 165-166, 207-209, 306, 317
Irenaeus, goodness of marriage, 48, 265-266
Irish bishops, conscience, 105, 281, 284

J

Janssens, Louis, proportionalist, 249, 276, 277, 278
Jensen, Joseph, OT on sex, 260, 316; fornication in NT, 263-264, 307
Jerome, 48, 149, 151, 256, 261, 295, 318
John Chrysostom, marriage and sex, 48, 49, 50, 266-267
John Damascene, marriage and sex, 49, 266
John Paul II (Karol Wojtyla), adultery, 141-142 ; anthropology, 161, 304; baptism and marriage, 133, 287; chastity, 127, 289; concupiscence and lustful desire, 37, 260, 294; conscience and its formation, 98, 100, 225, 281-282; contraception, 146, 148-149, 151-152, 296, 298, 299; dissent and ecclesial communion, 250, 287; *Evangelium Vitae*, overview and significance, 212-219; *Familiaris Consortio*, overview, 254; free choice, 70, 95, 222, 274, 280; fundamental option, 280; Genesis texts, 36, 256, 258, 259; immorality of extramarital sex, 31, 172, 174; infallibility of ordinary magisterium, 112-113, 252, 284, 285; law of love, the human good, and moral absolutes, 222-223; *Letter to Families*, 210-212; marriage, 25-26, 130, 255, 259, 290, 295; marital consent, 130, 290; marital love and procreation, 255, 295, 296; mortal sin, 183-184, 311-312; nuptial meaning of the body, 179, 258; object of human act, 276; original nakedness, 259; original solitude, 258; personalist norm, 279, 308; physicalism, 119, 158; proportionalism 79-88, 223-224; sensuality, concupiscence, sentiment 289; Sermon on the Mount, 262; *Veritatis Splendor*, overview, 221-225; virginity, 137-138
Joyce, Mary R., 292, 299, 303
Joyce, Robert, 289
Justin Martyr, goodness of marriage, 48, 266

K

Kambie, R.T., NFP, 302
Kathchadourian, Herant, 312
Keane, Philip, 249, 287, 297, magisterium and infallibility, 285; physicalism, 297; premarital sex, 309, 319
Keefe, Jeffrey, theories of homosexuality, 313
Kelly, Gerald, 273, 305, 306, 312
Kippley, John, 292, 299
Klaus, Hanna, NFP, 302
Kosnik, Anthony, et al., 176; adultery 261, 295; homosexuality, 315; masturbation 312; premarital sex, 309

L

Lactantius, 50, 53, 266
Lateran, Second and Fourth Councils, marriage, 22, 252
Lawler, Ronald, free choice vs. fundamental option, 280; magisterium, 251; mortal sin, 322
Lee, Patrick, critique of dualism, 302; Thomas Aquinas, 277
Le Maistre, Martin, 272
Leo IX, 178, 255, 310
Leo XIII, marriage teaching, 24, 253, 290, 291
Léon-Dufour, Xavier, 274, 275
Lerch, J.R., 286
Lercher, L., 286
Letter to Families, overview, 210-212; significance, 217-218
Letter to the Bishops of the Catholic Church on the Pastoral Care of Homosexual Persons, 201-205
Lombard, Peter, 57, 59-60, 269
London, Perry, 249
Lopez, T., 251
Lopez Trujillo, Alfonso Cardinal, 298
Lucas, John, 291
Luke, marriage texts, 263
Lunde, Donald T., 296, 312
Luño, Angel Rodriguez, on *Evangelium Vitae*, 320
Lumen Gentium, assent due magisterial teaching 20, 109-112, 287, 301; common holiness, 122 duty to teach, 316; infallibility, 59, 109, 111, 150, 250-251

M

Macedo, Stephen, 317

Macquarrie, John, 281

magisterium, conscience and, 105-121; moral absolutes, 80-92; moral theology and, 19-21; recent teaching on sexual ethics; 199-231

Mark, marriage texts, 41; sexual sins, 43

marital act, goodness of, 27-29, 49, 52-53, 60-63

marriage, baptism and, 132; family and, 136; Fathers on 47-53; goodness and holiness, 22-27; goods of, and chastity, 132-136; goods of 22, 52-53, 57-63; magisterium on, 22-30, 128-132; medieval theologians, on 63-67; OT on, 33-39; NT on, 39-43; vocation of chastity, 128-131

Maguire, Daniel, 251, 277, 287, 288

Martin, Francis, 257; John Paul II, anthropology of, 259

Matthew, marriage texts, 41-43; 262, list of sexual sins, 43; *"porneia"* exception clause, 42, 262

May, William E., 250, 252, 278, 282, 292, 301, 320; NFP vs. contraception, 303-304; reproductive technologies, 306, 317; sexual complementarity, 289

McAuliffe, Michael, 291

McCary, James, 312

McCombie, Sharon, rape protocol, 318

McCracken, Samuel, homosexuality, 316-317

McCreesch, Thomas, Wisdom literature and sex 260

McCormick, Richard A., adultery, 294; proportionalism, 276, 277, 278; magisterium, 287

McKenzie, John L., 33, 293, 310, 314; Baal myth vs. Genesis, 256; biblical meaning of "word," 290

McNeill, John T., penitentials, 269

McNeill, John, 249, defense of homosexual acts, 315

medieval theologians, sex and marriage, 58-63

Miguens, Manuel, 256; NT themes, 261; Paul's moral thought, 294; Sodom and Gomorrah story, 315

Milhaven, John, 277

Miller, Paula Jean, Bonaventure's teaching on marriage, 270

Moberly, Elizabeth, homosexuality, 313-314

Montagu, Ashley, 249, 296, 305

Montague, George, critique of Kosnik et al., 315; Paul's moral thought, 294

Mork, Wulstan, 302

Murphy, Roland, OT sexual teaching, 260

N

O

P

W

Weinberg, M., 185, 312
Wojtyla, Karol, see John Paul II

Y

Yarborough, O. Larry, Paul's moral teaching, 264, 265, 294, 295, 308

Z

Zalba, M., 285, 309, 310, 315, 318, 319
Zedda, Silverio, Paul's moral teaching, 44, 263-265, 307-308, 310

Our Sunday Visitor...
Your Source for Discovering the Riches of the Catholic Faith

Our Sunday Visitor has an extensive line of materials for young children, teens, and adults. Our books, Bibles, booklets, CD-ROMs, audios, and videos are available in bookstores worldwide.

To receive a FREE full-line catalog or for more information, call **Our Sunday Visitor** at **1-800-348-2440**. Or write, **Our Sunday Visitor** / 200 Noll Plaza / Huntington, IN 46750.

Please send me: __ A catalog
Please send me materials on:
__ Apologetics and catechetics   __ Reference works
__ Prayer books   __ Heritage and the saints
__ The family   __ The parish

Name_____
Address_____Apt._____
City_____State___Zip_____
Telephone ( )_____
                                             A89BBABP

Please send a friend: __ A catalog
Please send a friend materials on:
__ Apologetics and catechetics   __ Reference works
__ Prayer books   __ Heritage and the saints
__ The family   __ The parish

Name_____
Address_____Apt._____
City_____State___Zip_____
Telephone ( )_____
                                             A89BBABP

 Our Sunday Visitor
200 Noll Plaza
Huntington, IN 46750
1-800-348-2440
OSVSALES@AOL.COM

Your Source for Discovering the Riches of the Catholic Faith